W9-BUG-231

Apple Pro Training Series

OS X Server
Essentials 10.10

Arek Dreyer and Ben Greisler

Apple
Certified

Apple Pro Training Series: OS X Server Essentials 10.10
Arek Dreyer and Ben Greisler
Copyright © 2015 by Peachpit Press

Peachpit Press
www.peachpit.com

To report errors, please send a note to *errata@peachpit.com*. Peachpit Press is a division of Pearson Education.

Apple Series Editor: Lisa McClain	**Production Services**: Happenstance Type-O-Rama
Production Editor: Tracey Croom	
Technical Editor: Adam Karneboge	**Indexer**: Jack Lewis
Apple Reviewer: Susan Najour	**Cover Illustration**: Paul Mavrides
Apple Project Manager: Debra Otterstetter	**Cover Production**: Happenstance Type-O-Rama
Copy Editor: Kim Wimpsett	
Proofreader: Darren Meiss	

ISBN 13: 978-0-13-403350-1
ISBN 10: 0-13-403350-7
9 8 7 6 5 4 3 2 1 Printed and bound in the United States of America
Alternate Binding:
ISBN 13: 978-0-13-403417-1
ISBN 10: 0-13-403417-1
9 8 7 6 5 4 3 2 1 Printed and bound in the United States of America

Thanks to my lovely wife, Heather Jagman, for her cheerful support.

—Arek Dreyer

My love and appreciation to my wife, Ronit, and my children, Galee and Noam, for their continued support through this project.

—Ben Greisler

Acknowledgments With the memory of Steve Jobs still fresh in our minds, thank you to Tim Cook, Jonathan Ive, and everyone at Apple for continually innovating, surprising, and delighting customers.

Thank you to all the people who continue to help their users get the most out of OS X and iOS. Keep learning, and don't expect the pace of change to let up any time soon.

Thanks to the amazingly capable Lisa McClain, for gently making sure these materials made it into your hands, and to Scout Festa and Kim Wimpsett, for working their editorial and production magic.

Thanks to Adam Karneboge for adept corrections and suggestions.

Thanks to Schoun Regan for all his help.

Thank you, also, to the following people. Without your help, this book would be much less than what it is:

Mark Bulthaup	Scott George	Alby Rose
Craig Cohen	Charlie Heizer	John Signa
Gordon Davisson	Andre LaBranche	Cindy Waller
Weldon Dodd	Ben Levy	Simon Wheatley
Josh Durham	Tip Lovingood	Kevin White
Charles Edge	Jussi-Pekka Mantere	Josh Wisenbaker
Ed Faulkner	Sean Murphy	Eric Zelenka
Patrick Gallagher	Susan Najour	

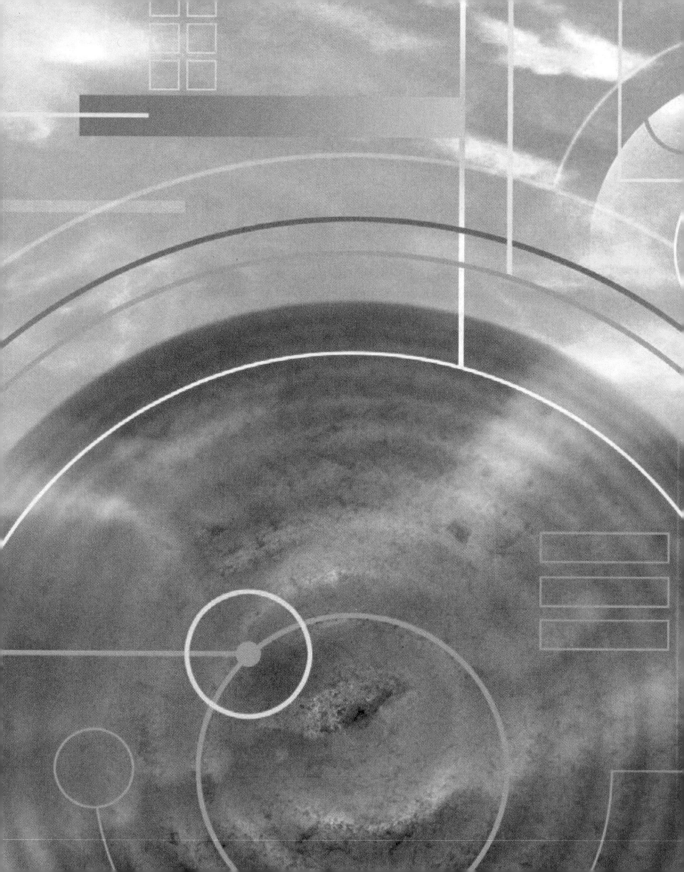

Contents at a Glance

Providing Network Services

Using Collaborative Services

Table of Contents

Providing Network Services

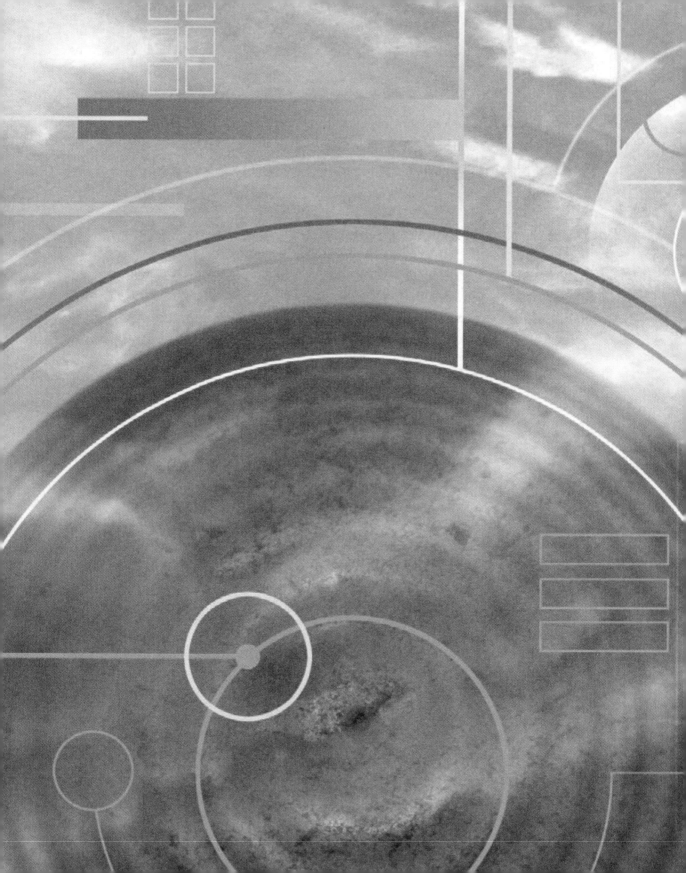

About This Guide

This guide serves as a tour of the breadth of functionality of OS X Server and the best methods for effectively supporting users of OS X Server systems. It is for both self-paced learners working independently and those participating in an instructor-led course. This guide is the curriculum for the Apple official training course Yosemite 201: OS X Server Essentials 10.10, a three-day, hands-on course that provides an in-depth exploration of how to configure and support OS X Server for Yosemite. This course is facilitated by an Apple Certified Trainer and is organized into multiple lessons, each containing instructor presentations followed by related student exercises.

GOALS

► Learn how this guide is organized to facilitate learning

► Set up an environment for self-paced exercises

► Introduce Apple Authorized Training and Certification

The primary goal of this guide is to prepare technical coordinators and entry-level system administrators for the tasks demanded of them by OS X Server; you will learn how to install and configure OS X Server to provide network-based services, such as configuration profile distribution and management, file sharing, authentication, and collaboration services. To help you become truly proficient, this guide covers the theory behind the tools you will use. For example, not only will you learn how to use Server app—the tool for managing services and accounts—but you will also learn about the ideas behind profile management, how to think about access to and control of resources, and how to set up and distribute profiles to support your environment.

You will learn to develop processes to help you understand and work with the complexity of your system as it grows. Even a single OS X Server computer can grow into a complicated system, and creating documentation and charts can help you develop processes so that additions and modifications can integrate harmoniously with your existing system.

This guide assumes you have some knowledge of OS X, because OS X Server is an app that you install on OS X (Yosemite). Therefore, you should be comfortable with basic navigation, troubleshooting, and networking in OS X. When working through this guide, a basic understanding and knowledge of OS X is preferred, including knowledge of how to troubleshoot the operating system. Refer to *Apple Pro Training Series: OS X Support Essentials 10.10* from Peachpit Press if you need to develop a solid working knowledge of OS X.

> **NOTE** ▶ Unless otherwise specified, all references to OS X refer to version 10.10 or later, and references to OS X Server refer to version 4.0, which at the time of this writing is the most current version available. Some screenshots, features, and procedures may be slightly different from those presented on these pages because of subsequent upgrades.

Learning Methodology

Each lesson in this guide is designed to give technical coordinators and entry-level system administrators the skills, tools, and knowledge to implement and maintain a network that uses OS X Server by doing the following:

▶ Providing knowledge of how OS X Server works

▶ Showing how to use configuration tools

▶ Explaining troubleshooting and procedures

The exercises contained within this guide are designed to let you explore and learn the tools necessary to manage OS X Server for Yosemite. They move along in a predictable fashion, starting with installing and setting up OS X Server and moving to more advanced topics such as performing multiprotocol file sharing, using access control lists, and permitting OS X Server to manage network accounts. It is required that you start from a Mac that is not yet running OS X Server and that you do not use this server as a production server.

This guide serves as an introduction to OS X Server and is not meant to be a definitive reference. Because OS X and OS X Server contain several open source initiatives and can be configured at the command line, it is impossible to include all the possibilities and permutations here. First-time users of OS X Server and users of other server operating systems who are migrating to OS X Server have the most to gain from this guide; still, others who are upgrading from previous versions of OS X Server will also find this guide a valuable resource.

OS X Server is by no means difficult to set up and configure, but how you use OS X Server should be planned in advance. Accordingly, this guide is divided into seven parts:

► Part 1, "Configuring and Monitoring OS X Server," covers planning, installation, initial configuration, and monitoring of OS X Server.

► Part 2, "Configuring Accounts," defines authentication and authorization, access control, and Open Directory and the vast functionality it can provide.

► Part 3, "Managing Devices with Configuration Profiles," covers managing devices with the Profile Manager service.

► Part 4, "Sharing Files," introduces the concept of sharing files over multiple protocols and controlling access to files with access control lists.

► Part 5, "Implementing Deployment Solutions," teaches you how to effectively use deployment services, NetInstall, the Caching service, and the Software Update service.

► Part 6, "Providing Network Services," introduces the network services, including Time Machine, VPN, DHCP, and Websites.

► Part 7, "Using Collaborative Services," focuses on setting up collaboration services together, starting with Mail, moving through Wiki, Calendar, and Contacts, and finishing with the Messages service.

Lesson Structure

Most lessons in this guide contain a reference section followed by an exercise section (the lessons on Caching and Software Update services do not contain exercises).

NOTE ► "Note" resources, like this one, offer important information to help clarify a subject. For example, some of the exercises in this guide may be disruptive. Consequently, it's recommended that you perform these exercises on an OS X computer that is not critical to your daily productivity.

The reference sections contain initial explanatory material that teaches essential concepts. The exercise sections augment your understanding of concepts and develop your skills through step-by-step instruction for both self-paced learners and the hands-on portions of an instructor-led course.

TIP ► "Tip" resources, like this one, provide helpful hints, tricks, or shortcuts. For example, each lesson begins with an opening page that lists the learning goals and necessary resources for the lesson.

MORE INFO ▶ The "More Info" resources, like this one, provide ancillary information. These resources are merely for your edification and are not considered essential for the coursework.

Throughout this guide you'll find references to Apple Support articles. You can find these articles at the Apple Support website (www.apple.com/support), a free online resource containing the latest technical information for Apple products. We strongly encourage you to read the suggested articles and search the Apple Support website for answers to any problems you encounter.

We encourage you to explore two additional resources that Apple provides specifically for OS X Server: OS X Server Support (https://www.apple.com/support/osxserver/) and OS X Server: Advanced Administration (https://help.apple.com/advancedserveradmin/mac/4.0/).

Lesson files and bonus materials are available online when you redeem the access code supplied with your guide at www.peachpit.com/redeem. Detailed instructions for downloading files are provided later in this guide. Appendix A, "Lesson Review Questions & Answers," recaps each lesson through a series of questions that reinforce the material you learned in the guide. Try to answer each question yourself before looking at the answer. You can refer to various Apple resources, such as the Apple Support website and OS X Server documentation, as well as the lessons themselves to help you answer these questions. Appendix B, "Additional Resources," lists relevant Apple Support articles and recommended documents related to the topic of each lesson. You'll also find supplemental exercise material for exercises in Lesson 20 and Lesson 23. An "Updates & Errata" document will contain updates and corrections to the guide if any are available.

Exercise Setup

This guide is written so that both the self-paced learner and the attendee at an Apple Authorized Training Center (AATC) or Apple Authorized Training Center for Education (AATCE) can complete most of the exercises using the same techniques. Those attending Yosemite 201 at an AATC or AATCE will have the appropriate exercise setup provided as part of the training experience. Self-paced learners attempting these exercises will have to set up an appropriate environment using their own equipment.

NOTE ► Some of these exercises can be disruptive (for example, turning on the DHCP service may prevent devices on the local network from being able to browse Internet), and some exercises, if performed incorrectly, could result in data loss or damage to files. As such, it's recommended that you perform these exercises on an isolated network, using OS X computers and iOS devices that are not critical to your daily productivity. Apple, Inc., and Peachpit Press are not responsible for any data loss or any damage to any equipment that occurs as a direct or indirect result of following the procedures described in this guide.

Mandatory Requirements

Here's what you will need to complete the lessons in the guide:

► Two Mac computers, each with OS X Yosemite. One Mac is referred to as your "administrator computer," and the Mac on which you will install OS X Server is referred to as your "server computer" or, more simply, your "server." After you are done using your server computer with this guide, you should erase and reinstall OS X on its startup volume before using it again in a production environment.

► An Apple ID that is associated with a verified email address so you can obtain Apple Push Notification service (APNs) certificates for Server app notifications and for the Profile Manager service. You can create an Apple ID at the appropriate time during an exercise if you don't already have an Apple ID.

► A valid licensed copy of OS X Server from the Mac App Store.

► An Internet connection for obtaining APNs certificates for alerts and for the Profile Manager service.

► An isolated network or subnet with an exercise-specific configuration. This can be facilitated with something as simple as a small network Wi-Fi router with multiple Ethernet ports. For example, Apple AirPort Extreme would be a good choice. You can find instructions for the general setup of an exercise network and specific instructions for the configuration of AirPort Extreme at www.apple.com/airport-extreme.

► A router (such as AirPort Extreme) to connect the small isolated network to the Internet. It will be helpful to be familiar with how to configure it.

► Two Ethernet network cables (to complete the NetInstall exercises); each Ethernet cable will connect a Mac to the Ethernet switch.

► Student Materials demonstration files, which you can download after registering your guide with Peachpit. Instructions for registration and download are included in "Exercise 1.1 Configure OS X Before Installing OS X Server on Your Server Computer " on page 21.

Optional Add-Ons

If a specific resource is required for an optional exercise, it will be listed as a prerequisite at the beginning of that exercise. Here are some examples:

▶ An iOS device to test access to OS X Server services, including the Profile Manager service

▶ A Wi-Fi access point (preferably the same AirPort base station) to provide wireless access for iOS devices to your private network

▶ For "Exercise 19.1 Configure the DHCP Service (Optional)" on page 544: To provide DHCP on an extra isolated network: either an additional built-in Ethernet port on your Mac (for example, if your server computer is a Mac Pro) or a USB to Ethernet adapter or a Thunderbolt to Gigabit Ethernet Adapter; and an extra Ethernet network switch

If you lack the equipment necessary to complete a given exercise, you are still encouraged to read the step-by-step instructions and examine the screenshots to understand the procedures demonstrated.

Network Infrastructure

As was previously stated, the exercises require an isolated network. You should replicate the instructor-led classroom environment, which is described in the next sections, as closely as possible so that you do not need to translate between the exercise instructions and your situation.

IPv4 Addresses

The instructor-led environment provides an IPv4 network with a gateway of 10.0.0.1 and subnet mask of 255.255.255.0; if possible, configure your internal network with the same parameters.

Many consumer-level routers are configured with a gateway of 192.168.1.1 and a subnet mask of 255.255.255.0. You might not be able to change this on your router; in many cases you will be able to replace the "10.0.0" portion of an IPv4 address in the exercise with a value appropriate for your isolated network (for example, 192.168.1.171 instead of

10.0.0.171 for a server address for student 17). You will need to remember to substitute your network prefix throughout the exercises.

DHCP
The classroom DHCP service provides IPv4 addresses in the range of 10.0.0.180 to 10.0.0.254; if possible, configure your internal network's DHCP service with the same parameters. It will be helpful to know how to define the IP addresses of DNS servers being provided by DHCP.

If you can configure your isolated network's DHCP service, configure it to use a similar range of IPv4 addresses. If you are unable to change the range of IPv4 addresses, there is a possibility that the DHCP service will assign to a device an IPv4 address already in use by your server computer or your administrator computer. This is another reason to keep your network isolated; do not introduce new devices to it.

Domain Names
The exercises and reference material in this guide use the Internet domains pretendco.com, pretendco.private, and megaglobalcorp.com, which are for learning environments only; do not attempt to use these in your production environment.

The exercises are written in such a way that any existing DNS service on your isolated network will be ignored so that you can experience your server setting up the DNS service for itself.

Advanced Administrators
If you already have advanced server administration skills, you may choose to use different settings, including your organization's Internet domain (instead of pretendco.com), your organization's DNS service, and a different IPv4 address scheme, but be warned that this introduces a high level of variability that the exercises cannot address in the given space, and be prepared to modify the exercises on your own as necessary.

Exercise Order
The exercises in this guide are designed to be relatively independent of each other so that you can perform them out of order or skip exercises you are not interested in. However, some exercises you must perform in the correct order, and where appropriate, an exercise lists these prerequisites. Here are some examples:

xxiv   About This Guide

▶ You must perform all the exercises in Lesson 1 "Installing OS X Server" to install OS X Server and configure your administrator computer before performing any other exercises.

▶ You must perform "Exercise 4.2 Configure an Open Directory Certificate Authority" on page 152 and "Exercise 9.1 Create and Import Network Accounts" on page 292 to create users who you will use in later exercises; otherwise, if the prerequisites for an exercise include the user account used in the lesson, you can simply create those user (and possibly) group accounts with the Server app's Users pane.

Apple Training and Certification

The Apple Training and Certification program is designed to keep you at the forefront of Apple technology. Certification creates a benchmark to demonstrate your proficiency in specific Apple technologies and can give you a competitive edge in today's evolving job market.

Certification exams are delivered at Apple Authorized Training Centers around the world.

Reading this guide or attending the Yosemite 201 class will help prepare you to pass the OS X Server Essentials 10.10 exam and become an Apple Certified Technical Coordinator. Passing both this exam and the OS X Support Essentials 10.10 exam earns Apple Certified Technical Coordinator (ACTC) 10.10 certification. This is the second level of the Apple certification program for Mac professionals, which includes the following:

▶ Apple Certified Support Professional (ACSP) certification verifies an understanding of OS X core functionality and an ability to configure key services, perform basic troubleshooting, and support multiple users with essential OS X capabilities. ACSP certification is designed for the help desk professional, technical coordinator, or power user who supports OS X users, manages networks, or provides technical support for the Mac. Students earn ACSP certification by passing the OS X Support Essentials 10.10 exam. Visit http://training.apple.com/certification/osxyosemite to review the OS X Support Essentials Exam Prep Guide. To prepare for this exam, attend the Yosemite 101 class or read *Apple Pro Training Series: OS X Support Essentials 10.10*.

▶ Apple Certified Technical Coordinator (ACTC) certification verifies a foundation in OS X and OS X Server core functionality and an ability to configure key services and perform basic troubleshooting. ACTC certification is intended for OS X technical coordinators and entry-level system administrators who maintain small to medium-size networks of computers using OS X Server. Students earn ACTC certification by passing the OS X Support Essentials 10.10 exam and OS X Server Essentials 10.10 exam. Visit http://training.apple.com/certification/osxyosemite review the OS X Server Essentials Exam Prep Guide.

MORE INFO ▶ To read OS X technical white papers and learn more about all Apple certifications, visit http://training.apple.com.

NOTE ▶ Although all the questions in the OS X Server Essentials 10.10 exam are based on material in this guide, nothing can substitute for time spent learning the technology. After you read the guide or take the class, spend time increasing your familiarity with OS X Server on your own to ensure your success on the certification exam.

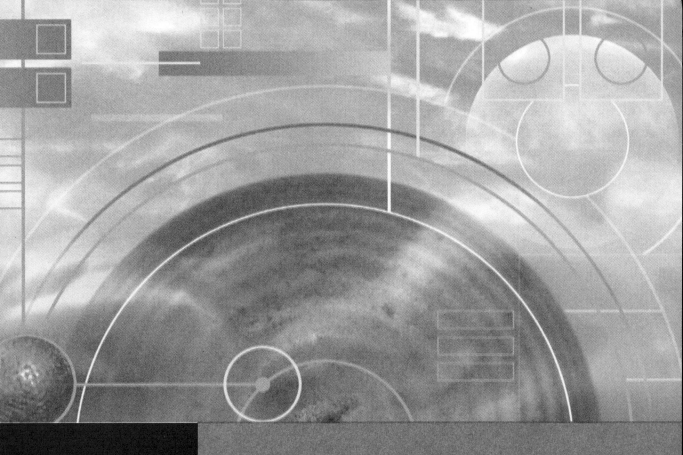

Configuring and Monitoring OS X Server

Lesson 1

Installing OS X Server

OS X Server for Yosemite helps your users collaborate, communicate, share information, and access the resources they need to get their work done, whether in business or in education.

OS X Server for Yosemite is an app (called "the Server app" in this guide) that runs on a Mac computer running Yosemite; if your Mac can run Yosemite, it can run OS X Server. You can use the Server app to provide services or to manage OS X Server running on a remote Mac computer.

Although you could dive right in and install and configure OS X Server, it's recommended that you divide working with OS X Server into four phases:

1. Planning and installation—Plan how the server will be set up, verify and configure the hardware, and install the OS X Server software; this is covered in this lesson.

2. Configuration—Use the Server app to configure your server; all the lessons in this guide use the Server app to configure your server.

3. Monitoring—Use the Server app to monitor the status of your server and optionally to specify an email address to receive notifications of specific alerts, which is covered in Lesson 5 "Using Status and Notifications".

4. Ongoing maintenance—Use the Server app to perform ongoing server and account maintenance and monitoring.

This lesson begins with planning and continues into the initial installation and configuration of OS X Server.

Reference 1.1
Evaluating OS X Server Requirements

Before you install the software, take the time to evaluate the server needs of your organization and the OS X Server hardware requirements.

Defining the Minimum Hardware Requirements

You can install the OS X Server app on any Mac computer running OS X Yosemite with at least 2 gigabytes (GB) of random-access memory (RAM) and 10 GB of available disk space or 50 GB if you plan on using the Caching service. Remember, those are the minimums, and you will need more RAM and disk space as you start using services. It wouldn't be unreasonable to run 16 GB or more RAM in a heavily used production server.

To run Yosemite, your Mac must be one of the following models:

▶   iMac (mid-2007 or later)

▶   MacBook (13-inch Aluminum, Late 2008; 1 3-inch, Early 2009 or later)

▶   MacBook Pro (Mid/Late 2007 or later)

▶   MacBook Air (Late 2008 or later)

▶   Mac mini (Early 2009 or later)

▶   Mac Pro (Early 2008 or later)

▶   Xserve (Early 2009)

Some features of OS X Server require an Apple ID, and some features require a compatible Internet service provider.

Verifying System Requirements

Before you install OS X Server, confirm that your system meets the hardware requirements. You can find this information on the label attached to the box of every Mac computer sold, or you can find it with the About This Mac window and System Information app.

To check whether a Mac computer can run Yosemite, you can start with the About This Mac window. The next few figures walk you through the process of determining whether this Mac can run OS X Server for Yosemite.

Under the Apple menu, choose About This Mac, which contains all the information you need in a single app. The Overview pane displays your Mac system's model and memory.

The Storage pane displays information about available storage.

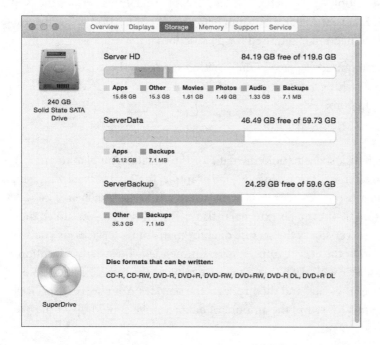

Addressing Other Hardware Considerations

Typical considerations when choosing server systems include network and system performance, potential disk usage and needed capacity, and RAM. You may find that using multiple servers, running a few services on each server, results in better performance than running all the services on a single server.

Network

Be sure to consider the speed of the network interface when making a server hardware decision. All Mac computers that can run Yosemite support Gigabit Ethernet; if your Mac ships with a built-in Ethernet port, that port supports Gigabit Ethernet. If your Mac is equipped with a Thunderbolt port, you can use the Apple Thunderbolt to Gigabit Ethernet Adapter.

You can combine two Ethernet interfaces to act as one to aggregate network throughput for services such as file sharing.

For learning and testing scenarios only, you could consider using Wi-Fi as your server's primary network connection. This opens the possibility of using a MacBook Air, which does not have a built-in Ethernet port. In this instance, you could use Wi-Fi, the Apple USB Ethernet Adapter for MacBook Air (which provides 10/100Base-T Ethernet), or the Apple Thunderbolt to Gigabit Ethernet Adapter. Although a wireless connection is OK for testing, a Gigabit Ethernet connection is required for production.

> **NOTE** ▸ Ethernet is required to provide the Caching service and the NetInstall service. See Lesson 15 "Caching Content from Apple" and Lesson 14 "Leveraging NetInstall" for more information.

Disk

Be sure you have enough disk space to hold the data for the services you plan to offer. If the services you plan to offer are disk intensive—for example, the Mail service with a high volume of mail—consider using a faster physical disk such as a serial-attached SCSI (SAS) disk, a solid-state disk (SSD), or even an external disk system. Although you can change the location where your server stores the service data for many of its services, as you will learn in Lesson 3 "Exploring the Server App", it is recommended you specify a location *before* populating your server with data; this is because moving the service data location stops your services, moves the data, and then restarts the services. Your server's services are not available during this time, and the amount of data to move could impact the amount of time the process takes.

RAM

In general, more RAM results in better system performance, but exactly how much RAM is ideal for your situation is impossible for this guide to prescribe. If making a choice, err on the higher side. A production server could easily have 16 GB or more of RAM.

You can use the Memory Usage and Memory Pressure statistics available in the Stats pane. See Lesson 5 "Using Status and Notifications" for more information.

Availability

To ensure that OS X Server stays up and running, you can select the Energy Saver system preference labeled "Start up automatically after a power failure" (not available on all Mac computers). If using external storage, do not use this option because the storage often takes longer to come online than the server, which can cause problems with data availability. See the following note.

It is highly recommended that you use an uninterruptible power supply (UPS) for your server, including any external volumes, to keep your server up and running in the case of a brief power outage.

It is also a good idea to check that the Energy Saver preference for computer sleep is set to never go to sleep. That will keep services available without having to wake the computer.

> NOTE ▶ If you use an external volume, do not select the checkbox "Start up automatically after a power failure" because you cannot guarantee that an external volume will be powered up correctly after a power failure. (You may have to manually confirm that the external volume is powered on and available before you start up your Mac with OS X Server; otherwise, a service may start before the volume that contains its data is available.)

Reference 1.2
Preparing to Install OS X Server

> NOTE ▶ This reference section describes the process of installing OS X Server in a general way; the exercises offer detailed step-by-step instructions, so do not perform any actions until you reach the exercises, which are at the end of this lesson.

Any Mac capable of running Yosemite can run OS X Server for Yosemite. As detailed in "Reference 1.4 Upgrading or Migrating to OS X Server" on page 18, the Mac App Store will not allow you to purchase OS X Server unless you are running OS X Yosemite.

Formatting/Partitioning Disks

After you confirm that your computer meets the hardware requirements, you can simply install Yosemite on your existing startup disk, or you can install Yosemite on another disk. You can also begin making decisions about the devices and subsequent formatting of those devices prior to installing the software.

Disk Utility is located in the Utilities folder, which is in the Applications folder. Using this utility, you can divide a disk into one or more partitions. Doing so allows you to first choose a partition scheme for your disk. Your choices are as follows:

▶ GUID Partition Table—Used to start up Intel-based Mac computers

▶ Apple Partition Map—Originally used to start up PowerPC-based Mac computers but also found on some preformatted external disk drives

> **NOTE** ▶ To install OS X Server on a volume, that volume's disk must be formatted with GUID Partition Table. You can examine a disk's partition scheme with the Disk Utility app, which lists this information as Partition Map Scheme, and with the System Information app, which lists this information as Partition Map Type.

Once you choose a partition scheme, you can divide your disk into as many as 16 logical disks, each with its own format. Each logical disk is called a "partition." Once you format a partition, it contains a volume. See *Apple Pro Training Series: OS X Support Essentials 10.10* for further information about the available volume formats.

To install OS X Server on a volume, it must have one of the two following journaled formats:

▶ Mac OS X Extended (Journaled)

▶ Mac OS X Extended (Case-Sensitive, Journaled)

Unless you have a compelling reason to use Mac OS X Extended (Case-Sensitive, Journaled) format, use Mac OS X Extended (Journaled).

You can use the other, nonjournaled formats for data partitions, but journaling eliminates the need for a lengthy disk check on a volume after a power outage or other failure.

By using separate partitions, you can segregate your data from the operating system. You may decide to store user or service data on a separate volume. Having the operating system on its own volume conserves space by keeping user files and service data from filling up the startup volume. In case you need to perform a clean install of OS X and OS X Server at a later time, you can erase the entire startup volume and install the operating system without touching the data on the other volumes.

NOTE ▶ OS X Server stores data for many of its services in /Library/Server/ on the startup volume by default, but as you will see later in this lesson, you can use the Server app to change the service data location. In any event, make sure you have a good backup of your server before erasing your server startup volume.

To create multiple partitions on a single disk, simply select your disk, choose the number of partitions from the Partition Layout menu, and choose the following for each partition:

▶ Name of partition—Using lowercase alphanumeric characters and removing spaces in volume names may help reduce troubleshooting of share points later.

▶ Format of partition—See the previous list for various acceptable OS X Server partition formats.

▶ Size of partition—Again, OS X Server requires at least 10 GB of available disk space for installation.

NOTE ▶ The following figure shows a volume for backup purposes. A backup target would typically be on a different physical drive. This is just for testing.

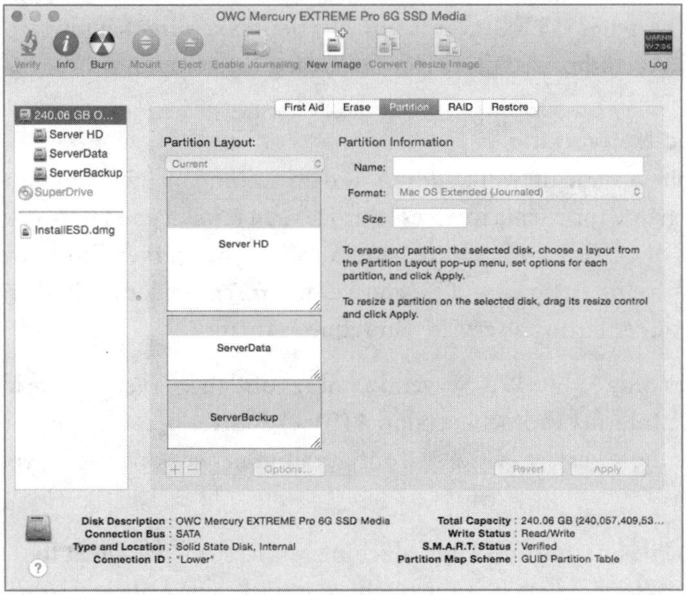

Before you click Apply, remember: *All previous data on the disk may be erased!*

Having multiple partitions does not increase speed, but installing multiple disks may increase server performance. Installing the operating system on one disk and installing additional disks to store user data can reduce connection times to the operating system and to data. If you add the second disk on a separate bus, the server can read and write to each of those buses independently.

Redundant Array of Independent Disks (RAID)

To provide increased availability or performance, it is possible to install OS X on a RAID volume before installing OS X Server. However, because an OS X Recovery system partition cannot exist on a RAID volume, you may want to create an external OS X Recovery system from which you can start up so you can access a variety of administration and troubleshooting utilities. For further information, you may want to read Lesson 3, "OS X Recovery," in *Apple Pro Training Series: OS X Support Essentials 10.10*.

FileVault Full-Disk Encryption

Because full-disk encryption requires a user to enter an encryption password after the computer starts up, full-disk encryption isn't recommended for use with OS X Server for the startup disk or for any disk that stores service data. If there is a concern regarding unintended access of the computer OS X Server is running on, make sure that physical security is set up to prevent unauthorized users from accessing the computer.

Configuring Naming and Networking

Traditionally, servers require a static network address and an accompanying Domain Name System (DNS) host name for clients to access services at a known good network address. Previous versions of OS X Server required you to verify your server's host name during its initial setup and configuration, but OS X Server for Yosemite doesn't bother you with those details unless you're starting a service that requires them.

Today, many of the services offered by OS X Server do not require the server to have a specific host name or static Internet Protocol version 4 (IPv4) address because clients on the local subnet can access those services via zero-configuration networking (using your server's Bonjour name).

Some services, such as the File Sharing and Time Machine services, allow a client to browse for the service; other services, such as the Caching service, automatically work for clients on the local network, even if the server's IPv4 address or host name changes.

For other services, such as the Open Directory and Profile Manager services, it is best practice to configure the server with a static IPv4 address and an accompanying DNS host name to ensure that clients can consistently access the service.

For example, if you intend to use OS X Server to provide only the File Sharing and Wiki services on the local network and have your clients access these services via your server's Bonjour name, you don't need to bother switching the server from Dynamic Host Configuration Protocol (DHCP) to a static IPv4 address.

Nevertheless, it's still best practice to manually assign your server a static IPv4 address rather than to rely on a DHCP service to provide a dynamically assigned IPv4 address.

> **TIP** ▶ To configure the DNS server or servers that your Mac uses, in Network preferences, select the primary network interface, click Advanced, and then click the DNS tab.

> **MORE INFO** ▶ When provided by DHCP or manually entered, OS X automatically appends the contents of the Search Domains field to the DNS names you enter in apps such as Safari.

Clients can access your server's services directly via IPv4 and IPv6 address or, more commonly, via various names, including the following:

▶ Computer Name

▶ Local Hostname

▶ Host Name

The following three sections explain each in detail.

Explaining the Use of the Computer Name

The "computer name" is used by clients on your server's local subnet when browsing using the following:

▶ Finder sidebar to access the File Sharing and Screen Sharing services on the server

▶ Apple Remote Desktop (ARD)

▶ AirDrop

The computer name can contain spaces.

If your server offers file- or screen-sharing services, Mac users in the same broadcast domain (usually a subnet) will see your server's computer name in the Shared section of the Finder sidebar, as in the following example.

Explaining the Use of the Local Hostname

Your server uses Bonjour to advertise its services on its local subnet. The "local hostname" is a name that ends in ".local" and follows the rules for DNS names. OS X automatically removes any special characters and replaces any space character with a dash in the local hostname.

> **MORE INFO** ▸ See www.apple.com/support/bonjour for more information about Bonjour zero-configuration networking.

Devices that use Bonjour (including PCs, Mac computers, and iOS devices) on the same subnet as your server can access services using your server's local hostname. The following figure is an example of using a local hostname to access the local Wiki service.

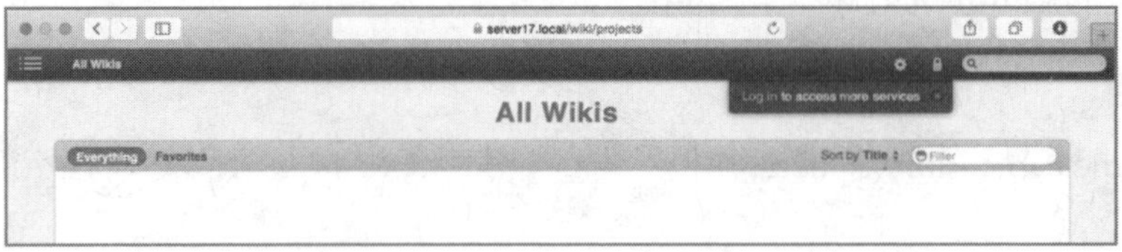

Explaining the Host Name

The "host name," or the primary DNS host name, is a unique name for your server, historically referred to as the fully qualified domain name (FQDN). Some services on OS X Server require a working FQDN or will work better if one is available. Computers and devices can access services on your server by using your server's DNS host name, even if they are not on the same local subnet.

If there is a DNS record for your Mac server's primary IPv4 address, OS X automatically uses DNS records to set your Mac server's host name. Otherwise, OS X automatically uses your Mac server's computer name to set a Bonjour-based host name, such as Locals-MacBook-Pro.local.

When you first configure OS X Server, it automatically creates a self-signed Secure Sockets Layer (SSL) certificate using your Mac system's host name, even if the host name is something like Locals-MacBook-Pro.local, so it's best practice to configure your Mac system with your desired host name before initially installing and configuring the Server app. You'll learn more about certificates in Lesson 4 "Configuring SSL Certificates".

> **MORE INFO** ▶ If you use Change Host Name Assistant, covered in the next section, to change your host name, the Server app automatically creates a new self-signed SSL certificate with your new host name.

If your environment's infrastructure already has a DNS service that provides DNS records for devices on your internal network, it's best to keep using that DNS service; create DNS records for your server using the appropriate tools for the existing DNS service.

If you don't have a DNS service already running for devices on your internal network and you don't have DNS records available at the time you install OS X Server, that's OK. If there are no appropriate DNS records available, your server can provide them, as you'll learn in the following section.

Changing Names and Addresses

After your initial installation and configuration of OS X Server, you can use the Server app to change the following attributes quickly (by clicking Edit next to the Computer Name attribute in the Overview pane):

▶ Computer Name

▶ Local Hostname

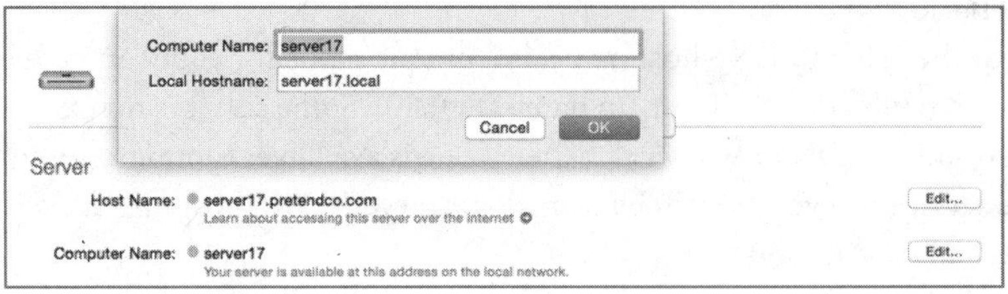

NOTE ▶ The Sharing pane of System Preferences also lets you change the Computer Name and Local Hostname attributes.

You can also use the Server app to start Change Host Name Assistant (by clicking Edit next to the host name in the Overview pane) to change the following attributes:

▶ Computer Name

▶ Host Name

▶ Network Address

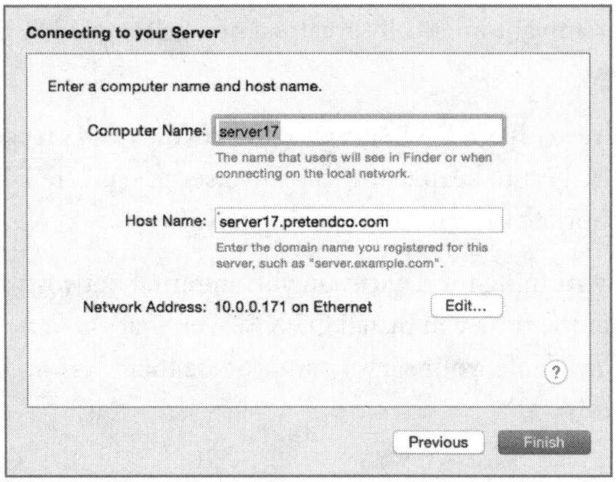

When you use Change Host Name Assistant, if the DNS service you specify in the DNS Server field of Network preferences does not supply forward and reverse DNS records for the address you specify in the IP Address field, the Server app asks if you'd like to start the DNS service. If you answer affirmatively, the Server app performs the following configuration steps:

▶ Configures the DNS service on your server computer to provide a forward DNS record for your primary DNS name and a reverse DNS record for its primary IPv4 address

▶ Starts the DNS service

▶ Configures your server's primary network interface to use its own DNS service (specifically, 127.0.0.1, which is the loopback address that always points back to the computer) as the primary DNS service, in addition to any DNS servers that were previously specified

▶ If appropriate, removes the old default self-signed SSL certificate and creates a new one with the new host name

This ensures your server will always be able to resolve its host name to its IPv4 address and its IPv4 address to its host name.

However, other computers and devices will not necessarily use these DNS records and therefore will not be able to access services on your server by its host name unless you configure them to use your server's DNS service. See Lesson 2 "Providing DNS Records" for more information about DNS.

Downloading OS X Server

OS X Server app is purchased and downloaded from the Mac App Store. The Mac App Store will not allow you to purchase OS X Server unless you are running OS X Yosemite.

NOTE ▶ The app is called OS X Server in the Mac App Store, and it's called Server in your Applications folder (once it finishes downloading from the Mac App Store). This guide refers to it as "the Server app."

NOTE ▶ You can use the Server app on another Mac to administer your server, but you must copy the Server app from your server to the other Mac. You will need to repeat this step whenever you update the Server app on your server. See Apple Support article HT202279, "How to administer OS X Server remotely using Server App," for more information.

Reference 1.3
Installing OS X Server

Once you have configured OS X on your server computer and have the Server app installed on your server computer, you can start installing OS X Server.

When you configure OS X Server, be sure to have an active network connection, even if it is only to a network switch that doesn't have anything else connected to it.

Open the Server app: If it isn't already in the Dock, you can click Launchpad in the Dock and then click Server; you can open the Server app from your Applications folder; or you can open it with a Spotlight search. From the introductory window, when you click Continue, you start the process of installing and configuring OS X Server.

> **NOTE ▶** If you want to use the Server app to manage an instance of OS X Server that has already been installed and configured on another server (rather than installing and configuring OS X Server on this Mac), instead of clicking Continue, click Other Mac.

As soon as you click Continue, you have to agree to the terms of the software license agreement. As with all software, carefully read the software license agreement.

Once you click Agree, you need to provide local administrator credentials. After your credentials have been confirmed, the Server app configures itself. When the process is complete, the Server app displays the Overview pane.

Once the Server app has been installed, do not move it from the Applications folder. That will cause the services to be stopped, and you will not have a functional server. You will need to reinstall the Server app to bring it back to functionality.

NOTE ▶ A previous version of OS X Server (for Mountain Lion) prompts you to confirm and possibly change the computer name and host name during its initial configuration. In comparison, the initial configuration of OS X Server for Mavericks and OS X Server for Yosemite is much more streamlined, but you should check that the naming is what you need it to be ahead of time.

Reference 1.4
Upgrading or Migrating to OS X Server

If you have an existing Mac with Snow Leopard Server, Lion Server, OS X Server for Mountain Lion, or OS X Server for Mavericks and your computer meets the hardware requirements for OS X Yosemite, you can "upgrade" to OS X Server for Yosemite. Otherwise, you can "migrate" from your old server to OS X Server for Yosemite on a Mac that meets the hardware requirements for Yosemite by first installing OS X Yosemite, then using OS X Setup Assistant or Migration Assistant, and finally installing OS X Server for Yosemite.

To upgrade to OS X Server for Yosemite, first you need to upgrade to Yosemite, and then you can install OS X Server for Yosemite. Remember that it is always best practice to back up any existing setup prior to running the upgrade so you can restore should anything go wrong.

Use the following steps:

1   Make sure your Mac can run Yosemite.

2   Make sure you have OS X Server for Mountain Lion, Lion Server, or the latest version of Snow Leopard Server. Use Software Update to update to the latest version of the appropriate software.

3   If your OS X Server computer is configured to use itself as a DNS server, replace its own IP address in Network preferences with an external DNS server. During the upgrade process the DNS service will be turned off and won't be available to provide DNS lookups. This will prevent a connection to the Internet, but providing an external DNS server will solve that problem.

4   Download OS X Yosemite from the Mac App Store.

5   Open Install Mac OS X Yosemite to perform the upgrade to OS X Yosemite.

6   Once running Yosemite, download OS X Server from the Mac App Store.

7   Open Server from Launchpad or the Applications folder to install OS X Server.

8   Once OS X Server is open, check that all of your services are running; some might need to be switched back on.

> **NOTE** ▶ Upgrading the server software should be a planned event. Always run updates on a test system before rolling out into production. In some cases, third-party solutions may not operate smoothly with the new software. You should preflight the update in isolation first and roll it once you have tested your implementation so that all features, functions, or services work as expected, especially when upgrading or migrating from the earliest versions of the operating system (OS) allowed for upgrades and migrations.

> **MORE INFO** ▶ See Apple Support article HT202848, "OS X Server: Upgrade and migration from Mavericks or Mountain Lion," for detailed instructions. Refer to the Apple Support site for updates and new articles.

Reference 1.5
Updating OS X Server

When an update for OS X Server becomes available, you can download and install it using the Mac App Store.

You may notice that the App Store icon in the Dock displays a badge with a number indicating the number of updates available.

To install the update, open the App Store, click Updates in the toolbar, and then click Update for the OS X Server update.

If you haven't already signed in to the Mac App Store, you will be prompted to do so.

Even though you see a message that services have been stopped, you'll find that most of your services are still running.

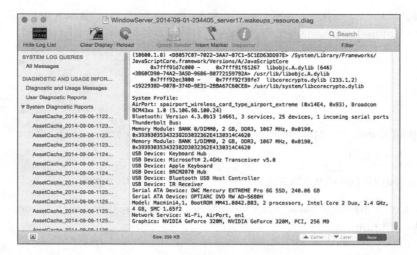

To complete the update of OS X Server, open the Server app. At the update pane, click Continue, and provide local administrator credentials. Wait while your services are updated.

Reference 1.6
Troubleshooting

One common problem found in server installations is incompatibility with third-party hardware and software configurations. Isolate the changes to your system when you run into problems, and keep the variables to a minimum.

Inspecting Logs

OS X and OS X Server log events to various log files. You can view logs in the Console app or select Logs in the sidebar of the Server app. In the following figure, the Console app displays the contents of system.log.

Throughout this guide, you will view various logs with the Console app or the Logs pane of the Server app.

Exercise 1.1
Configure OS X Before Installing OS X Server on Your Server Computer

> ► **Prerequisite**
>
> ► You must have a Mac that is running OS X Yosemite, that has never had OS X Server installed and configured on its startup volume, and that is qualified to run OS X Server.

In this exercise, you will configure your server computer in preparation for installing OS X Server on it.

You'll use one of two options to configure a local administrator account, depending on whether you are performing these exercises independently or are in an instructor-led environment with a Mac computer that has already been set up.

In both situations, you'll use System Preferences to configure the Network and Sharing settings. You will also download student materials that you'll use throughout this class. Finally, you will apply any necessary system software updates.

Establish Your Student Number

In this exercise, you will use a student number to provide unique names and addresses for your computers.

1   If you are in an instructor-led environment, obtain your student number from the instructor.

If you are performing the exercises independently, you can use any number from 1 to 17, but this guide uses student number 17 in its examples, so you might consider choosing 17 as your student number.

Configure OS X

It is most convenient to start with a fresh installation of OS X. If your Mac is at the Welcome screen when you turn it on, you can use the steps in "Option 1: Configure OS X on Your Server Computer with Setup Assistant" on page 22. If you need to use an existing OS X system, you should skip to "Option 2: Configure an Existing OS X System for Your

Server Computer" on page 25 so your Mac will be configured as expected for the rest of the exercises.

Option 1: Configure OS X on Your Server Computer with Setup Assistant

This option is necessary if your server computer has not already been set up, which is the situation in an instructor-led environment. If you are using a Mac with existing accounts, perform the steps in "Option 2: Configure an Existing OS X System for Your Server Computer" on page 25 instead.

Ensure that you have Yosemite installed on your server computer. If it isn't already installed, install it now using the Mac App Store, the Recovery HD, or a method specified by your instructor, and then continue when you reach the Welcome screen.

In this section, you'll step through OS X Setup Assistant for the initial system configuration of your server computer.

1   Ensure that your computer is connected to a valid Ethernet network connection.

2   If necessary, turn on the Mac that will run OS X Server.

3   At the Welcome screen, select the appropriate region, and click Continue.

4   Select the appropriate keyboard layout, and click Continue.

     Setup Assistant evaluates your network environment and tries to determine whether you are connected to the Internet. This can take a few moments.

5   If you are not asked about your Internet connection, your computer's network settings have already been configured via DHCP, and you may move on to step 6.

     If you are asked to select your Wi-Fi network, this could indicate any number of conditions, including the following:

     ▶ Your computer is not connected to Ethernet.

     ▶ Your computer does not have a built-in Ethernet port.

     ▶ Your computer's Ethernet port is connected to a network that does not supply the DHCP service.

     ▶ Your computer has not yet received DHCP configuration.

     ▶ Your computer's Ethernet port is connected to a network that is not connected to the Internet.

If you are performing the exercises in an instructor-led environment, ask your instructor how you should configure your computer; it is possible that the classroom DHCP service is not turned on or that your computer is not connected to the classroom network.

To configure your Mac to use an Ethernet port, click Other Network Options, select Local network (Ethernet), and click Continue.

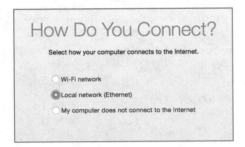

At the Your Internet Connection screen, set TCP/IP Connection Type to Using DHCP, and click Continue.

If you are performing the exercises independently and you plan to use Wi-Fi as your primary network connection, select an appropriate Wi-Fi network, provide the Wi-Fi network's password, and click Continue. Keep in mind that to perform the NetInstall exercises, both your server and your administrator computer need an Ethernet connection.

6   When asked about transferring information to this Mac, select "Don't transfer any information now," and click Continue.

7   At the Sign in with Your Apple ID screen, select "Don't sign in," click Continue, and then click Skip to confirm that you want to skip signing in with an Apple ID.

Note that if you do provide Apple ID credentials, some figures may look slightly different, and there may be extra steps. In an instructor-led environment, it is recommended that you not enter an Apple ID at this time.

8   At the Terms and Conditions screen, when you have finished reading, click Agree.

9   In the dialog to confirm that you have read and agree to the OS X software license agreement, click Agree.

Create your local administrator account.

> **NOTE** ► It is important that you create this account as specified here. If you do not, future exercises may not work as written. **Bold blue** text is used throughout this guide to indicate text that you should enter exactly as shown.

If your server is accessible from the Internet, use a strong password for the Local Admin account. Be sure to remember the password you have chosen because you will need to reenter it periodically as you use this computer.

> **NOTE** ► In a production environment, you should always use a strong password.

1   At the Create Your Computer Account screen, use the following settings:

   ► Full Name: **Local Admin**

   ► Account Name: **ladmin**

   ► Password: **ladminpw**

   ► (verify field): **ladminpw**

   ► Hint: Leave blank.

2   Deselect the checkbox "Set time zone based on current location."

3   Click Continue to create the account.

4   At the Select Time Zone screen, click your time zone in the map or choose the nearest location in the Closest City pop-up menu, and then click Continue.

5   At the Diagnostics & Usage screen, leave selected "Send diagnostics & usage data to Apple" and "Share crash data with app developers," and then click Continue.

Please skip Option 2 below and continue at the section "Confirm Your Computer Is Qualified to Run OS X Server" on page 26.

Option 2: Configure an Existing OS X System for Your Server Computer

This option is designed only for those who are performing the exercises independently and who have a computer that is already set up with an existing administrator account.

NOTE ▶ You may not use a Mac whose startup volume has already had OS X Server installed and configured.

If your computer has not been set up (that is, if the initial administrator account has not been created), perform the steps in "Option 1: Configure OS X on Your Server Computer with Setup Assistant" on page 22 instead.

Create a new administrator account in System Preferences; if your server is not accessible from the Internet, use the password ladminpw.

1   If necessary, log in with your existing administrator account.

2   Open System Preferences.

3   In System Preferences, open Users & Groups.

4   In the lower-left corner, click the lock icon.

5   In the dialog that appears, enter the password for your existing administrator account, and click Unlock.

6   Click the Add (+) button under the user list.

7   In the dialog that appears, use the following settings:

NOTE ▶ It is important that you create this account as specified here. If you do not, future exercises may not work as written. If you already have an account named Local Admin or ladmin, you will have to use a different name here and then remember to use your substitute name throughout the rest of the exercises. **Bold blue** text is used throughout this guide to indicate text that you should enter exactly as shown.

  ▶ New Account: Choose Administrator.

  ▶ Full Name: Local Admin

  ▶ Account Name: ladmin

8   Select "Use separate password."

If you are performing the exercises in an instructor-led environment, enter ladminpw in the two Password fields.

If your server is accessible from the Internet, use a strong password for the Local Admin account. Be sure to remember the password you have chosen because you will need to reenter it periodically as you use this computer.

9   Click Create User.

10   If automatic login was turned on and you are asked if you want to turn it off, click Turn Off Automatic Login.

11   Close System Preferences, and log out.

12   At the login screen, select the Local Admin account, and enter its password (ladminpw or whatever you specified earlier).

13   Press Return to log in.

14   At the Sign in with Your Apple ID screen, select "Don't sign in," click Continue, and then click Skip at the confirmation dialog.

Continue with the next section.

Confirm Your Computer Is Qualified to Run OS X Server

Before you go to the trouble of installing OS X Server, make sure your computer meets the technical requirements to run OS X Server. The first requirement is a Mac computer running Yosemite. The other two requirements are 2 GB of memory and 10 GB of available disk space.

1   From the Apple menu, choose About This Mac.

2   Confirm that you have at least 2 GB of memory.

3   If your Mac computer has more than one volume, About This Mac displays the name of your startup disk. Make a note of the name of your startup disk.

In the previous figure, there is only one volume, so About This Mac does not display the name of the startup disk.

4   Click the Storage tab.

5   Confirm that you have at least 10 GB free disk space on your startup disk.

6   If your Mac computer has only one volume, make a note of its name—it is the name of your startup volume.

7   Close the About This Mac window.

Change Your Startup Volume Name

In the previous section, you made a note of your startup volume name. Before you install OS X Server, confirm that your server computer's startup volume is what you want it to be. You can change that name now to avoid changing your startup volume name after you install OS X Server.

1   In the Finder, choose Go > Computer.

The Finder window displays the volumes.

2   Select your startup volume.

3   Press Return to edit the name.

4   Enter Server HD for the new startup volume name.

5   Press Return to save the name change.

6   Press Command-W to close the Finder window.

Set the Computer Name and Turn On Remote Management

After you create your first computer account, OS X automatically configures its Computer Name setting based on the first word in your computer account name followed by the model of your Mac computer. It also automatically configures a *local network name*, which is based on your computer's name, with any spaces replaced with hyphens, and with ".local" added; this appears in the Local Hostname field in the Sharing preferences.

If OS X detects a duplicate local network name on the same subnet, it silently adds a number to its local network name until it's no longer a duplicate.

You will specify a computer name associated with your student number; this automatically updates the local network name.

You will also turn on Remote Management, which will allow the instructor to observe your computer, control your keyboard and mouse, gather information, copy items to your computer, and otherwise help you if necessary.

> NOTE ► Even though you know administrator credentials for other students' computers and have the technical ability to remotely control their computers, please do not use that ability to interfere with their classroom experience.

Set the Computer Name

1   Open System Preferences.

2   Open Sharing.

3   For Computer Name, enter servern, replacing *n* with your student number.

For example, if your student number is 17, the computer name should be server17, in all lowercase and with no spaces.

4   Press Return.

Notice that the local network name listed under the Computer Name field is automatically updated.

Turn On Remote Management

Now you will allow your instructor (and yourself) to remotely manage your server computer from another Mac computer using Apple Remote Desktop or the Screen Sharing app.

1   Click somewhere over the phrase Remote Management, but don't select the checkbox yet.

2   For "Allow Access for," select "Only these users."

3   Click the Add (+) button, select Local Admin, and click Select.

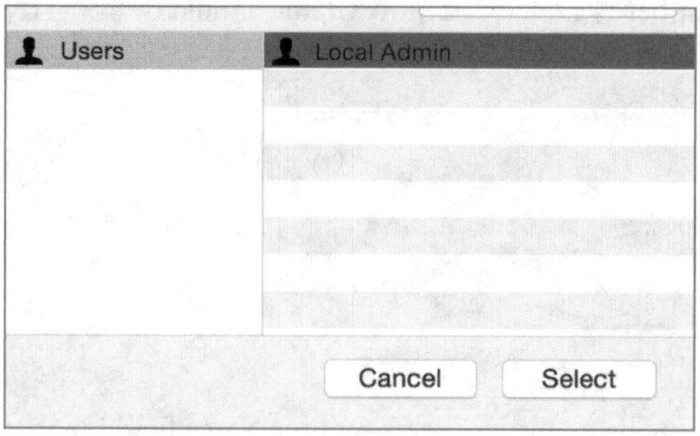

4   In the dialog that appears, hold down the Option key while selecting the Observe checkbox, which results in automatically selecting all the checkboxes, as shown in the following figure.

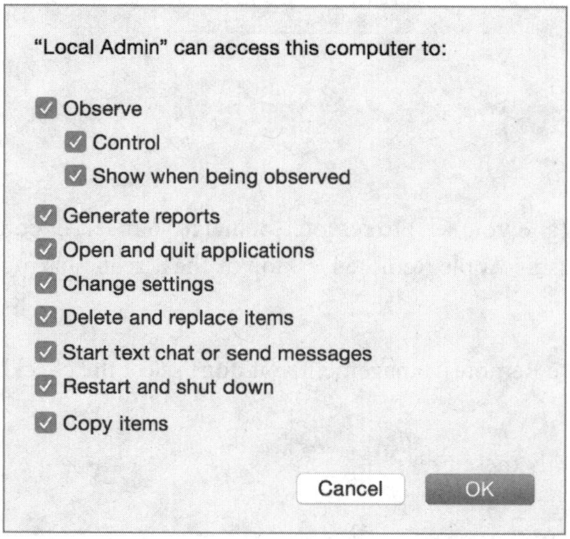

5   Click OK.

6   Select the checkbox Remote Management.

7   Confirm that the Sharing pane displays the text "Remote Management: On" and displays a green status indicator next to the text.

8   Click the Show All (looks like a grid) button to return to the main System Preferences pane.

```
●  ○ ○ ○     <   >   ▦            Sharing         Q Search         ⊗
```

Configure Network Interfaces

It is best practice to configure your network settings before you initially install and configure OS X Server. To get started, you will use your environment's DNS service, but keep in mind that during the course of these exercises, you will eventually use Change Host Name Assistant to configure, turn on, and use your server's DNS service.

NOTE ▶ The exercises are written for only one network interface to be active, but if you decide to use multiple network interfaces, this will not significantly impact your ability to complete the exercises.

NOTE ▶ As noted in ""Mandatory Requirements" on page xxi," the NetInstall exercises require an Ethernet port for your server. If you skip the NetInstall exercises, you can adapt the following instructions to configure an alternate network port, such as Wi-Fi.

1   In System Preferences, click Network.

2   In the instructor-led environment, configure your Mac computer's built-in Ethernet port to be the only active network service.

NOTE ▶ You may leave your Wi-Fi network interface turned on, but not joined to any network, to use AirDrop.

If you are performing the exercises independently, you may leave additional interfaces active, but be aware that this may cause differences between the way the exercises describe the windows and what you actually see.

In the list of network interfaces, select each network interface you will *not* use in the exercise (which should be all interfaces except one Ethernet port), click the Action (gear icon) pop-up menu, and choose Make Service Inactive.

3   If you will use multiple network interfaces, click the Action (gear icon) pop-up menu, choose Set Service Order, drag services to an appropriate order so that your primary interface is at the top of the list, and click OK.

4   Select the active Ethernet interface.

5   Click Advanced.

6   Click the TCP/IP tab.

7   In the Configure IPv4 pop-up menu, choose Manually.

8 In the instructor-led environment, enter the following information to manually configure the Ethernet interface (IPv4) for the classroom environment:

▶ IP Address: **10.0.0.***n***1** (where *n* is your student number; for example, student1 uses **10.0.0.11**, student 6 uses **10.0.0.61**, and student 15 uses **10.0.0.151**)

▶ Subnet Mask: **255.255.255.0**

▶ Router: **10.0.0.1**

	TCP/IP	DNS	WINS	802.1X	Proxies	Hardware

Configure IPv4:	Manually
IPv4 Address:	10.0.0.171
Subnet Mask:	255.255.255.0
Router:	10.0.0.1
Configure IPv6:	Automatically

If you are performing the exercises independently and choose to use different network settings, see "Exercise Setup" on page xx.

9 Click the DNS tab.

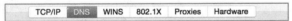

10 Even though you just switched Configure IPv4 from DHCP to Manually, you did not yet apply the change, so values assigned by DHCP are still listed, but once you click Apply, those values will not remain unless you deliberately add them.

MORE INFO ▶ In previous versions of OS X, DHCP-supplied values for DNS Servers and Search Domains were displayed dimmed.

11 In the DNS Servers field, click Add (+).

TCP/IP   DNS   WINS   8(

DNS Servers:

10.0.0.1

+ − IPv4 or IPv6 addresses

12 Enter 10.0.0.1.

If you are performing the exercises independently, enter the value or values appropriate for your environment.

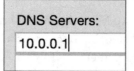

13 If there are any other values in the DNS Servers field, select another value, and then click Delete (–) to delete the value; do this until 10.0.0.1 is the only value in the DNS Servers field.

14 In the Search Domains field, any values assigned by DHCP are listed. In the Search Domains field, click Add (+), and enter pretendco.com.

If you are performing the exercises independently, enter the value or values appropriate for your environment.

TCP/IP	DNS	WINS	802.1X	Proxies	Hardware

DNS Servers:

10.0.0.1

Search Domains:

pretendco.com

15 If there are any other values in the Search Domains field, select another value, and then click Delete (–) to delete the value; do this until pretendco.com is the only value in the Search Domains field.

16 Click OK to save the change and return to the list of network interfaces.

17 Review the settings, and then click Apply to accept the network configuration.

Configure IPv4: Manually

IP Address: 10.0.0.171

Subnet Mask: 255.255.255.0

Router: 10.0.0.1

DNS Server: 10.0.0.1

Search Domains: pretendco.com

Update Software

If a local Caching service is available, your Mac will automatically use it to quickly download updates if they have already been downloaded on your network.

1 In System Preferences, click Show All.

2 Open App Store preferences.

3 Select the checkbox "Install app updates."

> **NOTE** ▸ The checkbox "Install app updates" enables automatic installation for Mac App Store items. However, you must manually install updates for the Server app; OS X prevents the Server app from being automatically updated. This is because any update to the Server app stops services and requires you to manually run the Server app to update the services.

4   Select the checkbox "Install OS X updates."

MORE INFO ▶ By default, the App Store preference "Install system data files and security updates" is selected so updates for important system and security software are installed automatically, except if the update requires a restart, in which case you will be presented with a notification stating "Updates Available." See Reference 4.1 Automatic Software Updates in *Apple Pro Training Series: OS X Support Essentials 10.10* for more information.

5   If the button at the bottom of the window is Check Now, click Check Now.

If the button at the bottom of the window is Show Updates, click Show Updates.

6   If you are in an instructor-led environment, ask your instructor what updates are appropriate to install; otherwise, if there are any updates, click Update All.

If there are no updates available, press Command-Q to quit App Store, skip the rest of this section, and continue with the section "Download Student Materials" on page 36.

7   If the "Some updates need to finish downloading before they are installed" dialog appears, click Download & Restart.

8   If the Restarting Your Computer notification appears, click Restart; after your Mac restarts, you will be automatically logged back in.

9   Quit App Store.

10 Quit System Preferences

Download Student Materials

Certain files are necessary for the completion of some of the exercises. If you are in an instructor-led environment, you can use the Option 1 section that follows. Otherwise, you should skip to Option 2.

Option 1: Download Student Materials in the Instructor-Led Environment

If you are performing the exercises independently, skip to "Option 2: Download Student Materials for the Independent Reader" on page 37.

If you are in an instructor-led environment, you will connect to the classroom server and download the student materials used for the course. To copy the files, you'll drag the folder to your Documents folder.

1   In the Finder, choose File > New Finder Window (or press Command-N).

2   In the Finder window sidebar, click Mainserver.

    If Mainserver does not appear in the Finder sidebar, in the Shared list click All, and then double-click the Mainserver icon in the Finder window.

    Because Mainserver allows guest access, your server computer logs in automatically as Guest and displays the available share points.

3   Open the Public folder.

4   Drag the StudentMaterials folder to the Documents folder in the Finder window sidebar.

5   Once the copy is complete, disconnect from Mainserver by clicking Eject next to the Mainserver listing.

In this exercise you configured your server computer in preparation for installing OS X Server. You have completed this exercise; skip the Option 2 section that follows.

Option 2: Download Student Materials for the Independent Reader

If you are in the instructor-led environment, skip this section.

If you are performing the exercises independently, download the materials from Peachpit's site and place them in your Documents folder.

You will use a redemption code—provided on the card in the back of the printed version of this guide or on the "Where Are the Lesson Files?" page in the electronic version of this guide—to access the student materials.

After you enter the provided redemption code on the Peachpit.com website, the related files will be added to your Peachpit account on the Lesson & Update Files tab.

1   Using Safari, open www.peachpit.com/redeem, enter the code provided, and click Redeem Code.

> **NOTE ▶** If you do not already have a free Peachpit account, you will be prompted to create one.

> **NOTE ▶** If you purchase or redeem a code for the electronic version of this guide directly from Peachpit, the lesson file link will automatically appear on the Lesson & Update Files tab without the need to redeem an additional code.

2   Click the Lesson & Update Files tab.

3   Click the lesson file links to download the appropriate files to your computer, which places the material in your Downloads folder.

4   In the Finder, choose File > New Finder Window (or press Command-N).

5   Choose Go > Downloads.

6   Double-click the StudentMaterials.zip file to decompress it.

7   Drag the StudentMaterials folder from your Downloads folder to your Documents folder in the Finder window sidebar.

8   Drag the StudentMaterials.zip file from your Downloads folder to the Trash in the Dock.

In this exercise, you used About This Mac, System Preferences, and the Finder to configure OS X on your server computer in preparation for installing OS X Server.

Exercise 1.2
Perform the Initial Installation of OS X Server on Your Server Computer

> ### Prerequisite
>
> ► "Exercise 1.1 Configure OS X Before Installing OS X Server on Your Server Computer " on page 21

Now that you have OS X configured on your server computer, it's time to install OS X Server on it and configure it so you can administer it remotely.

Install Server

It's recommended to download the latest version of OS X Server from the Mac App Store.

If you are in an instructor-led environment, use the Option 1 section that follows. Otherwise, you should skip to Option 2.

Option 1: In the Instructor-Led Environment, Copy Server

In the instructor-led environment, the classroom server has the Server app available in the StudentMaterials folder; move the Server app to the Applications folder on your server computer with the following steps:

1   In the Finder on your server computer, open a new Finder window, click Documents in the Finder window sidebar, open the StudentMaterials folder you downloaded, and then open the Lesson1 folder.

2   Drag the Server app into the Applications folder in the Finder window sidebar.

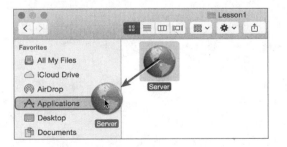

Please skip the Option 2 section; continue at the "Open Server" section that follows.

Option 2: For the Independent Reader, Download or Purchase Server in the Mac App Store

If you are performing the exercises independently, download OS X Server from the Mac App Store, which automatically places the Server app in your Applications folder.

Open Server

Once you have the Server app installed in the Applications folder, open the Server app.

1   In your Dock, click Launchpad.

2   You may need to swipe to the next page in Launchpad to see the Server app (hold down the Command key and press the Right Arrow key, or if you have a trackpad, swipe to the left with two fingers to get to the next page in Launchpad).

3   Click Server to open the Server app.

4   Keep the Server app in the Dock. Click and hold Server in the Dock, and then choose Options > Keep in Dock from the menu that appears.

5   At the "To set up OS X Server on this Mac, click Continue" pane, click Continue.

6   Read and agree to the terms of the software license agreement.

7   Ensure that "Use Apple services to determine this server's Internet reachability" is selected, and click Agree.

8   Provide local administrator credentials (User Name: Local Admin, Administrator Password: ladminpw) and click Allow.

9   Wait while OS X Server for Yosemite configures itself.

After its initial installation, the Server app displays the Overview tab in its Server pane.

NOTE ▶ The public IPv4 address in the following figure is obscured intentionally.

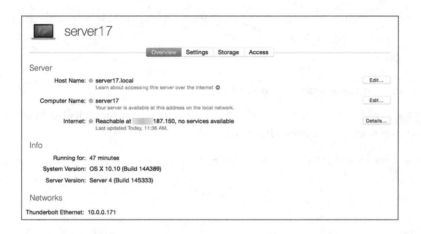

You have successfully installed OS X Server. Congratulations!

Configure Your Server's Host Name and DNS Records

In many production environments, DNS is already provided. This guide is carefully designed to be useful for students in an instructor-led environment as well as for independent readers, who may have any of a variety of different combinations of network infrastructure. This guide is written so that your server provides DNS and your administrator computer uses your server's DNS; in production environments, it is common to have different configurations.

Before you installed OS X Server, if you followed this guide, you configured your Mac to use a DNS service that does not have DNS records for the IPv4 address that you manually assigned for your Mac, so OS X automatically assigned the host name server*n*.local (where *n* is your student number).

> **NOTE ▶** It is recommended that you configure your server computer and your administrator computer according to the instructions in this guide, even if your environment provides DNS records, to experience what happens when the Server app configures your DNS service.

You will change your server's host name, which causes the Server app to offer to automatically configure, start, and use the DNS service, then you will use the alerts to address the "Host name changed" notification.

NOTE ▶ It is best practice to set up OS X Server with appropriate DNS records in place. This exercise illustrates a common scenario where DNS records are not already in place.

Update Your Server's Host Name and Start DNS Service

1   If the Server app window is not already displaying the Overview tab, select your server in the Server app sidebar, and then click the Overview tab.

2   Confirm that your server's Host Name is server*n*.local (where *n* is your student number).

3   Confirm that your server's Computer Name setting is server*n* (where *n* is your student number).

4   Next to the Host Name field, click Edit to change the host name.

5   In the Change Host Name pane, click Next.

6   If you see the Multiple Networks Detected pane, choose the network interface that you would like to use to configure your server's identity; the Server app will create forward and reverse records using the IPv4 address assigned to the network interface you choose (it should be 10.0.0.*n*1, where *n* is your student number). Click Next.

7   In the Accessing your Server pane, select Internet, and click Next.

You will learn more about these options in Lesson 2 "Providing DNS Records".

8 If necessary, set Computer Name to server*n*, where *n* is your student number.

9 In the Host Name field, enter server*n*.pretendco.com, where *n* is your student number.

10 Next to the Network Address field, click Edit to review your network settings.

11 If you have multiple interfaces, first select and then drag your intended primary network interface to the top of the network interface list, if it is not already at the top of the list.

12 Select your primary network interface, and confirm that it is configured as you want it configured; the settings should be as follows:

▶ Configure IPv4: Manually

▶ IP Address: 10.0.0.*n*1 (where *n* is your student number)

▶ Subnet Mask: 255.255.255.0

▶ Router: 10.0.0.1

▶ DNS Server: 10.0.0.1

▶ Search Domains: pretendco.com

Configure your server's network.

Thunderbolt... Private IP	Status: **Connected**
Bluetooth PAN Not Connected	Thunderbolt Ethernet is currently active and has the IP address 10.0.0.171.
Wi-Fi Not Connected	

Configure IPv4: Manually

IP Address: 10.0.0.171

Subnet Mask: 255.255.255.0

Router: 10.0.0.1

DNS Server: 10.0.0.1

Search Domains: pretendco.com

IPv6...   Ethernet...

Cancel   Apply

13 If you made any changes, click Apply to accept the network configuration changes. Otherwise, click Cancel to return to the Connecting to your Server pane.

14 At the Connecting to your Server pane, click Finish to accept the new names and network address settings.

15 At the "Do you want to set up DNS?" dialog, click Set Up DNS.

Do you want to set up DNS?

Server can automatically set up a DNS server that resolves your host name. Devices configured to use your server for DNS will be able to access your server using your host name. This will affect your server's network settings.

Skip   Set Up DNS

16 In the Overview pane, confirm that your Host Name and Computer Name fields are configured as you expect.

Server

Host Name: ● server17.pretendco.com   Edit...
            Learn about accessing this server over the internet ❷

Computer Name: ● server17   Edit...
                Your server is available at this address on the local network.

17 Confirm that the Advanced section of the Server app sidebar is now displayed and there is a green status indicator next to DNS, which indicates that DNS is running on this server.

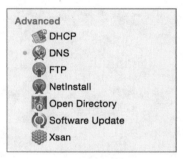

18 Open System Preferences, and click Network.

19 Select your primary network interface, click Advanced, and click DNS.

Configure the DNS Servers Field to Contain Only 127.0.0.1.

Note that 10.0.0.1 is also listed in the DNS Servers field. The Server app automatically adds your original DNS servers after adding 127.0.0.1 as a first entry as a fallback in case your server's DNS service is stopped or does not forward requests to other DNS servers properly. However, because other DNS servers may not reply with DNS records your server expects (for instance, replying with a public IPv4 address instead of a private IPv4 address), you should remove all entries other than 127.0.0.1 from the DNS Servers field.

1 Highlight the 10.0.0.1 entry, and then click Remove (–).

2 Confirm that the DNS Servers field contains 127.0.0.1 only and that the Search Domains field contains pretendco.com.

DNS Servers:	Search Domains:
127.0.0.1	pretendco.com

3   Click OK to save the change and return to the list of network interfaces.

4   Review the settings, and then click Apply to accept the network configuration.

5   Quit System Preferences.

View the Host Name Change Alert

After you change the server's host name, the server generates an alert about the change.

1   Click Alerts in the Server app

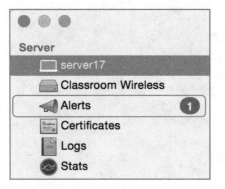

2   Double-click to open the "Host name changed notification" alert.

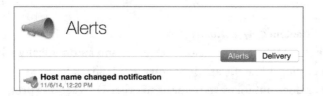

3   Review the information in the alert.

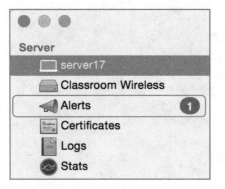

4   Click Done.

Configure Your Server to Allow Remote Administration

Configure your server so that you can administer it with the Server app on your administrator computer.

1   In the Server app, select your server in the sidebar.

2   Click the Settings tab.

3   Select the checkbox "Allow remote administration using Server."

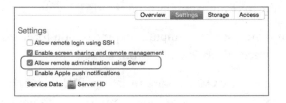

4   Because you're going to open the Server app on your administrator computer next, press Command-Q to quit the Server app.

It's recommended that you administer your server with only one instance of the Server app at a time.

In this exercise, you used the Server app to configure your server with OS X Server, and you turned on remote administration using the Server app, which leads nicely to the next exercise, which is to configure your administrator computer.

Exercise 1.3
Configure Your Administrator Computer

▶ **Prerequisites**

- ▶ "Exercise 1.1 Configure OS X Before Installing OS X Server on Your Server Computer" on page 21
- ▶ "Exercise 1.2 Perform the Initial Installation of OS X Server on Your Server Computer" on page 39
- ▶ You must have a Mac that is running OS X Yosemite and that has never had OS X Server installed and configured on its startup volume.

Your "administrator computer" is a Mac on which you will open the Server app and use it to administer your computer running OS X Server. Remember that your administrator computer must be running OS X Yosemite to administer OS X Server for Yosemite.

In this exercise, you will configure your administrator computer in preparation for using it to administer your server and to remotely access services from your server.

This exercise is similar to "Exercise 1.1 Configure OS X Before Installing OS X Server on Your Server Computer" on page 21, but you will configure your administrator computer to use the following:

- ▶ A different computer name
- ▶ A different primary IPv4 address
- ▶ Your server's DNS service

You'll use one of two options to configure a local administrator account, depending on whether you are performing these exercises independently or are in an instructor-led environment.

In both situations, you'll use System Preferences to configure the Network and Sharing settings (if you want, you can change the Energy Saver settings on your own). You will also download student materials that you'll use throughout this class. Finally, you will apply any necessary system software updates and then use the Server app to confirm that you can use it to connect to your server.

If your administrator computer has not yet been set up and is at the Welcome screen, use the Option 1 section that follows. Otherwise, you should skip to "Option 2: Configure an Existing OS X System for Your Administrator Computer" on page 51.

Option 1: Configure OS X on Your Administrator Computer with Setup Assistant

This option is necessary only if your administrator computer has not already been set up, which is the situation in an instructor-led environment. If you are using a Mac with existing accounts, perform "Option 2: Configure an Existing OS X System for Your Administrator Computer" on page 51 instead.

Ensure that you have Yosemite installed on your administrator computer. If it isn't already installed, install it now using the Mac App Store, OS X Recovery, or a method specified by your instructor, and then continue when you reach the Welcome screen.

In this section, you'll step through OS X Setup Assistant for the initial system configuration of your administrator computer.

1   Ensure that your administrator computer is connected to a valid network connection.

2   If necessary, turn on your administrator computer.

3   In the Welcome screen, select the appropriate region, and click Continue.

4   Select the appropriate keyboard layout, and click Continue.

Setup Assistant evaluates your network environment and tries to determine whether you are connected to the Internet. This can take a few moments.

5   If you are not asked about your Internet connection, your computer's network settings have already been configured via DHCP, and you may move on to step 6.

If you are performing the exercises in an instructor-led environment, ask your instructor how you should configure your computer.

If you are performing the exercises independently and you plan to use Wi-Fi as your primary network connection, select an appropriate Wi-Fi network, provide the Wi-Fi network's password, and click Continue. Keep in mind that to perform the NetInstall exercises, both your server and your administrator computer need an Ethernet connection.

6   When asked about transferring information to this Mac, select "Don't transfer any information now," and click Continue.

7   At the Sign in with Your Apple ID pane, select "Don't sign in," click Continue, and then click Skip to confirm that you want to skip signing in with an Apple ID. Note that if you do provide Apple ID credentials, some figures may look slightly different, and there may be extra steps.

8   In the Terms and Conditions pane, when you have finished reading, click Agree.

9   In the dialog to confirm that you have read and agree to the OS X software license agreement, click Agree.

Create your local administrator account.

> **NOTE ▶** It is important that you create this account as specified here. If you do not, future exercises may not work as written. **Bold blue** text is used throughout this guide to indicate text that you should enter exactly as shown.

1   In the Create Your Computer Account pane, use the following settings:

    ▶ Full Name: **Local Admin**

    ▶ Account Name: **ladmin**

    ▶ Password: **ladminpw**

    ▶ (verify field): **ladminpw**

    ▶ Hint: Leave blank.

    ▶ Deselect the checkbox "Set time zone based on current location."

    ▶ Deselect the checkbox "Send Diagnostics & Usage data to Apple."

> **NOTE ▶** In a production environment, you should always use a strong password.

2   Click Continue to create the local administrator account.

3   At the Select Time Zone pane, click your time zone in the map or choose the nearest location in the Closest City pop-up menu, and then click Continue.

Please skip the section "Option 2: Configure an Existing OS X System for Your Server Computer" on page 25; continue at the section "Set the Computer Name and Turn On Remote Management " on page 28.

Option 2: Configure an Existing OS X System for Your Administrator Computer

This option is designed only for those who are performing the exercises independently and who have a computer that is already set up with an existing administrator account.

NOTE ▶ You may not use a Mac whose startup volume has already had OS X Server installed.

If your computer has not been set up (that is, if the initial administrator account has not been created), perform "Option 1: Configure OS X on Your Administrator Computer with Setup Assistant" on page 49 instead.

Create a new administrator account in System Preferences.

1   If necessary, log in with your existing administrator account.

2   Open System Preferences.

3   In System Preferences, open Users & Groups.

4   In the lower-left corner, click the lock icon.

5   In the dialog that appears, enter the password for your existing administrator account, and click Unlock.

6   Click the Add (+) button under the user list.

7   In the dialog that appears, use the following settings:

NOTE ▶ It is important that you create this account as specified here. If you do not, future exercises may not work as written. If you already have an account named Local Admin or ladmin, you will have to use a different name here and then remember to use your substitute name throughout the rest of the exercises. **Bold blue** text is used throughout this guide to indicate text that you should enter exactly as shown.

▶ New Account: Choose Administrator.

▶ Full Name: Local Admin

▶ Account Name: ladmin

8   Select "Use separate password."

If you are performing the exercises in an instructor-led environment, enter ladminpw in the two Password fields.

If you are performing the exercises independently, you can select a more secure password for the Local Admin account. Be sure to remember the password you have chosen because you will need to reenter it periodically as you use this computer.

You may provide a password hint if you want.

If you entered your Apple ID, you can select or deselect the checkbox "Allow my Apple ID to reset this user's password"; it does not have a major effect on the exercises.

NOTE ▶ In a production environment, you should always use a strong password.

9   Click Create User.

10   If automatic login was turned on and you are asked if you want to turn it off, click Turn Off Automatic Login.

11   Quit System Preferences, and log out.

12   At the login screen, select the Local Admin account, and enter its password (ladminpw or whatever you specified earlier).

13   Press Return to log in.

14   At the Sign in with Your Apple ID pane, select "Don't sign in," click Continue, and then click Skip at the confirmation dialog.

Continue with the next section.

Set the Computer Name and Turn On Remote Management

You will specify a computer name associated with your student number. If you are performing the exercises independently, you can choose to skip this section.

You will also turn on Remote Management, which will allow the instructor to observe your computer, control your keyboard and mouse, gather information, copy items to your computer, and otherwise help you if necessary.

1   Open System Preferences.

2   Open Sharing.

3   For Computer Name, enter clientn, replacing n with your student number.

For example, if your student number is 17, the computer name should be client17, in all lowercase and with no spaces.

4   Press Return to make the change take effect.

Notice that the local network name listed under the Computer Name field is automatically updated.

5   Click somewhere over the phrase Remote Management, but don't select the checkbox yet.

6   In "Allow Access for," select "Only these users."

7   Click the Add (+) button, select Local Admin, and click Select.

8   In the dialog that appears, hold down the Option key while selecting the Observe checkbox, which results in automatically selecting all the checkboxes.

9   Click OK.

10   Select the checkbox Remote Management.

11   Click Show All to return to the main System Preferences pane.

Configure Networking

Configure your administrator computer to use your server's DNS service.

> **NOTE** ▶ The exercises are written for only one network interface to be active, but if you decide to use multiple network interfaces, this will not significantly impact your ability to complete the exercises.

NOTE ▶ As noted in "Mandatory Requirements" on page xxi, the NetInstall exercises require an Ethernet port for your administrator computer. If you skip the NetInstall exercises, you can adapt the following instructions to configure an alternate network port, such as Wi-Fi.

1 In System Preferences, click Network.

2 In the instructor-led environment, configure one of your Mac computer's Ethernet ports to be the only active network service.

   NOTE ▶ You may leave your Wi-Fi network interface enabled, but not joined to any network, to use AirDrop.

   In the list of network interfaces, select each network interface you will *not* use in the exercise (which should be each interface except for one Ethernet interface), click the Action (gear icon) pop-up menu, and choose Make Service Inactive.

   If you are performing the exercises independently, you may leave additional interfaces active, but be aware that this may cause differences between the way the exercises describe the windows and what you actually see.

3 If you will use multiple network interfaces, click the Action (gear icon) pop-up menu, choose Set Service Order, drag services to an appropriate order so that your primary interface is at the top of the list, and click OK.

4 Select the active Ethernet interface.

5 Click Advanced.

6 Click the TCP/IP tab.

7 In the Configure IPv4 pop-up menu, choose Manually.

8 Enter the following information to manually configure the Ethernet interface (IPv4) for the classroom environment:

   ▶ IP Address: 10.0.0.n2 (where n is your student number; for example, student1 uses 10.0.0.12, student 6 uses 10.0.0.62, and student 15 uses 10.0.0.152)

   ▶ Subnet Mask: 255.255.255.0

   ▶ Router: 10.0.0.1

TCP/IP	DNS	WINS	802.1X	Proxies	Hardware

Configure IPv4: Manually

IPv4 Address: 10.0.0.172

Subnet Mask: 255.255.255.0

Router: 10.0.0.1

Configure IPv6: Automatically

If you are performing the exercises independently and choose to use different settings, see the section "Network Infrastructure" on page xxii and be prepared to substitute network values that are appropriate for your environment throughout all the exercises in this guide.

9   Click the DNS tab.

10   Even though you just switched from DHCP to Manual, you did not yet apply the change, so values assigned by DHCP are listed but will not remain unless you deliberately add them.

11   In the DNS Servers field, click Add (+), and enter the IPv4 address of your server computer (10.0.0.n1, where n is your student number; for example, student1 uses 10.0.0.11, student 6 uses 10.0.0.61, and student 15 uses 10.0.0.151).

DNS Servers:

10.0.0.171

12   In the Search Domains field, values assigned by DHCP are listed.

If there are any manually entered values in the Search Domains field, the Delete (–) button is available; select each entry, and then click Delete to delete the entry until the Delete button is dimmed.

13   In the Search Domains field, click Add (+), and enter pretendco.com.

If you are performing the exercises independently, enter a value appropriate for your environment.

14   Click OK to close this pane.

15 Review the settings, and then click Apply to accept the network configuration.

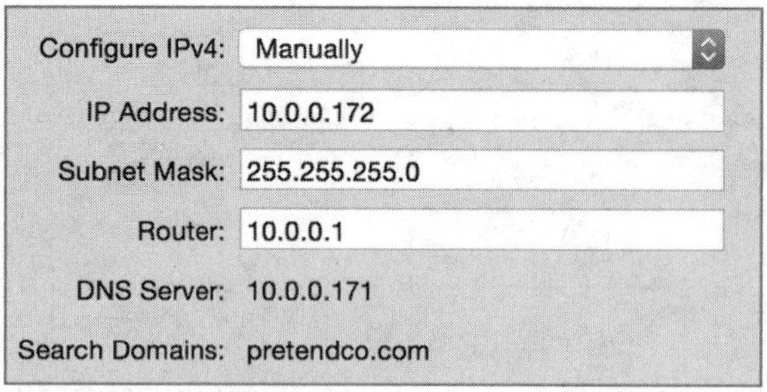

Configure IPv4:	Manually
IP Address:	10.0.0.172
Subnet Mask:	255.255.255.0
Router:	10.0.0.1
DNS Server:	10.0.0.171
Search Domains:	pretendco.com

16 Quit System Preferences.

Confirm DNS Records

Use Network Utility to confirm that your administrator computer can access your server's DNS service. Network Utility is located in /System/Library/CoreServices/Applications/, which is automatically indexed by Spotlight.

1 On your administrator Mac, click the Spotlight icon in the upper-right corner of the screen (or press Command–Space bar) to reveal the Spotlight search field.

> ⌕ Spotlight Search

2 Enter Network Utility in the Spotlight search field.

If there is no result for Network Utility, then choose Go > Go to Folder, enter /System/Library/CoreServices/Applications/, click Go, open Network Utility, and skip to step 4.

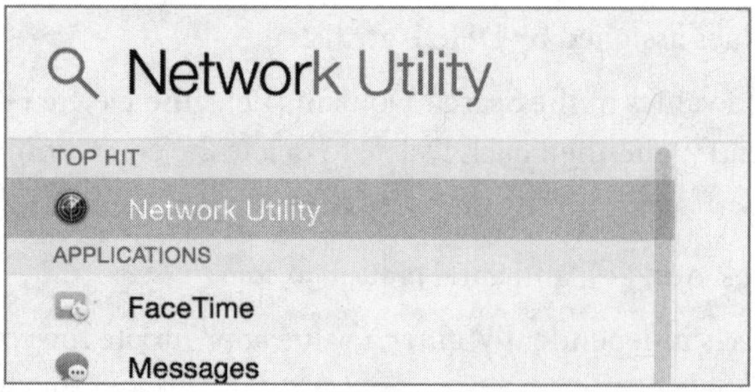

> ⌕ **Network** Utility
>
> TOP HIT
>
> 🌐 Network Utility
>
> APPLICATIONS
>
> 📷 FaceTime
>
> 💬 Messages

3 Press Return to open the "Top Hit" of your Spotlight search, which is Network Utility.

4   In Network Utility, click the Lookup tab.

5   Enter your server's primary IPv4 address in the field (10.0.0.n1, where n is your student number), and click Lookup.

6   Confirm that your server's host name appears in the results field.

7   Enter your server's host name in the field, and click Lookup.

8   Confirm that your server's primary IPv4 address appears in the results field.

9   Press Command-Q to quit Network Utility.

Update Software

If a local Caching service is available, your Mac will automatically use it.

1   Open System Preferences

2   Open App Store preferences.

3   Select the checkbox "Install app updates."

4   Select the checkbox "Install OS X updates."

5   If the button at the bottom of the window is Check Now, click Check Now.

If the button at the bottom of the window is Show Updates, click Show Updates.

6   If you are in an instructor-led environment, ask your instructor what updates are appropriate to install; otherwise, if there are any updates, click Update All.

If there are no updates available, press Command-Q to quit App Store; then skip the rest of this section, and continue with the section "Download Student Materials" on page 58.

7   If the "Some updates need to finish downloading before they are installed" dialog appears, click Download & Restart.

If the Restarting Your Computer notification appears, click Restart; after your Mac restarts, you will be automatically logged back in.

8   Quit App Store.

9   Quit System Preferences.

Download Student Materials

Certain files are necessary for the completion of some of the exercises. You have already downloaded them to your server computer, but you should also have them available on your administrator computer. If you are in an instructor-led environment, you can use the Option 1 section that follows. Otherwise, you should skip to Option 2.

Option 1: Download Student Materials in the Instructor-Led Environment

If you are in an instructor-led environment, you will connect to the classroom server and download the student materials used for the course. To copy the files, you'll drag the folder to your Documents folder.

If you are performing the exercises independently, skip to "Option 2: Download Student Materials for the Independent Reader" on page 59.

1   In the Finder, choose File > New Finder Window (or press Command-N).

2   In the Finder window sidebar, click Mainserver.

If Mainserver does not appear in the Finder sidebar, in the Shared list click All, and then double-click the Mainserver icon in the Finder window.

Because Mainserver allows guest access, your administrator computer logs in automatically as Guest and displays the available share points.

3   Open the Public folder.

4   Drag the StudentMaterials folder to the Documents folder in the Finder window sidebar.

5   Once the copy is complete, disconnect from Mainserver by clicking Eject next to the listing for Mainserver.

Skip the Option 2 section that follows, and resume with the section "Install the Server App" on page 60.

Option 2: Download Student Materials for the Independent Reader
If you are performing the exercises independently, copy the student materials from your server (or download the materials from Peachpit's site), place them in your Documents folder, and then apply any necessary system software updates.

If both of your Mac computers have AirDrop turned on, you can use AirDrop to copy the StudentMaterials folder from your server to your administrator computer. Click AirDrop in a Finder window on each Mac. On your server computer, open a new Finder window, open your Documents folder, drag the StudentMaterials folder to the picture for your administrator computer in the AirDrop window, and then click Send. On your administrator computer, click Save; then once the transfer has completed, open the Downloads folder, and drag StudentMaterials to your Documents folder in the Finder window sidebar. Finally, close the AirDrop window on your server computer and on your administrator computer.

Another option is to use a removable disk. If you have a universal serial bus (USB), FireWire, or Thunderbolt disk, you can connect it to your server, copy the StudentMaterials folder from your local administrator's Documents folder to the volume, eject the volume, connect the volume to your administrator computer, and drag the StudentMaterials folder to your Documents folder in the Finder window sidebar.

Alternatively, you can download the files from Peachpit again using the steps in "Download Student Materials" on page 36.

Everyone should continue with the next section, "Install the Server App."

Install the Server App

On your server computer, you ran the Server app to configure your server computer as a server. However, on your administrator computer, you will run the Server app to remotely administer your server.

Option 1: In the Instructor-Led Environment, Copy Server

In the instructor-led environment, the classroom server has the Server app available in the StudentMaterials folder; move the Server app to the Applications folder on your server computer with the following steps:

1   In the Finder on your server computer, open a new Finder window, click Documents in the Finder window sidebar, open the StudentMaterials folder that you downloaded, and then open the Lesson1 folder.

2   Drag the Server app into the Applications folder in the Finder window sidebar.

Option 2: For the Independent Reader, Download or Purchase Server in the Mac App Store

If you are performing the exercises independently, you should have already purchased OS X Server by the time you completed "Exercise 1.2 Perform the Initial Installation of OS X Server on Your Server Computer" on page 39; if this is the case, open the Mac App Store in your Dock or from the Apple menu, log in with the Apple ID you used to purchase OS X Server, and download OS X Server, which automatically places the Server app in your Applications folder.

Use the Server App to Administer Your Server

Using your administrator computer, open the Server app, connect to your server, and accept its SSL certificate.

1   On your administrator computer, open the Server app.

2   Click and hold Server in the Dock, and then choose Options > Keep in Dock from the menu that appears.

3   Click Other Mac.

4   In the Choose a Mac window, select your server, and click Continue.

5   Provide the administrator credentials (Administrator Name: ladmin, Administrator Password: ladminpw).

6   Leave the "Remember this password in my keychain" checkbox unselected so the credentials you provide will not be saved in your keychain (a secure store of passwords), which means that you must provide administrator credentials each time you connect to your server with the Server app. This facilitates using different administrator credentials, as is required for "Exercise 7.1 Create and Configure Local User Accounts" on page 219.

7   Click Connect.

8   Because your server is using a self-signed SSL certificate that has not been signed by a certificate authority (CA) that your administrator computer is configured to trust, you'll see a warning message that you are connecting to a server whose identity certificate is not verified. See Lesson 4 "Configuring SSL Certificates" for more information on SSL.

> **NOTE ▶** In a production environment, you might want to address this situation as soon as possible by using Keychain Access on your server computer to configure your server to use a valid SSL certificate for the com.apple.servermgrd identity, which is used to communicate with a remote instance of the Server app. This is outside the scope of this guide.

9   Click Show Certificate.

10 Select the checkbox to always trust com.apple.servermgrd when connecting to your server by its fully qualified domain name.

11 Click Continue.

12 You must provide your login credentials to modify your keychain.

Enter your password (ladminpw), and click Update Settings.

After you click Update Settings, the Server app connects to your server.

In this exercise, you prepared your administrator computer to remotely administer your server and to access services from your server.

Lesson 2
Providing DNS Records

The Domain Name System (DNS) is a critical service. It is so critical in fact that OS X Server sets up its own DNS service if one is not provided for it in certain circumstances. Without a properly working DNS, problems will occur with certain services, and as a result, it is important to understand what DNS is and how to manage it for OS X and other computers.

Although there are many aspects of DNS, this lesson concentrates on what is needed to make OS X work properly.

GOALS

▶ Deploy OS X Server as a DNS server

▶ Understand DNS

Reference 2.1
What Is DNS?

In its basic form, DNS is the system that helps identify computers, servers, and other devices on a network via an Internet Protocol version 4 (IPv4) number or name. Here are two examples:

server17.pretendco.com = 10.0.0.171 (a forward lookup)

10.0.0.171 = server17.pretendco.com (a reverse lookup)

UNIX operating systems such as OS X rely on DNS to keep track of resources on the network, including themselves. They are constantly doing "lookups," or finding out about the IP addresses and host names they need to contact, including their own information. The lookups can be triggered by authentication requests, access to resources, or almost anything else a server may be asked to do.

The flow of a DNS request goes like this:

1. A computer makes a DNS request to find out the IP address of a resource such as a web server or file server. That request is sent to the DNS server that the computer is configured to use. It got that information via Dynamic Host Configuration Protocol (DHCP) or a manual configuration of the DNS server. For example, where is www.apple.com?

2. The DNS server receives the request and determines whether it has the answer to the question either by being authoritative for the domain the request is for or by having it cached from a previous request. If it has the answer, it returns the answer to the requesting computer. It may have the answer because it has cached the answer from an earlier request, or it is "authoritative" for that domain (apple.com) and is configured with the answer. If not, it might forward the request to another DNS server it has been configured to use. This is known as the "forwarding server," and it now has the responsibility to get the result and report to the requesting DNS server.

3. If there is not a forwarding server, the DNS server consults a list of root servers located at /Library/Server/named/named.ca and sends a request to a root server.

4. The root server sends a response telling the DNS server where to find the DNS servers that handle .com requests because the original request was for a domain that had ".com" as the top-level domain (TLD).

5. The DNS server asks the TLD server where the domain "apple.com" is, and the server responds with that answer.

6. Now knowing where the DNS server that is authoritative for "apple.com" is, the DNS server asks for the answer to www.apple.com, and the server provides the answer.

7. The DNS server does two things with that answer: passes the answer to the original requestor and caches the answer in case another request comes in for it. The cached answer will live on the requesting server for a time specified in the DNS record, called "time to live" (TTL). After that time expires, the cached answer is purged.

As you can see, having the answer close speeds up the lookup process, so it is handy to host your own DNS server for your own users' computers and mobile devices.

Typical trouble caused by bad or nonexistent DNS includes the following:

▶ Resources that can't be connected to over the network, such as websites, wikis, calendars, and file shares

▶ Not being able to log in to a computer that uses Open Directory hosted by the server

▶ Single sign-on (SSO) via Kerberos not working

▶ Authentication problems

DNS has a number of pieces, including but not limited to the following:

▶ Requestor—The computer looking for information.

► DNS server—The service that provides all or some of the information the requestor asks for.

► Records—The information-defining information relating to the DNS zone, such as machines and name servers.

► Zone files—The text-based files that contain the DNS records. As of OS X Mavericks, these files reside in a new location, /Library/Server/named/.

► Primary zone—A group of records for a domain.

► Secondary zone—A replica of a primary zone, typically on another DNS server, that has its records created by a zone transfer.

► Zone transfer—The process of sending a copy of a primary zone to another server for use with a secondary zone.

► Forwarding server—Where requests are sent if the DNS server doesn't have the zone information to answer the request.

Reference 2.2
Evaluating OS X DNS Hosting Requirements

When first configuring OS X Server, the Server app checks to see whether a DNS host name correlating to the computer's IPv4 address is being provided by the DNS server listed in Network preferences. If it is, the computer is named with the host name information contained in the DNS records.

If DNS information for the computer's IPv4 address is not provided, OS X Server sets up the DNS service on that computer if the Host Name setting is edited. This is different from some versions of OS X Server prior to 10.9, which handled that task at the initial server configuration. This process guarantees that at least enough DNS information is available to the server to function properly. You can tell that the DNS service was turned on in the Server app list of services if you see a green status indicator next to the DNS service and in Network preferences if the value for DNS Server is 127.0.0.1.

Here are three typical scenarios for DNS services as they relate to OS X Server:

▸ Automatically configured DNS—If the server has its own DNS running and working, leaving it that way and not configuring the DNS service beyond that point may be appropriate. This may be when the server is the only server on the network, as might be the case in a small office. The client computers will contact the server via Bonjour for those services that support it. This assumes that the server is on the same segment (subnet) of the network as the client. This configuration is viable and might work well.

▸ Externally provided DNS—Other configurations may require externally provided DNS. An example of this is when the server will be connected to an Active Directory (AD) system for user and group information. In this situation, it is best to place a record for the server into the DNS service used by the Windows server hosting AD. Make sure there is an A record, used for forward lookups, of server17.pretendco.com = 10.0.0.171 and a reverse, or PTR, record of 10.0.0.171 = server17.pretendco.com. Check these details using Network Utility or command-line tools before configuring your server to use this external DNS server.

NOTE ▶ Windows DNS service prior to Windows 2008 R2 commonly doesn't provide a reverse zone. While making an A record, there is a checkbox to automatically make a PTR record, but unless the appropriate reverse zone already exists, the PTR record will not be made.

▶ OS X Server–hosted DNS—This differs from automatically configured DNS in that it is manually set up by the administrator and can be used by other computers and devices on the network to get DNS information. The DNS service on the server has new DNS zones set up and populated with records representing the computers, servers, and other devices on the network. This style of providing DNS is used when there are larger needs than simply identifying one server on the network, and all computers on your network will use your server for DNS information.

Dealing with Internal and External DNS

Today users expect to access their data from wherever they are, so you need to consider how to handle requests both from inside your own networks and from networks that are outside your control. Services such as Mail, Calendar, Websites, and device management are used from both types of networks, so you need to know how to handle DNS in both cases.

The concept is simple: For computers and devices on your internal network, just use your server's DNS service. But for computers and devices that are not on your internal network (and that do not have a VPN connection to your internal network), configure an external DNS server to provide authoritative DNS service for your domain with records that use public IP addresses, and configure your router to forward that traffic to your server's internal IP address. For simple setups, you can use an AirPort Base Station; see "AirPort" on page 102 for more information.

Here is an example of an internal request:

www.pretendco.com = 10.0.0.171

Here is an example of an external request:

www.pretendco.com = 203.0.113.10

For this to work, you need to populate the external DNS host server with the proper external IP address for your servers and allow the services access through your firewall based on the ports they use. This lets you provide the same services for users wherever they may be.

Here are some examples to show when to use what DNS service:

▶ Outside DNS only—If you don't have to serve clients internal to your network, you may not have to set up internal DNS except for the server. If you are hosting email, profile management, or websites that users access from outside your network, there is no need to configure extra DNS records for internal usage. You just need to use a DNS hosting company to provide your DNS and set up your domain to point to the authoritative DNS servers.

▶ Outside DNS, self-hosted—This is the same idea as the first one, but instead of using a commercially hosted DNS server, you configure your DNS service in OS X Server to provide the external DNS records. You need to populate the DNS zones with the appropriate records and allow outside requests to be answered by your server. You still need to configure the domain to point to your DNS service.

▶ Internal DNS only—If you are not exposing any of your services to the outside world, you need to configure only an internal DNS service that provides answers for internal resources. You can limit the requests to which the DNS service will reply to clients on your internal network. This allows you to have full control over your internal DNS system.

▶ Separate DNS—If you are providing services to both internal clients and external clients, it is a good idea to have your own internal DNS server and configure a separate external DNS server or use a hosted DNS service. Depending on where clients are, they will get answers to DNS queries from your internal DNS server with internal resources if they are inside your network or from your external DNS service with external resources if they are outside your network. Make sure the external requests coming into your network are routed to the correct internal resources.

Reference 2.3
Configuring DNS Service in OS X Server

Prior to setting up DNS services in OS X Server, you need to collect certain information. This includes the following:

▶ The domain you want to host. In this guide, you'll be using pretendco.com.

▶ The host names you want to have records for. Most of the examples in this guide use server17 as the host name, but you could also include records for devices such as printer01 or winserver02. These are used for the A records, or forward lookups, which map a DNS name to an IPv4 address.

▶ The IPv4 addresses for all the host names you want to include. These are used for the PTR records, or reverse lookups, mapping IPv4 addresses to DNS names. An example is 10.0.0.171.

▶ The IPv4 address of upstream DNS servers that will answer DNS requests the DNS server you are setting up doesn't have the answers for. This is called a "forwarder." If you don't provide a forwarder, top-down lookups involving the root DNS servers get used. It is more practical and better practice to use forwarding servers to reduce the load on the root DNS servers. You can use DNS servers provided by your Internet service provide (ISP) or any public DNS service.

▶ The range of IPv4 addresses or networks you want your DNS server to provide DNS lookups for. This prevents unwanted networks from using your DNS server.

▶ The information for any other type of record you want to include, such as the email server needed for MX records, the server you want to make an alias for when setting up a CNAME, or servers that need to advertise their services via a SRV record.

The general flow of setting up a DNS server includes defining the domain or domains that the server will be responsible for. The DNS service that is responsible for the "official" DNS information about a domain is the Start of Authority (SoA) of the domain and is contained in the DNS records. If you are hosting DNS records strictly for your internal domains, this is not a critical piece of information, but if you are hosting DNS for a domain that is accessible to the Internet, it is critical.

Since OS X Server can create its own default zone during the running of the Change Host Name assistant if an external DNS record isn't available for the server's IP address, you will end up with a zone that is authoritative for the fully qualified name of your server (server17.pretendco.com), not just the domain (pretendco.com). This is fine if you never plan to add more DNS records, but if you do, you will want to add the new zones based on your domain and remove the generated zones.

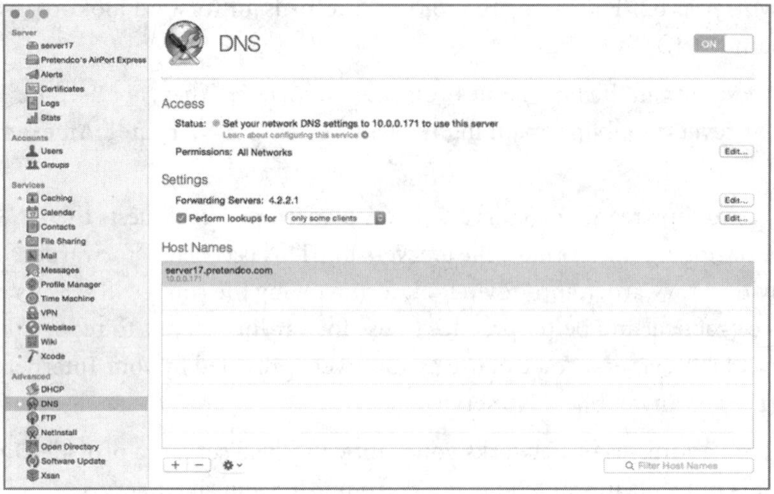

Reference 2.4
Troubleshooting DNS Service in OS X Server

Since DNS is a critical service, it helps to understand the basics of troubleshooting it:

► Is the server, computer, or device set up to use the proper DNS server? Many problems are related to the wrong information being delivered via an incorrectly defined DNS server.

► Are DNS services available on the defined DNS server? Check that the DNS service is running on the defined server. In Terminal, run the command telnet *<IPv4 address of server>* 53 and see whether a connection is made (after a successful connection, press Control-], and then type quit to close the connection). Port 53 is the port used by DNS.

▸ Are the proper DNS records available from the DNS server? Check all the pertinent records, forward and reverse, using Network Utility or command-line tools. Make sure both the forward and reverse records are available and match.

▸ Your computer might be caching old DNS information and needs to be flushed. To flush the DNS cache, run the command `sudo discoveryutil udnsflushcache` in Terminal app.

Exercise 2.1
Create DNS Zones and Records

▸ **Prerequisites**

  ▸ All exercises in Lesson 1 "Installing OS X Server"

When you performed the initial installation and configuration of OS X Server in Lesson 1 "Installing OS X Server", the DNS service you configured OS X to use did not contain records for your server's primary IPv4 address. When you used the Change Hostname Assistant, the Server app automatically configured a domain called server*n*.pretendco.com (where *n* is your student number) with one A (address) record in it, which facilities a forward lookup. Then the DNS service was automatically started for you.

Although this is fine for a single host system, in this exercise you will replace the limited primary zone of server*n*.pretendco.com (where *n* is your student number) with a new zone for pretendco.com, which can contain a broader set of records. You will create a machine record, an alias record, and an MX record in the zone you just created.

After you confirm that the Show All Records option is deselected in the Action (looks like a gear) menu, you will click the Add (+) button and create a new record in the form of server*n*.pretendco.com (where *n* is your student number), and the Server app will offer the following:

▶ The IP Addresses field for you to specify multiple addresses for the host name
▶ The Aliases field for you to specify multiple alias records for the host name
▶ The "Create an MX record for this host name" which creates an MX record (for the pretendco.com zone) with priority 0 for the host name

Once you enter the host name and click Create, the Server app will do the following:

▶ Create a new pretendco.com zone
▶ Create a nameserver record for the zone (using the host name you specified)

You will use Network Utility on your administrator computer to confirm your work.

To prevent confusion moving forward, after you confirm that your new zone is functional, you will remove the limited server*n*.pretendco.com zone (where *n* is your student number).

Collect DNS Configuration Data

Prior to setting up the DNS service, gather your information. For this exercise, use the following information:

▶ Forwarder server address (or addresses). In a classroom situation, your instructor will provide you with the appropriate IPv4 addresses for your classroom's Internet connection; if you are performing the exercises independently, use the IPv4 address of a DNS server or servers provided by your ISP.

▶ Additional record type. Use an MX record for pretendco.com, which is your server's hostname with a priority of 0.

▶ Alias record for vpn.pretendco.com to server*n*.pretendco.com (where *n* is your student number).

▶ Additional machine record for client*n*.pretendco.com with 10.0.0.*n2* (where *n* is your student number).

Configure Forwarding Servers

If your server's DNS service receives a request for a DNS record that it does not host and you have configured a forwarding server for your DNS service, then your server's DNS service sends that request to a forwarding server. If you do not specify any forwarding servers, then your server uses the root DNS servers. It is best practice to specify the DNS servers provided by your ISP (which has a much larger cache of entries from the Internet and may result in a quicker lookup), but you can specify any other DNS servers that perform successful lookups in response to requests from your server's DNS service.

You will specify DNS forwarders provided by your ISP (or by your instructor, if you are in an instructor-led environment). If you do not know what DNS forwarders to use, read this section, and resume by performing the steps in the next section, "Configure DNS Hosts " on page 76.

After you make the change, confirm that you can use your DNS service to look up records that your server's DNS service does not directly host.

1   On your server, open the Server app, and select the DNS service.

2   To the right of Forwarding Servers, click Edit.

Settings
Forwarding Servers: 10.0.0.1   Edit...

3   For each existing value, select the value, and then click the Remove (–) button.

4   Click the Add (+) button.

5   Enter the IPv4 address of a forwarding server, and click OK.

6   Repeat the previous step for each additional DNS server.

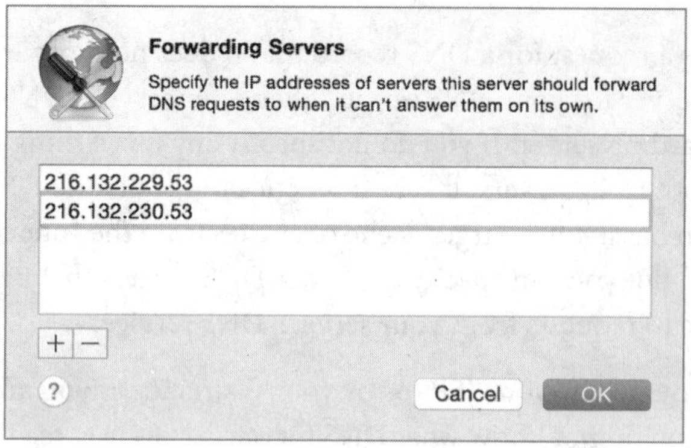

Forwarding Servers

Specify the IP addresses of servers this server should forward DNS requests to when it can't answer them on its own.

216.132.229.53
216.132.230.53

[+][−]

(?)   Cancel   OK

7   Click OK to save the change.

If you have one forwarder, it is listed. Otherwise, the number of forwarding servers is displayed.

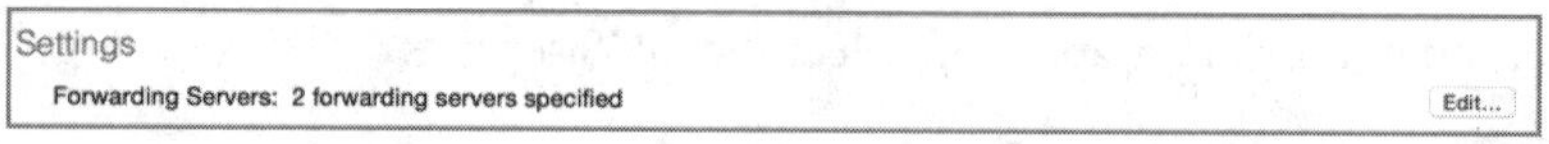

Settings

Forwarding Servers: 2 forwarding servers specified   Edit...

8   On your administrator computer, open Network Utility, using a Spotlight search if necessary.

9   Click the Lookup tab if it is not already selected.

10   Enter training.apple.com, and click Lookup.

11   Confirm that the Results field contains an IPv4 address. Your server requested that record from your ISP's DNS service and then delivered the answer to your administrator computer.

Enter an internet address to lookup.

[training.apple.com]   (ex. 10.0.2.1 or www.example.com)

Lookup

```
Lookup has started...

training.apple.com -> 17.151.20.254
```

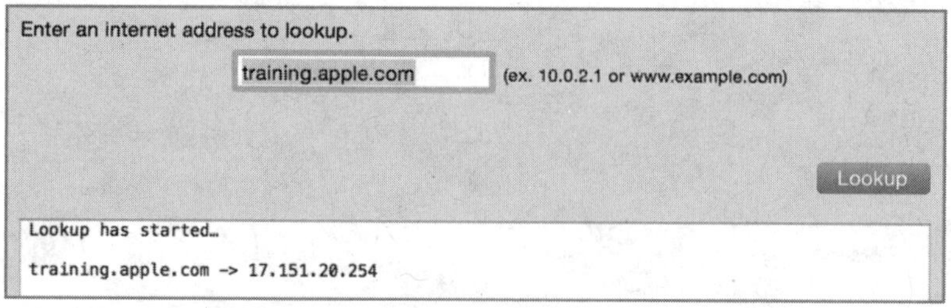

Inspect the Limited Default Zones

1   On your server, note that your server's name and IPv4 address are listed in the Host Names field.

2   Click the Action (gear icon) menu at the bottom of the DNS pane, and choose Show All Records.

This changes the simplified view into a more standard view illustrating the various zones configured.

3   Review the records listed in the pane. In the following figure, there are two zones: a primary named server17.pretendco.com and a reverse named 171.0.0.10.in-addr.arpa.

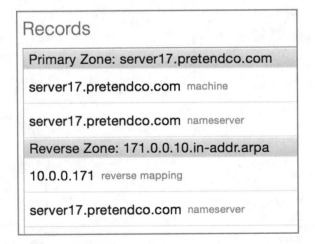

Each zone has a nameserver record, which defines your server as the authoritative DNS service for that zone. The primary zone has one machine record, and the reverse zone has one mapping record that corresponds to the primary zone's one machine record.

Configure DNS Hosts

Create a new DNS record that will automatically create a new pretendco.com zone, create an additional machine record, and then remove your original limited zones.

Create a New Record

1   Click the Action (gear icon) menu at the bottom of the DNS pane, and choose Show All Records so that the option is deselected.

2   Click the Add (+) button.

If clicking the Add (+) button displays a pop-up menu, click the Add (+) button again to close the pop-up menu; then go back to step 1.

3   In the Host Name field, enter server*n*.pretendco.com (where *n* is your student number).

4   Under the IP Addresses field, click Add (+), and then enter your server's IPv4 address, 10.0.0.*n*1 (where *n* is your student number).

5   Under the Aliases field, click Add (+), and then enter vpn.

6   Select the checkbox "Create an MX record for this host name."

7   Click Create.

Inspect the New Zones and Records

1   Click the Action (gear icon) menu at the bottom of the DNS pane, and choose Show All Records so that the option is selected.

2   Review the information displayed in the Records field.

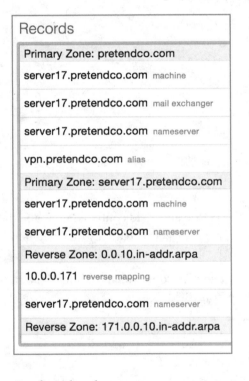

3   Confirm that there are two new zones:

▶   pretendco.com
▶   0.0.in-addr.arpa

4   Confirm that in the pretendco.com zone the following records exist:

▶   machine
▶   mail exchanger
▶   nameserver
▶   alias

5   Confirm that in the 0.0.in-addr.arpa zone the following records exist:

▶ reverse mapping
▶ nameserver

6   Double-click the mail exchanger record.

7   Confirm the zone is set to pretendco.com, the Mail Server field contains your server's host name, and the Priority field is set to zero.

8   Click Cancel to return to the list of DNS records.

9   Double-click the alias record.

10   Confirm that in the zone pretendco.com the Host Name field contains "vpn" and the Destination field contains your server's host name (also called a fully qualified domain name).

Note that the top of the pane contains vpn.pretendco.com, which is a combination of the contents of the Host Name field and the Zone field.

11   Click Cancel to return to the list of DNS records.

Create a New DNS Record While Show All Records Is Selected

As you saw, when you create a new record with Show All Records deselected, the Server app automatically creates a host name record, and you have the option to create an alias and to create an MX record with priority 0 for the zone.

When Show All Records is selected, the ability to create new records is more fine-grained.

1   In the main DNS pane, click the Add (+) button, and choose Add Machine Record.

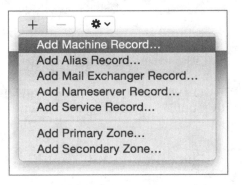

2   From the Zone menu, choose pretendco.com.

3   In the Host Name field, enter clientn (where *n* is your student number). Note that you should not enter the domain, just the first part of the host name.

4   Click the Add (+) button, and enter your administrator computer's IPv4 address, 10.0.0.*n*2 (where *n* is your student number).

5   Confirm that the new host name is displayed as expected next to the globe.

For example, if it is displayed as client*n*.pretendco.com.pretendco.com, you mistakenly entered pretendco.com in the Host Name field; remove pretendco.com from the Host Name field.

	client17.pretendco.com	
Zone:	pretendco.com	
Host Name:	client17	
IP Addresses:	10.0.0.172	

6   Click Create.

Remove the Redundant Zone

To prevent confusion in the future, remove the limited zone that the Server app originally created. Currently there are two zones that can answer the query for your server's host name, and you want only the more full-featured of the two, so you will remove the zone created during the host name configuration.

1 Select "Primary Zone: server*n*.pretendco.com" (where *n* is your student number).

2 Confirm that the server*n*.pretendco.com primary zone (where *n* is your student number) is selected, the text for the zone is slightly modified (it has a slight shadow), and the zone is not otherwise highlighted.

3 Confirm that the selected zone has only two records.

4 Click the Delete (–) button, but do not click Delete in the confirmation dialog yet.

5 Confirm that the confirmation dialog refers to server*n*.pretendco.com (where *n* is your student number).

If the confirmation dialog refers to only pretendco.com, click Cancel, and return to step 1.

6 Click Delete to delete the zone.

7 Note that the corresponding reverse zone, *n*.0.0.10.in-addr.arpa (where *n* is your student number), was also automatically removed.

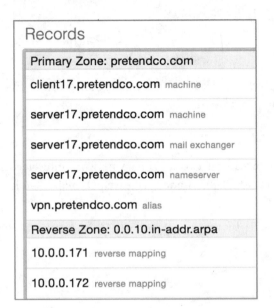

Add a Nameserver Record for the Reverse Zone

As of the current writing, removing the server*n*.pretendco.com (where *n* is your student number) zone results in the removal of the nameserver record for the 0.0.10.in-addr.arpa zone. Create one now.

> **NOTE** ▶ If the nameserver record already exists in the 0.0.10.in-addr.arpa zone, skip this section, and continue with "Confirm New DNS Records" on page 82.

1   In the main DNS pane, click the Add (+) button, and choose Add Nameserver Record.

2   From the Zone menu, choose 0.0.10.in-addr.arpa.

3   In the Nameserver field, enter server*n*.pretendco.com (where *n* is your student number).

4   Click Create.

Confirm New DNS Records

Now that you've created the records, use Network Utility and the host command to con-firm that you can look up the records you just created.

In the following steps , replace *n* with your student number:

1   On your server, open Network preferences, select your primary network interface, and confirm that the DNS Server field is set to 127.0.0.1 and the Search Domain field is set to pretendco.com.

Configure IPv4:	Manually
IP Address:	10.0.0.171
Subnet Mask:	255.255.255.0
Router:	10.0.0.1
DNS Server:	127.0.0.1
Search Domains:	pretendco.com

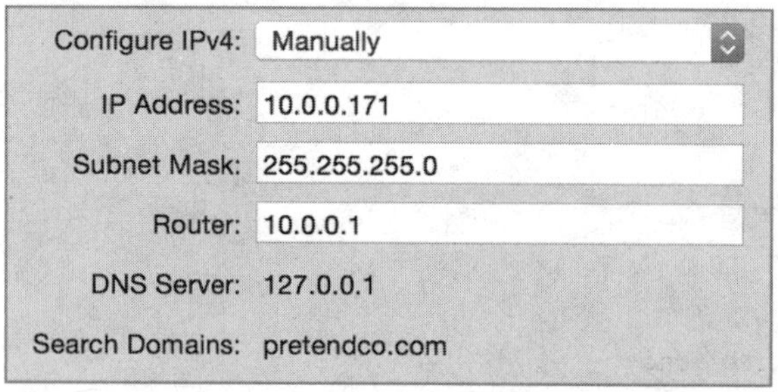

If they are not, click Advanced, click the DNS tab, and modify the DNS Servers and Search Domains fields.

2   Quit System Preferences on your server.

3   On your administrator computer, open Network preferences, select your primary net-work interface, and confirm that the DNS Server field is set to 10.0.0.*n* and the Search Domains field is set to pretendco.com.

Configure IPv4:	Manually
IP Address:	10.0.0.172
Subnet Mask:	255.255.255.0
Router:	10.0.0.1
DNS Server:	10.0.0.171
Search Domains:	pretendco.com

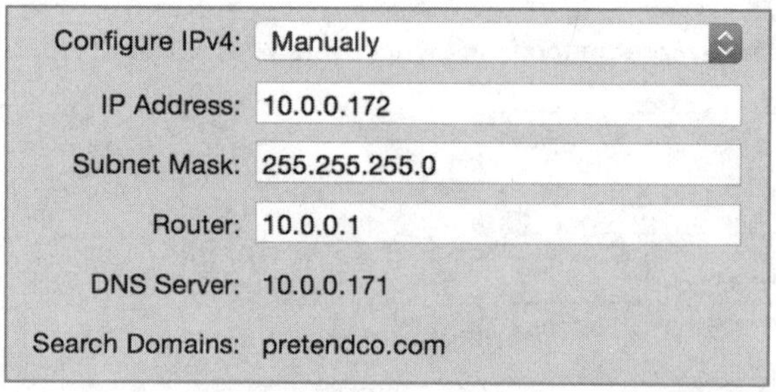

4   Quit System Preferences on your administrator computer.

5   On your administrator computer, open Network Utility (using a Spotlight search if necessary).

6   Click the Lookup tab if it is not already selected.

7   Enter server*n*.pretendco.com, and click Lookup.

8   Confirm that the expected IPv4 address is in the Results field: 10.0.0.*n*1.

9   Repeat steps 7 and 8 to confirm a query for client*n*.pretendco.com returns 10.0.0.*n*2.

10   Enter 10.0.0.*n*1, and click Lookup.

11   Confirm that the Results field contains your server's host name.

12   Repeat steps 10–11 to confirm that a query for 10.0.0.*n*2 results in client*n*.pretendco.com.

Network Utility does not look up MX records. You can use several command-line utilities instead; in this exercise, you will use the host command in Terminal.

1   On your administrator computer, use a Spotlight search to open Terminal.

2   Enter host pretendco.com.

```
●  ●  ●                    🏠 ladmin — bash — 80×24
Last login: Mon Nov 10 10:39:50 on ttys000
client17:~ ladmin$ (host pretendco.com█ )
```

3   Press Return to issue the command.

4   Confirm that the result contains information about the host that handles mail for the domain (the 0 indicates the priority).

```
●  ●  ●                    🏠 ladmin — bash — 80×24
Last login: Mon Nov 10 10:39:50 on ttys000
client17:~ ladmin$ host pretendco.com
(pretendco.com mail is handled by 0 server17.pretendco.com. )
client17:~ ladmin$ █
```

5   Enter host vpn.pretendco.com.

```
●  ●  ●              ⌂ ladmin — bash — 80×24
Last login: Sun Nov  9 11:54:56 on ttys000
client17:~ ladmin$ host pretendco.com
pretendco.com mail is handled by 0 server17.pretendco.com.
client17:~ ladmin$ host vpn.pretendco.com
vpn.pretendco.com is an alias for server17.pretendco.com.
server17.pretendco.com has address 10.0.0.171
client17:~ ladmin$ ▌
```

6   Press Return to issue the command.

7   Confirm that the result indicates that vpn.pretendco.com is an alias for server*n*.pretendco.com.

```
●  ●  ●              ⌂ ladmin — bash — 80×24
Last login: Mon Nov 10 10:39:50 on ttys000
client17:~ ladmin$ host pretendco.com
pretendco.com mail is handled by 0 server17.pretendco.com.
client17:~ ladmin$ host vpn.pretendco.com
vpn.pretendco.com is an alias for server17.pretendco.com.
server17.pretendco.com has address 10.0.0.171
client17:~ ladmin$ ▌
```

8   Leave Terminal open for the next exercise.

In this exercise, you created a full zone for pretendco.com, removed the automatically created zone, created a few extra records, and used Network Utility and the host command to confirm you can look up the records.

Exercise 2.2
Restrict Access to the DNS Service

▶ **Prerequisites**

   ▶   All exercises in Lesson 1 "Installing OS X Server"

By default, your DNS service provides service, for the zones it hosts, to anyone in the world who can connect to your DNS service. It also provides, by default, recursive lookups for requests that originate from the "local network."

In this exercise, you will restrict access to recursive lookups, then restrict access to the DNS service, and finally restore the default access, confirming your work along the way.

> **NOTE ►** When you use Network Utility to look up DNS records, it will return an answer if your computer has already performed a query and cached the answer. For this reason, Network Utility is not an appropriate tool to use to test whether your server's DNS service is available for queries. You will use the host command instead of Network Utility to test access to your server's DNS service.

> **MORE INFO ►** To flush the DNS cache on your administrator computer, you could reboot your administrator computer or use the following command, which is outside the scope of this guide: sudo discoveryutil udnsflushcache. However, for this exercise, you will use the host command, which does not use cached DNS records.

Configure Recursive Lookup Restrictions

Use the following steps to configure the DNS service to serve only the DNS information that it directly hosts.

> **NOTE ►** Your administrator computer will no longer be able to resolve any DNS records except for those hosted directly by your server. You will restore the service at the end of this exercise.

1   On your administrator computer, quit the Server app.

2   On your server, open the Server app, connect to your server, and then in the Server app sidebar select the DNS pane.

3   The "Perform lookups for" checkbox is selected by default.

   Next to "Perform lookups for," click Edit to configure for whom your DNS service will provide recursive lookups.

   | ☑ Perform lookups for | only some clients ⬦ | Edit... |

4   Select the checkbox "The server itself."

5   Deselect the checkbox "Clients on the local network."

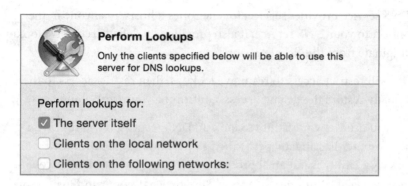

6   Confirm that the checkbox "Clients on the following networks" is deselected.

7   Click OK to save this configuration.

8   On your administrator computer, if you don't already have Terminal open, use a Spot-light search to open Terminal.

9   In the Terminal window, press Command-K to clear the Terminal window, leaving the current line at the top of the Terminal window.

10 In the Terminal window, enter host servern.pretendco.com (where *n* is your student number).

```
client17:~ ladmin$ host server17.pretendco.com
```

11 Press Return to issue the command.

12 Confirm that the reply contains the IPv4 address of your server; the DNS service provides the records in pretendco.com directly.

```
client17:~ ladmin$ host server17.pretendco.com
server17.pretendco.com has address 10.0.0.171
client17:~ ladmin$
```

13 In the Terminal window, enter host deploy.apple.com.

```
● ● ●                        ⌂ ladmin — bash — 80×24
client17:~ ladmin$ host server17.pretendco.com
server17.pretendco.com has address 10.0.0.171
client17:~ ladmin$ host deploy.apple.com
```

14 Press Return to issue the command.

15 Confirm that the host is not found; your server's DNS service does not host records for the apple.com zone and will not perform a recursive lookup for that request.

```
● ● ●                        ⌂ ladmin — bash — 80×24
client17:~ ladmin$ host server17.pretendco.com
server17.pretendco.com has address 10.0.0.171
client17:~ ladmin$ host deploy.apple.com
Host deploy.apple.com not found: 3(NXDOMAIN)
client17:~ ladmin$
```

16 If you get an answer instead of an error, it's possible that your administrator computer previously looked up that address and cached the answer; try again using a host name that you have not recently looked up, such as training.apple.com or developer.apple.com.

Configure DNS Service Permissions

In addition to specifying the hosts for which your DNS service will perform a recursive lookup, you can specify the hosts for which your DNS service will perform any lookup at all. You will configure your DNS service to respond to only your server.

NOTE ▶ Your administrator computer will no longer be able to resolve any DNS records. You will restore the service at the end of this exercise.

1 On your server, in the DNS pane of the Server app, click Edit next to Permissions.

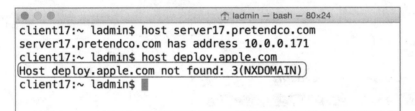

2 Click the "Allow connections from" pop-up menu, and choose "only some networks."

3 Click the Add (+) button, and choose This Mac. Note that the existing entry, "private networks," will automatically be replaced once you choose This Mac.

4 Click OK to save the change.

Inspect the Access Tab

Confirm that your change is reflected in the Access tab for your server.

1 In the Server app sidebar, select your server.

2 Click the Access tab.

3 Confirm that in the Custom Access field there is an entry for DNS with the restriction in the Network column to Only this Mac.

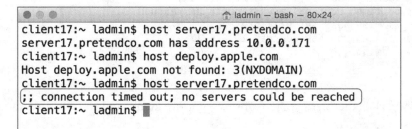

Confirm the DNS Service Is Restricted

1 On your administrator computer, in the Terminal window, enter host server*n*.pretendco.com (where *n* is your student number).

```
● ● ●                    ⬆ ladmin — bash — 80×24
client17:~ ladmin$ host server17.pretendco.com
server17.pretendco.com has address 10.0.0.171
client17:~ ladmin$ host deploy.apple.com
Host deploy.apple.com not found: 3(NXDOMAIN)
client17:~ ladmin$ host server17.pretendco.com
```

2 Press Return to issue the command.

3 Confirm that the reply is that the connection timed out and no servers could be reached; your server's DNS service does not accept any request from any requester other than itself.

```
● ● ●                    ⬆ ladmin — bash — 80×24
client17:~ ladmin$ host server17.pretendco.com
server17.pretendco.com has address 10.0.0.171
client17:~ ladmin$ host deploy.apple.com
Host deploy.apple.com not found: 3(NXDOMAIN)
client17:~ ladmin$ host server17.pretendco.com
;; connection timed out; no servers could be reached
client17:~ ladmin$ ▊
```

Clean Up DNS Permissions

Configure your DNS service to perform lookups for pretendco.com for private networks and to perform recursive lookups for the local network only.

1   On your server, in the DNS pane of the Server app, click Edit next to Permissions.

2   Click the "Allow connections from" pop-up menu, and choose "private networks."

DNS
Network Access

Allow connections from: private networks

Cancel   OK

3   Click OK to save the change.

4   On your administrator computer, in the Terminal window,
    enter host server*n*.apple.com (where *n* is your student number), and then press Return
    to issue the command.

5   Confirm that the IPv4 address of your server is returned.

```
                            ladmin — bash — 80×24
client17:~ ladmin$ host server17.pretendco.com
server17.pretendco.com has address 10.0.0.171
client17:~ ladmin$ host deploy.apple.com
Host deploy.apple.com not found: 3(NXDOMAIN)
client17:~ ladmin$ host server17.pretendco.com
;; connection timed out; no servers could be reached
client17:~ ladmin$ host server17.pretendco.com
server17.pretendco.com has address 10.0.0.171
client17:~ ladmin$
```

6   On your server, click the "Perform lookups for" pop-up menu, and choose "only some clients."

7   Leave the checkbox "The server itself" selected.

8   Select the checkbox "Clients on the local network."

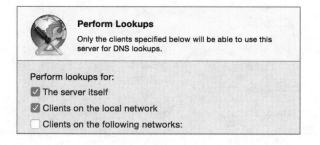

9 Click OK to save the change.

10 On your server, quit the Server app.

11 On your administrator computer, in the Terminal window, enter
host deploy.apple.com (or another host name that previously resulted in an error).

```
client17:~ ladmin$ host deploy.apple.com
```

12 Press Return to issue the command.

13 Confirm that you receive a valid response. In the following figure, the reply includes
information that deploy.apple.com is an alias and includes an IPv4 address.

```
client17:~ ladmin$ host deploy.apple.com
deploy.apple.com is an alias for deploy.apple.com.akadns.net.
deploy.apple.com.akadns.net has address 17.164.1.36
client17:~ ladmin$
```

14 Enter host client*n*.pretendco.com (where *n* is your student number), and press Return.

15 Confirm that you receive a valid response: 10.0.0.*n*2 (where *n* is your student number).

16 On your administrator computer, quit Terminal.

In this exercise, you restricted access to recursive lookups, then restricted access to the
DNS service, and finally restored the default access. In the next lesson, you will learn more
about using the Access tab of the Server pane to restrict access to other OS X Server services.

Lesson 3
Exploring the Server App

Once you've completed your initial installation of OS X Server, the Server app opens its main configuration pane, and you can continue configuring it. In this lesson, you'll learn about the various panes available in the Server app. You will learn how to enable remote access to the Server app and how to move the location your server uses to store much of its service data. You will also learn about a new feature in OS X Server for Yosemite where you can granularly control access to services from a single location.

GOALS

▶ Describe the Server app

▶ Use the Server app to administer a remote computer with OS X Server

▶ Move service data to a different volume

Reference 3.1
Allowing Remote Access

You can certainly administer OS X Server using the Server app on your server computer, but it's not recommended to use your server for your daily productivity applications.

You can use the Server app on any remote Mac with Yosemite to manage OS X Server, but only if the checkbox "Allow remote administration using Server" is selected. It is recommended that you do not simultaneously use the Server app on more than one Mac to administer a given server.

> **MORE INFO** ▶ When you select the "Allow remote administration using Server" checkbox, you enable other Mac computers to use the Server app to configure, manage, and monitor your server using TCP port 311.

Unlike earlier versions of OS X Server, you cannot perform a remote initial installation of OS X Server with the Server app; you have to use the Server app on the Mac on which you want to install OS X Server, at least for the initial installation and configuration.

However, sometimes you need direct control of your server computer, such as to perform a series of file or folder copy operations using the Finder. If you select the checkbox "Enable screen sharing and remote management," you can use tools like Screen Sharing (available from the Tools menu in the Server app and located in /System/Library/CoreServices/Applications/) and Apple Remote Desktop (available from the Mac App Store) to take control of the Mac running OS X Server.

When you select the "Enable screen sharing and remote management" checkbox, by default this allows access for all local accounts on the server computer that you configure as an administrator (if you have used Sharing preferences to configure specific users for specific levels of access, that configuration information will be preserved when you select or deselect the checkbox). If you want to allow access for other accounts or specify a password for software that uses Virtual Network Computing (VNC), configure this with Sharing preferences on the server computer.

NOTE ▶ If you have Sharing preferences open when you use the Server app to configure remote access, you may need to quit System Preferences and reopen the Sharing pane to see the updated settings.

The following figure illustrates the Remote Management checkbox in Sharing preferences that is selected when you select "Enable screen sharing and remote management." Note that the Screen Sharing checkbox is unavailable; if you select Screen Sharing, you will see the message "Screen Sharing is currently being controlled by the Remote Management service."

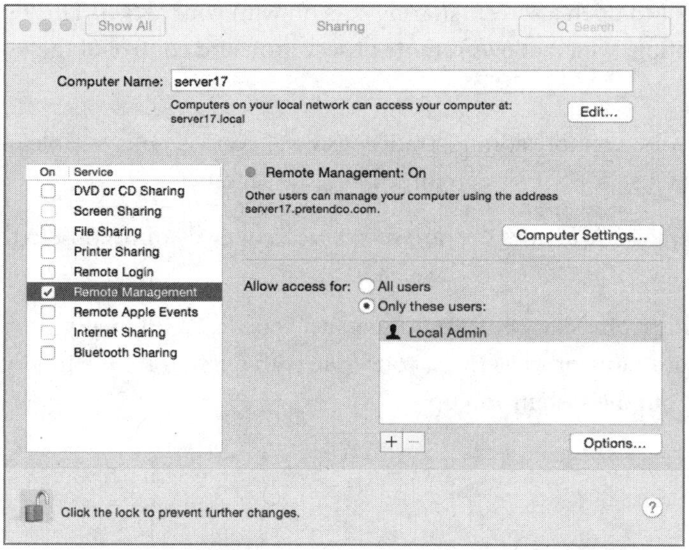

MORE INFO ▶ If you use Sharing preferences to deselect Remote Management and select Screen Sharing, then in the Server app the "Enable screen sharing and remote management" checkbox will display a dash (–) instead of a checkmark.

The "Allow remote login using SSH" checkbox in the Server app has the same effect as the Remote Login checkbox in Sharing preferences; selecting or deselecting either checkbox has the same effect on the checkbox in the other tool.

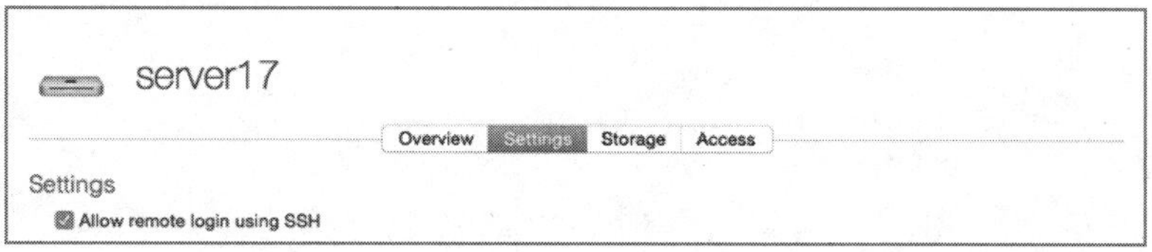

When you run the Server app on a remote administrator computer, if the "Allow remote login using SSH" checkbox is selected, an arrow appears next to it. If you click this arrow, the Server app opens Terminal and attempts to connect to your server using the Secure Shell (SSH) protocol, with the user name of the administrator account that you provided to the Server app to connect to your remote server computer. You must provide the password to successfully open an SSH connection.

Similarly, there is a shortcut to open a screen-sharing session with your server. This opens the Screen Sharing application, which allows remote observation and control of the remote server computer.

Of course, the checkbox "Allow remote administration using Server" is not available for you to configure unless you use the Server app directly on the server.

The following figure illustrates the arrows that are shortcuts to open a connection to the server.

NOTE ▶ If you upgrade from Mac OS X Snow Leopard version 10.6.8 or any version of OS X Lion, Mountain Lion, or Mavericks, your Mac with OS X Yosemite inherits the Sharing settings from the system you upgraded.

Reference 3.2
Using Server Sidebar Elements

The Server app sidebar contains four sections, which you'll use throughout this guide:

▶ Server

▶ Accounts

▶ Services

▶ Advanced Services

Server

The Server section displays your server and items that are not services or accounts:

▶ Your server

▶ An AirPort device, if there is one on your subnet

▶ Alerts

▶ Certificates

- ► Logs
- ► Stats

Lesson 4 "Configuring SSL Certificates" covers using SSL certificates to prove your server's identity and provide encryption for the network traffic associated with its services.

Lesson 5 "Using Status and Notifications" covers using the Alerts, Logs, and Stats panes to proactively monitor your server.

The following sections address the server and AirPort items in the Server section of the Server app sidebar.

Your Server

Once you select your server in the Server app sidebar, you see four tabs:

- ► Overview
- ► Settings
- ► Storage
- ► Access

Overview Pane

The Overview pane is the first thing you see after your initial installation and configuration of OS X Server. It displays information about how clients can access services, and it displays your server's host name and computer name. A new feature for OS X Server for Yosemite is the Internet field, which displays the total number of services that are reachable from the Internet and the external IPv4 address at which the services are reachable. The Server app communicates with servers at Apple to see what they can access on your server and report to the Server app. By clicking the Details button, you can see which services are available at that external IP address.

Note that clients in your local subnet can also use the Local Hostname setting, which is not displayed here.

The Server section of the Overview pane displays information about how long the server computer has been running since last starting up, as well as version information for OS X and OS X Server.

The bottom of the Overview pane lists each active network interface and its IPv4 address.

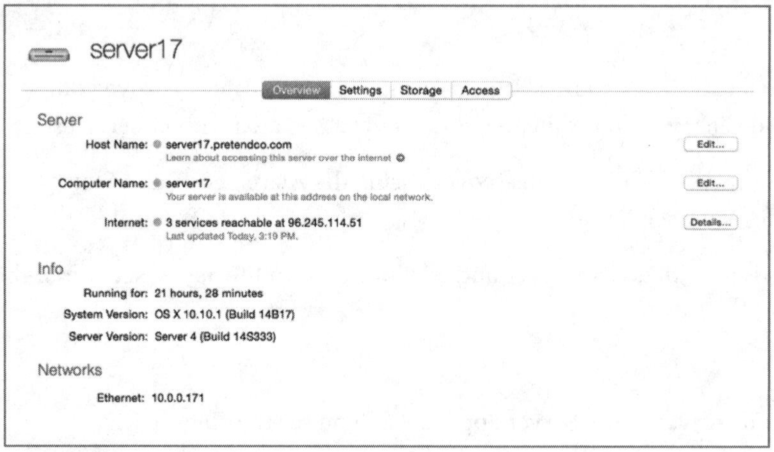

Settings Pane

The Settings pane offers a number of options to configure the following:

▶   Remote access and administration

▶   Push notifications

▶   The location to store service data

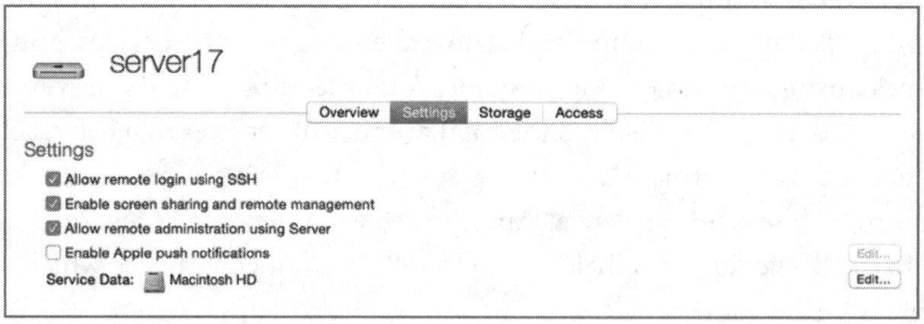

Lesson 5 "Using Status and Notifications" covers the "Enable Apple push notifications" checkbox.

The last option in the Settings pane allows you to configure your server to store data for various services on a volume other than the startup volume.

Moving Service Data Location

By default, most service data is stored in /Library/Server/ on your server's startup volume. Whether you want more space or more speed or simply want service data segregated from your operating system (OS), you can change the service data location. When you click Edit next to the Service Data field, you have the opportunity to change where your server stores most of its service data. The following figure shows what the pane looks like for a server with three internal volumes and one external volume.

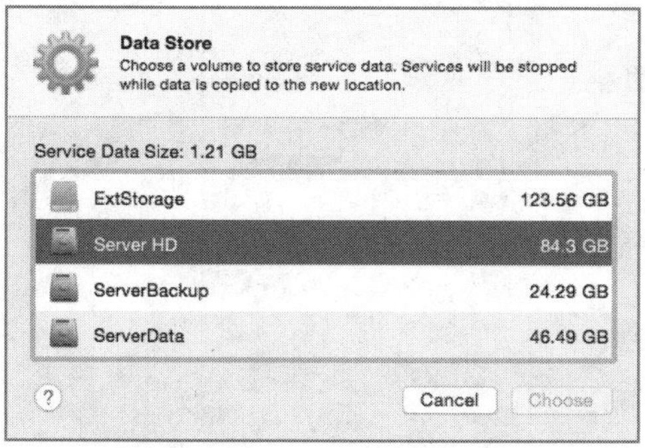

If you use the Server app to choose a different service data volume, it does the following:

► Automatically stops the appropriate services

► Creates a new folder on the volume you choose (/Volumes/*volume_name*/Library/ Server/)

► Copies the existing service data to the new folder

► Configures services to use the new location

► Starts the services again

Not all the service data is moved. For example, configuration and temporary files (such as the Mail spool file) remain on the startup volume, and many services, such as Caching, File Sharing, FTP, NetInstall, Time Machine, Websites, and Xcode, offer separate interfaces to choose where to store data for those services.

You should not change the name of your server's startup volume after you start offering services, nor should you change the name of the service data storage volume after you designate it in the Server app.

> **MORE INFO** ▶ If you choose to share the Websites root via FTP, it will share the /Library/Server/Web/Data/Sites/ folder on your server's startup volume, even if you choose a different data volume for your server's service data.

Storage Pane

The Storage pane displays an alphabetical list of the disks connected to your server computer; you can also drill down and edit file ownership, permissions, and access control lists (ACLs). You'll see more about this pane in Lesson 13 "Defining File Access".

> **TIP** ▶ If you have multiple volumes attached to your server, only the startup volume has special folder icons for the Applications, Library, System, and Users folders. Other volumes have regular folder icons in the Storage pane.

Access Pane

The Access pane is a new feature of OS X Server for Yosemite. It gives you one location to view the permissions for both user- and network-level authorization. The choices you see in the Access pane are, for the most part, duplicates of the controls available in the individual Services pane but with more visibility and with the addition of information such as the network ports involved. There are two major sections of the Access pane: Default Access and Custom Access.

The Default Access area allows you to define what the default rules are, including both user and network restrictions. Each rule is individually modifiable. The Users column can specify both users and groups of users for increased flexibility.

The default network definition can include multiple choices of network ranges if needed.

It allows custom range definitions.

In the Custom Access area of the Access pane, you have the ability to add custom rules. You can name a rule, assign network ports to it, and set availability from networks as needed.

AirPort

If you select an AirPort device in the Server app sidebar, you have the opportunity to provide authentication to manage the AirPort device. The AirPort pane is useful when the AirPort device sits between your internal network and your Internet connection; the option to expose services modifies the Network Address Translation (NAT) rules on your AirPort device to allow specific network traffic from the Internet to your server.

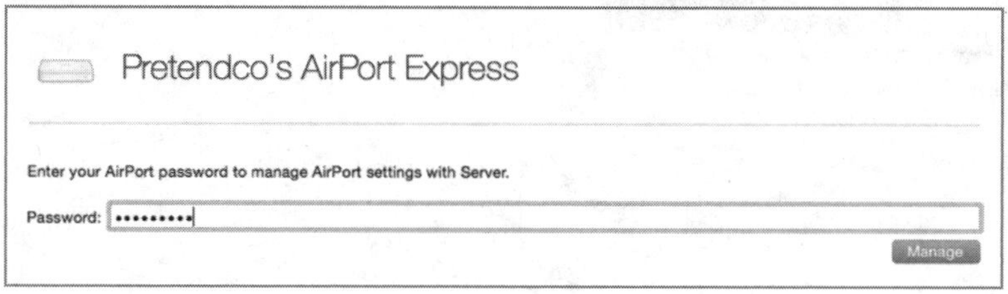

Once you authenticate to the AirPort device, you see the option to require users to provide network user credentials before gaining access to the wireless network (using Remote Authentication Dial-In User Service [RADIUS]). See Lesson 8 "Configuring Open Directory Services" for more information about network accounts.

You can expose services manually by clicking Add (+) in the AirPort pane, or you can have the Server app automatically expose the service when you start a service.

The following figure illustrates the menu that appears when you click Add (+).

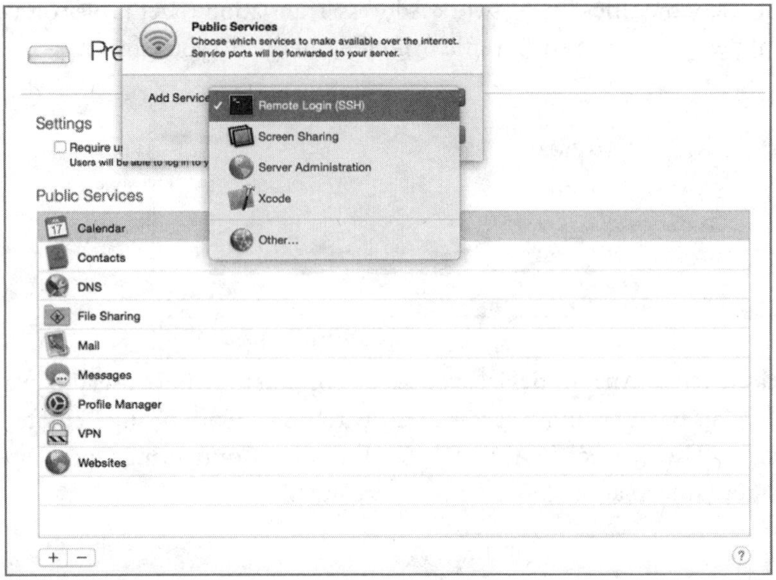

The following figure shows what it looks like when you start some services for the first time.

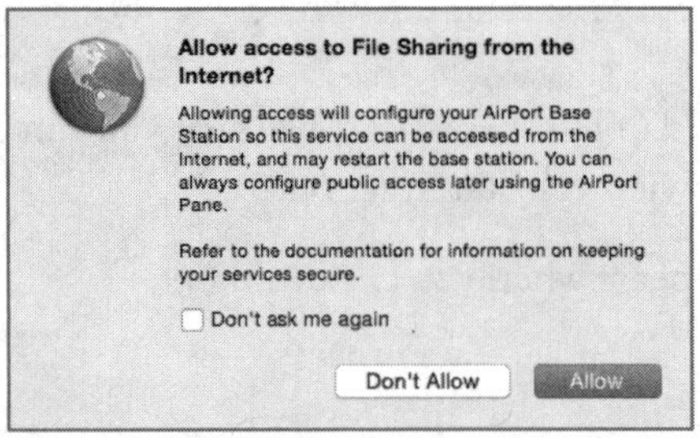

The AirPort pane lists the services that are exposed. In the following figure, the File Sharing service is listed.

Pretendco's AirPort Express

Settings

☐ Require user name and password login over Wi-Fi
Users will be able to log in to your wireless network using RADIUS

Public Services

| ⬦ File Sharing |

This view of exposed services simplifies some complexity. The following figure from editing the NAT rules via AirPort Utility illustrates that File Sharing consists of two protocols: 139 (Windows file sharing) and 548 (AFP for Mac clients).

Firewall Entry Type: IPv4 Port Mapping

Description: File Sharing

Public UDP Ports:

Public TCP Ports: 139, 548

Private IP Address: 10.0.0.171

Private UDP Ports:

Private TCP Ports: 139, 548

Cancel   Save

Accounts

The Accounts section of the Server app sidebar contains the Users and Groups panes. You'll make extensive use of the Users and Groups panes in Lesson 7 "Managing Local Users" and Lesson 9 "Managing Local Network Accounts".

Services

The Services section is a list of the services that OS X Server offers. A green status indicator appears next to the services that are currently running. Select any service to configure it.

Table 3-1 describes the available services.

TABLE 3.1   Basic OS X Server Services

Service Name	Description
Caching	Automatically speed up the download of software and other assets distributed by Apple for Windows PCs, Mac computers, and iOS devices.
Calendar	Share calendars, book conference rooms and meeting-related resources, and coordinate events using the CalDAV protocol.
Contacts	Share and synchronize contacts information among multiple devices using the CardDAV protocol.
File Sharing	Share files among Windows PCs, Mac computers, and iOS devices, using standard file sharing protocols, including SMB3, AFP, and WebDAV.
Mail	Provide mail service for multiple email clients using the SMTP, IMAP, and POP standards.
Messages	Securely provide the collaborative power of instant messaging, including audio and video conferencing, file transfer, and sharing presentations with the ability to archive chat transcripts.
Profile Manager	Configure and manage iOS devices and Mac computers over the air via configuration profiles.

Service Name	Description
Time Machine	Provide a centralized backup location for Mac computers that use Time Machine.
VPN	Provide secure encrypted virtual private network services to facilitate secure access to local resources by remote Windows PCs, Mac computers, and iOS devices.
Websites	Host websites based on the combination of host name, IP address, and port number.
Wiki	Enable groups to quickly collaborate and communicate using wiki-powered websites, blogs, and calendars, including QuickLook for viewing attachments and WebDAV support for iOS.
Xcode	Allow developer teams to automate the building, analyzing, testing, and archiving of Xcode projects.

Advanced Services

By default, the list of advanced services is hidden. This list includes services that are not used as often as the other services, and it includes services, such as Xsan, that are a little more advanced than the regular services. To display the list of advanced services, hover your pointer above the word "Advanced," and then click Show. To hide the list, hover your pointer above the word "Advanced," and then click Hide.

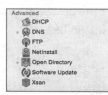

Table 3-2 describes the advanced services.

TABLE 3.2 Advanced OS X Server Services

Service Name	Description
DHCP	Dynamic Host Configuration Protocol assigns networking information to networked computers and devices.
DNS	Domain Name System provides resolution of names to IP addresses and of IP addresses to names.
FTP	File Transfer Protocol is a legacy protocol but is widely supported for uploading files to, and downloading files from, a server.
NetInstall	Allow multiple Mac computers to install OS X, install software, restore disk images, or start up (boot) from a common OS configuration by starting from a network disk rather than a locally attached disk.
Open Directory	Provide a centralized location to store information about users, groups, and other resources, and integrate with existing directory services.
Software Update	Host and manage software updates for OS X clients.
Xsan	Provide a shared storage area network using Fibre Channel storage for clients on your local network.

MORE INFO ▶ Appendix B's "Lesson 1 Resources Installing OS X Server" section lists Apple Support articles that address services that have been offered in previous versions of OS X Server but do not appear in this list of services. For the print version of this guide, the appendix is available as part of the downloadable lesson files.

Reference 3.3
Using the Manage Menu

The Server app Manage menu offers two main menu items.

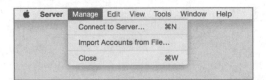

When you choose Connect to Server on a Mac that is not yet configured as a server, it opens a window that offers the following buttons:

► Other Mac: To open the Choose a Mac window

► Cancel: To close the window and quit the Server app

► Continue: To set up OS X Server on this Mac

► Help: To open Server Help in the Help Center

When you choose Connect to Server on a Mac that is already configured as a server, it opens the Choose a Mac window that includes the following:

► Your Mac

► Servers on your local subnet that allow remote administration

► Other Mac, which allows you to specify another Mac by its host name or IP address

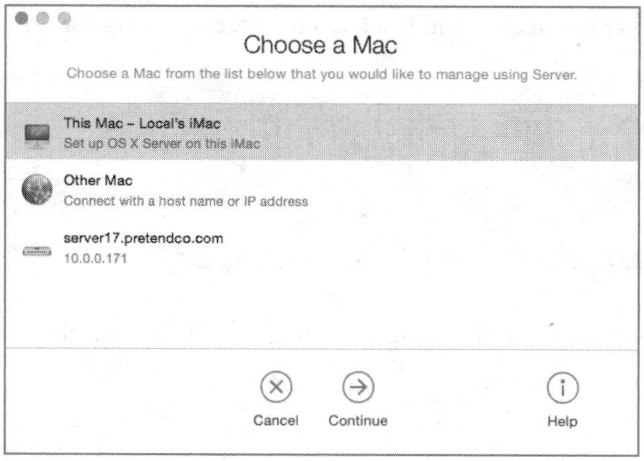

You can find more information about the "Import Accounts from File" menu item in Lesson 7 "Managing Local Users" and Lesson 9 "Managing Local Network Accounts".

Reference 3.4
Using the Tools Menu

The Tools menu allows you to quickly open three administration applications:

► Directory Utility

► Screen Sharing

► System Image Utility

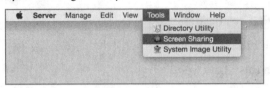

These three applications are located in /System/Library/CoreServices/Applications/ on every Mac with OS X Yosemite.

Reference 3.5
Using Help and Server Tutorials

A new feature that arrived with OS X Server for Mavericks and continues in OS X Server for Yosemite is Server Tutorials. Server Tutorials offers information and step-by-step instructions for several OS X Server services. From the Help menu, choose Server Tutorials.

In the Server Tutorials window, select one of the topics, and then scroll through the content.

You can close the Server Tutorials window when you're done using it.

Don't underestimate the power of Server Help. After you enter search terms into the Search field, Server Help lists help resources matching your query.

Once you choose a topic from the list of results, the Help Center window stays in the foreground until you close it.

Reference 3.6
Troubleshooting

If you attempt to administer to a remote server via its host name but your administrator computer does not have access to a Domain Name System (DNS) server with records available for that remote server, you will not be able to authenticate to that server with the Server app. A simple workaround is to use its local hostname or IP address, as in server17.local or 10.0.0.171, respectively. Keep in mind that this is just a workaround, and you should fix any DNS-related issues.

On your server, do not delete the Server app or move the Server app from the Applications folder on your startup volume. If you do, you will see a dialog that all your services have stopped, and you will need to reinstall OS X Server (or just move the Server app back into the Applications folder of the server's startup volume). Depending on your original configuration, you may need to reenter your Apple ID to renew your Apple Push Notification service certificates.

It is recommended that you do not change the name of any volume associated with your server after you've configured your Mac as a server because some file paths are hard-coded into configuration files and won't be automatically updated.

You can provide feedback about OS X Server by choosing Server > Provide Server Feedback.

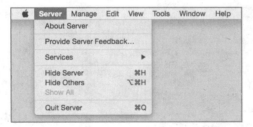

Exercise 3.1
Turn On Screen Sharing and Remote Management

▶ **Prerequisites**

- ▶ All exercises in Lesson 1 "Installing OS X Server"
- ▶ "Exercise 2.1 Create DNS Zones and Records" on page 71

In "Exercise 1.2 Perform the Initial Installation of OS X Server on Your Server Computer" on page 39, you confirmed that your server allows remote administration using the Server app. Now you will turn on screen sharing and remote management as well. If you have a copy of Apple Remote Desktop, performing this action would allow you to use it to control your server. In this exercise, you will use Screen Sharing to control your server.

Confirm Screen Sharing and Remote Management Are Turned On

Open a connection to your server with the Server app if you don't already have one open, and then turn on screen sharing and remote administration.

1   Perform these exercises on your administrator computer. If you do not already have a connection to your server computer with the Server app on your administrator computer, then connect to it with the following steps: Open the Server app on your administrator computer, choose Manage > Connect to Server, select your server, click Continue, provide administrator credentials (Administrator Name ladmin and Administrator Password ladminpw), deselect the "Remember this password" checkbox, and then click Connect.

2   Select your server in the sidebar if it is not already selected, and then click the Settings tab.

3   Confirm that the "Enable screen sharing and remote management" checkbox is selected.

Confirm You Can Make a Screen-Sharing Connection

Open a Screen Sharing connection.

1   Click the arrow next to the "Enable screen sharing and remote management" check-box.

This attempts to make a connection to your server with the Screen Sharing app.

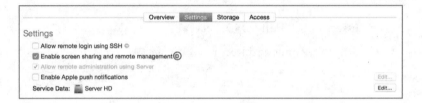

2   Enter local administrator credentials for your server computer (Name: ladmin; Password: ladminpw).

3   Click Connect.

4   Confirm that you have remote control of your server.

5   Click the Close button in the Screen Sharing window.

In "Exercise 1.1 Configure OS X Before Installing OS X Server on Your Server Computer" on page 21, you selected the Remote Management checkbox in Sharing preferences on your server, so the checkbox "Enable screen sharing and remote management" is selected. Therefore, you are able to take control of your remote server computer using Screen Sharing, right from the Server app shortcut.

Exercise 3.2
Inspect the Service Data Volume

▶ **Prerequisite**

   ▶ "Exercise 3.1 Turn On Screen Sharing and Remote Management" on page 113

In this exercise, you will go through the procedure to relocate your service data volume, but you will not actually change it.

Inspect Options to Move the Service Data to a Different Volume

Using the Server app, you can choose a different volume for service data. It's a good idea to perform this task as early as possible so that you don't have to wait with services turned off while a large amount of data is moved to the new volume.

1   On your administrator computer, if you are not already connected to your server, open the Server app, connect to your server, and authenticate as a local administrator.

2   In the Server app sidebar, select your server, and click Settings.

3   Next to the Service Data field, click Edit.

4   Inspect the current Service Data Size entry, as well as how much space is available on any listed volume. If you have another volume available on which to store the service data, you can select that volume and click Choose.

It is possible that you do not have any extra volumes in your test environment, so the rest of the exercises for this guide are written with the assumption that the service data is stored on the startup volume.

5   For the purposes of this exercise, click Cancel to close the window.

Even though you went through the procedure to relocate your service data volume, you didn't actually change it in this exercise. You can use this procedure in a production environment with an additional storage volume.

Exercise 3.3
Explore the Access Tab

> **Prerequisite**
>
> ▸ "Exercise 3.1 Turn On Screen Sharing and Remote Management" on page 113

In this exercise, you will explore the Access tab. If a particular service does not have a custom access rule, when someone tries to access that service, your server uses whatever is specified in the Default Access section to determine whether to grant access to the service. You have not created any users yet, so you will modify network access. You will create a custom network range based on your student number and use that range to limit default access to services. After confirming that a Mac outside that range cannot access your server, you'll create a custom rule for the Remote Administration service, and this rule will allow service for a new network range that incorporates your classmate's Mac. After confirming that this custom rule allows your classmate's Server app to see your server, you'll return your access rules to their defaults.

If you are performing these exercises on your own, you can modify the access rules, but without a third Mac, you cannot confirm that the rules actually do anything. You can simply read along with the exercise instead.

Modify Default Access Rules

Start by modifying the default access to services on your server (these rules apply to all services that don't otherwise have a custom access rule defined).

> **NOTE ▶** Be careful when managing network access rules remotely. No one wants to have to travel to the Mac computer running Server just to reconfigure network access rules after accidentally preventing remote access.

1   On your administrator computer, with your server selected in the Server app sidebar, click the Access tab.

2   Note that the Default Access section allows all users when connecting from all networks.

3   Click the "When connecting from" pop-up menu, and choose "only some networks."

4   In the Default Network Access pane, click the Add (+) button, and choose "Create a new network."

5   Enter the following information (where *n* is your student number):

▶   Name: Student *n* Range
▶   Starting IP Address: 10.0.0.*n*1
▶   Ending IP Address: 10.0.0.*n*9

NOTE ▶ As of the current writing, once you click Create, you cannot edit the name or range of this network, and you cannot remove this network, so double-check your entries before clicking Create.

6   Click Create.

7   In the Default Network Access pane, select Private Networks, then click Remove (-).

8   Confirm that your new range is the only item in the Default Network Access pane.

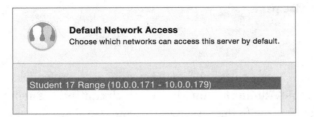

9   Click OK to save the change.

10 Confirm that in the Default Access section the settings include "all users" and "only some networks" and that in the Custom Access section the entries for Screen Sharing and SSH, which are set to Default in the Network column, reflect the network range you just created: Student *n* Range (where *n* is your student number).

11 If you are in an instructor-led environment, tell a classmate that you are ready for her to test whether her Server app can see your server. Otherwise, skip to the next section, "Modify Custom Access Rules" on page 120.

Confirm Modified Default Access Rules Are in Effect

If you are in an instructor-led environment, wait until a classmate confirms that she is ready for you to verify that your Server app cannot see her server because you have a Mac that uses an IPv4 address outside the network range that she specified.

1   On your administrator computer, choose Manage > Connect to Server.

2   In the Choose a Mac pane, confirm that your classmate's server no longer appears.

3   Click Cancel in the Choose a Mac pane.

Modify Custom Access Rules

Now that you've modified the default access rules, modify the custom access rules. Customize the access rules for the Remote Administration service, which controls the ability to connect to and administer your server with the Server app. If you are performing these exercises on your own, choose a number between 1 and 17, different from your own student number, to use as a fictional classmate's student number.

1   On your client computer, with your server selected in the Server app sidebar, click the Access tab.

2   Click the Add (+) button, and choose Remote Administration.

3   In the Remote Administration pane, click the Add (+) button, and choose "Create a new network."

4   Enter the following information (where m is your classmate's student number):

▶   Name: Student m Range
▶   Starting IP Address: 10.0.0.m1
▶   Ending IP Address: 10.0.0.m9

> **Create A New Network**
> Enter the IP Address range for which you want to manage access.
>
> Name: Student 2 Range
>
> Starting IP Address: 10.0.0.21
>
> Ending IP Address: 10.0.0.29
>
> (?)   Cancel   Create

5   Click Create.

6   Confirm that two networks are now listed: one based on your student number and the other based on your classmate's student number.

Allow connections from:	only some networks	⬍

Student 2 Range (10.0.0.21 - 10.0.0.29)
Student 17 Range (10.0.0.171 - 10.0.0.179)

7   Click OK to save the change.

8   In the Custom Access field, note that in the Custom Access section the new rule for Remote Administration contains information about which network ranges can access the service, as well as the port type and number associated with the service.

	Overview	Settings	Storage	Access	

Default Access

Allow connections from:	all users	⬍		Edit...
When connecting from:	only some networks	⬍		Edit...

Custom Access

Name	Users	Network	Ports
Caching	All users	Local Subnets	
DNS	All users	Private Networks	TCP/UDP 53
Remote Administration	All users	Student 2 Range, Student 17...	TCP 311
Screen Sharing	Administrators	Default (Student 17 Range)	TCP 5900
SSH	Administrators	Default (Student 17 Range)	TCP 22

Confirm the Custom Access Rule Is in Effect

If you are in an instructor-led environment, wait until your classmate confirms that she is ready for you to verify that your Server app can now see her server because you have a Mac that uses an IPv4 address in the network range for which she granted access to the Remote Administration service on her server.

1   On your client computer, choose Manage > Connect to Server.

2   In the Choose a Mac pane, confirm that your classmate's server appears.

3   Click Cancel in the Choose a Mac pane.

Restore Default Access

To prevent issues in future exercises, restore your server's default access, and remove the rule you created for the Remote Administration service.

1   In the Default Access section, click the "When connecting from" pop-up menu, and choose "all networks."

2   In the Custom Access section, select the Remote Administration custom rule, and then click the Remove (–) button.

3   Click Remove to confirm removing the custom rule.

4   Confirm that your Default Access and Custom Access sections appear as shown in the following figure.

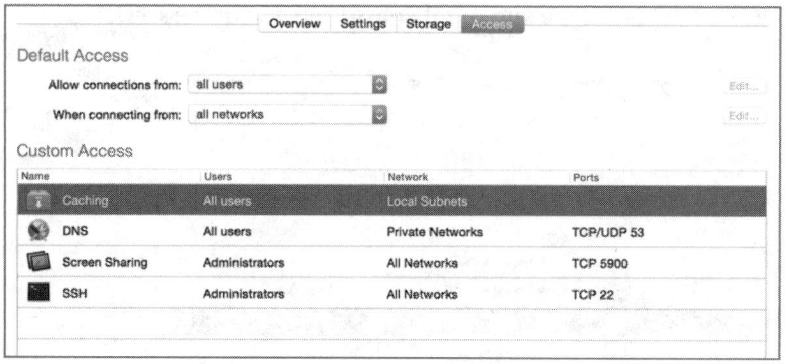

In this exercise, you modified the default access to your server's services, added a custom access rule for a service, reset the default access to their default settings, and removed your custom access rule.

Lesson 4
Configuring SSL Certificates

You can use OS X Server without doing any additional work to secure its services. However, you can use the Secure Sockets Layer (SSL) technology to prove your server's identity to client computers and devices and to encrypt communication between your server and client computers and devices. This lesson starts by describing the basics of SSL and then shows you how to configure SSL certificates for use with OS X Server.

Reference 4.1
Describe SSL Certificate Basics

You want the users who use your server's services to trust your server's identity and to be able to encrypt network traffic with your server.

The OS X solution is to use SSL, which is a system for transmitting data securely between hosts. You can configure your server to use an SSL certificate, which provides the ability to use the SSL system.

An "SSL certificate" (also referred to as simply a "certificate") is a file that identifies the certificate holder. A certificate specifies the permitted use of the certificate and has an expiration date. Importantly, a certificate includes a public key infrastructure (PKI) public key.

GOALS

▸ Describe the basics of SSL certificates

▸ Create a certificate signing request

▸ Create a self-signed SSL certificate

▸ Import a certificate signed by a certificate authority

▸ Archive your certificate

▸ Renew your certificate

▸ Configure which certificate your OS X Server services use

PKI involves the use of public and private keys. Grossly simplified, a "key" is a cryptographic blob of data, and within PKI, public and private keys are created in a way that they are mathematically linked: Data encrypted with one key can be decrypted only by using the other key. If you can decrypt data with one key, it proves that the data was encrypted with the other key. The public key is made publicly available, and the private key should be kept private. Fortunately, all of this encryption and decryption happens behind the scenes and is the basis for establishing secure communications.

Here are some definitions:

A "digital identity" (or more simply, an "identity") is an electronic means of identifying an entity (such as a person or a server). An identity is the combination of a certificate (which includes the public key) and the corresponding private key. If you don't have your private key, you can't prove your identity. Similarly, if another entity has your private key, that other entity can claim your identity, so be sure to keep your private key private!

Again simplifying, a "digital signature" is a cryptographic scheme that uses PKI private and public keys to demonstrate that a given message (a digital file such as an SSL certificate) has not been changed since the signature was generated. If a message, which has been signed, changes or is otherwise tampered with, it will be clear that the signature no longer matches the underlying data. Therefore, you can use a digital signature on a certificate to prove its integrity.

A certificate must be either self-signed or signed by a "certification authority" (also known as a "certificate authority" or, more simply, a "CA"). In other words, you can sign your own certificate using your private key (remember that a certificate is a file that identifies the holder of the certificate and includes the public key), or you can have someone else, namely, a CA, use their private key to sign your certificate.

An "intermediate CA" is a CA whose certificate is signed by another CA. So, it's possible to have a hierarchical "chain" of certificates, where an intermediate CA, which in turn is signed by yet another CA, signs a certificate.

In the following figure, the certificate for www.apple.com is signed by an intermediate CA with the name of Symantec Class 3 EV SSL CA - G3, and that intermediate CA is signed by a CA with the name of VeriSign Class 3 Public Primary Certification Authority - G5.

You can follow a chain of certificates, starting with a signed certificate, up to the intermediate CA and ending at the top of the chain. The certificate chain ends with a CA that signs its own certificate, which is called a "root CA." It is not required to have an intermediate CA involved—you could simply have a root CA sign your certificate—but in practice, an intermediate CA is often involved.

How do you know if you can trust a CA? After all, since a root CA has signed its own SSL certificate, this effectively means that the organization in control of a root CA simply asserts that you should trust that it is who it claims to be.

The answer is that trust has to start somewhere. In OS X and iOS, Apple includes a collection of root and intermediate CAs that Apple has determined are worthy of trust (see the Apple Root Certificate Program page on the Apple site for the acceptance process: www.apple.com/certificateauthority/ca_program.html). Out of the box, your Mac computers and iOS devices are configured to trust those CAs. By extension, your Mac computers and iOS devices also trust any certificate or intermediate CA whose certificate chain ends with one of these CAs. In OS X, these trusted CAs are stored in the System Roots keychain. (See Lesson 8, "Keychain Management," in *Apple Pro Training Series: OS X Support Essentials 10.10* for more information about the various keychains in OS X.) You can use Keychain Access to view this collection of trusted root CAs. Open Keychain Access (in the Utilities folder). In the upper-left Keychains column, click System Roots. Note that in the following figure the bottom of the window states that there are more than 200 trusted CAs or intermediate CAs by default in Yosemite.

MORE INFO ▶ Some third-party software companies, such as Mozilla, do not use the System Roots keychain and have their own mechanism to store CAs that their software is configured to trust.

In Lesson 8 "Configuring Open Directory Services", you will learn that when you configure your server as an Open Directory master, the Server app automatically creates a new CA and a new intermediate CA and uses the intermediate CA to sign a new SSL certificate with your server's host name as the common name (the Common Name value is part of what identifies the certificate holder). It is recommended that if you haven't engaged a widely trusted CA to sign an SSL certificate for your server, you should use the SSL certificate signed by your Open Directory intermediate CA; in Lesson 10 "Configuring OS X Server to Provide Device Management", you will learn how to use the Trust Profile to configure your iOS devices and OS X computers to trust your Open Directory CA and, by extension, the intermediate CA and the new SSL certificate.

But what about computers and devices that are outside your control and that you cannot configure? When people use computers and devices that are not configured to trust your server's self-signed SSL certificate or your server's Open Directory CA or intermediate CA and they try to securely access services on your server, they will still see a message that the identity of your server cannot be verified.

One way to prove your identity is for your server to use an SSL certificate that's signed by a CA that most computers and devices are configured to trust or trust inherently.

Deciding What Kind of Certificate to Use

Before going through the process of getting a widely trusted CA to sign a certificate for you, consider the services you'll use with the certificate, as well as the computers and devices that will access those services.

If you use a self-signed certificate, there is no additional server configuration to install the certificate on your server, but you do need to configure each client to trust that self-signed certificate. For a Mac client, this involves not only distributing the certificate to the Mac and adding it to the System keychain but also configuring how the operating system (OS) will trust the certificate.

> **NOTE ▶** If you use a self-signed certificate and are not able to configure all devices to trust that self-signed certificate, when users encounter a service that uses the self-signed certificate, they will be presented with a dialog informing them that the certificate may not be trustworthy and that to access services they must click Continue. This may undermine your efforts to train users not to automatically trust untrusted, expired, or otherwise invalid certificates.

If you use a certificate signed by a widely trusted CA, you need to generate a certificate signing request (CSR), submit the CSR to a CA, and then import the signed certificate.

Of course, it is possible to use a mix of certificates for different services; if your Websites service responds to multiple host names, you'd want a certificate for each host name that you use for web services secured by SSL.

In all cases, you need to configure your server's services to use the appropriate certificates.

The next section shows you how to obtain a certificate that's signed by a widely trusted CA so that you can use it to prove the identity of your server and to encrypt communications between your server and the users of your server's services.

Reference 4.2
Configuring SSL Certificates

Your server has a default SSL certificate that's self-signed. That's a good start, but no other computers or devices will trust services that use that certificate without additional configuration. To get a CA to sign a certificate, start by using the Server app to create a certificate signing request. Specific steps to accomplish this objective follow in more detail, but generally they include the following:

► Generating a new CSR

► Submitting your CSR to a CA that is generally trusted

► Importing the signed certificate

► Configuring your server's services to use your newly signed certificate

The CA's process of using your CSR and signing your SSL certificate with its own private key includes verifying your identity (otherwise, why would anyone trust the CA if it signed certificates from unverified entities?) and optionally charging you money.

To finish the story, computers and devices can now use your server's services without getting a warning that your SSL certificate is not verified (as long as those computers and devices trust the CA you've chosen to sign your certificate). Additionally, your server and the users of its services can use your server's SSL certificate in the process of encrypting communications for services that use that SSL certificate.

Before you start creating new certificates, take a moment to inspect what you already have.

Viewing Your Server's Default Certificate

You can use the Server app to display certificates (if you're logged in at the server, you can also use the Keychain Access app). By default, the Server app doesn't display the default certificate. To display all certificates, select Certificates in the Server app sidebar, and then from the Action (gear icon) pop-up menu, choose Show All Certificates.

Once Show All Certificates is selected, you see your default certificate. In the following fig-ure, the certificate has the server's host name and expires in two years.

> **MORE INFO** ▶ When you use the Server app Change Host Name Assistant to change your server's host name, it automatically creates a new self-signed certificate for the new host name.

To get more details, double-click the certificate; alternatively, select it, click the Action (gear icon) pop-up menu, and choose View Certificate. When you choose View Certificate, the details of the certificate appear. You'll need to scroll to inspect all of the certificate's information.

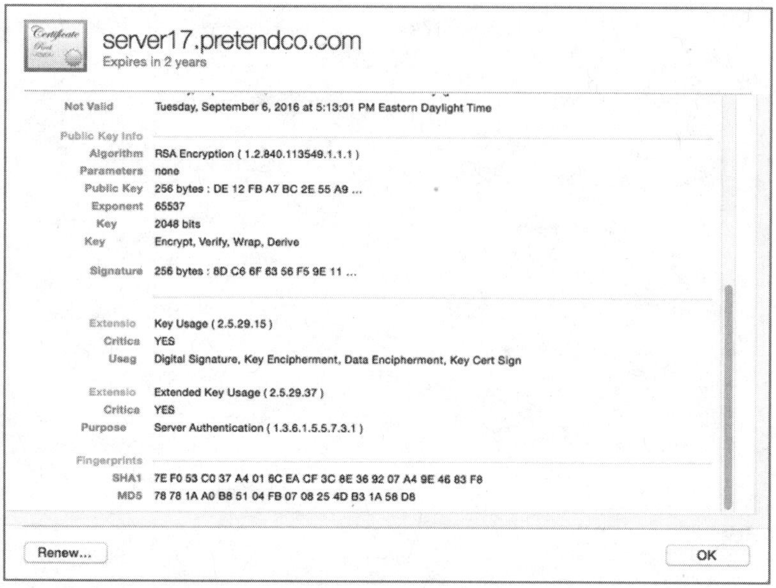

Click OK to return to the Certificates pane.

The following figure illustrates what you'd see after you configure your server as an Open Directory master or replica. At first glance, it looks like there is just one additional certificate, the code signing certificate, but the certificate with the server's host name is no longer a self-signed certificate but a certificate signed by your Open Directory CA; that certificate icon is blue, whereas the original self-signed certificate was bronze.

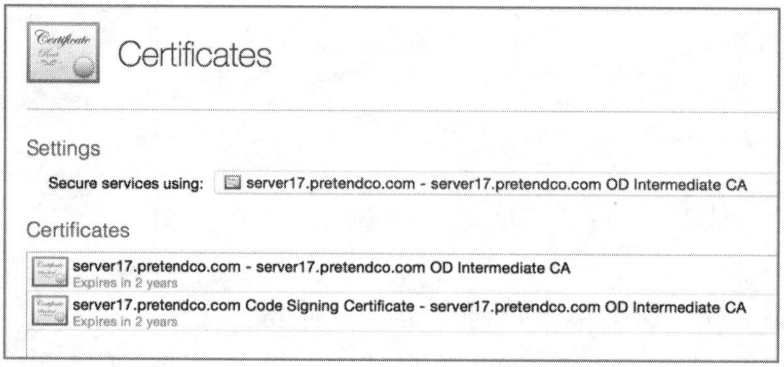

Explaining Options for Adding New Certificates

In the Server app Certificates pane, if Show All Certificates is not selected in the Action (gear icon) pop-up menu, then the text in the Trusted Certificates field instructs you to "Click (+) to get a trusted certificate." This is the path to getting a CA to sign a certificate for you.

> **NOTE** ▶ To reveal the menu choice to create a new self-signed certificate, you must first click the Action (gear icon) pop-up menu and choose Show All Certificates.

After Show All Certificates has been selected, click Add (+) to reveal three menu commands:

▶ Get a Trusted Certificate has the same effect as clicking Add (+) if Show All Certificates is not selected; it allows you to quickly generate a certificate signing request.

▶ Create a Certificate Identity is the command to choose to create a new self-signed certificate.

▶ Import a Certificate Identity allows you to import a signed certificate or a certificate and private key that you've archived.

Obtaining a Trusted Certificate

You can choose to get a CA to sign a certificate for you so that users around the world can use your server's services without being notified that your server's identity is not verified.

> **NOTE** ▶ In versions of OS X Server previous to 2.2, you need to first create a self-signed certificate and then create a CSR from that certificate. This process has been streamlined as of OS X Server version 2.2. However, be aware that when you use the following procedure to generate a CSR, the Server app generates a public and private key pair, but it doesn't generate a self-signed certificate.

The path to generating a self-signed certificate depends on whether Show All Certificates is selected in the Action (gear icon) pop-up menu:

- ► If Show All Certificates is not selected, simply click Add (+) in the Certificates pane.
- ► If Show All Certificates is selected, click Add (+), and then choose Get a Trusted Certificate.

After that, you'll see the Get a Trusted Certificate wizard.

In the next pane you can enter all the information that is necessary to establish an identity. A CA uses these details to verify your identity.

In the Host Name field, enter the host name you'll use for the services that will use this certificate. Use your organization's full legal name for the Company or Organization field, or if it's for personal use, just use your full name. The Department field is flexible; you can enter information such as your department name, but you should enter some value. To be fully compliant with standards, do not abbreviate your state or province. The following figure illustrates all of the fields completed.

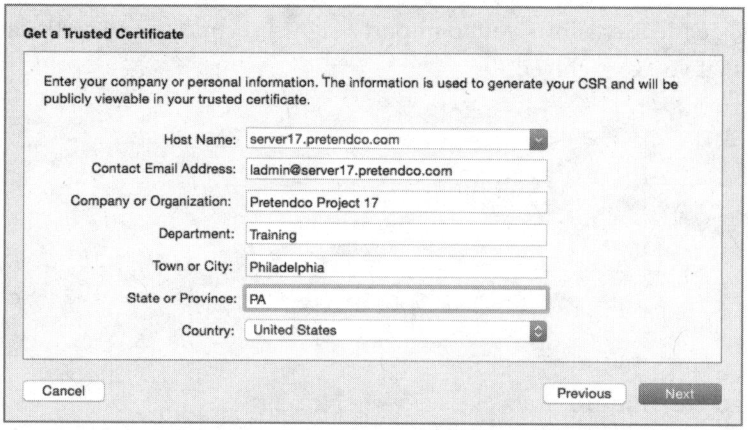

The next pane displays the text of your CSR, which you will submit to the CA of your choice. You can wait and access this text later, or you can select and copy this text, or click Save, now.

After you click Finish, the Server app displays the pending request.

If you didn't copy the text of your CSR earlier, you can access it again: Select the certificate that's marked "Pending," click the Action (gear icon) pop-up menu, and choose View Certificate Signing Request (or just double-click the pending certificate item).

Your course of action depends on how your CA accepts CSRs. If your CA allows you to upload a text file, then use the Save dialog to save the CSR as a text file. If your CA requires you to paste the text of the CA into a web form, click the disclosure triangle, and then copy the text of the CSR.

You need to choose an appropriate CA for your organization's needs (choosing a CA is outside the scope of this guide), send the CSR to the CA, and prove your identity to the CA. After some period of time, you will receive a signed certificate from the CA.

Importing a Signed Certificate

Once you receive the signed certificate from the CA, it's time to import it with the Server app. If you are still at the list of certificates, double-click your pending certificate to reveal the field into which you can drag your signed certificate.

> **NOTE ▶** If the CA provides you with the certificate in text form rather than in a separate file, you'll need to convert that text into a file. A quick way to do this is to select and copy the text, open TextEdit, press Command-N to create a new file, and choose Format > Make Plain Text (if that is an available command). Paste the text into the text file, and save it with a .cer extension.

Double-click the pending CSR, and drag the file containing a signed certificate, as well as any ancillary files provided by the CA, into the Certificate Files field (this is also where you could import a certificate and private key that you've exported with Keychain Access). Once the certificate is in the Certificate Files field, its color will be blue, as long as the top of the certificate chain is a root CA that your server trusts.

> **NOTE ▶** If you click Edit next to Certificate Request and then click Edit in the confirming dialog, a new public and private key pair and a new CSR will be generated, and you'll lose the original CSR.

Click OK to save your changes.

Generating a Self-Signed Certificate

In addition to generating a CSR, you can also use the Server app to generate a new self-signed certificate. This is useful if your server offers services at an alternative host name that corresponds to your server's Internet Protocol version 4 (IPv4) address or another IPv4 address that your server is configured to use and if you have the ability to configure computers and iOS devices to trust the self-signed certificate.

MORE INFO ▶ In versions of the Server app prior to version 2.2, the workflow was to create a self-signed certificate, then generate a CSR, and finally replace the self-signed certificate with the signed certificate. In version 2.2 and later, the Server app does not offer a way to replace a self-signed certificate with a signed certificate.

In the Certificates pane, when you click Add (+) and choose Create a Certificate Identity, you see a blank Name field.

NOTE ▶ The Show All Certificates option must be selected in the Action (gear icon) pop-up menu for the Create a Certificate Identity command to be available from the Add (+) button.

Enter the host name for the self-signed certificate, and then click Create.

NOTE ▶ You can select the "Let me override defaults" checkbox if you have more specific needs, but for most purposes, the defaults will suffice.

At the warning that you are about to create a self-signed certificate, click Continue.

At the Conclusion window, click Done. Finally, click either Always Allow or Allow to allow the Server app to copy the public and private key pair and the certificate from your login keychain to the System keychain and to /private/etc/certificates/.

You'll see the certificate in the Certificates field, as long as the Show All Certificates option is selected in the Action (gear icon) pop-up menu.

Inspecting a Certificate

You can inspect your certificates with the Server app, as well as with the System keychain of your server computer (the System keychain contains items that are not user specific and that are available to all users of a system). The following figure shows a certificate that's been signed by a CA for test purposes. Note that the OS has not yet been configured to trust the CA that signed this certificate.

You can also use Keychain Access to inspect a certificate and its associated private key. Because the certificate and private key are stored in the System keychain on the server, you need to log in directly on your server (or use a screen-sharing method to control your server) to use Keychain Access to access the private key.

Keychain Access is in the /Applications/Utilities/ folder on your startup volume; you can use Spotlight or Launchpad to search for it (in Launchpad, it is in the folder named Other). Select the My Certificates category to filter the items that Keychain Access displays. If necessary, toggle the show/hide button in the lower-left corner of the Keychain Access window until you can see all keychains. Select the System keychain to show items that are for the entire system, not just for the user who is currently logged in.

At least three items are listed (if you provided an Apple ID for push notifications, you will see more items):

► com.apple.servermgrd, which is used for remote administration with the Server app

► A certificate named Server Fallback SSL Certificate, which the Server app automatically uses if the default SSL certificate is removed

► An SSL certificate with the host name of your server

When you select a certificate that is not signed by a trusted CA, Keychain Access displays a warning icon, along with the text that explains the issue. In the following figure, the warning for the self-signed certificate is "This certificate has not been verified by a third party."

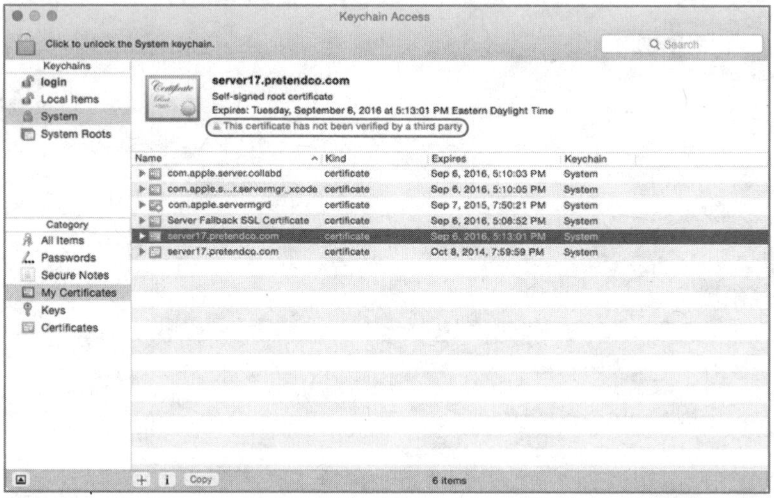

If you double-click your default self-signed SSL certificate to open it, you'll see a warning icon and the text "This certificate has not been verified by a third party."

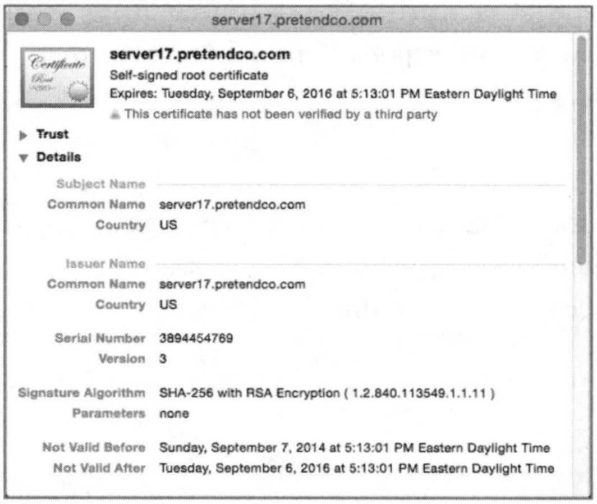

If a service on your server uses this self-signed certificate, when users attempt to use services that use that SSL certificate, they may be warned that your SSL certificate is not trusted, as shown in the following figure.

It's recommended to train your users that when they see an SSL warning, they should *not* continue using the service that uses the unverified SSL certificate.

Archiving Your Certificate

Whether you have a self-signed certificate or a certificate signed by a CA, you should take steps to archive your certificate and its private key. You may need to reinstall your server in the future, or an administrator might accidentally remove your certificate and its private key; if you have an archive of your certificate and private key, you can easily use the Server app to re-import your certificate and its private key.

You use the Keychain Access app to export your certificate and private key. Keychain Access prompts you to specify a password to protect your private key; it is recommended that you use a strong password.

You use the Server app to import the certificate and private key. You need to provide the password that was entered when the certificate was exported in the first place; otherwise, you will not be able to import.

Renewing Your Certificate

SSL certificates do not last forever. Luckily, it is simple to renew SSL certificates. The Server app issues an alert when an SSL certificate expiration date approaches. To renew a self-signed SSL certificate, simply click Renew when viewing the certificate in the Certificates pane or when viewing the alert.

Once you click Renew, the Server app takes care of renewing the certificate, and the alert displays that the issue has been resolved.

NOTE ▶ Do not click Renew for an Open Directory CA because this causes changes to the CA properties, and your Open Directory intermediate CA will no longer be signed by a trusted authority.

If you have a certificate signed by a widely trusted CA, when you click Renew, you will see the message that you need to generate a new CSR. See the earlier section "Obtaining a Trusted Certificate" on page 131 for more details.

Configuring OS X Server Services to Use a Certificate

Once you have taken steps to obtain a signed certificate or create a new self-signed certificate or have configured your server as an Open Directory server, you should use the Server app to configure services to use that certificate. You start in the Certificates pane of the Server app.

With the pop-up menu, you can do either of the following:

▶ Choose one certificate to specify that all services use that certificate.

▶ Choose Custom to configure each service separately to use or not use a certificate.

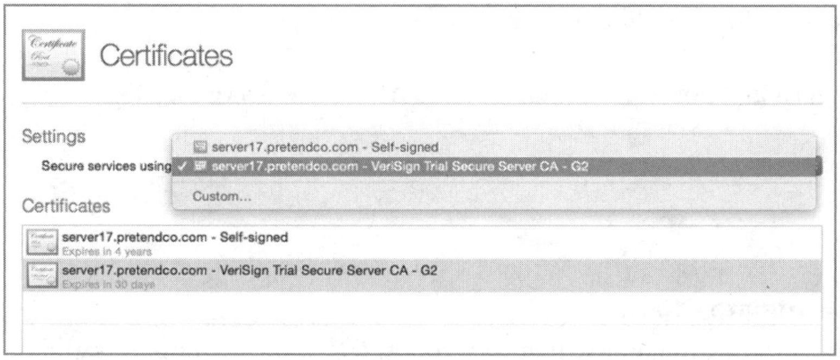

The following figure shows an example of choosing Custom and then editing the value for the default secure site of the Websites service. Note that there are some extra certificates in the figure. This illustrates that you can configure your server to respond to requests at multiple host names, create a certificate for each host name, and configure each secure site to use the appropriate certificate.

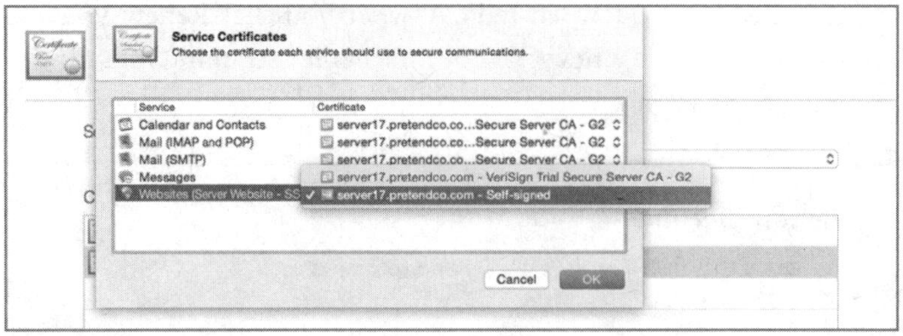

You can use the Server app to configure the following OS X Server services to use SSL:

▶   Calendar and Contacts

▶   Mail (IMAP and POP)

▶   Mail (SMTP)

▶   Messages

▶   Open Directory (appears only after starting Open Directory services)

▶   Websites

You will see in Lesson 20 "Hosting Websites" that you can granularly specify an SSL certificate for each website you host, and you can use the Profile Manager pane to specify the SSL certificate to use for the Profile Manager service.

A few other services use SSL but do not appear in the Server app:

▶   com.apple.servermgrd (for remote administration with the Server app)

▶   VPN

▶   Xcode

Following the Certificate Chain

When choosing a CA to use, make sure that it's a root CA that most computers and devices are configured to trust. It's not useful for you to have a CA sign your certificate if not many computers or devices will trust that certificate. As an example, the following figure shows how an SSL certificate signed by a trial CA appears in Keychain Access.

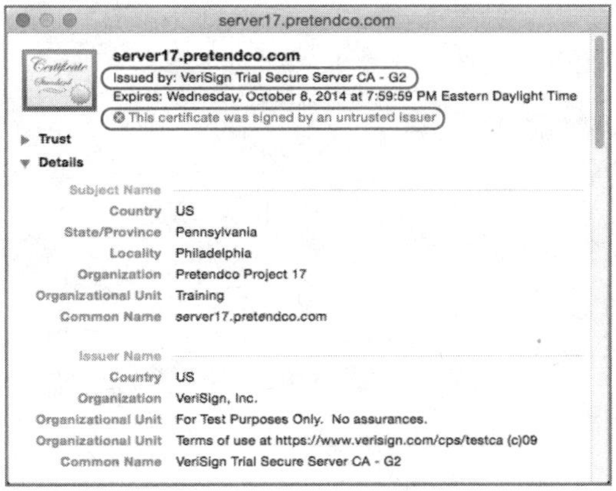

You can see that the "Issued by" field near the top of the window shows VeriSign Trial Secure Server CA – G2. Note the red X icon and the text "This certificate was signed by an untrusted issuer." This is a CA that is by default not trusted by computers and devices, so even if you used this signed certificate for OS X Server services, the people who access your services would experience trouble. In some cases, the service might silently fail, or the user may be alerted that the identity of the service cannot be verified. The following figure illustrates that on a client Mac Safari notifies the user that Safari can't verify the identity of the website.

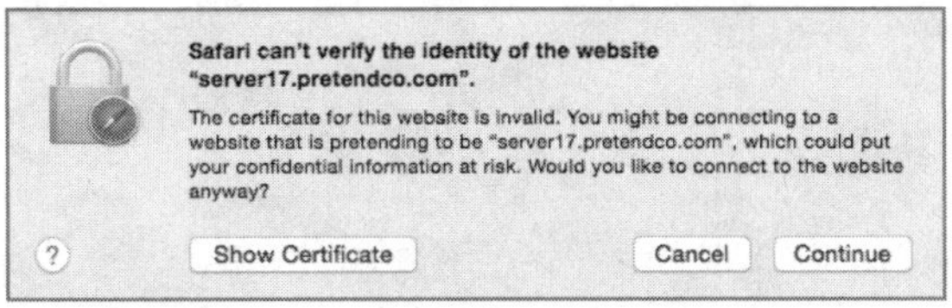

If you click Show Certificate, Safari displays the certificate chain. The following figure shows what you see when you select the server's certificate at the bottom of the certificate chain: that the certificate was signed by an untrusted issuer.

The following figure illustrates that if you click the Details disclosure triangle, you'll see information about the identity of the certificate holder, as well as information about the issuer (the entity that signed the certificate). In this case, the issuer's common name is VeriSign Trial Secure Server CA – G2.

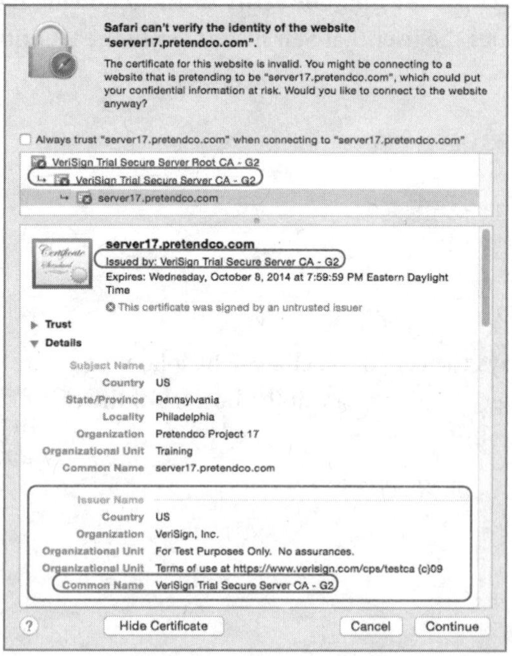

When you select the certificate in the middle of the certificate chain, you see that this is an intermediate CA; the window states "Intermediate certificate authority," and the Issuer Name information shows you that the common name of the issuer (or signer) is VeriSign Trial Secure Server Root CA – G2.

Finally, when you select the certificate at the top of the certificate chain, you see that this is a root CA; the window states "This root certificate is not trusted." This root CA is not in this computer's System Root keychain, so Safari doesn't trust the intermediate CA, and it doesn't trust the server17.pretendco.com certificate either.

Since that example root CA is for trial use only, it is not recommended to configure your Mac to always trust it outside of a learning or testing environment.

Configuring Trust

You can configure your Mac to always trust a certificate for the currently logged-in user. Returning to the previous example of your server using its self-signed SSL certificate for a website, you can click Show Certificate and then select the "Always trust..." checkbox.

After you select "Always trust...," OS X asks for your login credentials. After you successfully authenticate, OS X adds the certificate to your personal login keychain and configures your system to always trust the certificate for SSL purposes so that your Mac trusts it when you are logged in with the account that you were logged in as when you clicked the "Always trust..." checkbox. This will not affect any other computers or devices or any other users who log in to that Mac.

In Keychain Access, you can open and inspect the self-signed certificate you just added. Note the blue plus (+) icon with the text that states the certificate is marked as trusted for server17.pretendco.com.

After you visit the site again in Safari, if you click the encryption icon in the Address and Search field and then click Show Certificate, you see similar information.

A further option for Mac computers is to download and install the certificate in the System keychain, with the "Always trust..." checkbox selected for SSL. Keep in mind that you would need to do this for *every* Mac that uses SSL-enabled services from your server.

For an iOS device, when you open Safari to a page protected by the server's self-signed certificate, you can tap Details.

Then tap Trust.

Cancel	**Certificate**	Trust

server17.pretendco.com
Issued by IntermediateCA_SE...

Not Trusted

Expires   11/1/16, 12:31:56 PM

More Details   >

Now your iOS device is configured to trust that certificate.

Note that you can use a configuration profile to distribute a certificate to Mac computers and iOS devices. This automatically configures the device to trust the certificate. See Lesson 11 "Managing with Profile Manager" for more information about profiles.

See "Exercise 4.3 Configure Your Administrator Computer to Trust an SSL Certificate" on page 159 for complete instructions.

Reference 4.3
Troubleshooting

Certificate Assistant uses the IPv4 address of the Mac from which you run the Server app, so if you're using an administrator computer to configure a remote server and generate a new self-signed certificate, be sure to use the server's host name and IP address where appropriate.

When you configure your server as an Open Directory server, if you have a self-signed certificate with your server's host name in the certificate's Common Name field, the Server app replaces the original self-signed SSL certificate with a new certificate. This new certificate will be signed by a newly created intermediate CA associated with your server's Open Directory service.

However, if you have a certificate with your server's host name in the certificate's Common Name field and the certificate is signed by a CA or an intermediate CA (that is not associated with your Open Directory service), then the Server app doesn't replace it with a new one signed by the Open Directory intermediate CA (however, the Server app still creates the Open Directory CA and intermediate CA).

Each certificate has an expiration date; if the current date is later than a certificate's expiration date, the certificate is not valid.

> **MORE INFO** ▸ Some files associated with certificates are stored in /private/etc/certificates/, and possibly /private/var/root/Library/Application Support/Certificate Authority/, on your server.

Exercise 4.1
Examine the Default SSL Certificate

▶ **Prerequisites**

- ▶ All exercises in Lesson 1 "Installing OS X Server"
- ▶ "Exercise 2.1 Create DNS Zones and Records" on page 71

In this exercise, you will examine the default self-signed certificate.

1   Perform these exercises on your administrator computer. If you do not already have a connection to your server computer with the Server app on your administrator computer, then connect to it with the following steps: Open the Server app on your administrator computer, choose Manage > Connect to Server, select your server, click Continue, provide administrator credentials (Administrator Name: ladmin Adminis-

trator Password: ladminpw), deselect the "Remember this password" checkbox, and then click Connect.

2   In the Server app sidebar, select Certificates.

3   Note that by default your server's services use a certificate that is self-signed.

4   Click the Action (gear icon) menu, and choose Show All Certificates.

5   Select the self-signed certificate.

6   View the details of the certificate. Double-click the self-signed certificate, or click the Action menu and choose View Certificate.

7   Click OK return to the Certificates pane.

Note that there is little identifying information associated with this certificate. For example, there is no email address, organization name, department, or city. By default, no other computer or device trusts this self-signed certificate. To use this self-signed certificate to secure your server's services, you could configure your client computers and devices to trust this certificate.

Alternatively, you could click the Add (+) button and choose Get a Trusted Certificate, send the resulting certificate signing request to a widely trusted certificate authority to sign, and then import the signed certificate. However, this is outside the scope of this guide, so the next exercise is a compromise between using a self-signed certificate with little information and using a certificate signed by a widely trusted CA.

Exercise 4.2
Configure an Open Directory Certificate Authority

When you configure your server as an Open Directory (OD) master, the Server app automatically creates an OD CA, an intermediate CA, a signed certificate, and a code signing certificate that you can use with the Profile Manager service. When you enroll your Mac computer or your iOS device with your server's Profile Manager service, your computer automatically trusts your server's OD CA. Additionally, if you bind your Mac to your OD server, it automatically trusts your server's OD CA. This guide has not yet covered binding or enrolling, so in "Exercise 4.3 Configure Your Administrator Computer to Trust an SSL Certificate" on page 159 you will use Safari to configure your administrator computer to trust your server's OD CA.

In this exercise, you will configure your OD CA. You will examine the new CA, the intermediate CA, and two new certificates and verify that the Server app automatically removes your server's old default self-signed certificate, updates services to use the certificate signed by the intermediate CA, and configures your server to trust the new certificates.

Configure Open Directory

Because the Server app creates keychain entries on your server, perform the following steps on your server.

Correct DNS records are crucial to the proper functioning of Open Directory services, so double-check DNS before starting the Open Directory service.

1   On your administrator computer, quit the Server app if it is open.

2   On your server computer, open Network Utility (use Spotlight if necessary).

3   Click the Lookup tab.

4   Enter your server's host name in the field, and then click Lookup.

5   Confirm that your server's IPv4 address is returned.

6   Enter your server's primary IPv4 address in the field, and then click Lookup.

7   Confirm that your server's host name is returned.

Once you've confirmed your DNS records, configure your server as an Open Directory master.

1   On your server, open the Server app, select your server, click Continue, provide administrator credentials (Administrator Name: ladmin, Administrator Password: ladminpw), deselect the "Remember this password" checkbox, and then click Connect.

2   If the Server app does not display the list of advanced services, hover the pointer above the word "Advanced" in the sidebar, and then click Show.

3   Select Open Directory.

4   Click On to turn on the Open Directory service (or in the Server app sidebar, Control-click Open Directory, and choose Start Open Directory Service).

5   Select "Create a new Open Directory domain," and click Next.

6   In the Directory Administrator pane, deselect the checkbox "Remember this password in my keychain."

Name:	Directory Administrator
Account Name:	diradmin
Password:	
Verify:	
	☐ Remember this password in my keychain

7   Configure a password.

If your server is not accessible from the Internet, in the Directory Administrator pane, enter diradminpw in the Password and Verify fields.

Of course, in a production environment, you should use a secure password and consider using an account name different from the default "diradmin" so that it is more difficult for unauthorized people to guess the username and password combination.

8   Click Next.

9   In the Organization Information pane, enter the appropriate information.

If the following fields do not already contain the information shown, enter it, and click Next.

▶   Organization Name: Pretendco Project *n* (where *n* is your student number)

▶   Admin Email Address: ladmin@server*n*.pretendco.com (where *n* is your student number)

10   View the Confirm Settings pane, and click Set Up.

The Server app displays its progress in the lower-left corner of the Confirm Settings pane.

When it has completed the configuration, the Server app displays the Settings tab of the Open Directory pane, with your server listed as the master in the Servers list.

Inspect the OD Certificates

Inspect the certificates that the Server app automatically created.

1   In the Server app sidebar, select Certificates.

2   Click the Action (gear icon) pop-up menu, and choose Show All Certificates.

3   Confirm that the "Secure services using" pop-up menu is no longer set to a self-signed certificate but rather a certificate signed by your server's OD intermediate CA.

4   Confirm that the self-signed certificate is no longer listed in the Certificates field.

5   Double-click the certificate with your server's host name, signed by your OD intermediate CA (the first entry in the Certificates field).

6 Confirm that in the Issuer Name section, the first field (which is the common name) has a value made up of the following strings:

► "IntermediateCA_"
► Your server's host name in all capital letters
► "_1"

7 Click OK to close the certificate information pane.

8 Double-click the code signing certificate (the second entry in the Certificates field).

9 Confirm that this is also issued by your OD intermediate CA.

Use Keychain Access to inspect your OD CA, your OD intermediate CA, and the two signed certificates.

1 On your server, use a Spotlight search to open Keychain Access.

2 In the Keychains column, select System.

3 In the Category column, select My Certificates.

4 Select your OD CA. Its name is Pretendco Project *n* Open Directory Certificate Authority (where *n* is your student number).

5   Double-click your OD CA to examine it.

6   Confirm that the second line of text identifies it as "Root certificate authority" and that the Subject Name information matches the Issuer Name information.

7   Note that the certificate's color is bronze, which signifies that it is a root certificate.

8   Click the Trust disclosure triangle to display more details.

9   Confirm that your server is set to always trust this certificate.

▼ **Trust**		
When using this certificate:	Always Trust	⟨?⟩
Secure Sockets Layer (SSL)	Always Trust	

10 Close your OD CA.

11 Double-click your OD intermediate CA.

12 Confirm that its second line of text identifies it as "Intermediate certificate authority." Because your server trusts your OD CA and your OD CA signed this intermediate CA, this certificate is marked as valid with a green checkmark.

Note that the color of the certificate is blue, which signifies that it is an intermediate or leaf certificate.

```
●  ●  ●         IntermediateCA_SERVER17.PRETENDCO.COM_1

  Certificate   IntermediateCA_SERVER17.PRETENDCO.COM_1
  Standard      Intermediate certificate authority
                Expires: Thursday, September 26, 2019 at 1:06:06 PM Central Daylight
                Time
                ⊘ This certificate is valid

  ▶ Trust
  ▼ Details
            Subject Name
           Common Name   IntermediateCA_SERVER17.PRETENDCO.COM_1
           Organization  Pretendco Project 17
     Organizational Unit MACOSX OpenDirectory Intermediate CA
          Email Address  ladmin@server17.pretendco.com

             Issuer Name
           Common Name   Pretendco Project 17 Open Directory Certificate Authority
           Organization  Pretendco Project 17
     Organizational Unit MACOSX OpenDirectory Root CA
          Email Address  ladmin@server17.pretendco.com

          Serial Number  1358348142
               Version   3

       Signature Algorithm  SHA-256 with RSA Encryption ( 1.2.840.113549.1.1.11 )
```

13 Close your OD intermediate CA.

14 Double-click the certificate with your server's host name.

15 Confirm that the second line of text indicates that it is signed by your OD intermediate CA. Your server is configured to trust your OD CA, which signed your OD intermediate CA, which signed this certificate, so it is marked as valid with a green checkmark.

16 Double-click your code signing certificate, inspect it, and close it.

17 Quit Keychain Access.

In this exercise, you configured your server to be an Open Directory master. The Server app automatically configured a new OD CA, intermediate CA, and two new certificates; it removed your server's old default self-signed certificate, and it updated services to use the certificate signed by the intermediate CA. It automatically configured your server to trust its own OD CA, which means that your server also trusts the OD intermediate CA and the two other certificates that are signed by the OD intermediate CA.

Exercise 4.3
Configure Your Administrator Computer to Trust an SSL Certificate

▶ **Prerequisite**

- ▶ "Exercise 4.2 Configure an Open Directory Certificate Authority" on page 152

NOTE ▶ If you obtained a certificate from a widely trusted CA, you do not need to perform this exercise.

In a production environment, it is best to use a valid SSL certificate that's been signed by a trusted CA. If that isn't possible, you should configure your users' computers and devices to trust your server's certificate so that your users do not get into the habit of configuring their devices to trust unverified SSL certificates.

This lesson shows you how to configure an individual computer to trust your server's OD CA; it is beyond the scope of this exercise to show you how to replicate the end result on multiple computers and devices.

Turn On the Web Service Temporarily

Turn on your server's Websites service so you can quickly access the SSL certificate your server's services use.

1   In the Server app sidebar, Control-click Websites, and then choose Start Websites Service.

Visit Your Server's Website Protected by SSL

In this exercise, you will use your administrator computer and confirm that you are using your server's DNS service; otherwise, you will not be able to connect to its web service using its host name. Then you'll open Safari to your server's default HTTPS website. Finally, you'll configure your administrator computer to trust the SSL certificate.

1   On your administrator computer, open System Preferences.

2   Open the Network pane.

3   Select the active network service, and confirm that your server's IP address is listed for the DNS Service value.

    If you are using Wi-Fi, you need to click Advanced and then click the DNS tab to view the DNS Service value.

4   Quit System Preferences.

5   On your administrator computer, open Safari, and in the Address and Search
field, enter https://server*n*.pretendco.com (where *n* is your student number).

6   Press Return to open the page.

Your certificate is not signed by a CA that your administrator computer is configured to
trust, so you'll see the message that Safari can't verify the identity of the website.

> **Safari can't verify the identity of the website
> "server17.pretendco.com".**
>
> The certificate for this website is invalid. You might be connecting to a
> website that is pretending to be "server17.pretendco.com", which could put
> your confidential information at risk. Would you like to connect to the website
> anyway?
>
> ?   Show Certificate   Cancel   Continue

Configure Your Administrator Computer to Trust This SSL Certificate

Once you see the dialog that Safari can't verify the identity of the website, you can click
Show Certificate and configure the currently logged-in user to trust the SSL certificate
used by the website.

1   Click Show Certificate.

2   Note that the certificate with your server's host name is marked in red, "This certificate was signed by an untrusted issuer."

Safari can't verify the identity of the website "server17.pretendco.com".

The certificate for this website is invalid. You might be connecting to a website that is pretending to be "server17.pretendco.com", which could put your confidential information at risk. Would you like to connect to the website anyway?

☐ Always trust "server17.pretendco.com" when connecting to "server17.pretendco.com"

> ⊠ Pretendco Project 17 Open Directory Certificate Authority
>   ↳ ⊠ IntermediateCA_SERVER17.PRETENDCO.COM_1
>   ↳ ⊠ server17.pretendco.com

server17.pretendco.com
Issued by: IntermediateCA_SERVER17.PRETENDCO.COM_1
Expires: Sunday, September 25, 2016 at 1:06:07 PM Central Daylight Time
⊘ This certificate was signed by an untrusted issuer

▶ Trust
▶ Details

?   Hide Certificate   Cancel   Continue

3   In the certificate chain, select your OD CA.

4   Click the Details disclosure triangle, and inspect the details.

5   Select the checkbox "Always trust 'Pretendo Project *n* Open Directory Certificate Authority'" (where *n* is your student number).

☑ Always trust "Pretendco Project 17 Open Directory Certificate Authority"

⊠ Pretendco Project 17 Open Directory Certificate Authority
  ↳ ⊠ IntermediateCA_SERVER17.PRETENDCO.COM_1
      ↳ ⊠ server17.pretendco.com

6   Click Continue.

7   Provide your login credentials, and click Update Settings.

This updates the settings for the currently logged-in user; this does not affect any other user on this computer.

8   Confirm the Safari Address and Search field displays a lock icon, which indicates that the page was opened using SSL.

🔒server17.pretendco.com   ↻

9   Keep Safari open for the next section of this exercise.

Confirm That Your Mac Trusts the SSL Certificate

To view the SSL certificate the Websites service is using, perform the following steps.

1   In the Safari Address and Search field, click the lock icon.

2   In the pane that informs you that Safari is using an encrypted connection, click Show Certificate.

3   Confirm that the certificate is listed as valid with a green checkmark.

Safari is using an encrypted connection to server17.pretendco.com.

Encryption with a digital certificate keeps information private as it's sent to or from the https website server17.pretendco.com.

Pretendco Project 17 Open Directory Certificate Authority
↳ IntermediateCA_SERVER17.PRETENDCO.COM_1
    ↳ server17.pretendco.com

server17.pretendco.com
Issued by: IntermediateCA_SERVER17.PRETENDCO.COM_1
Expires: Sunday, September 25, 2016 at 1:06:07 PM Central Daylight Time
⊘ This certificate is valid

▶ **Trust**
▶ **Details**

?   Hide Certificate   OK

4   Press Command-Q to quit Safari.

You confirmed that the Websites service uses the SSL certificate you configured in the previous exercise. You confirmed that by trusting a CA, you trust a certificate that was signed by an intermediate CA that was signed by the CA (at least for the currently logged-in user).

Exercise 4.4
Clean Up

To ensure that the rest of the exercises are consistent, turn off the Websites service.

1   In the Server app sidebar, select the Websites service, and click Off to turn the service off.

2   Confirm that no green status indicators appear next to the Websites service.

This indicates that the service is off.

You are ready to complete the tasks of any other lesson's exercises.

Lesson 5

Using Status and Notifications

A server can perform its functions only when it is in good health and has the resources it needs. OS X Server for Yosemite, via its Server app, provides monitoring and issues notifications if something triggers a threshold or condition. Using the monitoring and notifications features can help keep the server running properly.

Reference 5.1
Using Monitoring and Status Tools

Servers, even OS X Server computers, need some attention from time to time and can't be left to their own devices. It is inefficient to regularly peruse all the operating parameters to make sure the server is healthy. You can use the built-in capabilities of the server to tell you when things go wrong or show you when certain trigger points are reached. When these points are reached, OS X Server can notify you via an alert. This doesn't remove the need to look over the server once in a while, but it can help you recognize that a situation is happening or could happen shortly.

Four major sections in the Server app help you monitor the server:

▶ Alerts—Choose which items to monitor and add the email address or addresses of those who will get the alerts.

▶ Logs—Quickly access and search logs for the services provided by OS X Server.

▶ Stats—View graphs for processor and memory usage, network traffic, and Caching service usage for time periods ranging from one hour to seven days. New are the abilities to view memory pressure, which is a measure of random-access memory (RAM) usage, and to view the number of connected users in file sharing.

▶ Storage—See a list of all visible volumes available to the server and the amount of storage space left.

You can use Screen Sharing or Apple Remote Desktop to view the server remotely, and you can install the Server app on a nonserver computer (as you did on your administration computer). This allows you to monitor and manage the server from a different computer.

Reference 5.2
Configuring OS X Server Alerts

In the Server section of the Server app, the Alerts pane allows you to configure both the list of email addresses to receive alerts and what alerts will be sent. The Alerts pane has two tabs:

▶ Alerts—Where the messages are shown.

▶ Delivery—Where the email recipients are listed and what will be delivered to them. There is also the choice for push notifications.

NOTE ▶ Push notification is available only once the Apple Push Notification service on the server is configured and turned on.

When choosing an email address for notifications, it is recommended to create a separate email account that can link to multiple people rather than sending it to specific users from the Server app. This prevents a situation where a person responsible for the server leaves the group and notifications go unnoticed. An account such as *alerts@server17.pre-tendco.com* could be used for multiple purposes and decouples the alerts from individuals.

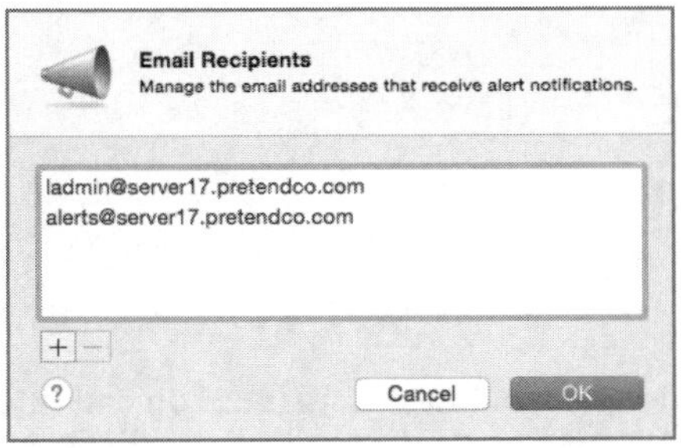

The email is sent directly from the server using its built-in Simple Mail Transfer Protocol (SMTP) service. This can cause issues with some receiving email servers treating the incoming alert email as spam and blocking it. If you are in control of your own email server, you can "whitelist" the Internet Protocol (IP) address of the server so the emails don't get rejected. Alternatively, you can select the "Relay outgoing mail through ISP" checkbox in the Mail service of OS X Server and enter an SMTP server and credentials. This channels the email through any standard mail server, reducing the chance of the alert being tagged as spam. The Mail service does not need to be turned on.

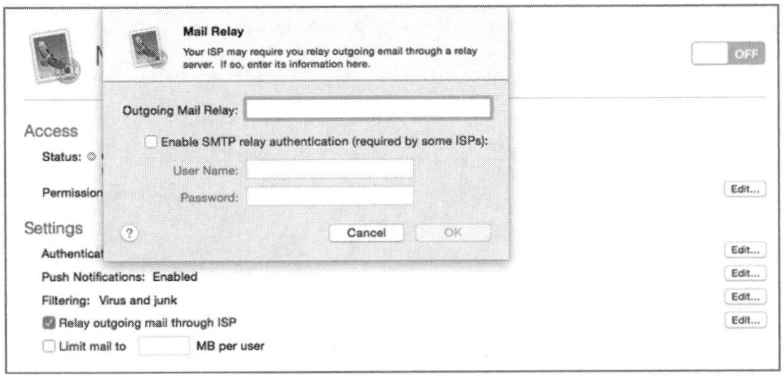

After you use the Server app to enable Apple push notifications and supply an Apple ID for push notifications, your server can send alerts to any Mac with OS X Yosemite that has the Server app installed and logged into the server. These alerts appear in the Server app and in Notification Center of these computers. In the following figure, the server is configured to send alerts to any computer running the Server app that is connecting to server17.

Push Notification Recipients

Choose which administrators receive push alerts. Administrators will be added to the recipient list when they connect using Server.

Recipient	Enable
ladmin - server17	☑
ladmin - server18	☑

| + | − |

[Cancel] [OK]

Alert messages are displayed with a brief description of what has occurred. You can filter the result by adding a term at the bottom of the pane. Double-click the alert, or click the Action (gear icon) menu and choose View Alert, to get additional information regarding the alert. In some cases, a button is available to help rectify the error, but you must understand what caused the error and how clicking the button may help or hurt the server. Sometimes the alert is not a problem but a message that a software update is available, and the action is to run the update.

Network IP Address change notification
9/9/14, 2:50 PM

Summary

The IPv4 network address of server17.pretendco.com has changed from 10.0.0.171 to 192.168.254.10. Some services may not work correctly until they have been updated to use the new configuration.

Actions

✓ This issue has successfully been resolved.

Reference 5.3
Using Logs in OS X Server

In the Server section of the Server app, the Logs pane allows quick access to the logs for the various services running on the server. A search box gives you a way to track down specific items in the logs.

Certain logs will always be available, but others become available once you have turned on the service.

Additional logs are available using the Console app, located at /Applications/Utilities/.

Reference 5.4
Using Stats in OS X Server

In the Stats pane, six performance graphs are available:

▶ Processor Usage—Divided into System CPU and User CPU to help determine what is using the most CPU cycles

▶ Memory Usage—Shows how much physical RAM is being used

▶ Memory Pressure—Shows the impact of RAM use on virtual memory

▶ Network Traffic—Shows outbound and inbound traffic

▶ Caching, Bytes Served—Shows Caching service data transfer

▶ File Sharing, Connected Users—Shows how many users are using file sharing connections

All six graphs are adjustable to show time intervals from the past hour to the past seven days.

When using the graphs, realize that the numbers on the graph don't tell the whole story. Often, the shape of the graph is most important. Review the graphs once in a while to get used to what is normal and be able to identify when a change is happening.

A normal Processor Usage graph might show a certain percentage during the workday, with spikes corresponding to heavy server utilization. It may indicate a problem when the graphs show a higher than usual percentage with no usage changes to account for it. This would indicate that it is time to do some more research.

Memory usage might creep up over time if an application isn't releasing RAM. The graph might also show that all available RAM is being used continuously, which may indicate that the server needs a RAM upgrade.

Network traffic should also follow the usage patterns. Heavy access will be shown in the graphs, but traffic at night or other times of low usage might indicate a backup process or access that isn't planned.

Reviewing the Caching service in Stats can give you an idea of the network usage and activity associated with it.

The Memory Pressure graph is new in OS X Server for Yosemite although the underlying measurement was available in Mavericks. It is a relative measure of RAM usage as it applies virtual memory paging. If the memory pressure goes up, it might indicate the computer needs more RAM to operate efficiently. A high level might mean that RAM contents are being sent to the hard drive, resulting in poor performance. It is expected for the measurement to go up during periods of high usage, especially in high RAM requirement services such as file transfers.

Reference 5.5
Viewing Storage Space

Storage is listed under the server's name in the Server section of the Server app. Select the server in the sidebar, and then click the Storage tab. Each volume attached to the server is listed, and the available amount of storage capacity is listed next to it with a bar graph for quick review. You can review each volume and view and change permissions (covered further in Lesson 12 "Configuring the File Sharing Service" and Lesson 13 "Defining File Access").

Exercise 5.1
Use the Server App to Monitor Your Server

▶ **Prerequisites**

- ▶ All exercises in Lesson 1 "Installing OS X Server"
- ▶ "Exercise 2.1 Create DNS Zones and Records" on page 71

It's a good idea to use the Server app to proactively monitor your server so you can address any issues that crop up, rather than reacting to an alert in a crisis situation. In this exercise, you will configure alerts, send a test alert, and explore the Stats pane.

Configure Alerts

Configure alerts to inform you when there's something you need to notice about your server.

Turn On Apple Push Notifications

1   Perform these exercises on your administrator computer. If you do not already have a connection to your server computer with the Server app on your administrator computer, then connect to it with the following steps: Open the Server app on your administrator computer, choose Manage > Connect to Server, select your server, click Continue, provide administrator credentials (Administrator Name: ladmin, Administrator Password: ladminpw), deselect the "Remember this password" checkbox, and then click Connect.

2   Select your server in the sidebar.

3   Click the Settings tab.

4   If the "Enable Apple push notifications" checkbox is not already selected, select it now.

5   If you haven't already configured an Apple ID to be used for push notifications, in the dialog, provide your Apple ID credentials to obtain the push notification certificate. In an instructor-led environment, your instructor may provide one. Click OK when done.

If you do not already have an Apple ID, click the link under the credential fields to create an Apple ID.

Configure Email Recipients

Configure the email recipients of alerts from the Server app.

1 In the Server app sidebar, select Alerts.

2 Click the Delivery tab, and click the Email Addresses Edit button.

3 Click the Add (+) button.

4 Enter an email address (you can use your own) that will receive alerts, and then press Tab to stop editing.

5 If you want, repeat steps 3–4 to add more recipients.

6 Click OK to save the change.

Inspect Push Recipients

Configure the recipients of push alerts from the Server app.

1 Next to the Push Notifications field, click the Edit button.

2 In the Push Notification Recipients pane, confirm that the name of the currently logged-in user (ladmin) and the name of the computer that you have been using (client*n,* where *n* is your student number) appear.

3   Note that the Add (+) button is not available because you are already added for this user from this Mac computer.

4   Click Cancel to close the Push Notification Recipients pane.

5   On your administrator computer, quit the Server app.

Add a Push Recipient from Your Server

1   On your *server computer*, open the Server app ; at the Choose a Mac pane, select your server, click Continue, provide administrator credentials (Administrator Name: ladmin, Administrator Password: ladminpw), deselect the "Remember this password" checkbox, and then click Connect.

2   In the Server app sidebar, select Alerts, and then click the Delivery tab.

3   Next to the Push Notifications field, click the Edit button.

4   Click the Add (+) button.

5   Confirm that the name of the currently logged-in user (ladmin) and the name of your server (server*n*, where *n* is your student number) appear.

6 · Click OK to save the change.

Inspect the Alerts to Send

Inspect the list of alerts and the mechanisms for them to be sent.

1 In the Settings field, inspect the alert types you want to be sent.

Send a Test Alert

Now that you've configured alerts, confirm that you are receiving the alerts. Send a test alert from your server. Confirm the alert was delivered by push notification to your administrator computer.

> **NOTE ▶** Confirming the email delivery of the test alert is outside the scope of this exercise because this test environment may result in a bounced email message. The resulting alert email message will have a Return-Path field with the value of *root@servern.pretendco.com* and a From field with the values of Server Alerts and *alerts@servern.pretendco.com* (where *n* is your student number). In this exercise, an external email server cannot access an MX record for your server. This message might not be accepted by an external email server, or it might be considered spam by an email filter. You may need to configure your spam filters to accept email from that address.

You will generate a test alert from your server computer, view it on your administrator computer even though the Server app is not running on your administrator computer, and then view the test alert on your server computer.

1   While still using your server to run the Server app, confirm that you are in the Alerts pane in the Delivery tab.

2   Click the Action (gear icon) pop-up menu, and choose Send Test Alert.

Confirm the Alert

> **NOTE ▶** If you do not receive the alert in this test environment, don't worry; read this exercise, and continue performing the steps of "Perform Ongoing Monitoring" on page 179.

Within a few moments, your administrator computer (and your server) will receive a notification about the alert and increase the count in the badge for the app icon in the Dock (your Server app may appear in a different location in the Dock than as shown in the following figure).

A notification for the test alert appears in the upper-right corner of the screen.

Within a few moments, the notification disappears.

> **TIP** In Notification Center preferences you can select Server in the left column and then change the Server alert style from its default type of Banners to Alerts, which do not disappear.

1   On your *administrator computer*, click the Notification Center icon in the upper-right corner of the screen of your administrator computer.

2   Click the Notifications tab.

3   Confirm that in the Server section your test alert appears.

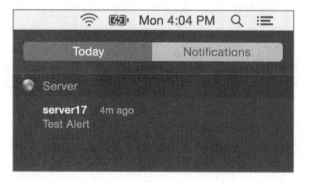

4   Still on your administrator computer, click the test alert in Notification Center.
    The Server app opens.

5   On your administrator computer, at the Choose a Mac pane, select your server, click Continue, provide administrator credentials (Administrator Name: ladmin, Administrator Password: ladminpw), deselect the "Remember this password" checkbox, and then click Connect.

6   In the Server app sidebar, select Alerts.

7 Click the Alerts tab in the Alerts pane.

8 Double-click the test alert.

9 Review the information, and click Done.

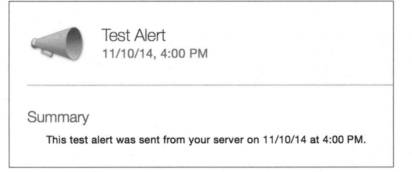

10 Click the Action (gear icon) menu, and choose Clear All.

This removes all the alerts from the list of alerts on your administrator computer.

Clear the alerts on your server computer as well.

1 On your server computer, click the Alerts tab.

2 Click the Action (gear icon) menu, and choose Clear All.

This removes all the alerts from the list of alerts on your server.

3 Quit the Server app on your server.

The steps you have taken for creating alerts and setting up monitoring are recommended for all servers.

Perform Ongoing Monitoring

It's a good idea to periodically check the amount of free disk space and to check the graphs in the Stats pane.

Monitor Disk Space

One of the alerts is for low disk space; instead of waiting for an alert, regularly use the Server app to display information about available disk space.

1 On your administrator computer, in the Server app sidebar, select your server.

2 Click the Storage tab.

3 Select the List View button in the bottom-left corner of the Storage pane.

4 Review the amount of available space for each volume.

Monitor the Available Graphs

Although no alert exists for an abnormally high amount of processor usage, memory usage, or network traffic, monitoring these occasionally is still a good idea. The Server app displays a graph of each of the following categories of information:

▶ Processor Usage (including System CPU and User CPU)

▶ Memory Usage

▶ Memory Pressure

▶ Network Traffic (including Outbound Traffic and Inbound Traffic)

▶ Caching — Bytes Served

▶ File Sharing — Connected Users (for AFP and SMB)

Explore the graphs that are available in the Server app

1 In the Server app sidebar, select Stats.

2 Use the pop-up menu on the left to choose the attribute to display; the following figure displays the Network Traffic graph.

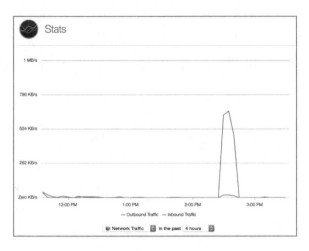

3   Click the pop-up menu on the right to choose the duration of time to include for the graph.

4   Take a look at each of the available graphs to get a feel for the stats that are available.

In this exercise, you configured email and push delivery of alerts, sent a test alert, and confirmed that it was sent via push notification; you also explored the Stats pane.

Lesson 6
Backing Up OS X Server

At some point you may have to recover a server whose hardware or software has failed. To help protect against failures, you need to implement a proven backup system. Although there are many backup choices on the market, OS X since Mac OS X v10.5 has had Time Machine built in. When used with OS X Server, it can provide a functional, low-cost, and simple backup solution that works properly with OS X. Time Machine is the recommended backup for OS X Server because it protects all of the operating system configurations and data needed for a successful restore.

GOALS

▶ Back up OS X Server

▶ Restore OS X Server

Reference 6.1
Describing Backup Concepts

There are a number of considerations when it comes to backing up a computer. You need to decide when and how often it gets backed up, where it gets backed up to, and how often the backup media is rotated.

The commercial products available to back up OS X Server offer a wide range of backup techniques and choice of media. With these products you can define exactly how often the server gets backed up and what gets backed up. You can decide whether you are going to back up to tape, hard drives, or cloud storage. You get to decide what style of backup to use, such as one of the following:

▶ Full image—The entire server's drive is replicated block by block, but it requires that the server be stopped and copied while booted from another volume.

▶ Full file-level copy—The entire volume is copied file by file. This takes longer and doesn't require the server to be started from another volume, but unless certain services, especially ones that use a database, are stopped, the backup may not be totally valid.

- ▶ Incremental—Only the changes from the previous backup are copied. This backup takes less time and space, but it can take longer to restore because it may need to read from multiple incremental copies to get the full amount of data.

- ▶ Continuous—This is also known as continuous data protection (CDP) and is where changes are committed to the backup in short intervals rather than waiting for the end of the day. This allows for more granular backups. This is the technology that Time Machine uses.

When deciding on the media, consider capacity, life span, and portability. Some popular choices include the following:

- ▶ Tape—While tape's death has been reported for years, it stays viable by offering large capacities, portability, and increasing speed. The downside is that the tape drives and libraries tend to require care and effort to keep running.

- ▶ Disk

- ▶ Cloud-based storage—Storing data on a remote host over the Internet is becoming extremely popular and viable with increasing bandwidth and the availability of inexpensive data storage plans. The downside is the reliance on a third party to keep your data safe and the length of time to restore data over the Internet. Some hosts will allow you to make a local backup and send it to them for "seeding," where they copy your data from disk to their infrastructure and send you a disk for restores.

Regardless of the choice of backup technique and media, testing the restores is immensely critical. Data has been lost because a trusted backup turned out to have a problem when a restore was needed. Backups should be tested on a regular basis and verified as valid.

Backup Diversity

It is wise to have a backup of your backup. Backups sometimes fail or can't be recovered, so it is a good idea to use different techniques to provide additional coverage. Maybe use a local backup plus a cloud backup. Each has its advantages and disadvantages, but you can cover multiple bases by using multiple techniques.

Local backups are great because they are fast and easy to recover with, but if there is a problem at that location that damages those backups along with the original source, such as a fire or flood, you have lost all of your data and operating system configurations.

Cloud backups or remote backups are good because they protect against local damages, but they take longer to both back up and recover. This could make them inappropriate for situations in which time is of the essence. Just be careful that you don't exclude information that you can't recover from the loss of.

Combining local and remote backups can give you the best of both worlds as long as you use them appropriately. For example, you might back up only data remotely and leave the operating system out. This might speed up backups because you can always rebuild the operating system. Local backups can be made so they are bootable to make recovery fast.

Reference 6.2
Backing up with Time Machine

Apple has provided a simple-to-use and effective backup application in all versions of OS X since Mac OS X v10.5. Time Machine was originally conceived to make it easy to back up computers with little effort. The process of setting up Time Machine is simply to connect an external hard drive and turn on Time Machine.

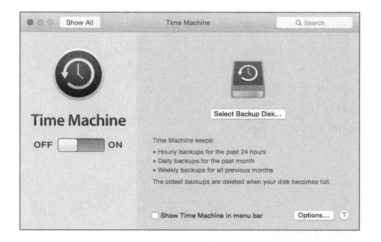

Time Machine has grown in capability and is a viable choice to back up OS X Server. Time Machine can be considered a form of continuous data protection, and it properly handles the databases OS X Server uses. Time Machine is the supported backup process for OS X Server.

> **NOTE ▶** If you have moved your service data off the startup volume, you need to refer to Apple Support article HT202406, "Restoring OS X Server from a Time Machine backup," for instructions on how to use command-line tools to restore the service data properly.

Backup targets for Time Machine are limited to hard drive volumes visible to the server and Time Machine–enabled network AFP share points.

NOTE ▶ For more information regarding Time Machine, refer to Lesson 16, "Time Machine," in *Apple Pro Training Series: OS X Support Essentials 10.10*.

For OS X Server, Time Machine can back up service data, including the following:

▶ Contacts

▶ File Sharing

▶ Calendar

▶ Messages

▶ Mail

▶ Open Directory

▶ Profile Manager

▶ Time Machine (the service for providing a backup target across a network)

▶ VPN

▶ Web

▶ Wiki

Time Machine will not back up the following:

▶ /tmp/

▶ /Library/Logs/

▶ /Library/Caches/

▶ /Users/<username>/Library/Caches/

Time Machine has the ability to back up to more than one target. This makes it easy to connect a hard drive to the server for continuous protection and connect a second drive that is rotated offsite. With two or more hard drives being rotated offsite, a disaster recovery plan can be implemented while providing instant recovery of data from the local drive as needed.

Time Machine is capable of taking snapshots and backing up onto its own startup volume. The snapshots feature is a convenience designed for laptops but shouldn't be considered for production servers.

Time Machine makes a backup once an hour for 24 hours. Beyond 24 hours it saves a daily backup for a month and then weekly backups from that point on until the target volume fills up. The oldest backups are deleted at that point. If you don't want to lose your backups, replace the backup targets as they become close to full.

One feature of Time Machine running on OS X Server is triggering a script that automatically archives the content of Open Directory each time Time Machine runs. The resulting file is placed in /private/var/backups/ and is copied along with other files during Time Machine operation. The archive can be recovered from that path in the backup location and used to re-create the Open Directory environment if required. To recover the file, you will need root access at the command line, and you will need to enable the root user and log in with the root credentials. See Apple Support article HT1528, "Enabling and using the 'root' user in Mac OS X," for more information.

```
bash-3.2# pwd
/Volumes/ServerBackup/Backups.backupdb/server17/2014-09-11-113501/Macintosh HD/var/backups
bash-3.2# ls -l
total 8200
-rw-rw----@ 1 root  admin  4198400 Sep 11 11:34 ServerBackup_OpenDirectoryMaster.sparseimage
bash-3.2#
```

Exercise 6.1
Use Time Machine to Back Up OS X Server

▶ **Prerequisites**

- ▶ All exercises in Lesson 1 "Installing OS X Server"
- ▶ "Exercise 2.1 Create DNS Zones and Records" on page 71

It is important to consider your backup strategy when planning your IT environment. With Time Machine, backup and restore are easy. This exercise guides you through the basics of using Time Machine to back up your server. In this exercise, you will specify a Time Machine destination and then start your initial Time Machine backup.

Prepare a temporary destination for the Time Machine backup.

Option 1: Use an External Disk as a Time Machine Destination

If you have an external HFS+–formatted disk that you can erase before and after you perform the exercises, follow these steps. Otherwise, skip to the next section, "Option 2: Use an Internal Volume as the Time Machine Destination" on page 189.

> **NOTE ▶** Do not erase your disk unless you are sure you do not need any information stored on it. If there is any question, skip this option, and continue with "Option 2: Use an Internal Volume as the Time Machine Destination" on page 189.

1   Physically connect the external disk to your server computer.

2   If you are asked if you want to use this disk to back up with Time Machine, click Don't Use.

3   On your server, press Command–Space bar to open a Spotlight search, enter Disk Utility, and open Disk Utility.

4   In the Disk Utility sidebar, select your external disk (select the disk, which is on the left, not the volume, which is indented to the right).

5   Click the Erase tab.

6   Click the Format pop-up menu, and choose Mac OS Extended (Journaled).

7   In the Name field, enter Server Backup.

8   Click Erase.

9   When you are asked if you want to use this disk to back up with Time Machine, click Decide Later.

10 Quit Disk Utility.

Skip the Option 2 section, and continue with the section "Configure Time Machine" on page 191.

Option 2: Use an Internal Volume as the Time Machine Destination

Alternatively, considering that access control lists (ACLs) prevent you from removing backup files from a Time Machine destination and that this is a test environment, you can follow the steps in this section to use Disk Utility to create a new temporary volume on your existing disk. In a production environment, a Time Machine destination should be a volume on a physically separate disk.

> **NOTE ►** Using the same disk or partitioning a disk for a Time Machine backup location is OK only for demonstration and learning. Do not do this on a real production computer. Also, make sure you have a good backup before live-partitioning a disk that already has data on it. For more information regarding disk partitioning, refer to Lesson 10, "File Systems and Storage," in *Apple Pro Training Series: OS X Support Essentials 10.10*.

1   On your server, press Command–Space bar to open a Spotlight search, enter Disk Utility, and open Disk Utility.

2   In the Disk Utility sidebar, select the element (either a disk or a Core Storage logical volume group) that contains your server's startup volume.

3   Click the Partition tab.

4   Select a volume with extra space, such as your startup volume. If you have only one volume, it is automatically selected.

Partition Layout:

Current

Server HD

5   Click Add (+).

6   Select the new volume you just created.

7   In the Name field, enter Server Backup.

Note that if your server's startup volume is contained in a Core Storage logical volume group, various elements of the Disk Utility window will be different from what you see in the following figure. For more information on Core Storage, see "Reference 9.1 File System Components" in *Apple Pro Training Series: OS X Support Essentials 10.10.*

8   This is just for demonstration purposes, so you can leave the Size field at its default.

9   Click Apply, and in the dialog to confirm your action, click Partition.

10 Wait until the operation completes (there is a progress bar in the lower-right corner of the Disk Utility window).

11 Quit Disk Utility.

Configure Time Machine

1   On your server, open System Preferences, and select the Time Machine preferences pane.

2   In Time Machine preferences, select the checkbox "Show Time Machine in menu bar."

3   Click Select Backup Disk.

4   Select Server Backup, and then click Use Disk.

5   Click Use Selected Volume if you are asked "Are you sure you want to back up to the same device your original data is on?" because this is for demonstration purposes only.

If you are asked to erase the disk, click Erase.

6   In the main Time Machine preferences pane, click Options to review the list of items that you could select to exclude from backups. If you have any other volumes that you do not want to include the backup, click the Add (+) button, choose the volume in the sidebar, and then click Exclude.

If you change the volume that stores your server's service data, you should include that volume in the backup.

7   Close the exclusions pane: Click Save if you made any changes, or click Cancel otherwise.

8   From the Time Machine menu, choose Back Up Now.

Time Machine prepares for the backups and makes a complete copy of all the nonexcluded files at the first backup. You can watch the progress in the Time Machine preferences pane.

After the first backup has completed, the next time Time Machine runs, it copies only the files that have changed since the last backup.

In this exercise, you specified a Time Machine destination and completed a Time Machine backup.

Exercise 6.2
Inspect Time Machine Backup Files

▶ **Prerequisite**

   ▶   "Exercise 6.1 Use Time Machine to Back Up OS X Server" on page 187

Because it takes a while to complete a backup, consider continuing with another lesson and then returning to this exercise after the backup has completed. Don't worry, you can work while a backup is being made; just be sure to follow the steps of this exercise to initiate one last backup before you restore.

In this exercise, you will inspect the files related to OS X Server that are part of the backup. You will use the Finder to confirm critical server files are backed up. You will use the Server app Logs pane to confirm that special steps were taken to back up a sample service, namely, the Open Directory service.

Use the Finder to Examine Backup Files

Because some files are readable only with root user privileges, you will change permissions to read some files.

Wait for the Backup to Complete

1 On your server, after you see the notification that the Time Machine backup has completed, close the notification.

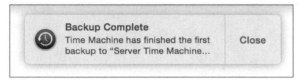

2 Quit System Preferences.

Inspect Backup Files in Finder

1 In the Finder, choose Go > Go to Folder.

2 You can use tab completion to help you quickly enter the next value: In the Go to the folder field, enter **/Volumes/Server Backup/Backups.backupdb/server*n*/Latest/Server HD/**, and click Go (where *n* is your student number).

3 Open Library, and then open Server.

This folder contains many (but not all) files related to your server's services.

4 Open named.

This folder contains files for the DNS records you created.

5 Close the named folder.

6 In the Finder, choose Go > Go to Folder; in the "Go to the folder" field, enter /Volumes/ Server Backup/Backups.backupdb/server*n*/Latest/Server HD/var/ (where *n* is your student number), and click Go.

The var folder is hidden in the Finder unless you request it in the Go to Folder command. Many of the folders in the var folder are readable only by root, so in the next few steps you will make a copy and change the permissions; after you inspect the files, you will remove the copy you made.

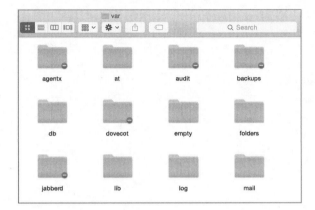

7   Drag the backups folder to your desktop.

8   At the warning that you need to enter the name and password for an administrator, click Continue.

9   Provide local administrator credentials, and click OK.

10 Close the var folder.

11 Select the backups folder, and then choose File > Get Info.

12 Click the disclosure triangle next to Sharing & Permissions.

13 Click the lock icon in the lower-right corner of the Info window, provide local administrator credentials, and click OK.

14 Click the Add (+) button.

15 Select Local Admin, and click Select.

This adds the Local Admin user (short name: ladmin) to the access list with "Read only" permissions.

16 Close the Info window to save the changes.

17 From your desktop, open the backups folder.

18 Open the item named ServerBackup_OpenDirectoryMaster.sparseimage.

The ldap_bk volume is mounted and appears on the desktop.

19 Open the ldap_bk volume.

20 Open the certificates folder.

21 Confirm that files related to your OD CA and your OD intermediate CA are there.

22 Close the following folders: certificates, ldap_bk folder, and backups.

23 Select the ldap_bk volume on the desktop, and then choose File > Eject "ldap_bk".

24 Drag the backups folder to the Trash, provide local administrator credentials, and then click OK.

Use the Logs Pane to View a Backup Log

Use the Server app Logs pane to view a log related to backing up the Open Directory service. You will learn more about the Open Directory service in Lesson 9 "Managing Local Network Accounts".

1   Perform this exercise on your administrator computer. If you do not already have a connection to your server computer with Server app on your administrator computer, then connect to it with the following steps: Open the Server app on your administrator computer, choose Manage > Connect to Server, select your server, click Continue, provide administrator credentials (Administrator Name: ladmin, Administrator Password: ladminpw), deselect the "Remember this password" checkbox, and then click Connect.

2   In the Server app sidebar, select Logs.

3   Click the pop-up menu, scroll to the Open Directory section, and choose Configuration Log.

4   Note that there are five steps involved with backing up the Open Directory service.

Also note that the timestamps for this log are displayed in the Coordinated Universal Time (UTC) standard.

In this exercise, you examined the data in the Time Machine backup related to your server's services.

You can keep Time Machine running throughout the rest of the exercises. If you ever want to go back to an earlier state, you can restart in OS X Recovery mode and restore from the Time Machine backup.

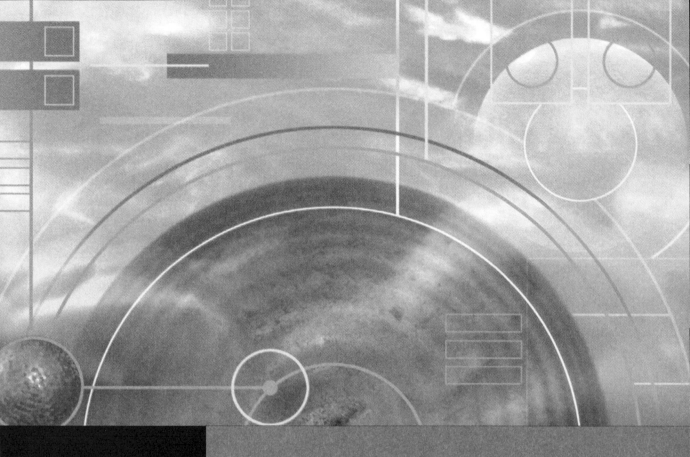

Configuring Accounts

Lesson 7
Managing Local Users

Authentication is the process by which people identify which user account they want to use on the system. This is similar to, but slightly different from, saying that authentication is how a person proves his or her identity to a system. The distinction is useful because multiple people may share the same user name and password, or one person may have multiple user accounts on the same system. In each case, the person supplies user account *credentials* (which usually consist of a name and a password) to identify the user account the person wants to use, and if the supplied credentials are valid, the person successfully authenticates. Although there are other methods of authenticating a user account, such as smart cards or biometrics, the combination of name and password is the most common (and is assumed for this lesson).

Authorization is the process that determines what an authenticated user account is allowed to do on the system. OS X Server can disallow authorization to use OS X Server services unless a user is explicitly granted authorization to use the service. In Lesson 12 "Configuring the File Sharing Service", you will learn more about authorization to access a particular file.

In this lesson, you will use the Server app to do the following:

► Configure local user and group accounts
► Import local accounts
► Configure access to services

GOALS

► Describe authentication and authorization

► Create and configure local user accounts

► Create and configure local group accounts

► Import local accounts

► Manage service access authorization

Reference 7.1
Describing Authentication and Authorization

When configuring any server for access by users, you'll need to determine what services the server will provide and what levels of user access to assign. For many of the services this guide covers, such as File Sharing, you'll need to create specific user accounts on your server.

When considering the creation of user accounts, you'll want to determine how to best set up your users, how to organize them into groups that match the needs of your organization, and how to best maintain this information over time. As with any service or information technology task, the best approach is to thoroughly plan your requirements and approach before starting to implement a solution.

Using Authentication and Authorization

Authentication occurs in many different contexts in OS X and OS X Server, but it most commonly involves using a login window. For example, when you start up an OS X computer, you may have to enter a user name and password in an initial login window before being allowed to use the system.

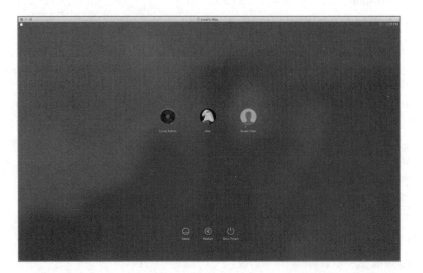

Authentication also occurs when you attempt to connect to a network file service, whether via Apple Filing Protocol (AFP) or Server Message Block (SMB); in the following figure, you need to provide a name and a password to authenticate for the AFP service.

A user must authenticate before accessing these services, even if logging in just as a guest user. Depending on what he is trying to access, the user may or may not get feedback on whether he entered the wrong password (authentication) or is not allowed access to the service (authorization). For instance, if the user *enters a wrong password* at the login window, the login window will simply shake and return you to the login window; this is the behavior for many authentication dialogs in OS X.

If the user *does not have authorization* to log in at a computer, even if the user name and password are correct, the login window will again shake and return to the login window. The user experience is the same, despite the different reasons for the user not being able to access a service.

Reference 7.2
Creating and Administering User and Administrator Server Accounts

A number of tools are available to create and administer user and group accounts. You use Users & Groups preferences in OS X to define local users and perform basic administration of local groups. However, System Preferences does not have a remote mode; you have to use tools such as Screen Sharing or Apple Remote Desktop to remotely administer System Preferences on an OS X Server computer.

NOTE ▶ It is common to drop the word "account" from the term "user account."

This lesson focuses on using the Server app to remotely manage local user and group accounts and to remotely manage access to the services OS X Server provides.

OS X stores local user and group accounts in the local directory domain (also known as local directory node). You will learn about managing local network accounts in Lesson 9 "Managing Local Network Accounts".

To administer a server with the Server app, you must authenticate as an administrator. This is required whether you use the Server app at the server locally or remotely from another computer.

Using the Server App to Configure User Accounts

To grant a person specific permissions on OS X Server, you must set up a user account for that person. The Server app is the primary tool you will use in this lesson for creating and configuring user accounts on OS X Server. You'll use the Server app to create network user accounts in Lesson 9 "Managing Local Network Accounts".

Standard local user accounts on OS X enable a person to access files and applications local to that computer. After you install OS X Server, local user accounts continue to allow access to files and services, whether you use a local user account to log in on the OS X Server computer or you use a local user account to access OS X Server services such as Mail and File Sharing. When you use another computer, you can use a server's local user account to remotely access various services offered by that server. But you cannot use that local user account at another computer's login window to log in to that computer, unless that other computer also has a local user account with the same name and password defined in its local directory domain. This is a complication you should avoid by using a centralized directory, which is covered in Lesson 9 "Managing Local Network Accounts".

When you use the Server app to create a user, you can specify the following settings:

- ▶ Full name
- ▶ Account name
- ▶ Email addresses
- ▶ Password
- ▶ Whether the user can administer the server
- ▶ Home folder
- ▶ Disk quota
- ▶ Keywords
- ▶ Notes

A user account's full name is also known as a long name or name; it is common practice to use a person's full name, with the first letter of each name capitalized, and a space between each word in the name. The name can contain no more than 255 bytes, so character sets that occupy multiple bytes per character have a lower maximum number of characters.

The account name, also known as a short name, is an abbreviated name, usually consisting of all lowercase characters. A user can authenticate using the full name or account name. OS X uses a user's account name when creating a home folder for that user. Carefully consider the account name before assigning it because it is not a trivial task to change a user's account name. You are not permitted to use spaces in a user's account name; it must contain at least one letter, and it can contain only the following characters:

▶ a through z

▶ A through Z

▶ 0 through 9

▶ _ (underscore)

▶ – (hyphen)

▶ . (period)

Using Keywords and Notes

Keywords and notes allow you to quickly search and sort accounts and can help you quickly create groups or edit groups of users. These features are useful for organizing users or searching for particular users based on something other than name or user ID. This provides for a more realistic search pattern should you need to specify a range of users without adding them to a specific group.

To add a new keyword , simply enter it in the Keyword field, and then press Tab or Return.

NOTE ▸ Local accounts and network accounts (see Lesson 8 "Configuring Open Directory Services") have separate keyword lists.

You can add a note to a user account with information that may be useful later, such as who created the account, the year of graduation, or the purpose of the account.

To search for users with the same keyword or note, enter text in the Filter Users field, and then choose the appropriate item from the menu.

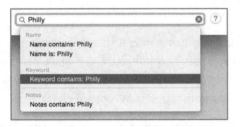

You can add more filtering options by entering more search terms.

After filtering the user list, don't forget that you can click the Clear button in the Filter Users field to remove the filter terms and display all users again.

Using Advanced Options

For a little more information about the user, select the user in the Users pane, Control-click (or secondary-click), and choose Advanced Options from the shortcut menu.

In the advanced settings pane, you can view and modify several attributes of a user account.

The full list of attributes listed in the advanced settings pane is as follows:

► User ID

► Group

► Account Name

► Aliases

► Login shell

► Home Directory

You should not modify these attributes without completely understanding the ramifications of a change.

NOTE ► Invalid settings can prevent the user from logging in or accessing resources.

A full explanation of all of these attributes is outside the scope of this guide, but some are important enough that they are explained in the following sections.

The user ID (UID) is a numerical value that the system uses to differentiate one user from another. Though users gain access to the system with a name or short name, each name is associated with a UID, and the UID is used in making authorization decisions. In the unlikely event that two users are logged in with different names and passwords but with the same UID, when they access documents and folders, the system will consider them to be the same owner. Because of this, the system will provide both users with the same access to documents and folders, a situation you should avoid.

NOTE ▶ The Server app allows you to configure multiple users with the same UID, but this is not recommended.

The group is the primary group the user is associated with, even though you can configure the user to be associated with multiple groups. You do not need to explicitly add a user to its primary group. Note that when you view a group's list of members, a user who is a member of a group because the group is the user's primary group will *not* be listed as a member of the group, even though that user effectively is a member of that group.

It is recommended that you do not change the account name in the advanced settings pane; this could prevent the user from accessing resources.

You can assign one or more aliases for a user account. An alias allows a user to access services by authenticating with one of her aliases and her password. An alias is sometimes a shorter or otherwise more convenient string of text than the account name.

Creating Templates

You can create user and group templates from an existing account to cut down on the time it takes you to create new users with the attributes you desire. From the pop-up menu that appears when you Control-click (or secondary-click) an account, choose either Create Template from User or Create Template from Group. After you've created a template, when you create a new account, a Template pop-up menu appears, and you can choose to use a template or not.

Configuring Local User Accounts

OS X Server maintains a list of local user accounts for managing access to resources. In this section, you will learn how to use the Server app to do the following:

▶   Create local users who can access services and files on your server

▶   Give a local user the ability to administer your server

▶   Create local groups

▶ Assign local users to a local group

▶ Assign local groups to a local user

▶ Assign local groups to a local group

Creating Local Users Who Can Access Services and Files on Your Server

In the Users pane in the Server app, simply click the Add (+) button to create a new user.

Enter values for the new user's attributes, and then click Create.

Giving a Local User the Ability to Administer Your Server

An administrator account is a special type of user account on OS X Server that enables the user to administer the server. A user with an administrator account can create, edit, and delete user accounts, as well as modify the settings of various running services on the server where the administrator account exists. The administrator uses the Server app to perform basic account and service management.

> **NOTE** ▶ An administrator account is powerful, so carefully consider the ramifications before configuring an account to be able to administer your server.

It is simple to make a local user an administrator. Just select the checkbox "Allow user to administer this server." You can do this when you create the user or at any time afterward. You'll create a user and make it an administrator.

When you make a user account an administrator, the operating system makes that user account a member of the local group that has the full name of Administrators. Any member of the Administrators group can use the Server app and can unlock all the preferences in System Preferences. Any member of the Administrators group can also change file ownership, can make any systemwide change, and can run commands as the root user in the command-line environment, so consider carefully before enabling a user account to be a member of the Administrators group.

> **NOTE ▶** You can also use Users & Groups preferences to specify a user as an administrator.

> **NOTE ▶** When you select "Allow user to administer this server" for a user, you add him or her to the local group named admin. You can use the credentials for any user in the admin group to access secure system preferences, such as Users & Groups and Security preferences, among other privileges. Be careful about which users you assign to be part of the local group admin.

In the list of users, there is no indication that any user is an administrator user.

To remove administrator status for a user, simply deselect the checkbox "Allow user to administer this server," and click Done.

Creating Local Groups

Groups allow you to assign privileges to groups of users so you don't have to modify each user individually. In the Server app sidebar, click Groups.

To create a group, click Add (+), enter information in the fields, and click Create.

Assigning Local Users to a Local Group

The most common approach for populating groups with users is to select a group and add one or more users to it. On your server, you will select a group, click Add (+), and then add users to the group. When you use the Server app to add a user to a group, you can't just enter the name; you have to choose a user from a list that appears when you start typing.

To browse, choose Show Accounts Browser from the Window menu in the Server app.

Select users and groups from the window that appears, and then drag them into the list of members.

Assigning Local Groups to a Local User

Just as you can assign a user to a group, you can edit a user to add groups to that user. The effect is the same: The user becomes a member of a group.

After you add a group to a user, you can verify your action by looking at that group's list of members.

Assigning Local Groups to a Local Group

You can make a group a member of another group. This way, when you want to allow a group of groups to access the same resource, you can configure the parent group instead of separately configuring each group. This is called nested groups.

Importing Accounts

You can create accounts individually, or you can import them from a properly formatted file. The file could be created on your own, created with a third-party tool, or created with command-line tools.

Anytime you import users from a file and that file does not specify a password for the users, you will need to set their passwords after you import the users.

Importing a List of Users with the Server App

The Server app can import a list of users and user account data. The first line must be a header line that defines what kind of data is contained in the file and how the text is formatted. The user data must follow the header line.

> **MORE INFO** ▶ If you don't already have a valid header line to copy, you can use an app such as Passenger from http://macinmind.com to generate a proper header line.

To import accounts, choose Manage > Import Accounts from File.

In the Import Users pane, navigate to select your input file. Be sure to provide administrator credentials; otherwise, you'll get an error message (by default, the Server app supplies administrator credentials).

If the import file does not contain plain text passwords, set the user passwords: Select the users you just imported, Control-click (or secondary-click), and choose Change Password from the shortcut menu.

Of course, you should always use secure passwords in a production environment.

The following figure shows an example of an import file with an appropriate header line that describes the content of the file.

Reference 7.3
Managing Access to Services

By default, if you have not configured your server to be an Open Directory server, it does not check for authorization before granting access to OS X Server services such as Mail, File Sharing, and Calendar. In this state, if a given service is running and someone can connect to it and successfully authenticate, OS X Server grants authorization to use the service.

> **NOTE** ▸ You can also use the Access pane of the Server app to specify access for users and groups. Refer to "Access Pane" on page 100 for more information.

However, you can choose to manage service access control manually. Once managed, after someone attempts to connect to a given service and successfully authenticates with a user account, OS X Server checks to see if that user is authorized to use the service before granting access to it. As you'll learn in Lesson 9 "Managing Local Network Accounts", managing access control is set up automatically after you configure your server as an Open Directory server.

Manually Managing Service Access

When you Control-click (or secondary-click) a user and choose Edit Access to Services from the shortcut menu, you see a list of services and a few buttons. Each service's check-box is selected because at this point you are not managing access to the service yet; every authenticated user can access the service if the service is running.

When you click a services box and after you click OK, you are asked whether you want to manually manage service access. Even after you click Manage, every user you create with the Server app is automatically granted authorization to each of your OS X Server services by default (of course, no user can access a given service if the service isn't running).

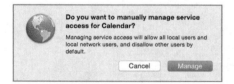

When you Control-click (secondary-click) a user and choose Edit Access to Services from the shortcut menu, you see a list of services, and each service has a checkbox you can select or deselect. When you deselect a checkbox, you remove authorization for that user to access the service.

OS X Server grants authorization to a service for a user if the user, or any group that the user is a member of, has the access checkbox selected for that service. Therefore, when you try to edit a user's access to services and the checkbox for a service is dimmed, you won't be able to deselect it.

MORE INFO ▶ If you create an account with Users & Groups preferences, the account does not automatically have access to any services.

Using Groups to Manage Access to Files and Services

You may find that long-term administration will be easier if you manage access to services based on organizational roles assigned to groups rather than to individual people. This will make it much easier when changes occur within your organization because you'll need to change only group membership rather than individual file and service permissions for each person.

When you turn on File Sharing with the Server app, it automatically turns on the AFP and SMB file-sharing protocols. (You will learn more about these services in Lesson 12 "Configuring the File Sharing Service".)

> **MORE INFO** ▶ Some system groups are normally hidden from view, with names like com.apple.access_afp and com.apple.access_backup. These contain the names of users and groups that have authorization to use a given service. You can view these groups by choosing View > Show System Accounts. You may see this referred to as service access control lists (SACLs) in other places. In most circumstances, it is best not to directly modify these system group files; instead, use the Server app to configure user or group access to services.

Reference 7.4
Troubleshooting

Keep the concepts of authentication and authorization separate in your head; just because you can authenticate doesn't mean you're authorized for a given action.

Troubleshooting Importing Users

When you use the Server app to import users or groups, a log file is automatically created in a folder named ImportExport in your home folder's Logs folder (~/Library/Logs/ImportExport). You can use the Console app to view these logs.

Note that this log file shows an example of successfully importing six user records. Some problems associated with importing accounts, if they occur, will appear in these log files.

NOTE ▶ The ImportExport logs are stored on the Mac on which you run the Server app to perform the import.

Troubleshooting Accessing Services

It can be somewhat confusing if a user is trying to connect to a service for which she doesn't have authorization. Despite that she has entered her password correctly, she may believe that she hasn't because she sees the authentication window shake or sees an error message. It may be useful to have users try to authenticate to a service they do have access to so you can confirm that their passwords aren't the problem.

Other potential failures can include a stacking of access rights based on individual access and group access. If the user is in one or more groups, you need to check the access rights across all of the user's groups.

Exercise 7.1
Create and Configure Local User Accounts

▶ **Prerequisites**

- ▶ All exercises in Lesson 1 "Installing OS X Server"
- ▶ "Exercise 2.1 Create DNS Zones and Records" on page 71

For users to access many services on your server, they need to have accounts that the server knows about. This lesson focuses on local user accounts, as opposed to local network users (Open Directory users) or users from another directory node.

In this exercise, you will use the Server app, the primary tool for creating and managing user accounts for OS X Server, to create users. You will create a new local user with administrator rights to your server and then use this account to create a new local user. You'll use the Keynotes and Comments fields, create a template from an existing user, and create a new user based on that template.

NOTE ▶ If you did not turn on Open Directory as part of the Lesson 4 exercises, ignore references to the Type pop-up menu in this lesson's exercises.

Create a New User

It is quick and easy to create a new user account. After creating the user, you will edit this user's basic attributes again.

1   Perform these exercises on your administrator computer. If you do not already have a connection to your server computer with the Server app on your administrator computer, then connect to it with the following steps: Open the Server app on your administrator computer, choose Manage > Connect to Server, select your server, click Continue, provide administrator credentials (Administrator Name: ladmin, Administrator Password: ladminpw), deselect the "Remember this password" checkbox, and then click Connect.

2   In the Server app sidebar, select Users.

3   Click the pop-up menu, and choose Local Users.

NOTE ▶ If you did not perform the exercises in "Exercise 4.2 Configure an Open Directory Certificate Authority" on page 152, then your server will not be configured as an Open Directory master, the Users pane will not display a pop-up menu, any editing you do in the Users pane will affect local users, and any editing you do in the Groups pane will affect local groups.

4   In the lower left of the Users pane, click the Add (+) button to add a new user.

5   If you have your directory administrator credentials stored in your keychain, then the Type pop-up menu appears; if this happens, confirm that the Type pop-up menu is set to Local Users.

6   Use the following settings:

   ▶   Full Name: Localuser 1

   ▶   Account Name: localuser1

   ▶   Email Address: Leave blank.

   ▶   Password: local

▶ Verify: local

7 For now, leave the "Allow user to administer this server" checkbox unselected.

8 Leave the Home Folder pop-up menu set to Local Only.

9 Leave the "Limit disk usage to" checkbox unselected.

10 In the Keywords field, enter demo, and then press Return so it becomes a distinct keyword.

11 In the Keywords field, enter class, and then press Return.

12 In the Notes field, enter Employee #408081.

13 Review the settings for this new user.

Full Name:	Localuser 1
Account Name:	localuser1
Email Addresses:	
Password:	•••••
Verify:	•••••
	☐ Allow user to administer this server
Home Folder:	🗂 Local Only
	☐ Limit disk usage to MB ◌
Keywords:	demo class
Notes:	Employee #408081

14 Click Create to create the user.

Edit a User

Use the Server app to edit the basic attributes for this user: Change the picture for the user, and allow the user to administer the computer. Selecting the checkbox to allow the user to administer the computer automatically adds the user to the system group whose full name is Administrators and whose account name is admin.

1 In the list of users, double-click Localuser 1 to edit this user's basic attributes.

NOTE ▶ Additional methods of editing the user's basic attributes include clicking the Action (gear icon) pop-up menu and choosing Edit User, Control-clicking the user and choosing Edit User from the shortcut menu, and pressing Command–Down Arrow.

2   Click the silhouette for the user, and select a picture from the available pictures.

3   Select the checkbox "Allow user to administer this server."

4   Note that you can edit the list of groups that this user is a member of. Leave this field blank for now.

5   Click OK to save the changes you just made.

Use the Server app to inspect and edit additional attributes for this user. Add an alias (you can use an alias instead of your full name or account name for some kinds of authentication, and the Mail service accepts messages addressed using aliases).

6   In the list of users, Control-click Localuser 1, and choose Advanced Options from the shortcut menu.

NOTE ▶ If the Users pane displays a pop-up menu and it is set to All Users, then the Advanced Options command is not available; in this case, click the pop-up menu, and choose Local Users.

7   In the Aliases field, enter localuserone.

WARNING! ▶ Even though you have the ability to change various options here, your user may have difficulty logging in or accessing files if you change the value for some attributes. Update only the Aliases field in this exercise.

8   Click OK to close the advanced settings pane.

Use a Different Account with the Server App

Next, use the Localuser 1 account to connect to your server and create another local user.

1   Quit and reopen the Server app.

2   At the Choose a Mac pane, select your server, and click Continue.

NOTE ▶ If your local administrator credentials for the Server app are stored in your keychain, then the Server app automatically connects and does not offer an authentication dialog. In this case, choose Manage > Connect to Server, and close the Server app window that was automatically opened and connected to your server; then at the Choose a Mac window, select your server, and click Continue.

3   For Administrator Name, enter localuser1; for Administrator Password, enter local.

4   Leave the checkbox "Remember this password in my keychain" unselected.

> **NOTE ▶** Be sure to leave the checkbox "Remember this password in my keychain" unselected; otherwise, the Server app automatically enters these temporary credentials the next time you connect to the server, until you remove the keychain entry.

```
Host Name or IP Address:   server17.pretendco.com
     Administrator Name:   localuser1
 Administrator Password:   •••••
                           ☐ Remember this password in my keychain
  ?                                      Cancel      Connect
```

5   Click Connect.

6   In the Server app sidebar, select Users.

7   If the Users pane displays a pop-up menu, click it, and choose Local Users.

8   At the lower left of the Users pane, click the Add (+) button to add a new user.

9   Click the silhouette for this new user, and choose Edit Picture.

10   If your administrator computer has a camera, you can click the Camera tab, take a photo of yourself to use for this user, and click Done to use that photo for this user.

  If you do not want to use your photo or if your administrator computer does not have a camera, click Cancel, and then click the silhouette for the user and select an existing picture.

11   Use the following settings for this new user:

  ▶   Full Name: Localuser 2

  ▶   Account Name: localuser2

  ▶   Email Address: Leave blank.

  ▶   Password: local

  ▶   Verify: local

12   Leave the checkbox "Allow user to administer this server" unselected.

13 Select the checkbox "Limit disk usage to," and enter 750 in the text field. Leave the unit pop-up menu at MB.

14 In the Keywords field, type demo, and then press Return.

15 In the Keywords field, type class, and then press Return.

16 In the Notes field, enter Another local user.

17 Click Create to create the user account.

You've proven that you can do something powerful—create a new user account—by using an account that you configured as an administrator of this server (Localuser 1).

Create a User Template

In the previous exercise, you entered the keywords "demo" and "class," along with a note. Wouldn't it be nice to be able to create new users with a common set of settings such as keywords and notes? You can with the template feature.

Perform the next steps using your original administrator account to illustrate that it doesn't matter which administrator creates a template; a template is available to any administrator.

1 Quit and reopen the Server app.

2 At the Choose a Mac pane, select your server, and click Continue.

3 For Administrator Name, enter ladmin; for Administrator Password, enter ladminpw.

4 Leave the checkbox "Remember this password in my keychain" unselected.

5 Click Connect.

Now that you're connected as a different administrator than the one who created the user account, create a new template from that newly created user account.

1 In the Server app sidebar, select Users.

2 If the Users pane displays a pop-up menu, click it, and choose Local Users.

3 In the list of users, Control-click the new user you just created, and choose Create Template from User.

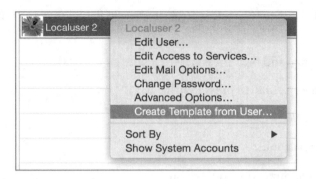

4   In the Template Name field, replace the contents with Lesson 7 user template.

5   Confirm that the disk usage quota, Keywords field, and Notes field values are part of the template.

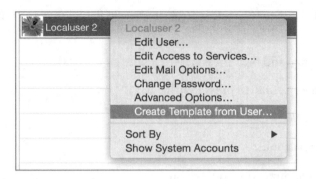

6   Click Done to create the template.

Use a User Template

Now that you have a template, you can use it when creating new accounts.

1   In the Users pane, click Add (+) to create a new user.

2   Click the Template pop-up menu, and choose the template you just created and edited.

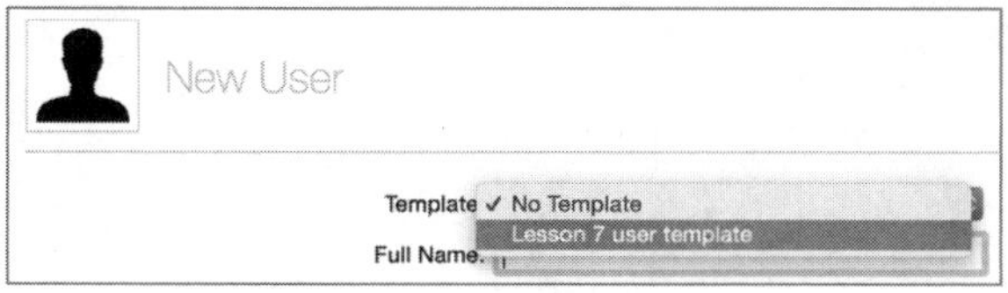

Use the following settings for this new user:

▶ Full Name: Localuser 3

▶ Account Name: localuser3

▶ Email Address: Leave blank.

▶ Password: local

▶ Verify: local

3 Leave the following fields populated from the template:

▶ Home Folder: Local Only

▶ Limit disk usage to: 750 MB

▶ Keywords: demo and class

▶ Notes: Another local user.

4   Click Create to create the user account.

Try to Use the Server App as a Nonadministrator User

You were able to create a new local user after you connected as Localuser 1 to your server with the Server app because earlier you selected the checkbox to allow Localuser 1 to administer the server. Try to use Localuser 2's credentials to connect to your server with the Server app; you won't be able to, which will confirm that only users in the Administrators group have the ability to administer the server.

1   Quit and reopen the Server app.

2   At the Choose a Mac pane, select your server, and click Continue.

> **NOTE ▶** If your local administrator credentials for the Server app are stored in your keychain, then the Server app automatically connects and does not offer an authentication dialog. In this case, choose Manage > Connect to Server, and close the Server app window that was automatically opened and connected to your server; then at the Choose a Mac window, select your server, and click Continue.

3   For Administrator Name, enter localuser2; for Administrator Password, enter local.

4   Leave the checkbox "Remember this password in my keychain" unselected.

> **NOTE ▸** Be sure to leave the checkbox "Remember this password in my keychain" unselected; otherwise, the Server app automatically enters these temporary credentials the next time you connect to the server, until you remove the keychain entry.

5   Click Connect.

The connection window shakes, indicating an authentication or authorization issue.

In this case, the user does not have authorization to connect to the server using the Server app.

6   Click Cancel.

In this exercise, you used the Server app to create and configure local user accounts, including a local administrator account. You created and used a user template. You demonstrated that you cannot use the Server app with an account that is not an administrator account.

Exercise 7.2
Import Local User Accounts

In this scenario, you have a tab-separated text file that was generated from the employee information database. It includes some information about each employee, including a first name, a last name, a full name, a shortened name to use for the account name, keywords, a note, and a password for the user. This file also has a properly formatted header line.

You also have a character-delimited text file with user account information exported from another server. Because OS X Server cannot export user passwords, this file does not contain passwords, so you will reset user passwords after you import them.

MORE INFO ▶ Although outside the scope of this guide, you can use the `dsexport` command-line tool to create a similar file. For more information about creating a character-delimited text file with accounts information, you can use `man dsexport` in Terminal.

Import User Accounts from a Delimited Text File

1   On your administrator computer, at the Choose a Mac pane, select your server, click Continue, provide administrator credentials (Administrator Name: ladmin, Administrator Password: ladminpw), deselect the "Remember this password" checkbox, and then click Connect.

2   In the Server app sidebar, select Users.

3   Choose Manage > Import Accounts from File.

4   In the open file dialog, click Documents in the sidebar, open StudentMaterials, and then open Lesson7.

5   Select (but do not double-click) the employees-tabdelimited.txt file.

6   Press the Space bar to get a Quick Look preview for this file.

The header line (the first line) contains a 9, which indicates that each record contains nine attributes. In the right column of the Import window, you get a preview of the contents of the text file.

7   In this scenario, the text file contains the following nine attributes:

▶   Last name

▶   First name

▶   Full name

▶   Account name

▶ Password

▶ User Shell

▶ Primary Group ID

▶ Keywords

▶ Comment (the Server app displays this field as Notes)

8 Press the Space bar again to close the Quick Look preview.

9 Leave the Template for Users checkbox unselected.

10 If your directory administrator credentials are stored in your keychain and the Type field displays a pop-up menu, click it, and choose Local Accounts.

11 Enter your local administrator credentials.

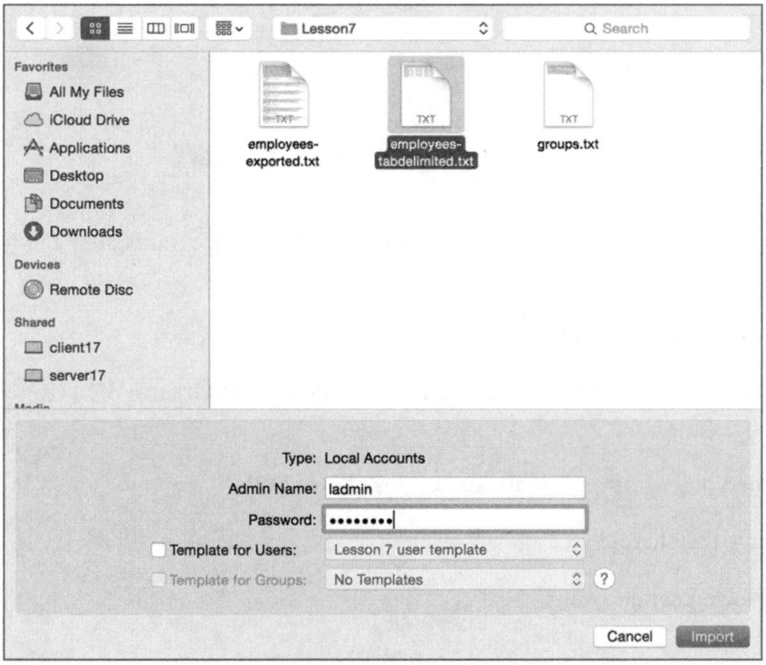

12 Click Import.

After the import has completed, the Server app displays the Users pane.

13 Inspect one of the users to confirm that it was correctly imported; double-click Alice Aymar.

14 Note that the Home Folder value is set to Custom. You will address this after the next step.

15 Click Cancel to return to the Users pane.

16 Select the users you just imported (Alice Aymar through Greta Green); then Control-click, and choose Edit Users.

17 Click the Home Folder pop-up menu, and choose Local Only.

18 Click OK to save the change.

You just imported local user accounts.

Import Users from an Exported Formatted File

You'll use the Server app to import users from a second text file, this one exported from another server (exporting users is outside the scope of this guide). This import file has more users with "Localuser" as the first name to reenforce the idea that you are still working in the server's local directory.

1 On your administrator computer, in the Server app, choose Manage > Import Accounts from File.

2 If the Lesson7 folder is not already displayed, click the Documents icon in the sidebar, and then open the /StudentMaterials/Lesson7/ folder.

3 Select the employees-exported.txt file, and press the Space bar to get a Quick Look preview of the file.

The header line is much longer than the previous header line. This header line states that each user record contains 40 attributes (as opposed to the previous file, in which each user record contains nine attributes).

4 Press the Space bar to dismiss the Quick Look preview of the file.

5 If you have your directory administrator credentials stored in your keychain, then the Type pop-up menu appears; if this happens, confirm that the Type pop-up menu is set to Local Users.

6 Enter your local administrator credentials.

7 Leave the Template for Users checkbox unselected.

8 Click Import to import the file.

When the Server app displays the list of users, you'll see that an additional five users have been imported (Localuser 4 through Localuser 8).

Update Passwords for the Imported Users

Because passwords are not included in this import file, you need to set a password for each of the new accounts. For now, you'll set each account to use the password "local."

1 If you have your directory administrator credentials stored in your keychain, then the Type pop-up menu appears; if this happens, confirm that the Type pop-up menu is set to Local Users.

2 Scroll to the bottom of the list of users.

3 Select all the newly imported accounts, Localuser 4 through Localuser 8, by selecting Localuser 4, holding down the Shift key, and then selecting Localuser 8.

4 Control-click while your pointer is still over one of the selected users to reveal the shortcut menu. Text at the top of the menu indicates how many users are part of your selection.

5 Choose Change Password.

6 In both the New Password and Verify fields, enter local.

7 Click Change Password.

8 Control-click while your pointer is still over one of the selected users to reveal the shortcut menu, and then choose Edit Users.

9 Click the Home Folder pop-up menu, choose Local Only, and click OK.

You've imported users from two types of files. The first was a simple text file, as if exported from some external list of employees, with attributes separated by the tab character. This file included passwords, so you did not need to reset these user passwords.

The second import file was exported from another server, so it did not include passwords, so you had to set passwords for these users.

Both files included a header line that specified which characters were used as attribute and value delimiters, as well as which fields in the text file corresponded with which attributes.

Neither import file defined user home folders, so you had to set that value after you imported the users.

You will review the logs related to importing these users in "Exercise 7.4 Troubleshoot Problems with Importing Accounts" on page 240.

Exercise 7.3
Create and Configure Local Groups

▶ **Prerequisite**

- ▶ "Exercise 7.2 Import Local User Accounts" on page 229

You can use the Server app to create and organize groups as well as users. You will create groups with the Server app and associate users and groups with each other.

1   On your administrator computer, if you are not already connected to your server, open the Server app, connect to your server, and authenticate as a local administrator.

2   In the Server app sidebar, select Groups.

Create a Group

1   In the Groups pane, click the Add (+) button.

2   Click the Type pop-up menu, and choose Local Group.

3   Enter the following information for the first new group:

- ▶   Full Name: Engineering
- ▶   Group Name: engineering

4   Click Create to create the group.

Import Groups

Rather than spend a lot of time creating more groups, import some groups with a group import file. You will use these groups for the rest of the exercise.

1 Choose Manage > Import Accounts from File.

2 If the Lesson7 folder is not already displayed, click the Documents icon in the sidebar, and then open the /StudentMaterials/Lesson7/ folder.

3 Select the groups.txt file.

4 Press the Space bar to get a Quick Look preview for this file.

Note in the file preview that this text file has a header line that defines the special characters, the account type (Groups), and the names of the attributes included.

5 Click the Type pop-up menu, and choose Local Accounts.

6 Enter your local administrator credentials.

7 Click Import.

The Server app displays the groups you just created and imported.

8 Double-click the Projects group.

The import file includes a list of users who are members of the Projects group, so you see them listed as members of the group.

9   Click OK to go back to the list of groups.

Add Users to Groups

You'll use the Server app to add users to groups. Even though you used an import file that had a number of groups populated with users, you may need to update group membership later.

In this scenario, a few people in your organization were added to a new Engineering department, so you should add their user accounts to the Engineering group. Add Alice Aymar and Ben Bond to the Engineering group.

1   Double-click the Engineering group.

2   Click the silhouette for the Engineering group, and select a picture for the group.

3   From the Window menu, choose Show Accounts Browser (or press Command-B).

4   Drag Alice Aymar and Ben Bond from the accounts window to the Members list.

5   Press Command-B to hide the accounts browser.

6   Click OK to save the changes to the list of groups.

Add Group Membership to a User Account

Although you could easily use the same process you used in the previous section to add users to the newly created groups, this time you'll try an alternate approach by adding groups to a user's account. In this scenario, Cindy Choi joined both the Marketing group and the Engineering group. Add these groups to that user's account.

1   In the Server app sidebar, select Users.

2   If necessary, click the Type pop-up menu, and choose Local Users.

3   Double-click Cindy Choi.

4   Press Command-B to show the accounts browser.

5   In the accounts browser, Command-click Marketing and Engineering, and then drag them to the Groups field.

6   Press Command-B to hide the accounts browser.

7   Click OK to save the change.

Add Groups to Groups

Nesting groups, or adding groups to groups, is critical to simplifying user and group management. In this scenario, each Pretendco employee is a member of one of three departments: Marketing, Engineering, or Management. There is a group named Employees, and you plan to use this group to allow all employees access to resources. Although you could populate the Employees group with all the individual Marketing, Engineering, and Management user accounts, the easiest approach is to add the three groups to the Employees group. When the structure of your organization changes over time—for example, if a new department is created—you would need to use the Server app to create a new group for this department and add its group to the Employees group.

When you are finished with this exercise, the Pretendco Employees group will consist of three groups: Marketing, Engineering, and Management.

1   Select Groups in the Server app sidebar.

2   Double-click the Employees group.

3   Press Command-B to display the accounts browser.

4   Command-click the Engineering, Management, and Marketing groups to select these groups.

    You can resize the accounts browser window to display a larger list of accounts.

5   Drag these three groups to the Members list of the Employees group.

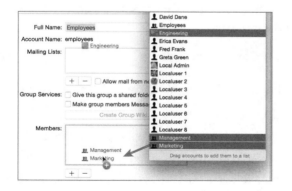

Note that even though you have three groups selected while holding the Command key, all three groups might not appear in the Members field of the accounts browser until you drop the accounts into the field.

6   Press Command-B to hide the accounts browser.

7   Click OK to save the changes to the group.

8   Double-click the Employees group to confirm that the new groups are listed in the Members field.

All members of the Marketing, Engineering, and Management groups now have access to the resources that members of the Employees group can access.

You just used the Server app to create and organize groups as well as users. You created groups with the Server app and associated users and groups with each other.

Exercise 7.4
Troubleshoot Problems with Importing Accounts

▶ **Prerequisite**

    ▶   "Exercise 7.2 Import Local User Accounts" on page 229

When you use the Server app to import users or groups, a log file is automatically created in a folder named ImportExport in the Library/Logs/ folder of your home folder on the computer you performed the import on. Since you imported users in an earlier exercise, you can use the Console app to inspect the import log.

On your administrator computer, open the Console app.

1   If the Console app is not already running, press Command–Space bar to use a Spotlight search to open Console.

2   If no sidebar is displayed for the Console window, click Show Log List in the toolbar.

    The Console app displays logs from several locations on your computer. The tilde character (~) is a symbol for your home folder, so ~/Library/Logs/ is a folder in your home folder and is for logs specifically related to your user account. The /var/log/ and /Library/Logs/ folders are for system logs. You will look for a log file in the ImportExport folder in your ~/Library/Logs/ folder.

3 Click the disclosure triangle for ~/Library/Logs/ to display the contents of that folder, and then click the disclosure triangle for ImportExport to display the contents of that folder.

4 Select a log file under ImportExport.

Note that this log file shows that you imported a number of records without error. Some problems associated with importing accounts, if they occur, will appear in these log files.

You just used the Console app to inspect the logs that were created when you imported accounts. Remember that the import log is stored on the computer that you used to perform the import, not necessarily on the server.

Exercise 7.5
Manage Service Access

▶ **Prerequisite**

▶ "Exercise 7.3 Create and Configure Local Groups" on page 235

You can limit access to services at the user and group levels.

You may not want all users with accounts on your server to access all the services your server offers. In this exercise, you'll limit access to the File Sharing service. You'll learn more about the File Sharing service in Lesson 12 "Configuring the File Sharing Service".

Use the Server app to allow only members of the Employees group to access the File Sharing service. In "Exercise 7.3 Create and Configure Local Groups" on page 235, you added Engineering, Marketing, and Managing groups to the members list of Employees.

Restrict Access to a Service

Start by restricting access to the File Sharing service.

1   On your administrator computer, if you are not already connected to your server, open the Server app, connect to your server, and authenticate as a local administrator.

2   In the Server app sidebar, select your server, and then select the Access tab.

3   Under the Custom Access field, click the Add (+) button, and then choose File Sharing.

4   Click the "Allow connections from" pop-up menu, and choose "only some users."

```
┌─────────────────────────────────────────────┐
│  ⬨   File Sharing                             │
│      Account Access, Network Access           │
├─────────────────────────────────────────────┤
│  Allow connections from:  [ only some users ▾]│
│  ┌─────────────────────────────────────────┐ │
│  │                                         │ │
│  │        Click (+) to add accounts        │ │
│  │                                         │ │
│  └─────────────────────────────────────────┘ │
│  [ + │ − ]                                    │
│  When connecting from:  [ all networks     ▾] │
│  (?)               [ Cancel ]  [   OK   ]     │
└─────────────────────────────────────────────┘
```

5   Press Command-B to display the accounts browser.

6   Drag Employees to the "Allow connections from" field.

    This restricts access to the File Sharing service for all users except those who are in the Employees group.

7 Press Command-B to hide the accounts browser.

8 Click OK to save the change.

9 Confirm that the File Sharing entry is active in the Custom Access list.

You just removed access to the File Sharing service for all accounts except those accounts that are members of the Employees group (which includes three other groups).

Inspect Membership in Groups for Various Users

1 In the Server app

2 Double-click Alice Aymar.

3 Confirm that Engineering appears in the Groups field; Alice Aymar is a member of the Engineering group (which is in turn a member of the Employees group).

4 Click Cancel to return to the list of users.

5 Double-click Localuser1.

6 Confirm that Contractors appears in the Groups field; this user is not a member of a group that is a member of the Employees group.

7 Click Cancel to return to the list of users.

Inspect Access to Services for Various Accounts

Confirm the following:

► The user Localuser 1 does not have explicit access to the service.
► The Employees group has explicit access to the service.
► The Engineering group has implicit access to the service.
► The Contractors group does not have explicit access to the service.

1 Control-click Localuser1, and choose Edit Access to Services.

2 Confirm that the checkbox File Sharing is unselected.

3   Click Cancel to close the services access sheet.

4   In the Server app sidebar, select Groups.

5   Click the Type pop-up menu, and choose Local Groups.

6   Control-click the Employees group, and choose Edit Access to Services (note that if the Type pop-up menu is set to All Groups, the shortcut menu displays fewer commands).

7   Confirm that the File Sharing checkbox is selected.

Select which services these groups can access:

- ☑ Calendar
- ☑ Contacts
- ☑ FTP
- ☑ File Sharing
- ☑ Mail
- ☑ Messages
- ☐ SSH

Cancel   OK

8   Click OK to return to the list of groups.

9   Control-click the Engineering group, and choose Edit Access to Services.

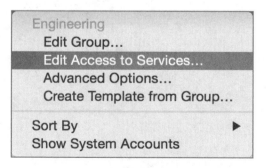

10 Confirm that the File Sharing checkbox is unavailable; you cannot modify this setting because the Engineering group has access to the service since it is a member of the Employees group.

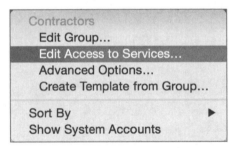

11 Click Cancel to close the services access sheet.

12 Control-click Contractors (which is not a member of the Employees group), and choose Edit Access to Services from the shortcut menu.

Contractors
Edit Group...
Edit Access to Services...
Advanced Options...
Create Template from Group...

Sort By   ▶
Show System Accounts

13 Confirm that the File Sharing checkbox is unselected.

Select which services these groups can access:

☑ 🗓 Calendar
☑ 📕 Contacts
☑ 🌐 FTP
☐ 📀 File Sharing
☑ 🖂 Mail
☑ 💬 Messages
☐ 🖥 SSH

Cancel   OK

14 Click Cancel to close the services access sheet.

Turn On File Sharing and Verify Authorization

Turn on File Sharing, and use it to verify authorization and lack of authorization to use the service. By default, there is a shared folder for each local user on your Mac before you configure OS X Server on that Mac; this explains why Local Admin's Public Folder is listed as a shared folder.

1 In the Server app sidebar, select File Sharing.

2 Click On to turn on the service.

3 Confirm that the Permissions field reflects permissions are limited to the Employees group.

From your administrator computer, attempt to connect to your server's File Sharing service.

1 On your administrator computer, in the Finder, press Command-N to open a new Finder window.

2 In the Shared section of the Finder window sidebar, select your server. If your server does not appear because there are too many other servers available, click All, and then double-click your server.

3 Click Connect As.

4 In the connection dialog, attempt to authenticate with the Localuser 1 account, which is not authorized to use the File Sharing service.

Select Registered User, in the Name field enter localuser1, in the Password field enter local, and leave the checkbox unselected.

> Enter your name and password for the server "server17".
>
> Connect as: ○ Guest
> ● Registered User
>
> Name: localuser1
>
> Password: •••••|
>
> ☐ Remember this password in my keychain
>
> Cancel   Connect

5   Click Connect.

The account you used does not have authorization to connect to the File Sharing service, even though it is an administrator account.

At the access dialog, click OK.

> **Access to your account on the server "server17" has been denied.**
> Contact your system administrator for more information.
>
> OK
>
> Name: localuser1
>
> Password: •••••
>
> ☐ Remember this password in my keychain
>
> Cancel   Connect

6   In the Name field enter aaymar, in the Password field enter bit-kw-543 (this password is defined in the first user import file), and leave the checkbox unselected.

Enter your name and password for the server "server17".

Connect as: ◯ Guest
             ⦿ Registered User

Name: aaymar

Password: ••••••••••

☐ Remember this password in my keychain

Cancel   Connect

7 Click Connect.

8 A list of available volumes appears.

9 Open the aaymar folder.

10 Confirm that you can see the usual folders of a user's home folder: Desktop, Documents, Downloads, Library, Movies, Music, Pictures, and Public.

11 In the Finder window sidebar, click the Eject button next to your server's icon to disconnect.

Shared
    🖳 server17   ⏏

You just verified that when you restrict authorization to use a service, only authorized user accounts can access the service. You demonstrated that Alice Aymar did not have explicit access to the File Sharing service, but because she is a member of a group (Engineering) that is a member of a group that has explicit access to the File Sharing service (Employees), she has access to the service.

Exercise 7.6
Clean Up

In the next lesson, you will configure your server to manage network accounts. Your server will then have multiple directories: the local directory and the network directory. You'll have network users and groups to work with in the next lesson.

To prevent confusion in later exercises, you will do the following:

▶ Delete the local user and local group accounts you were just working with

▶ Stop the File Sharing service

▶ Remove the access restriction for File Sharing

Make sure you connect to your server with the local administrator you had been using before you started the exercises in this lesson, rather than with the Localuser 1 account. Start by closing the active Server app window.

1 On your administrator computer, in the Server app, choose Manage > Close (or press Command-W) to close the Server app window.

Open the Server app again, and connect with credentials for the local administrator that you had been using before you started the exercises in this lesson. To be sure that you do not delete system accounts (accounts that are normally hidden and that are crucial to the normal operation of the system), confirm that the Server app is not displaying system accounts.

1 Open the Server app, select your server, and authenticate as the local administrator you had been using before you started the exercises in this lesson (for Administrator Name, enter ladmin; for Administrator Password, enter ladminpw).

2 Click the View menu, but do not choose any options. Confirm that the second menu choice is Show System Accounts.

🍎	**Server**	Manage	Edit	View	Tools	Window	Help
				Refresh		⌘R	
				Show System Accounts		⇧⌘-	

NOTE ▶ Do not choose Show System Accounts.

If the second menu choice is Hide System Accounts, choose Hide System Accounts, and then click the View menu again to confirm that Show System Accounts is the second menu choice.

Now that you are sure you will not accidentally delete system accounts, delete the other accounts you created in the exercises for this lesson.

1 In the Server app sidebar, select Users.

2 Confirm that the Type pop-up menu is set to Local Users.

3 For each user (except for the local administrator you had been using before you started the exercises in this lesson), select the user, click the Delete (–) button, and then at the dialog click Delete.

TIP ▶ If you accidentally click Delete after you select the user you are currently using to authenticate to the Server app, you will see a dialog informing you that the Server app will not allow you to delete this user. If you have multiple users selected, it will offer to delete the other selected users.

Delete the groups you created and imported.

1 In the Server app sidebar, select Groups.

2 Confirm that the Type pop-up menu is set to Local Groups.

3 Select one group, and then press Command-A (or choose Edit > Select All).

4 Click the Delete (–) button.

5 At the confirmation pane, click Delete to delete the groups.

Stop the File Sharing service.

1   In the Server app sidebar, select File Sharing.

2   Click Off to turn off the service.

Remove the access restriction for File Sharing.

1   In the Server app sidebar, select your server, and then click the Access tab.

2   In the Custom Access list, select File Sharing, click Remove (-), and then click Remove at the confirmation dialog.

You are ready to continue with the other exercises in this guide.

Lesson 8

Configuring Open Directory Services

This lesson describes how using a directory service can help you manage users and resources on your network. You will learn about the features of Apple Open Directory services and how to use these services. You will also learn how to set up and manage directories and user accounts with the Server app. Finally, you'll become familiar with common Open Directory service issues and learn how to resolve them.

Open Directory is extremely versatile when dealing with a variety of other directory services, such as Active Directory, eDirectory, and OpenLDAP, but mixed-platform directory service scenarios are outside the scope of this guide.

The management of computers via Open Directory is replaced by the use of profiles, but Open Directory is a requirement for running the Profile Manager service.

If you are performing the exercises independently and do not have an extra server computer, study and review, but do not perform, the tasks that involve the other directory server.

GOALS

▶ Describe the Open Directory service roles you can configure on OS X Server

▶ Configure OS X Server as an Open Directory server

▶ Bind OS X Server to another Open Directory server

▶ Locate and identify Open Directory–related log files

Reference 8.1
Introducing Directory Service Concepts

Giving a user multiple user accounts on different computers can cause problems. For instance, if each computer in a network has its own authentication database, a user might have to remember a different name and password for each computer. Even if you assign the user the same name and password on every computer, the information can become inconsistent over time because the user may change a password in one location but forget to do so in another. You can solve this problem by using a single source of identification and authentication information.

Directory services provide this central repository for information about the computers, applications, and users in an organization. With directory services, you can maintain consistent information about all the users—such as their names and passwords—as well as about printers and other network resources. You can maintain this information in a single location rather than on individual computers. The result is that you can use directory services to do the following:

▶ Provide a common user experience

▶ Provide easier access to networked resources such as printers and servers

▶ Allow users to log in on multiple computers using a single account

For example, once you "bind" OS X computers to an Open Directory service (to bind is to configure one computer to use the directory services offered by another), users can freely log in to any bound OS X computer. They will have their session managed based on who they are, what group they belong to, what computer they logged in at, and what computer group the computer belongs to. Using a shared directory service also permits a user's home folder to be located on another server and to be mounted automatically on whatever computer the user logs in to, as long as that computer is bound to the shared directory.

What Is Open Directory?

Open Directory is the extensible directory services architecture that is built into OS X. Open Directory acts as an intermediary between directories (which store information about users and resources) and the applications and system software processes that want to use the information.

In the context of OS X Server, the Open Directory service is a set of services that provide identification and authentication.

Many services on OS X require information from the Open Directory service to function. The Open Directory service can securely store and validate the passwords of users who want to log in to client computers on your network or use other network resources that require authentication. You can also use the Open Directory service to enforce global password policies, such as password expiration and minimum length.

You can use the Open Directory service to provide authentication to users on other platforms for file services, as well as other services that OS X Server provides.

Overview of Open Directory Service Components

Open Directory provides a centralized source for identification and authentication. For identification, Open Directory uses OpenLDAP, an open source implementation of the Lightweight Directory Access Protocol (LDAP), a standard protocol used for accessing directory service data. Open Directory uses LDAPv3 to provide read and write access to the directory data.

The Open Directory service leverages other open source technologies, such as Kerberos, and combines them with powerful server administration tools to deliver robust directory and authentication services that are easy to set up and manage. Because there are no per-seat or per-user license fees, Open Directory can scale to the needs of an organization without adding high costs to an IT budget.

After you bind an OS X computer to use an Open Directory server, that bound computer automatically gets access to network resources, including user authentication services, network home folders, and share points.

You can configure OS X Server in four basic Open Directory states:

▶ A standalone server

▶ An Open Directory master

▶ An Open Directory replica

▶ Connected to another directory service or multiple directory services (also referred to as a member server)

   NOTE ▶ You can configure your server to simultaneously connect to one or more other directory services at the same time as serving as an Open Directory master or replica.

As you plan directory services for your network, consider the need to share user, resource, and management information among multiple computers and devices. If the need is low, little directory planning is necessary; everything can be accessed from a server's local directory. However, if you want to share information among computers, you need to set up at least one Open Directory server (an Open Directory master). Furthermore, if you want to provide high availability of directory services, you should set up at least one additional server to be an Open Directory replica.

Describing the Standalone Server Role

The default state is for your server to host its local accounts. People must use accounts that are local users created on your server to access your server's services. User accounts in a standalone configuration will not be able to be used on another server to allow access to services.

Describing the Open Directory Master Role

When OS X Server is configured to host network accounts and provide directory services, this is referred to as an "Open Directory master" (or a "master," which is covered in the next section). The action you will select to perform in the Server app is "Create a new Open Directory domain." A "domain" is an organizational boundary for a directory; you are creating a shared directory domain, also referred to as a "node."

When you use the Server app to configure your server as an Open Directory master, it performs the following actions:

► Configures the OpenLDAP, Kerberos, and Password Server databases

► Adds the new directory service to the authentication search path

► Creates a local network group named Workgroup

► Adds the local group Local Accounts to the network group Workgroup

► Creates a new root Secure Sockets Layer (SSL) certification authority (CA) based on the organization name you provide at the time of configuration

► Creates a new intermediate SSL certification authority, signed by the same CA

► Creates a new SSL certificate with your server's host name, signed by the same intermediate CA (if you don't already have a signed SSL certificate with your server's host name)

► Adds the CA, intermediate CA, and SSL certificate to the System keychain of your server

► Creates a folder for the intermediate CA and the CA in /private/var/root/Library/Application Support/Certificate Authority/, each with files for Certificate Assistant and a copy of the certificate

► Grants local accounts and local network accounts authorization to access OS X Server services

OS X Server for Mountain Lion introduced a new set of terms: local accounts and local network accounts. "Local accounts" are those accounts that are stored in your server's local node. "Local network accounts" are those accounts that are stored in your server's shared Open Directory node (in its OpenLDAP database). The word "local" in the term "local network" differentiates these network accounts from other nodes' directories; local network accounts are from the local network–shared OpenLDAP node.

Once you have set up your server to be an Open Directory master, you can configure other computers on your network to access the server's directory services.

To recap, your server has local user and group accounts; after being configured as an Open Directory master, this local database still exists. Creating an Open Directory master creates a secondary, shared LDAP database. The administrator of that database has the default short name of diradmin. Each database is separate, and managing either one requires different credentials. You have also created a Password Server database to store user passwords, as well as a Kerberos Key Distribution Center (KDC). You will learn about those later in this lesson.

Describing the Open Directory Replica Role

Once you have a server configured as an Open Directory master, you can configure one or more Mac computers with OS X Server as a directory replica to provide the same directory information and authentication information as the master. The replica server hosts a copy of the master's LDAP directory, its Password Server authentication database, and its Kerberos KDC. Open Directory servers notify each other whenever there is a change in directory information, so all Open Directory servers have a current store of information.

You can use replicas to scale your directory infrastructure, improve search and retrieval time on distributed networks, and provide high availability of Open Directory services. Replication also protects against network outages because client systems can use any replica in your organization.

When authentication data is transferred from the master to any replica, that data is encrypted while it is copied over.

> **TIP** ▶ Because replication and Kerberos use timestamps, it's best to synchronize the clocks on all Open Directory masters, replicas, and member servers. You can use Date & Time preferences to specify the time server; you can use Apple time servers or an internal Network Time Protocol (NTP) server.

You can create nested replicas—that is, replicas of replicas. One master can have up to 32 replicas, and those replicas can have 32 replicas each; one master plus 32 replicas plus 32 × 32 replicas of those replicas totals 1,057 Open Directory servers for a single Open Directory domain. Nesting replicas is accomplished by joining one replica—referred to as a "tier-one replica"—to your Open Directory master and then joining other replicas to the tier-one replica. Any replica created from a tier-one replica is referred to as a "tier-two replica." You cannot have more than two layers of replicas.

The following figure has one Open Directory master and one replica that is also a relay, a replica that in turn has at least one replica.

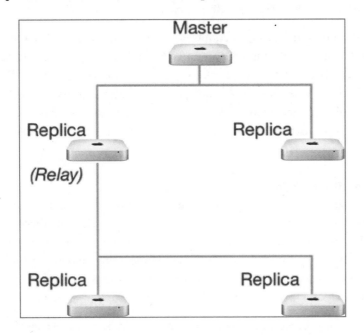

In the case of a disaster, you can promote an Open Directory replica to be the new master, but you must have either a Time Machine backup of your server that's configured as your Open Directory master to recover the automatically created Open Diretory archive or a manually created Open Directory archive. Search for "Archive and restore Open Directory data" in Server Help for more information.

Promote Open Directory replica to master

Enter the information for the directory administrator to promote this Open
Directory replica to master of the domain.

Directory Admin Name:

Password:

To restore your Certificate Authority keys, specify an archive:

Choose...

Cancel   Previous   Next

Describing Open Directory Locales

Open Directory locales make it easy for you to distribute the load among appropriate
Open Directory servers. An Open Directory locale is a grouping of one or more Open
Directory servers that service a specified subnet; you use the Server app to define a locale
and then associate one or more Open Directory servers and one or more subnets with that
locale. When a client computer (OS X v10.7 or later) is bound to any of your Open Directory servers, if that client computer is in a subnet associated with a locale, that client computer will prefer the Open Directory server or servers associated with that locale for
identification and authentication.

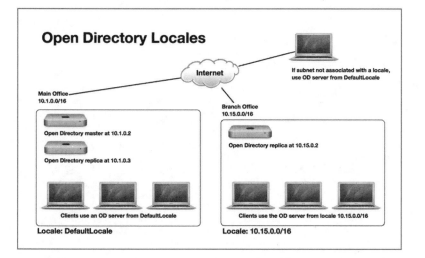

As soon as you configure your first Open Directory replica, OS X Server creates two additional locales:

▶ The locale named Default Locale is a fail-safe and includes the master and all of the replicas, even if they are not in the same subnet as your master; this is the locale that an OS X client uses if no locale is available for the client's subnet.

▶ The second locale is based on the subnet of the Open Directory master and includes the master and any replicas that are on the same subnet as the master; Open Directory clients on the same subnet use this locale.

▶ As you add more locales, they are displayed in the Locales pane.

To create a new Open Directory locale, click the Locales tab, click Add (+), and specify information for the new locale.

When configuring a new locale, you need to click Add (+) under the Servers field and select one or more of the Open Directory servers listed.

See https://help.apple.com/advancedserveradmin/mac/4.0 for more information on configuring Open Directory locales.

Describing the Role of Using Another Open Directory Server

If you intend to set up multiple servers, populating each server with the same user accounts would be extremely inefficient. Instead, you can bind your server to another directory system, in which case your server is referred to as a "bound server" or a "member server." In this role, each server gets authentication, user information, and other directory information from some other server's directory service. This way, users can authenticate to your server with an account defined in your server's local directory or with an account defined in any directory node that your server is bound to. The other directory node is commonly an Open Directory or an Active Directory system but could include other kinds of directories as well.

The Profile Manager service requires that your server be configured as an Open Directory master. That's fine because it is possible for your server to both be an Open Directory master and be bound to another directory service. This is particularly useful for providing services to groups within a larger organization. If you are the administrator for a group of users within a larger organization, you can use OS X Server to provide additional services to existing groups defined in your larger organization or to create additional groups of people for your smaller groups. You can achieve this without having to contact the people who administer resources for the larger organization, regardless of what directory service your larger organization uses.

Describing Access to Services

In the standalone state, your server by default does not check for authorization to access OS X Server services (except the SSH service); see "Reference 7.3 Managing Access to Services" on page 215 for more information.

If you configure your server as an Open Directory master, the Server app configures your server to start checking for authorization to access OS X Server services. When you create new local accounts and new local network accounts with the Server app, the Server app grants the new accounts authorization to access OS X Server services.

If you configure your server as an Open Directory master and then bind to another directory server, you may need to grant authorization to use your server services to accounts from the other directory node. You may find it convenient to grant authorization to access

OS X Server services to the other directory node's groups so you do not need to configure individual user accounts from the other directory node.

Reference 8.2
Configuring Open Directory Services

To provide the full range of Open Directory services, each server participating in the Open Directory domain, whether a master, replica, or member server, needs to have consistent access to forward and reverse Domain Name System (DNS) records for all the other servers in the domain. You should use Network Utility (or command-line tools) to confirm that DNS records are available.

You use the Server app to configure your server as an Open Directory master or replica, and you use Users & Groups preferences or Directory Utility to bind to another directory server.

Configuring OS X Server as an Open Directory Master

If your server is not already configured as an Open Directory master or connected to another directory service, you can turn on the Open Directory service, and the Server app walks you through configuring your server to be an Open Directory master or replica.

Start by selecting "Create a new Open Directory domain" and clicking Next.

You are prompted to create a new user, with the default name of Directory Administrator and the short name of diradmin.

You are also prompted to provide an organization name and an administrator email address. This organization name will identify this Open Directory server to Mobile Device Management (MDM) systems such as Profile Manager that use it.

Once you confirm these settings, the Server app configures your server as an Open Directory master.

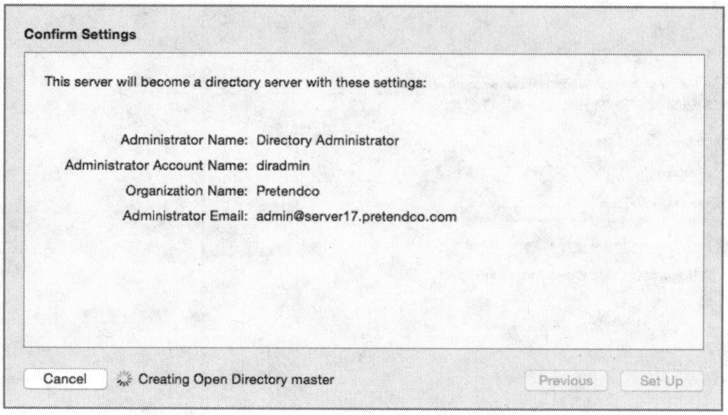

Confirm Settings

This server will become a directory server with these settings:

Administrator Name: Directory Administrator
Administrator Account Name: diradmin
Organization Name: Pretendco
Administrator Email: admin@server17.pretendco.com

Cancel   ⚙ Creating Open Directory master   Previous   Set Up

Afterward, the Open Directory pane displays your server, listed as the master. The Server app displays the Internet Protocol version 4 (IPv4) address of each active network interface for each server in the list of Open Directory servers.

Open Directory   ON

Settings   Locales

Access

Status: ● Available at server17.pretendco.com
Learn about configuring this service ⊙

Servers

🗄 server17.pretendco.com (master)
    10.0.0.171

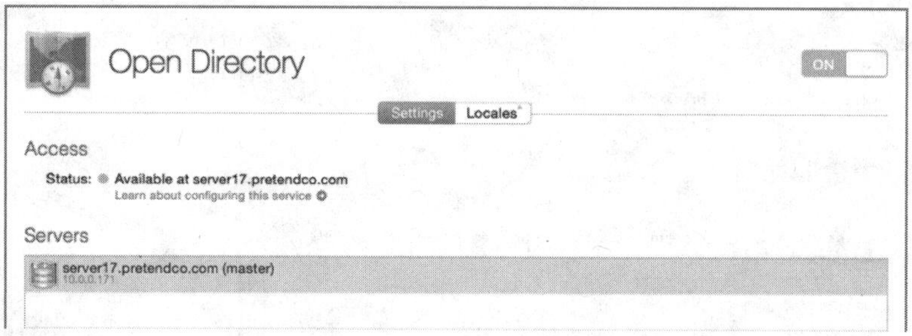

You can turn off the Open Directory service by using the switch without destroying the directory configuration. If you need to remove the Open Directory service, selecting the server in the Servers window and then clicking the Delete (–) button at the bottom of the window destroys the configurations permanently.

NOTE ▶ Even if a network interface has a self-assigned IPv4 address starting with 169.254, it will be displayed in the list of Open Directory servers. For example, if you find it convenient to use AirDrop on your server, it is possible to configure a Wi-Fi network interface to be active but not connected to any particular Wi-Fi network.

Creating an Open Directory Archive

When you back up your server with Time Machine, you automatically get a periodic archive of all identification and authorization components of your Open Directory server, including the following:

▶ The OpenLDAP directory database and configuration files, which include authentication information

▶ Kerberos configuration files

▶ Keychain data used by Open Directory

You can also create an Open Directory archive manually. Start by clicking the Action (gear icon) pop-up menu and choosing Archive Open Directory Master.

> **TIP** You need an Open Directory archive in order to promote an Open Directory replica to an Open Directory master.

The next step is to specify a location to create the archive file. Because the archive contains sensitive authentication information, be sure to protect the archive with a secure password.

Once the archive is created, you will find it as a password-protected sparseimage-style disk image.

Configuring OS X Server as an Open Directory Replica

If you already have an Open Directory master on another Mac with OS X Server, you use the Server app to configure your server as a replica of another Open Directory master.

You can configure a server to be a replica by using the Server app on an existing master or replica or by using the Server app on a server you want to configure as a replica. The replica server you're adding must have remote administration access enabled before you can add it as a replica.

If you're using the Server app on an existing master or replica, in the Open Directory pane, click the Servers tab, and click Add (+). Then do the following:

▶ Enter the host name (you could also enter an IP address or local hostname, but this guide recommends using the host name to verify that the crucial DNS host name records are available).

▶ Enter administrator credentials for the server you want to configure as the replica.

▶ Choose the parent server.

▶ Enter the directory administrator's credentials, and click Next.

If, instead, you're using the Server app on the server you want to configure as an Open Directory replica, select Open Directory in the Server app sidebar. Click the On/Off switch to On, select "Join an existing Open Directory domain as a replica," and click Next.

Configure Network Users and Groups

To continue, you'll need to configure your server as a network directory. This directory will store important information such as your user and group accounts.

- ○ Create a new Open Directory domain
- ● Join an existing Open Directory domain as a replica
- ○ Restore Open Directory domain from an archive

Cancel   Previous   Next

In the Parent Server field, enter another Open Directory server's host name (enter the master's host name to configure this server as a replica or enter a replica's host name to configure this server as a replica of the replica), enter directory administrator credentials, and click Next.

Join an existing Open Directory domain as a replica

Replicas provide failover and load balancing for Open Directory clients. Enter the information for the parent server in the Open Directory domain for which this server should become a replica.

Parent Server:
Directory Admin Name:
Password:

Cancel   Previous   Next

Afterward, the Server app displays your server as a replica of the master. In the Open Directory pane's Servers field, you may need to click the disclosure triangle to view the master and its replica (or replicas). In the following figure, server17 is the master, and server18 is the replica.

If you configure a replica of a replica, or a tier-two replica, the Servers field looks like the following figure, where server19 is a replica of server18, which is a replica of server17.

Configuring OS X Server to Use Another Open Directory Server

If you want your server to simply take advantage of a centralized directory service and not offer directory services itself, you can bind your server to another directory service so users can use credentials hosted by the centralized directory service to access services on your server. This lesson focuses on binding to another Open Directory system.

> **MORE INFO** ▶ Just as you can bind your server to another Open Directory service, you can bind your server to an Active Directory domain. This is outside the scope of this guide. See the section for this lesson in the "Additional Resources" appendix, which is provided when you download the lesson files.

Use the Users & Groups pane in System Preferences to bind your server to another directory. Open System Preferences, select Users & Groups, select Login Options, and click Join; if the server is already an Open Directory server, click Edit instead of Join.

Enter the host name of an Open Directory server, or click the pop-up menu to browse for one.

When you see the message "This server provides SSL certificates," click Trust. This adds the Open Directory's CA, intermediate CA, and SSL certificate to the System keychain so your Mac trusts services that use SSL certificates signed by the intermediate CA.

By default, OS X does not always use SSL when it makes an LDAP connection to an Open Directory server; for many organizations, this is not a concern because the information stored in the LDAP directory is not considered sensitive. Configuring OS X to use SSL for LDAP is outside the scope of this guide.

When you see the Client Computer ID window, leave the Client Computer ID field, which is generated from your host name, as it is.

You have the option to bind anonymously or set up authenticated binding.

Anonymous binding is appropriate when binding with OS X clients, but you should use authenticated binding, which mutually authenticates the member OS X Server and the Open Directory service, when binding a server to an Open Directory server. An authenticated bind creates a computer record in the Open Directory service; this computer record is used to mutually authenticate the bind between the two servers.

> **NOTE** ▶ Provide directory administrator credentials for the authenticated bind.

As an alternative, you can use Directory Utility or the command-line environment because they offer some advanced binding options, especially if you're binding to an Active Directory node.

Using Directory Utility Remotely

You can still use Directory Utility instead of System Preferences; in fact, using Users & Groups preferences offers a shortcut to Directory Utility, which is located in /System/Library/CoreServices/Applications/. Directory Utility offers more control than the Join button of Users & Groups preferences when binding to a directory service, and it allows you to make changes to a remote computer's directory services from OS X.

Binding OS X to Your Open Directory Service

Once you have an Open Directory master (and perhaps one or more replicas) set up, you can also configure the client computers to bind to the directory service so your client computers can take advantage of Open Directory services. On each client computer, you use Users & Groups preferences to specify a server that hosts an Open Directory service, or if you need more-advanced binding options, you use Directory Utility to create an LDAP configuration that has the address and search path for an Open Directory server.

Reference 8.3
Troubleshooting

Open Directory includes several services, so several log files are used for tracking status and errors. You can use the Server app to view status information and logs for Open Directory services. For example, you can use the password-service logs to monitor failed login attempts for suspicious activity, or you can use the Open Directory logs to see all failed authentication attempts, including the IP addresses that generated them. Review the logs periodically to determine whether there are numerous failed tries for the same password ID, which would indicate that somebody might be generating login guesses. It is imperative that you understand where to look first when troubleshooting Open Directory issues.

Accessing Open Directory Log Files

Generally, the first place to look when Open Directory issues arise is the log files. Recall that Open Directory comprises three main components: the LDAP database, the Password Server database, and the Kerberos Key Distribution Center. The Server app allows for easy viewing of many server-related Open Directory log files. The main log files are as follows:

► Configuration log—Contains information about setting up and configuring Open Directory services (/Library/Logs/slapconfig.log)

► LDAP log—Contains information about providing LDAP services (/private/var/log/slapd.log)

► Open Directory log—Contains information about core Open Directory functionality (/private/var/log/opendirectoryd.log)

▶ Password Service Server log—Contains information about successes and failures authenticating with local network user credentials (/Library/Logs/PasswordService/ApplePasswordServer.Service.log)

▶ Password Service Error log—If it exists, contains information about errors in the Password service (/Library/Logs/PasswordService/ApplePasswordServer.Error.log)

To view these log files, select Logs in the toolbar, click the pop-up menu, scroll to the Open Directory section of the pop-up menu, and choose one of the logs.

You can use the search field in the lower-right corner of the window. Keep in mind that you can resize the Server app window to view more log information in a single line, which can help you quickly read or skim the log files.

Interpreting log files can be a difficult task, and you may need the help of a more experienced system administrator. You can email the appropriate log file to that person.

Troubleshooting Directory Services

If a bound OS X computer experiences a startup delay or the login window displays a red status indicator with the text "network accounts unavailable," the bound computer could be trying to access a directory node that is not available on your network.

There are several ways to begin troubleshooting when you are unable to connect to a directory service:

▶ Using Network Utility to confirm DNS records

▶ Using Login Options in Users & Groups preferences to confirm that the network server is available

▶ Using Directory Utility to make sure the LDAP and other configurations are correct

▶ Using Network preferences to make sure the computer's network location and other network settings are correct

▶ Inspecting the physical network connection for faults

▶ Using the Console app while logged in with a local user account to monitor the Directory Services login /private/var/log/opendirectoryd.log

MORE INFO ▶ You can increase the level of logging detail for the Open Directory log; see the Apple Support article HT202242, "OS X Server: Changing opendirectoryd logging levels."

TIP ▶ If you update DNS records but still don't see the results you expect, you can reset (flush) the DNS cache using the command-line method in Terminal app by entering the following: **sudo discoveryutil udnsflushcaches**.

Exercise 8.1
Inspect Your Open Directory Master

▶ **Prerequisite**

▶ "Exercise 4.2 Configure an Open Directory Certificate Authority" on page 152

In Lesson 4 you turned on the Open Directory service so you could inspect and use the certificate authority and SSL certificates that were automatically created, but you didn't learn about Open Directory itself. When you turned on the Open Directory service, three new network services started running: an LDAP service, which provides access to shared directory data, and two authentication services, Password Server and Kerberos.

As mentioned in "Describing the Open Directory Master Role" on page 256, users and groups in the shared Open Directory node are called local network users and local network groups.

Inspect the Group Workgroup

The Server app automatically created a group named Workgroup. When you create a new local network user with the Server app, the Server app automatically places the new local network user in the Workgroup group.

1 Perform these exercises on your administrator computer. If you do not already have a connection to your server computer with the Server app on your administrator com-

puter, then connect to it with the following steps: Open the Server app on your administrator computer, choose Manage > Connect to Server, select your server, click Continue, provide administrator credentials (Administrator Name: ladmin, Administrator Password: ladminpw), deselect the "Remember this password" checkbox, and then click Connect.

2   In the Server app sidebar, select Groups.

3   Click the pop-up menu, and choose Local Network Groups.

4   Double-click the group Workgroup.

5   From the View menu, choose Show System Accounts.

For now, the only entity listed as a member of the group named Workgroup is the group account named Local Accounts. This is a special system group account that doesn't actually have any members listed, but the operating system treats all local accounts as a member of this group, so all local accounts on the server computer are therefore treated as members of the group Workgroup.

Full Name:	Workgroup
Account Name:	workgroup
Mailing Lists:	
	+ − ☐ Allow mail from non-group members
Group Services:	☐ Give this group a shared folder ⊙
	☑ Make group members Messages buddies
	Create Group Wiki...
Members:	👥 Local Accounts
	+ −
Keywords:	
Notes:	

6   From the View menu, choose Hide System Accounts.

7   Click Cancel to return to the list of groups.

In this exercise, you inspected the new network group named Workgroup.

Exercise 8.2
Use Logs to Troubleshoot Using Open Directory

▶ **Prerequisite**

    ▶ "Exercise 4.2 Configure an Open Directory Certificate Authority" on page 152

The logs on your server relating to being an Open Directory master are located in various folders, but you can access them all quickly with the Server app.

1   On your administrator computer, if you are not already connected to your server, open the Server app, connect to your server, and authenticate as a local administrator.

2   In the Server app sidebar, select Logs.

3   In the Logs pop-up menu, scroll to the Open Directory section, and note the five logs related to Open Directory.

4   Choose Configuration Log.

5   In the search field, enter Intermediate as an example.

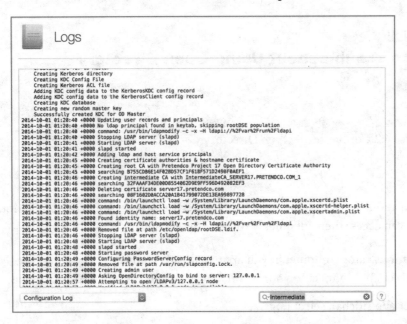

Note that the first instance of this word is highlighted. Each time you press Return, the next instance of the search term flashes.

6   Click the pop-up menu that currently displays Configuration Log, and choose LDAP Log as another example.

7   Scroll through the LDAP log, and then inspect the other logs.

In this exercise, you used the Server app to view logs related to configuring your server as an Open Directory master. Even though the logs are stored on the server, you can use the Server app to view them.

Lesson 9

Managing Local Network Accounts

Once you have created shared Lightweight Directory Access Protocol (LDAP) directories, you need to populate them with information. User account information is probably the most important type of information you can store in a directory. User accounts stored in your server's shared directory are accessible to all the computers that search that directory; those accounts are now referred to as "local network user accounts," though you may also see the terms "Open Directory user accounts," "network user accounts," or just "network users."

Reference 9.1
Using the Server App to Manage Network User Accounts

Use the Server app for basic and advanced management of users and services. The Server app automatically adds authorization for OS X Server services to local network users you create and adds these users to the built-in group called Workgroup.

The Server app gives you the basic options for account management, including the account details, email address, services that a user is authorized to use, groups to which a user belongs, and global password policy.

GOALS

► Configure local network accounts

► Import local network accounts

► Describe authentication types

► Understand basic Kerberos infrastructure

► Configure global password policy

To create a new user, select Users in the Server app sidebar, and then click the pop-up menu to choose the directory domain Local Network Users.

Click Add (+) to create a new user, and then configure the user. As with creating local user accounts, you can click the Password Assistant (key icon) button for help choosing a more secure password.

After you click Create, the Server app returns you to the list of users. When you double-click the user you just created to edit it, you'll see that when you create a user with the Server app, the user is automatically added to the local network group named Workgroup. You can modify the user's icon, among other attributes.

If you select "administer this server" for "Allow user to," the user gets added to the Open Directory Administrators group in LDAP and the Administrators group in the local directory. This means the user can add and remove users from both Local Users and Local Network Users, plus manage the server's configurations and settings.

When you secondary-click (Control-click) the user and choose Edit Access to Services from the shortcut menu, you'll see that the user has authorization to access each of the listed services.

MORE INFO ▸ When you create network user accounts outside the Server app, such as via command-line tools, those users are not automatically added to the group named Workgroup, nor are they given authorization to access any service. Therefore, be careful when you use both the Server app and other methods to create network user accounts.

Using the Server App to Allow Access to Services for Accounts from Another Directory Node

If you configure your server to be an Open Directory server, after you bind to another directory service, users from the other directory service are not automatically authorized to use services on your server unless you explicitly give users or groups from the other directory node access to these services.

Simply select one or more external accounts (users or groups), secondary-click, choose Edit Access to Services from the shortcut menu, and then select the checkboxes for the services you want those accounts to be allowed to access. Of course, adding users to a group and then authorizing services for that group is less tedious than editing access to services for each user.

Importing Local Network Accounts

Just like importing local accounts, you can import local network accounts. The import file must be a properly formatted file containing a header that defines the contents of the file.

MORE INFO ▸ For more information on creating a properly formatted file for importing accounts, see the section "Create a file to import users or groups" in Server Help.

Choose Manage > Import Accounts from File, select an import file, make sure the Type pop-up menu is set to Local Network Accounts, provide directory administrator credentials (as opposed to local administrator credentials), and click Import.

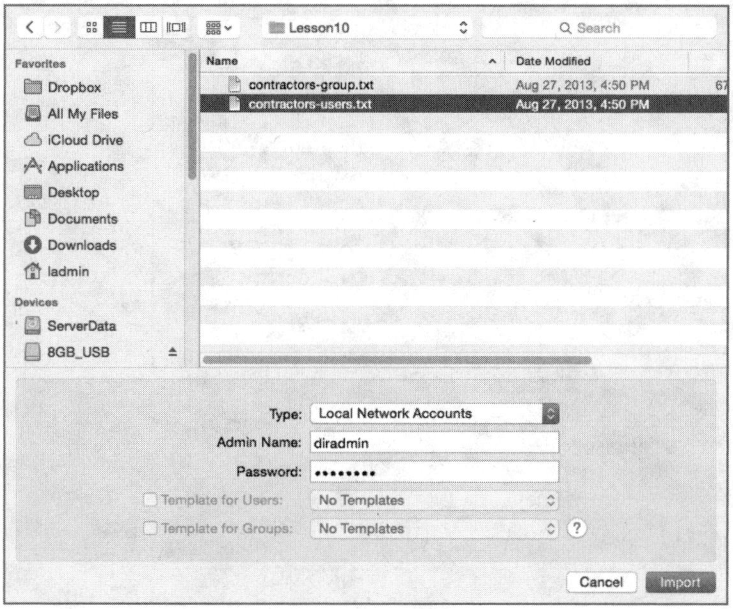

If your import file doesn't contain passwords, after you click Import and after the Server app has completed importing the accounts, select your newly imported users, secondary-click, and choose Reset Password.

You can also import local network groups. Note that the only thing that determines whether you are importing users or groups is the header of the import file. In the following figure, dsRecTypeStandard:Groups specifies that the file contains group accounts whereas dsRecTypeStandard:Users would specify that the file contains user accounts.. Remember to use the pop-up menu to specify into which directory node the Server app imports the accounts and to provide appropriate credentials.

Reference 9.2
Configuring Authentication Methods on OS X Server

For authenticating users whose accounts are stored in shared directories on OS X Server, Open Directory offers a variety of options, including Kerberos and the many authentication methods that various network services require. Open Directory can authenticate users by using the following:

► Single sign-on with the Kerberos Key Distribution Center (KDC) built in to OS X Server

► A hashed representation of a password that is stored securely as part of the Open Directory LDAP database, in a way that only the root user (or a process running with root privileges) can access

► An older crypt password for a user record stored in a third-party LDAP directory, for backward compatibility with legacy systems

► A shadow password for local (not network) accounts, in which a password is stored in the user record in a way that only the root user (or process running with root privileges) can access

MORE INFO ▶ See the man pages for pwpolicy and mkpassdb for more information on hashes and authentication methods.

In addition, Open Directory lets you configure the "global password policy" that affects all users (including administrators in Yosemite) in the LDAP domain, such as automatic password expiration and minimum password length.

Disabling a User Account

To prevent a user from logging in or accessing services on your server, you can temporarily disable that user by using the Server app to remove access to his account. Simply edit the user, and for "Allow user to," deselect the "log in" checkbox.

Doing so does not delete the user, nor does it change his user ID or any other information. It also doesn't delete any of the user's files. It simply prevents that user from authenticating and gaining access to the server via any method.

When a user account is disabled, you'll see the word "Disabled" next to the user in the list of users.

Setting Global Password Policies

Open Directory enforces global password policies. For example, a user's password policy can specify a password expiration interval. If the user is logging in and Open Directory discovers that the user's password has expired, the user must replace the expired password. Open Directory can then authenticate the user.

Password policies can disable a user account on a certain date, after a number of days, after a period of inactivity, or after a number of failed login attempts. Password policies can also require passwords to be a minimum length, contain at least one letter, contain at least one numeral, be mixed case, contain a character that is neither a number nor a letter, differ from the account name, differ from recent passwords, or be changed periodically.

Open Directory applies the same password policy rules to Password Server and Kerberos.

Kerberos and the Open Directory Password Server maintain password policies separately. The Kerberos password policy rules are kept in sync with the Open Directory Password Server password policy rules whenever a change is made.

After global password policies are put into effect, they are enforced only for users who change their passwords or users you subsequently create or import. This is because the account's password was established prior to the establishment of the global policy. In other words, if you change the policy to be either more or less restrictive, users will not be bound by the conditions of the new policy until they change their password.

> **MORE INFO** ▶ You can use command-line tools to apply policies for individual user accounts, but this is outside the scope of this guide. User account settings may override global policies.

To configure the global password policy, select Users in the Server app sidebar, and confirm that the directory node pop-up menu displays Local Network Users. Click the Action (gear icon) pop-up menu, and choose Edit Password Policy.

Configure the options to match your organization's policy, and then click OK.

It is important to obtain your organization's password policies prior to setting these options. If you miss certain criteria required by your organization and all users have been imported and have passwords set, changing these parameters may require users to change their passwords again to conform to the newer standards.

Unlike some earlier versions, the global password policy now impacts administrators also. This could lead to the administrator being locked out of the account. Refer to Apple Support article HT203114, "OS X Server (Yosemite): Global policies can lock out Admin accounts."

You can use either the Server app Users pane or the Server app Open Directory pane to configure the global password policy; they have the same options and the same effects (although the Open Directory pane offers the global password policy only for the local network users node, not for the local users node).

Remember that the global password policy may not be applied when a user attempts to authenticate; it is applied only at the following times:

▶ You create a new user.

▶ A user (with a password that was established before the password policy was established) changes her password.

Reference 9.3
Using Single Sign-On and Kerberos

Frequently, a user who is logged in on one computer needs to use resources located on another computer on the network. Users typically browse the network in the Finder and click to connect to the other computer. It would be a nuisance for users to have to enter a password for each connection. If you've deployed Open Directory, you've saved them that trouble. Open Directory provides single sign-on, which relies on Kerberos. Single sign-on essentially means that when users log in, they automatically have access to other services they may need that day, such as the Mail, File Sharing, Messages, and Calendar services, as well as VPN connectivity, without again entering their user credentials; in this way, Kerberos provides both identification and authentication services.

Defining Kerberos Basics

A complete Kerberos transaction has three main players:

▶ The user

▶ The service the user is interested in accessing

▶ The KDC, which is responsible for mediating between the user and the service, creating and routing secure tickets, and generally supplying the authentication mechanism

Within Kerberos there are different realms (specific databases or authentication domains). When you configure your server to be an Open Directory master, the realm name is the same as your server's host name, in all capital letters. Each realm contains the authentication information for users and services, called Kerberos principals. For example, for a user with a full name of Barbara Green and an account name of barbara on a KDC with the realm of SERVER17.PRETENDCO.COM, the user principal is barbara@SERVER17.PRE-TENDCO.COM. By convention, realms use all uppercase characters.

For a service to take advantage of Kerberos, it must be Kerberized (configured to work with Kerberos), which means that it can defer authentication of its users to a KDC. Not only can OS X Server provide a KDC when configured to host a shared LDAP directory, but it can also provide several Kerberized services. An example of a service principal is afpserver/server17.pretendco.com@SERVER17.PRETENDCO.COM.

Finally, Kerberos enables you to keep a list of users in a single database called the KDC, which is configured on OS X Server once an Open Directory master has been created.

The process can be simplified into three major steps, which are illustrated in the following figure.

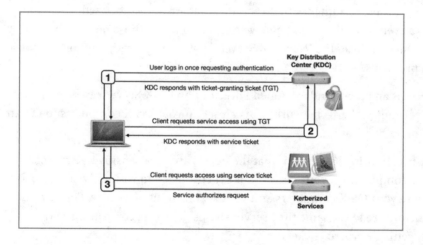

1. When a network user logs in on a Mac OS X v10.4 or later client computer, that computer negotiates with the KDC. If the user provides the correct user name and password, the KDC provides an initial ticket called a ticket-granting ticket (TGT). The TGT enables the user to subsequently ask for service tickets so she may connect to other servers and services on the network for the duration of the login session.

2. When the user on the client computer wants to access a Kerberized service, her computer presents her TGT to the KDC to obtain a service ticket.

3. The user's computer presents the service ticket to the Kerberized service to provide identification and authentication. The server that provides the Kerberized service

grants the user access to the service (as long as the user is authorized to use the service).

When a user with a valid Kerberos TGT tries to access a Kerberized service, she does not need to provide her user name because the TGT contains her identity. Likewise, she does not need to provide a password because the TGT provides authentication. In this way, Kerberos provides identification and authentication.

For example, when you have a TGT and attempt to access a Kerberized Apple Filing Protocol (AFP) or Server Message Block (SMB) service, you immediately see a list of shared folders to which you have access; the service uses Kerberos to identify and authenticate you, so you do not need to provide your user name or password.

Kerberos is one of the components of Open Directory. The reason a user's authentication information is stored in both the Password Server database and the Kerberos principal database is to allow users to authenticate to services that are not Kerberized. Users must enter a password every time they make a new connection to use those non-Kerberized services. Open Directory uses the Password Server database to provide support for those authentication protocols.

Because Kerberos is an open standard, Open Directory on OS X Server can be easily integrated into an existing Kerberos network. You can set up your OS X computers to use an existing KDC for authentication.

One security aspect to using Kerberos is that the tickets are time sensitive. Kerberos requires that the computers on your network be synchronized to within five minutes by default. Configure your OS X computers and your servers to use Network Time Protocol (NTP), and synchronize to the same time server so this doesn't become an issue that prevents you from getting Kerberos tickets.

To obtain Kerberos tickets on a Mac, that Mac must be either of the following:

▶   Bound to a directory node that provides Kerberos services (such as an Active Directory domain or forest or an Open Directory master or replica)

▶   A Mac running OS X Server that is an Open Directory master or replica

Examining Kerberos Tickets

You can use Ticket Viewer to confirm that you're able to obtain Kerberos tickets for a network user (you could also use command-line tools).

To use Ticket Viewer, open it in /System/Library/CoreServices/. Unless you've already used Ticket Viewer as the currently logged-in user, Ticket Viewer displays no identity by default; you must provide an identity by clicking Add Identity in the toolbar and entering a network user's principal or account name and password.

TIP ▶ If you're using Ticket Viewer as a troubleshooting tool, deselecting the "Remember password in my keychain" checkbox is probably a good idea so that Ticket Viewer doesn't automatically use your keychain to obtain a ticket for you; leave the checkbox unselected so that you always have to enter an identity and a password.

After you click Continue, Ticket Viewer attempts to obtain a TGT. If Ticket Viewer successfully obtains a TGT, it displays the expiration date and time, which by default is ten hours from the time you obtain the ticket.

To see detailed information about the tickets associated with your identity, select the entry for your identity, and choose Ticket > Diagnostic Information (or press Command-I). In the following figure, the first line includes the user account name (barbara), and the line that starts with "krbtgt" contains information about the TGT.

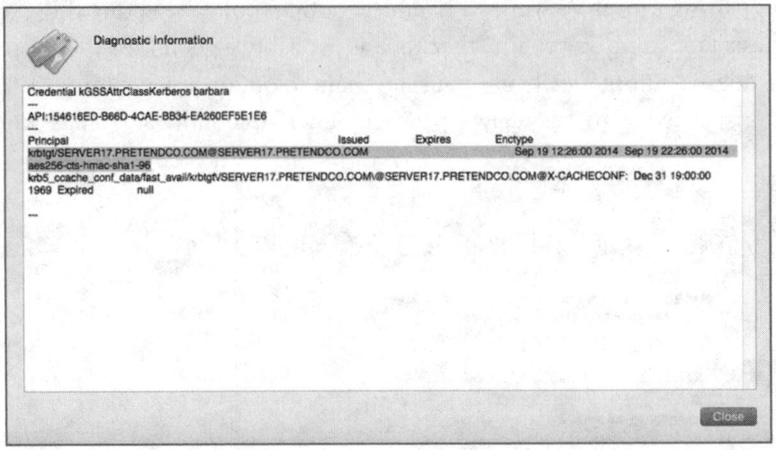

Once you have a TGT, you should be able to seamlessly access Kerberized services because OS X automatically obtains a service ticket for each Kerberized service. In the following figure, the line that starts with "cifs" represents the service-granting ticket OS X automatically obtained after the user attempted to access an SMB file-sharing service.

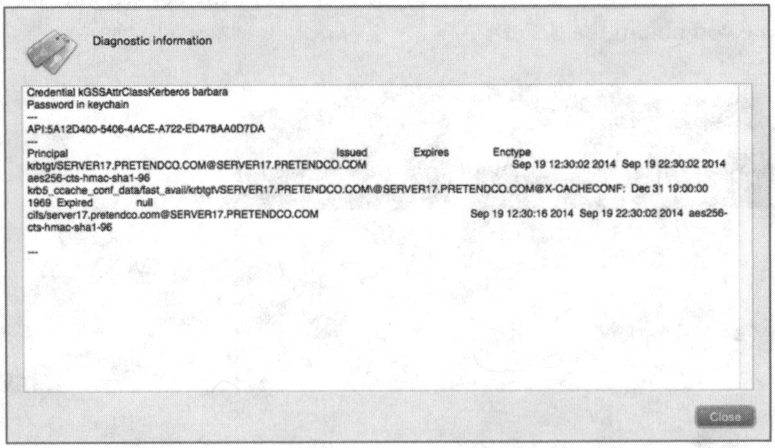

NOTE ► Ticket Viewer does not automatically update the diagnostic information pane, so you need to click the Close button in the lower-right corner of the diagnostic information pane and then choose Ticket > Diagnostic Information again to refresh the information.

Once you've confirmed your ability to obtain tickets, you should relinquish the ticket so it will not interfere with further investigation: Click the Clear button in your identity entry (next to the Refresh button).

Even though you may be logged in at the login window as a local user, you are able to get a Kerberos ticket as a network user. This is because although you authenticated *locally* to your administrator computer, you authenticated against the Open Directory service for your network user account with Ticket Viewer.

Reference 9.4
Troubleshooting

See the "Troubleshooting" section of Lesson 7 "Managing Local Users" for troubleshooting importing local accounts and accessing services, and apply the same knowledge and procedures to troubleshoot problems importing network accounts and accessing services.

See the "Troubleshooting" section of Lesson 8 "Configuring Open Directory Services" for general troubleshooting of Open Directory services.

Troubleshooting Kerberos

When a user or service that uses Kerberos experiences authentication failures, try these techniques:

► Ensure that the Domain Name System (DNS) service you use is resolving addresses correctly. This is especially important at the time you are configuring a server to be an Open Directory master. If the DNS doesn't resolve addresses correctly, the incorrect address will be written to the Kerberos configuration files. Kerberos tickets won't be usable.

► Kerberos authentication is based on encrypted timestamps. If there's more than a five-minute difference between the KDC, client, and server computers, authentication may fail. Make sure that the clocks for all computers are synchronized using the NTP service of OS X Server or another network time server.

► Make sure that Kerberos authentication is enabled for the service in question.

▶ View the user's Kerberos ticket with the Ticket Viewer application.

▶ When you browse for services using the Finder window, OS X may not automatically use the expected Kerberos identity; choose Go > Connect to Server, and enter a uniform resource locator (URL) instead.

MORE INFO ▶ You can use the `klist` command in the command-line environment to list information about your Kerberos credentials; see the man page for `klist`.

Exercise 9.1
Create and Import Network Accounts

▶ **Prerequisites**

▶ "Exercise 4.2 Configure an Open Directory Certificate Authority" on page 152

▶ You need the text files from the student materials, which you obtained as part of "Exercise 1.1 Configure OS X Before Installing OS X Server on Your Server Computer " on page 21 and "Exercise 1.3 Configure Your Administrator Computer" on page 48.

You create local network user accounts and local network group accounts just like you create local user accounts and local group accounts, except that you specify the local network node in the pop-up menu.

NOTE ▶ See Lesson 7 "Managing Local Users" for more information about using the new features such as keywords, notes, quotas, and templates.

In this scenario, within the greater Pretendco company, there is a main directory server that you do not have access to edit. Your group within Pretendco is working with some contractors. You need to give them access to your server's services, but these users don't need access to the services of any other servers in your larger organization. Therefore, you aren't going to ask the directory administrator of Pretendco's main directory server to create user accounts for these contractors.

Import Users into Your Server's Shared Directory Node

To expedite the exercise, in the student materials is a text file with contractors your group is working with for the Pretendco scenario. This text file has a properly formatted header line. The import file defines these users with the password of "net." Of course, in a production environment, each user should have his own unique password or passphrase that is secret and secure.

1 Perform these exercises on your administrator computer. If you do not already have a connection to your server computer with the Server app on your administrator computer, then connect to it with the following steps: Open the Server app on your administrator computer, choose Manage > Connect to Server, select your server, click Continue, provide administrator credentials (Administrator Name: ladmin, Administrator Password: ladminpw), deselect the "Remember this password" checkbox, and then click Connect.

Unlock the local network users node.

1 In the Server app sidebar, select Users.

2 Click the pop-up menu, and choose Local Network Users.

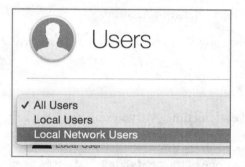

3 If the lock icon at the bottom of the Users pane is locked, click it to authenticate.

4 Deselect the checkbox "Remember this password in my keychain."

5 If necessary, enter your directory administrator credentials (Administrator Name: diradmin, Administrator Password: diradminpw).

6   Leave the checkbox "Remember this password in my keychain" unselected.

7   Click Authenticate.

Import the accounts into your server's shared directory node.

1   In the Server app, choose Manage > Import Accounts from File.

2   In the sidebar, click Documents. Open StudentMaterials, and then open the Lesson9 folder.

3   Select the contractors-users.txt file.

4   Press the Space bar to get a Quick Look preview of the import file.

```
                              contractors-users.txt                          ⬆
0x0A 0x5C 0x3A 0x2C dsRecTypeStandard:Users 12 dsAttrTypeStandard:FirstName dsAttrTypeStandard:UserShell
dsAttrTypeStandard:GeneratedUID dsAttrTypeStandard:PrimaryGroupID dsAttrTypeStandard:RecordName
dsAttrTypeStandard:UniqueID dsAttrTypeStandard:LastName dsAttrTypeStandard:Password dsAttrTypeStandard:RealName
dsAttrTypeStandard:NFSHomeDirectory dsAttrTypeStandard:HomeDirectory base64:dsAttrTypeStandard:JPEGPhoto
Carl:/bin/bash:FB96C6E3-E091-4103-B61B-A424C0A89F1A:20:carl:1092:Dunn:net:Carl Dunn:/Users/carl::/9j/
4AAQSkZJRgABAQAAAQABAAD/
4gxYSUNDX1BST0ZJTEUAAQEAAAxITGlubwIQAABtbnRyUkdCIFhZWiAHzgACAAkABgAxAAAhY3NwTVNGVAAAAABJRUMgc1JHQgAAAAAAAAAAAAAAAA9tY
AAQAAAADTLUhQICAAAAAAAAAAAAAAAAAAAAAAAAAAAAAAAAAAAAAAAAAAAAAAAAABFjcHJ0AAABUAAAADNkZXNjAAABhAAAAGx3dHB0AAAB8AAA
ABBAAAABRia3B0AAACBAAAABRyWFlaAAACGAAAABRnWFlaAAACLAAAABRiWFlaAAACQAAAABRkbW5kAAACVAAAAHBkbWRkAAACxAAAAIh2dWVkAAADTAAAA
IZZaWV3AAAD1AAAACRsdW1pAAAD/pAAAD
```

5   Press the Space bar to dismiss the preview.

6   Click the Type pop-up menu, and choose Local Network Accounts.

7   Enter your directory administrator credentials (Admin Name: diradmin, Password: dir-adminpw).

8   Click Import to start importing the file.

9   At the "Importing these accounts may take a long time. Are you sure you want to continue?" dialog, click Import.

10   Select Users in the Server app sidebar, select one of the newly imported users, Control-click, and choose Edit Access to Services.

Local Network Users

- Barbara Green
- Carl Dunn
- Enrico Baker
- Gary Pine
- Lucy Sanchez
- Maria Miller

Barbara Green
Edit User...
Edit Access to Services...
Edit Mail Options...
Change Password...
Advanced Options...
Create Template from User...

Sort By ▶
Show System Accounts

Note that every service's checkbox is selected, meaning that the Server app has granted each imported local network user account the authorization to use each listed service.

Select which services these users can access:

- ☑ Calendar
- ☑ Contacts
- ☑ FTP
- ☑ File Sharing
- ☑ Mail
- ☑ Messages
- ☑ SSH

Cancel   OK

11 Click Cancel to close the Service Access pane without making any changes.

You now have added eight local network user accounts.

On the computer you used to import the users, open the Console app, and view the import log.

1 Use a Spotlight search to open Console.

2 If no sidebar is displayed for the Console window, click Show Log List in the toolbar.

The Console app displays logs from several locations on your computer. The tilde (~) character is a symbol for your home folder, so ~/Library/Logs/ is a folder in your home folder, and it is for logs specifically related to your user account. The /var/log/ and /Library/Logs/ folders are for system logs. You will look for a log file in the ImportExport folder in your ~/Library/Logs/ folder.

3   Click the disclosure triangle for ~/Library/Logs to display the contents of that folder, and then click the disclosure triangle for ImportExport to display its contents.

4   Select a log file under ImportExport.

Note that this log file shows that you imported a number of users without error. Some problems associated with importing accounts, if they occur, will appear in these log files.

Import a Group into Your Server's Shared Directory Node

To expedite the exercise, you have an import file with a properly formatted header line that defines all the imported users as members of the Contractors group (Account Name: contractors). You will confirm that this local network group has no explicit access to your server's services. However, local network user accounts you create with the Server app or import with the Server app automatically have access to all the services in this list, so this isn't a big concern.

1   In the Server app, choose Manage > Import Accounts from File.

2   If the contents of the Lesson9 folder are not displayed, in the sidebar, click Documents. Open StudentMaterials, and then open Lesson9.

3   Select the contractors-group.txt file.

4   Press the Space bar to get a Quick Look preview of the file.

```
⊘                              contractors-group.txt                              ⬆
0x0A 0x5C 0x3A 0x2C dsRecTypeStandard:Groups 6 dsAttrTypeStandard:Member dsAttrTypeStandard:GeneratedUID
dsAttrTypeStandard:RecordName dsAttrTypeStandard:GroupMembers dsAttrTypeStandard:RealName
dsAttrTypeStandard:GroupMembership
enrico,lucy,barbara,maria,sue,gary,carl,todd:1F5BB153-C50A-4EA6-A6FF-43602CB1EEA7:contractors:7D3460FE-48F4-451F-B6CB-
B947A906686F9,AA241A6C-BA4F-42E7-93CD-90DBCF2BB55E,C7D826AE-FD8F-4065-87BB-893B92FE5AEB,1AEC004F-5D6B-4BE5-
BDA9-51256A822C89,F896C6E3-E091-4103-B61B-A424C0AB9F1A,BE962FDE-C038-4B20-97B6-422C81C60660,6115B57B-89EE-4F0F-
BD74-4A42BD0C770D,6D633E23-4634-4B80-88AE-8B48893F67AC:Contractors:enrico,lucy,barbara,maria,sue,gary,carl,todd
```

5   Press the Space bar to dismiss the preview.

6   Click the Type pop-up menu, and choose Local Network Accounts.

7   Enter your directory administrator credentials (Admin Name: diradmin, Password:diradminpw).

8   Click Import to start importing the file.

9   In the Server app sidebar, select Groups.

10   Click the Type pop-up menu, and choose Local Network Groups.

11   Control-click the Contractors group, and then choose Edit Access to Services from the shortcut menu.

12   Note that for the SSH and Screen Sharing services, the checkbox is unselected.

But remember that if a user has access to a service, it doesn't matter if one of that user's groups doesn't have access to a service.

13   Click Cancel to close the Service Access pane without making any changes.

You now have a new local network group populated with the local network users you previously imported.

Verify That Newly Imported Users Can Connect to Your Server's File Sharing Service

Turn on the File Sharing service if it isn't already on, and then use the Finder on your administrator computer to connect to your server's File Sharing service with a local network user account.

1   In the Server app, if the File Sharing service is not already on, with a green status indicator next to the service name in the sidebar, select File Sharing in the sidebar, and click On to turn it on.

2   On your administrator computer, open the Finder.

If you don't already have a Finder window open, press Command-N to open a new one.

3   If an Eject button appears next to your server in the Finder window sidebar, click the Eject button.

4   In the Finder window sidebar, select your server.

If your server does not appear in the Finder window sidebar, click All under Shared, and then select your server.

5   Click Connect As.

6   Provide credentials for one of the users you imported:

▶   Name: gary

▶   Password: net

7   Click Connect.

The Finder window displays the user account you are connected as and displays the shared folders this user has access to; this confirms that you have access to the File Sharing service. Note that unless you open a folder, you will not actually mount a network volume.

8   In the upper-right corner of the Finder window, click Disconnect.

In this exercise, you imported user and group accounts into your server's shared directory domain. You confirmed that when you use the Server app to import user accounts, those users are automatically granted access to all your server's services.

Exercise 9.2
Configure Password Policies

▶   **Prerequisite**

▶   "Exercise 9.1 Create and Import Network Accounts" on page 292

Configure Password Policy

It's easy to set up password policies using the Server app. The settings you specify affect all local and local network users, even those in the Administrators group. Requirements related to password complexity take effect only when a user changes her password. For this exercise, you'll configure the password policy such that it requires the following:

► Users to become disabled after ten failed attempts

► Passwords to contain at least one numeric character

► Passwords to contain at least eight characters

You'll create a new local network user account and then use the Change Password feature of making an Apple Filing Protocol (AFP) connection to change the user's password in compliance with password policy requirements. You'll attempt to change it to something that does not match the policy you just configured and then change it to a password that does conform to the policy.

1   On your administrator computer, if you are not already connected to your server, open the Server app, connect to your server, and authenticate as a local administrator.

2   In the Server app sidebar, select Users.

3   Click the pop-up menu, and choose Local Network Users.

4   From the Action (gear icon) pop-up menu, choose Edit Password Policy.

5   Select the checkbox "Passwords must contain at least one numeric character."

6   Select the checkbox "Passwords must contain at least __ characters," and enter 8 in the field.

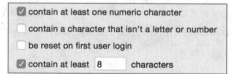

7   Click OK.

Create a new local network user for this exercise.

1   In the Users pane, confirm the pop-up menu is set to Local Network Users.

2   Click the Add (+) button.

3 Enter the following values, with a password that matches the previous password policy:

▶ Full Name: Rick Reed

▶ Account Name: rick

▶ Password (and Verify): rickpw88

▶ Leave the other fields at their defaults.

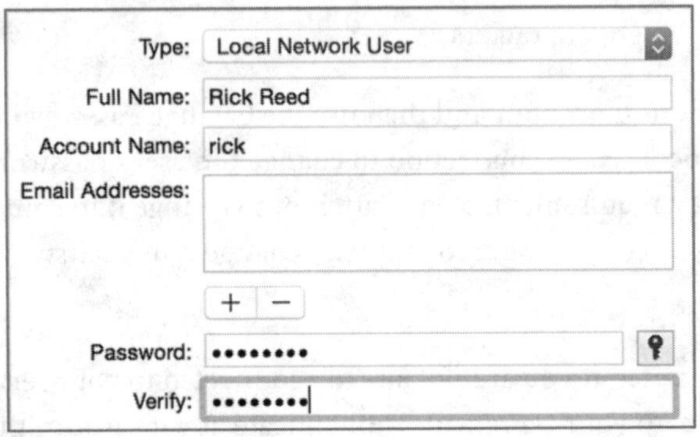

Type:	Local Network User ⌄
Full Name:	Rick Reed
Account Name:	rick
Email Addresses:	
	➕ ➖
Password:	•••••••• 🔑
Verify:	••••••••

4 Click Create to save the changes.

Confirm the Password

Make an AFP connection, and use the Change Password feature. Even though Server Message Block (SMB) is the default file-sharing protocol for OS X Mavericks and later, use the AFP file-sharing protocol because it offers the facility to change your password.

1 In the Server app, if the File Sharing service is not already on, with a green status indicator next to the service name in the sidebar, select File Sharing, and click the On/Off switch to turn it on.

2 On your administrator computer, open the Finder.

3 If an Eject button appears next to your server in the Finder window sidebar, click it.

4 Choose Go > Connect to Server.

5 Enter afp://servern.pretendco.com (where *n* is your student number).

6 Click Connect.

7   In the Name field, enter rick.

8   Click Change Password.

9   Enter the old password as well as a new password, without following the password policy that it must be at least eight characters and must include at least one numeric character:

▶   Old Password: rickpw88

▶   New Password: net

▶   Verify: net

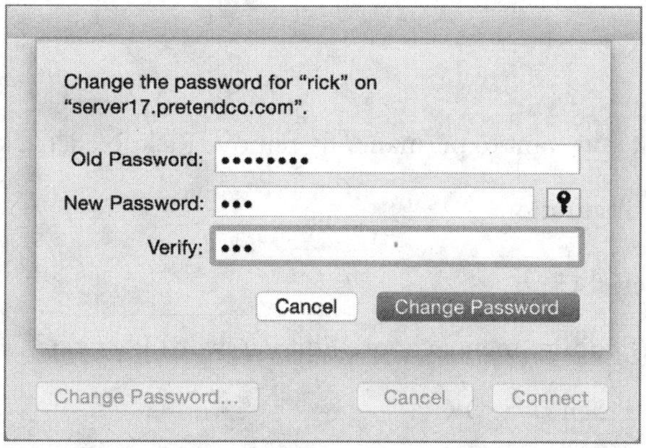

10   Click Change Password to try to change to the new password.

11   At the message that your password does not meet the policy, click OK.

12 Enter the old password as well as a new password, but this time follow the password policy that it must be at least eight characters and must include at least one numeric character:

   ▶ Old Password: rickpw88

   ▶ New Password: rickpw12345

   ▶ Verify: rickpw12345

13 Click Change Password.

   Once you've successfully changed the password, you are authenticated and authorized to use the File Sharing service. The Finder displays the user account you are connected as and displays the shared folders this user has access to.

14 Select the shared folder named rick, and click OK.

15 In the Finder sidebar, click Eject next to your server name.

Clean Up Password Policy

To prevent confusion in future exercises, remove the Rick Reed user, and remove your password policy configuration.

1 In the Server app sidebar, select Users.

2 Select Rick Reed.

3 Click the Delete (–) button.

4 When asked to confirm that you want to permanently remove Rick Reed, click Delete.

Remove the password policy configuration.

1 In the Server app sidebar, select Users.

2 From the Action (gear icon) pop-up menu, choose Edit Password Policy.

3 Deselect each checkbox, and then click OK.

In this exercise, you used the Server app to set password policy, and then you confirmed that the policy is in effect when a user attempts to make a password change that does not conform to the policy.

Managing Devices with Configuration Profiles

Lesson 10

Configuring OS X Server to Provide Device Management

The OS X Server Profile Manager service lets you manage OS X and iOS devices, and it allows your users to perform basic management of their devices. This lesson introduces you to Profile Manager.

Profile Manager provides functionality in three ways:

► Over-the-air (OTA) configuration of iOS and OS X devices

► Mobile device management (MDM)

► App and book distribution

In this lesson, you'll prepare the Profile Manager service for use and turn it on. The following lesson will describe how to apply it to managing iOS and OS X devices.

Reference 10.1
Administering the Profile Manager Service

Profile Manager is an account management tool that allows you to develop and distribute configurations and settings that control the experience on Mountain Lion and later computers and on iOS 6 and later devices. The configurations and settings are contained in Extensible Markup Language (XML)–based text files called profiles. Profile Manager includes three tools for its administration:

► Profile Manager web app

► A user portal website

► MDM server

Profile Manager Web App

The web tool allows easy access to the Profile Manager functionality from any browser that can connect to the server that has OS X Server installed with the Profile Manager service turned on. You can use the web interface to create profiles for use on iOS devices and OS X computers. You can also use it to create and manage device accounts and device group accounts. Users and groups are created in the Server app or read from a connected directory service but are displayed in the Profile Manager web app and can be used to manage by the user or user group level as well. When configured, Profile Manager is available at https://*server.domain.com*/profilemanager/.

User Portal

The user portal website is a simple way for users to enroll their own devices, obtain profiles, and wipe or lock their devices. When configured, the user portal is available via a web browser at https://*server.domain.com*/mydevices/ and lists users' enrolled devices and available profiles.

Device Management

You can configure and turn on the MDM functionality to allow you to create profiles for devices. When you or your users enroll Mountain Lion or later computers and iOS 6 or later devices, this allows over-the-air management of devices, including remote wipe and lock. App and book assignment is supported on Mac computers with OS X Mavericks or later, and on iOS devices with iOS 7.0 or later installed. Some features require OS X Yosemite or iOS 8.0 or later.

> **NOTE ▶** Profile Manager, the user portal website, and device management will be covered in more detail in Lesson 11 "Managing with Profile Manager".

Reference 10.2
Configuring Profile Manager

To be able to assign profiles, you must turn on the Profile Manager service. Using profiles is a significantly different way to manage clients than earlier versions of OS X Server offered.

Terminology

In the context of device management, a profile is a collection of settings that tells a device how to configure itself and what functions to allow or restrict. Configuration profiles contain payloads that define settings such as Wi-Fi settings, email accounts, calendaring accounts, and security policies. Enrollment profiles allow the server to manage your device.

Preparations for Profile Manager

Prior to configuring Profile Manager, you'll need to set up a few items to make the process more streamlined:

▶ Configure your server as a network directory server. In other words, create an Open Directory master

▶ Obtain and install a Secure Sockets Layer (SSL) certificate. It is recommended to use one signed by a trusted certificate authority. You could use the certificate that is automatically generated when you configure your server as an Open Directory master, but if you use this certificate, you need to first configure devices to trust that certificate. In some cases, the trust is created during enrollment such as when using the user portal website.

▶ Obtain an Apple ID for use when you request a push certificate from Apple through the https://appleid.apple.com website. Prior to using this ID, make sure you log in at that site and verify the email address. Otherwise, you might not have success requesting the push certificate. Use an institutional ID when setting up Profile Manager for an institution. This separates users, who can be transient, from the institution itself. Make sure you record this information and have it available for a later date.

Apple ID and Primary Email Address

deploy@server17.pretendco.com   Edit

Verified ✓

Enabling the Profile Manager Service

When enabling the Profile Manager service, you can do each step manually or let OS X Server do them for you. The steps required, regardless of them being done manually or automatically, are listed here in the general order. The exercises will include the actual setup for testing.

▶ Configure the Push Notification service. When you do this manually, you can find it in the Settings pane under your server.

▶ Configure Open Directory service as an Open Directory master, and connect to any external directory service you may want to use.

▶ Configure device management in the Profile Manager service pane. If the previous two bullet points weren't completed prior to this step, you would be prompted to configure them.

▶ Configure any access limitations you may need via the permissions in the Profile Manager service pane and/or in the Access pane under your server.

▶ Turn on the Profile Manager service via the On button.

⚙ Profile Manager   ON

Access

    Status: ● Available over the Internet at 96.245.114.51/profilemanager
             Learn about configuring devices for this service ⊙
    Permissions: All Networks   Edit...

Settings

    Device Management: Enabled
    ☐ Enroll devices using the Device Enrollment Program   Edit...
    ☐ Distribute apps and books from the Volume Purchase Program   Edit...

Configuration Profiles

    Default Configuration Profile: Settings for Everyone   Edit...
    ☐ Sign configuration profiles   Edit...
    Profiles are available to all users for download and devices can be enrolled for management. Visit user portal ⊙

Open Profile Manager ⊙

Once the Profile Manager service is running, you can perform management via the web app.

Enabling Volume Purchase Program (VPP)

The Volume Purchase Program allows you to purchase multiple copies of apps and books from the VPP store and distribute them to users and groups of managed iOS and OS X devices via Profile Manager.

VPP is designed for organizations needing to buy multiple copies of apps and books for distribution. All purchases made through VPP show up automatically in Profile Manager, ready to be deployed to your users.

For information on joining VPP, refer to the following pages:

https://www.apple.com/education/it/vpp/

https://www.apple.com/business/vpp/

Once you're a member of the VPP, you need to set up Profile Manager to allow a secure connection to the VPP. You do this by downloading a token available from the VPP store site in the Account Summary page.

You create the link between the VPP account and Profile Manager when you place the downloaded VPP token into the dialog that appears when you select the "Distribute apps and books from the Volume Purchase Program" checkbox in the Server app under Profile Manager.

You will need to replace the token if the account password is changed or it expires. It is best to replace the token prior to the expiration date.

You must purchase paid apps as managed distributions to be used with Profile Manager. Free apps will always come as managed distributions. In some cases, you can convert redeemable codes into managed distributions via VPP Support, available in the Apple Deployment Programs (ADP) site at https://deploy.apple.com.

The applications and books are available in the appropriate section of the Profile Manager web app. Even free apps indicate how many copies are available. If you run out, you can simply buy more, and the number of copies will increment by that amount.

Enabling the Device Enrollment Program (DEP)

The Device Enrollment Program provides automatic MDM enrollment for iOS devices and OS X computers with no or limited user interaction. A device or computer that is included in DEP will contact the Apple servers at initial startup and get information about its assigned MDM server, whether third party or Profile Manager. This avoids having to manually enroll the device or computer in the MDM and preserves the out-of-box experience for the end user.

DEP is for business and education clients who have the proper type of account with Apple. Check with your Apple sales group to get set up with a DEP customer ID. Only devices purchased using the DEP customer ID will be available to be used with the DEP.

For information on joining the DEP, see https://deploy.apple.com and https://deploy.apple.com/enroll/files/dep_help.pdf.

The process of using DEP with Profile Manager involves configuration in both Profile Manager and the DEP administration website. You need to export your public key for OS X Server from the Server app and download the DEP token from the DEP administration site. During the configuration, these items get imported into the other to create the trust between DEP and Profile Manager or any other MDM system used.

Logging into your DEP account requires using the two-factor authentication set up for the Apple ID. Upon initial login with your username and password to the DEP administration website, the two-factor authentication process is initiated, and a code is sent to a previously defined mobile phone. Once you receive the code, enter it, and you will be granted access.

The DEP management console is where you define an MDM server such as Profile Manager to be used with DEP-eligible devices.

You can assign devices to MDM services such as Profile Manager via order number or serial number. Newly purchased devices can be automatically added to an MDM service if you pick that option during the initial setup in Add MDM Server.

Any devices that are assigned to Profile Manager become available as placeholders. A placeholder is a special type of record that allows you to manage the device prior to its actual enrollment. The device's placeholder can be assigned to a user, included in a group of devices, or managed independently.

Exercise 10.1
Turn On Profile Manager

▶ **Prerequisite**

    ▶   "Exercise 2.1 Create DNS Zones and Records" on page 71

Turn On Basic Device Management

In this section, you'll turn on the Profile Manager service to manage devices, including specifying which certificate to use for signing configuration profiles. If you have a Deployment Enrollment Program account that you have not yet used in production, there is an optional section to enable your Profile Manager service to enroll devices using DEP. Likewise, if you have a Volume Purchase Program account that you have not yet used in production, there is an optional section to enable your Profile Manager service to distribute apps and books from the VPP.

1 Perform these exercises on your administrator computer. If you do not already have a connection to your server computer with the Server app on your administrator computer, then connect to it with the following steps: Open the Server app on your administrator computer, choose Manage > Connect to Server, select your server, click Continue, provide administrator credentials (Administrator Name: ladmin, Administrator Password: ladminpw), deselect the "Remember this password" checkbox, and then click Connect.

2 Select Profile Manager in the services sidebar.

3 Click the Configure button next to Device Management.

The service gathers some data and gives a description of its capabilities.

4 At the Configure Device Management pane, click Next.

5 If your server is already configured as an Open Directory master, you won't see the following steps. Skip the following steps, and continue at step 12.

6 If your server is not already configured as an Open Directory master, you will do so now. Click Next.

7 At the Directory Administrator pane, leave the Name and Account Name fields at their default settings. Enter diradminpw in the Password and Verify fields (of course, in a production environment, you should always use a strong password).

8 Click Next.

9 At the Organization Information pane, if necessary, in the Organization Name field, enter Pretendco Project *n* (where *n* is your student number), and in the Admin Email Address field, enter ladmin@server*n*.pretendco.com (where *n* is your student number).

10 Click Next.

11 If your server is *not* already configured as an Open Directory master, then at the Confirm Settings pane, review the information, and click Set Up. It may take a few moments for the Server app to configure your server as an Open Directory master. You can watch the status of the process in the lower-left corner of the pane.

12 In the Organization Information pane, the Name and Email address fields are already filled out.

Enter some text in the Phone Number and Address fields. You do not need to use real information for this exercise, but you should use valid information in a production environment.

13 Click Next.

14 At the Configure an SSL Certificate pane, leave the Certificate field at its default value of your Open Directory CA–created SSL certificate, and click Next.

15 If you haven't already set up push notifications, you are prompted for an Apple ID, which the Server app uses to request Apple Push Notification certificates.

If you do not already have an Apple ID, click the link under the credential fields to create an Apple ID.

When you create an Apple ID, you need to click the verification link that Apple sends to the email address that you used when you created the new Apple ID.

NOTE ▶ It is possible to have been regularly using an Apple ID for other services, even if you have never verified it. If you have not yet verified your Apple ID, open http://appleid.apple.com in Safari, click Manage your Apple ID, sign in with your Apple ID, click Send Verification Email to resend a verification email message to your email address, check your email, and finally click the verification link.

Once you have an Apple ID that you've verified, enter your Apple ID credentials, and click Next.

16 At the Confirm Settings pane, click Finish.

17 Select the "Sign configuration profiles" option, and then in the pop-up menu, choose the code signing certificate that was automatically created and signed by your Open Directory intermediate CA.

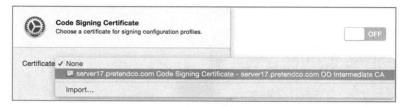

18 Click OK.

By signing profiles with a certificate, you provide a way to validate that the profiles came from where they were supposed to and that they have not been tampered with.

19 Click On to turn on Profile Manager.

Connect Profile Manager with Your Device Enrollment Program Account (Optional)

> **NOTE>** ▸ This exercise assumes that you followed the steps at https://help.apple.com/deployment/programs/ to establish your program agent account, create an administrator account for DEP, agree to the terms and conditions, and establish two-factor authentication.

> **NOTE** ▸ Do not perform this exercise with your production DEP account. This requires you to be a member of the Device Enrollment Program. You can sign up at https://deploy.apple.com.

1 To configure Profile Manager to enroll devices using DEP, select the "Enroll devices using the Device Enrollment Program" checkbox.

Settings

Device Management: Enabled

☐ Enroll devices using the Device Enrollment Program

☐ Distribute apps and books from the Volume Purchase Program

2 At the Device Enrollment pane, click the link, which opens http://deploy.apple.com in Safari.

3 In Safari, enter your DEP credentials, and then click Sign In.

4 At the "Would you like to save this password?" dialog, click Never for This Website.

5 At the "Verify your identity" pane, select a device to receive a verification code, and then click Send.

6 Enter your verification code, and then click Continue.

7 If there are terms and conditions to read and agree to, read them, select the checkbox, and then click Agree.

8 In the sidebar, select Device Enrollment Program.

9 At the Manage Servers pane, click Add MDM Server.

10 In the MDM Server Name field, enter **Pretendco Project** *n* (where *n* is your student number), and then click Next.

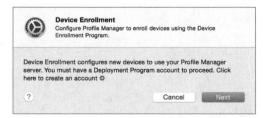

11 In the Server app, at the first Device Enrollment pane, click Next.

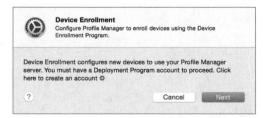

12 Enter some text in the Phone Number field, and click Next.

13 Next to Public Key, click Export.

14 At the Save As dialog, press Command-D to switch locations to your desktop.

15 Leave the default filename, and click Save.

16 In Safari, click Choose File.

17 Press Command-D to switch to the Desktop folder.

18 Select DeviceEnrollmentPublicKey.pem, and click Choose.

19 Now that you specified the public key, click Next.

Edit "Pretendco Project 17"

2. Upload Your Public Key.

Choose File...   ☐ DeviceEnrollmen...

The public key certificate is used to encrypt the Authentication Token file for
secure transfer to your MDM Server.

Previous   Cancel   Next

20 To download your server token, click Your Server Token.

Edit "Pretendco Project 17"

3. Download and Install your Server Token.

☐ Your Server Token

Contact your MDM vendor for installation instructions.

Previous   Done

The server token is automatically placed in your Downloads folder.

21 Click Done.

22 In the Server app, click Choose.

23 Select Downloads in the sidebar.

24 Select the server token. It is a file that starts with your server's name, contains a string
of characters that represents the timestamp, and ends with "smime.p7m."

25 Click Choose.

26 Click Continue.

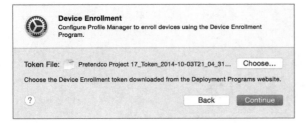

27 Click Done.

Device Enrollment
Profile Manager is configured with the following token for the Device Enrollment Program.

Apple ID: depadmin@arekdreyer.com

Token Expires: Saturday, October 3, 2015

Organization: Dreyer Network Consultants, Inc

Replace Token...   Done

28 In Safari, log in again at the deployment programs site if necessary.

29 In the Manage Servers section, select your server.

30 Review the details, and then click OK.

Server Details

Server Name:
Pretendco Project 17   Rename...

Public Key:
DeviceEnrollmentPublicKey.pem   Replace Key...

Server Token:
Created on 10/3/2014   Generate New Token...

Delete Server   OK

31 In the upper-left corner of the Safari window, click your name, and then choose Sign Out.

32 Close the Safari window.

Connect Profile Manager with Your Volume Purchase Program Account (Optional)

> **NOTE** ▶ This exercise assumes that you followed the steps at https://help.apple.com/deployment/programs/ to establish your program agent account, create an administrator account for VPP, agree to the terms and conditions, and establish two-factor authentication.

> **NOTE** ▶ Do not perform this exercise with your production VPP account. This requires you to be a member of the Volume Purchase Program. You can sign up at https://deploy.apple.com.

1 To configure Profile Manager to distribute apps and books, select the "Distribute apps and books from the Volume Purchase Program" checkbox.

Settings
Device Management: Enabled
☑ Enroll devices using the Device Enrollment Program   Edit…
☐ Distribute apps and books from the Volume Purchase Program   Edit…

2 Click the link to download your VPP service token.

This opens Safari and allows you to choose which VPP you signed up for, Business or Education.

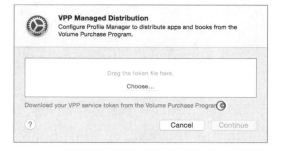

VPP Managed Distribution
Configure Profile Manager to distribute apps and books from the Volume Purchase Program.

Drag the token file here.
Choose…

Download your VPP service token from the Volume Purchase Program ⊙

?   Cancel   Continue

3 Select the appropriate VPP store.

4   Sign in with your VPP credentials.

5   If asked to save this password, click Never for This Website.

6   If you see the message that this Apple ID has not yet been used with the VPP, click Continue.

7   If there are terms and conditions to read and agree to, read them, select the checkbox, and then click Agree.

8   Click your Apple ID in the upper-right corner of the window, and choose Account Summary.

9   Click Download Token.

This automatically downloads your VPP token to your Downloads folder.

10 Click your Apple ID in the upper-right corner of the window, and choose Sign Out.

11 Close the Safari window.

12 In the VPP Managed Distribution pane, click Choose.

13 If necessary, click Downloads in the sidebar.

14 Select your VPP token. It is a file that starts with the string "sToken," contains your Apple ID for VPP, and ends with the string "vpptoken."

15 Click Choose.

16 Confirm that your token appears, and then click Continue.

> **⚙ VPP Managed Distribution**
> Configure Profile Manager to distribute apps and books from the
> Volume Purchase Program.
>
> ---
>
> 📄 sToken for bizvpp@arekdreyer.com.vpptoken
>
> Choose…
>
> ---
>
> Download your VPP service token from the Volume Purchase Program ⊙
>
> ?   Cancel   Continue

17 If you see a dialog that this token is already in use, click Cancel unless you are sure that the token has been in use only for testing. Otherwise, click Continue.

18 Review the VPP summary information, and then click Done.

> **⚙ VPP Managed Distribution**
> Configure Profile Manager to distribute apps and books from the
> Volume Purchase Program.
>
> ---
>
> Apple ID: bizvpp@arekdreyer.com
>
> Token Expires: Saturday, October 3, 2015
>
> Organization: Dreyer Network Consultants, In
>
> Replace Token…   Done

Clean Up

Remove your server key, your DEP token, and your VPP token, if applicable.

1 In the Finder, from your desktop, drag DeviceEnrollmentPublicKey.pem to the Trash.

2 In the Finder, open your Downloads folder.

3 Drag the file that ends in smime.p7m to the Trash.

4 Drag the file that ends in vpptoken to the Trash.

In this section, you turned on the Profile Manager service so you can manage devices. You configured the Profile Manager service to sign all configuration profiles using the code signing certificate that was signed by your OD intermediate CA. There was an optional section to enable your Profile Manager service to enroll devices using DEP and an optional section to enable your Profile Manager service to distribute apps and books from the VPP.

Lesson 11

Managing with Profile Manager

If you run an organization with several hundred users or even just a handful, how can you manage their experience with OS X and iOS? In previous lessons, you learned management techniques involving the user name and password. There are many other aspects to user account management, and it is important to understand how these various aspects interact with each other.

OS X Server provides the Profile Manager service, which allows you as the administrator to assign preferences and allow or deny certain settings to iOS and OS X devices.

Reference 11.1
Introducing Account Management

OS X Lion introduced the concept of profiles that contain configurations and settings, and OS X Yosemite expands on the idea. By assigning profiles to users, user groups, devices, or groups of devices, you can more effectively control them.

With profiles, you can achieve a range of results including but not limited to the following:

► Controlling settings on mobile devices and computers

► Restricting resources to specific groups or individuals

► Securing device use in key areas such as offices, classrooms, or open labs

► Customizing the user experience

► Providing apps and books to the users

GOALS

► Configure Profile Manager

► Construct management profiles

► Deliver profiles

► Install and delete profiles

► Manage users, groups of users, devices, and groups of devices using profiles

Levels of Management

You can create settings for four types of accounts:

▶ User—This usually relates to a specific person. This is the account that the person identifies herself with when logging in to the computer. A user's short name or user ID (UID) number uniquely identifies the user on a system.

▶ Group—This represents a group of users, a group of groups, or a mixture of both.

▶ Device—Similar to a user account, this is the singular entity that represents a given piece of hardware. This can be either a computer or an iOS device. Device accounts are uniquely identified by their Ethernet ID (MAC address), serial number, international mobile equipment identity (IMEI), or mobile equipment identifier (MEID).

▶ Device group—This represents a grouping of computers or iOS devices or both. A device group can include other device groups nested in it or a mixture of both individuals and nested groups.

Not all management levels make sense for all purposes, so when setting policy, you have to decide what is appropriate. For example, you might want to define printers by device group because a typical situation has a group of computers located geographically close to a specific printer. You may want to set virtual private network (VPN) access via a group of users such as remote salespeople. And individuals might have specific application access rights granted to them.

Each level can have a default group of settings and then custom settings. Mixing and layering profiles with conflicting settings is not recommended. The results may not be what you expected.

If a user or user group has an assigned profile and the user logs in to the user portal website to enroll an OS X computer, the profiles assigned to that user will be applied to that computer regardless of who logs in to that computer. The same applies if they have an iOS device assigned to them as a user.

Managing Preferences for Users in a Group

Although you can set up preferences individually for users with network accounts, it's more efficient to manage preferences for the groups to which they belong. Like with individual users, group management is applied if the user enrolling the device is a member of a group that has management set for it. Groups can also be used for applying Volume Purchase Program (VPP) enrollment to a wide swath of users rather than inviting users individually.

Managing Device Group Accounts

A device group account is set up for a group of OS X computers or iOS devices that have the same preference settings and are available to the same set of users and groups. You create and modify these device groups in Profile Manager.

When you set up a device group, make sure you have already determined how the devices are identified. Use descriptions that are logical and easy to remember (for instance, the description might be the computer name). This also makes it easier to find the devices to add them to the correct device group.

You can import lists of devices into Profile Manager via a comma-separated value (CSV) file. The file needs to be structured like this:

name, serial number, UDID, IMEI, MEID

Leave a field empty if you're not using that value.

Managing Apps

Apps—both Enterprise and those purchased via VPP—can be assigned to users and groups. Only Enterprise apps can be assigned to devices and device groups. Enterprise apps are ones that are developed "in-house" by a company, typically for internal needs, and are not distributed via the App Store.

Apps purchased through VPP automatically show up in the Apps pane in Profile Manager. Enterprise apps need to be uploaded into Profile Manager.

The VPP apps will be assigned to the devices at the next push, but in-house Enterprise apps get automatically pushed.

Delivering Profiles

Once created, profiles can be delivered in a number of ways:

▶ Via the user portal website—Users log in to the portal with their account credentials and are presented with the profiles assigned to them.

▶ Via an email to the user—The profile is a simple text file formatted in Extensible Markup Language (XML), so it is easily transported.

▶ Web link—The profile can be published on a website for users to visit and download.

▶ Automatic push—The profile gets automatically pushed to the device with no user interaction (the device must be enrolled for this to work).

Automatic push relies on the Apple Push Notification service (APNs). This service is hosted by Apple and is provided to allow secure push notification to client devices. Once a server is configured to utilize APNs, client devices enrolled for management in Profile Manager check in with APNs and wait for notification signals to be sent by the Profile Manager via APNs. No data is included in the notification beyond informing the client that Profile Manager has something for it. This keeps data secure between Profile Manager and the client.

Here is the push notification process:

1. An enrolled device makes contact with APNs and keeps a lightweight communication going between them. This happens any time the enrolled device has a network chance, as would occur when being turned on, changing networks, or switching network interfaces.

2. The Profile Manager service contacts APNs when it needs to notify an enrolled device or group of devices of a new or changed profile. APNs has the ability to send feedback to the Profile Manager service.

3. APNs notifies the device to get in touch with the associated Profile Manager service in which it is enrolled.

4. The device communicates with the Profile Manager service once notified.

5. The Profile Manager service sends the profile to the device.

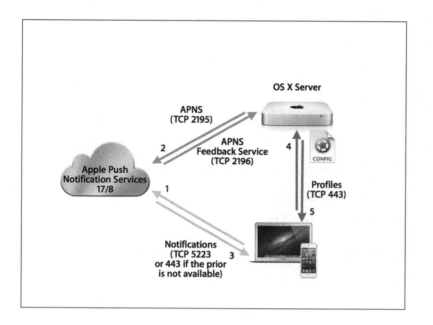

A list of installed profiles is available in OS X in Profile preferences. An equivalent list is available in iOS when you tap Settings > General > Profiles.

Remotely Locking or Wiping a Device

Once enrolled, a device or group of devices can be remotely locked or wiped. In this example, a remote lock will be performed. A remote wipe can be attempted, but do it only on a device you don't mind reconfiguring. Administrators can lock the device via Profile Manager, and users can lock it via the user portal website.

Upon requesting a lock, a confirmation pane will appear, a passcode will be requested, and the lock command will be sent. Mac computers are shut down, and an Extensible Firmware Interface (EFI) passcode is set, so it needs to be entered to use the computer again. For iOS devices, the screen is locked, and the passcode is enforced.

There are two ways devices can be locked or wiped:

▶   Profile Manager—Log in to the Profile Manager web app, and select the device or group of devices to be locked. In the Action (gear icon) pop-up menu, choose Lock. The content of the Action menu will vary depending on whether it is a device or device group.

▶ User portal—Once users log in, each device they enrolled will be displayed in the Devices pane. The lock and wipe choices are presented in each device listed.

Which Preferences Can Be Managed?

In addition to various other settings for user, group, device, and device group accounts, Profile Manager provides control over the preferences in Table 11-1. Table 11-2 describes the manageable preferences payloads for devices and device groups.

TABLE 11.1   **Manageable Preferences Payloads for Users and Groups**

Preference	OS X	iOS	Description
General	✓	✓	Profile distribution type, how the profile can be removed, organization, and description
Passcode	✓	✓	Define passcode requirements such as length, complexity, reuse, and so on
Mail	✓	✓	Configure email settings such as servers, account name, and so on
Exchange	✓	✓	Configure Exchange ActiveSync settings
LDAP	✓	✓	Configure connection to LDAP server
Contacts	✓	✓	Configure access to CardDAV server
Calendar	✓	✓	Configure access to CalDAV server
Network	✓	✓	Configure network setting on the device, including wireless and wired
VPN	✓	✓	Configure VPN settings: L2TP, PPTP, IPSec (Cisco), CiscoAnyConnect, Juniper SSL, F5 SSL, SonicWALL Mobile Connect, and Aruba VIA
Certificate	✓	✓	Allow the installation of PKCS1 and PKCS12 certificates
SCEP	✓	✓	Define connection to Simple Certificate Enrollment Protocol (SCEP) server
Web Clips	✓	✓	Display defined Web Clips as application icons
Fonts	✓	✓	Distribute fonts
Airplay	✓	✓	Define which AirPlay devices can be used
Global HTTP Proxy		✓	Define a proxy to be used by the device
Airprint		✓	Define settings for the device to connect to AirPrint printers

Preference	OS X	iOS	Description
Content Filter		✓	Define which URLs can be reached by the device
Domains		✓	Define email domains that won't be marked in Mail and web domains from which documents will be considered managed
Security and Privacy	✓	✓	Control if diagnostic and usage data gets sent to Apple; define password and lock restrictions, plus whether user can override Gatekeeper (OS X only)
Identification	✓		Configure identification information of user
Restrictions	✓	✓	Define application and content restrictions (separate OS X and iOS versions)
Subscribed Calendars		✓	Configure calendar subscriptions
APN		✓	Configure carrier settings such as the access point name (advanced use only)
Messages	✓		Configure connection to Jabber or AIM chat servers
AD Certificate	✓		Specify the settings for retrieving a certificate for your computer from Active Directory
Login Items	✓		Specify applications, items, and network mounts to launch at login
Mobility	✓		Define mobility settings for OS X clients to allow cached credentials and portable home directories
Dock	✓		Configure Dock behavior
Finder	✓		Configure Finder settings
Printing	✓		Configure printing settings and access to printers or print queues

Preference	OS X	iOS	Description
Parental Controls	✓		Define settings for Parental Controls such as content filtering and time limits
Accessibility	✓		Manage Accessibility settings
Single Sign-On		✓	Configure Kerberos settings
Custom Settings	✓		Apply custom preferences for items not defined in other payloads; similar to applying preference manifests in WGM

TABLE 11.2 Manageable Preferences Payloads for Devices and Device Groups

Preference	OS X	iOS	Description
General	✓	✓	Profile distribution type, how the profile can be removed, organization, and description
Passcode	✓	✓	Define passcode requirements such as length, complexity, reuse, and so on
Fonts	✓	✓	Distribute fonts
Single App Mode		✓	Define an app that will be the only one the device will open
Global HTTP Proxy		✓	Define a proxy to be used by the device
Airprint		✓	Define settings for the device to connect to AirPrint printers
Content Filter		✓	Define which URLs can be reached by the device
Domains		✓	Define email domains that won't be marked in Mail and web domains from which documents will be considered managed
Airplay	✓	✓	Define which AirPlay devices can be used

Preference	OS X	iOS	Description
Mail		✓	Configure email settings such as servers, account name, and so on
Exchange		✓	Configure Exchange ActiveSync settings
LDAP		✓	Configure connection to LDAP server
Contacts		✓	Configure access to CardDAV server
Calendar		✓	Configure access to CalDAV server
Network	✓	✓	Configure network setting on the device, including wireless and wired
VPN	✓	✓	Configure VPN settings: L2TP, PPTP, IPSec (Cisco), CiscoAnyConnect, Juniper SSL, F5 SSL, SonicWALL Mobile Connect, and Aruba VIA
Certificate	✓	✓	Allow the installation of PKCS1 and PKCS12 certificates
AirPlay	✓	✓	Define AirPlay destination settings
SCEP	✓	✓	Define connection to Simple Certificate Enrollment Protocol (SCEP) server
Web Clips		✓	Display defined Web Clips as application icons
Identification	✓		Configure identification information of user
AD Certificate	✓		Specify AD certificate settings
Directory	✓		Specify OD server settings
Restrictions	✓	✓	Define application and content restrictions (separate OS X and iOS versions)
Subscribed Calendars		✓	Configure calendar subscriptions

Preference	OS X	iOS	Description
APN		✓	Configure carrier settings such as the access point name (advanced use only)
Login Items	✓		Specify applications, items, and network mounts to launch at login
Mobility	✓		Define mobility settings for OS X clients to allow cached credentials and portable home directories
Dock	✓		Configure Dock behavior
Printing	✓		Configure printing settings and access to printers or print queues
Parental Controls	✓		Define settings for parental controls such as content filtering and time limits
Security and Privacy	✓	✓	Control if diagnostic and usage data gets sent to Apple; define password and lock restrictions, FileVault, plus whether user can override Gatekeeper (OS X only)
Custom Settings	✓		Apply custom preferences for items not defined in other payloads (similar to applying preference manifests in WGM)
Directory	✓		Configure binding to directory services
Time Machine	✓		Configure Time Machine preferences
Single Sign-On		✓	Configure Kerberos settings
Login Window	✓		Configure login window options, such as messages, appearance, access, and Login/LogoutHooks
Finder	✓		Configure Finder settings
Software Update	✓		Define an Apple Software Update server to be used by the computer
Accessibility	✓		Manage Accessibility settings

Preference	OS X	iOS	Description
Energy Saver	✓		Define Energy Saver policy such as sleeping, timed actions, and wake settings
Xsan	✓		Define Xsan membership
Custom Settings	✓		Apply custom preferences for items not defined in other payloads; similar to applying preference manifests in WGM

Layering and Multiple Profiles Considerations

In previous versions of OS X management, you could create different behaviors by layering management techniques reflecting users, groups of users, devices, and groups of devices. Although Profile Manager also shows those same four management levels, you need to be careful when building profiles.

The general rule is to avoid layering profiles that manage the same preferences, but this is not a strict rule. Some profiles can be additive, and others can collide, so you need to be aware of which are which.

Multiple profiles that contain different settings for the same preferences result in undefined results. There is no order of preference applied to the multiple profiles, so you will not have a predictable outcome.

Payloads that should remain exclusive include the following:

▶ AD Certificate

▶ APN

▶ Directory

▶ General

▶ Global HTTP Proxy

▶ Identification

▶ Restrictions

▶ Security & Privacy

▶ Single App Mode

▶ Single Sign-On

► Xsan

Payloads that can be combined include the following:

► Accessibility

► AirPlay

► AirPrint

► Calendar

► Certificate

► Contacts

► Content Filter

► Custom Settings

► Dock

► Domains

► Energy Saver

► Finder

► Fonts

► Exchange

► LDAP

► Login items

► LoginWindow

► Mail

► Messages

► Mobility

► Network

► Passcode

► Parental Controls

► Printing

► SCEP

► Software Update

► Subscribed Calendars

▶ Time Machine

▶ VPN

▶ Web Clips

Reference 11.2
Troubleshooting

Occasionally you'll have to troubleshoot profiles if things aren't working as you expect. Even a robust service such as Profile Manager can have an occasional issue.

Viewing Logs

The Profile Manager–related logs are at /Library/Logs/ProfileManager/; you can view them with Console by double-clicking the log file. Errors may be reported and listed in the logs. You can also view logs in the Server app.

Viewing Profiles

If a device is not behaving as expected, look at the list of installed profiles on the device and see whether the proper profiles have been installed. The solution may be as simple as applying the expected profile to the device.

Installing Profiles

If you're having problems installing a profile, you may have improper certificates. Review your Secure Sockets Layer (SSL) certificates for validity and make sure the Trust Profile has been installed on the device.

Problems Enrolling a Device

A trust profile must be installed prior to enrolling a device, unless you are using a certificate signed by a trusted certificate authority.

Pushing Profiles

If you're having problems pushing a profile, you may not have appropriate outbound ports open. Ports 443, 2195, 2196, and 5223 are APNs-related. Also, iOS uses the cellular network whenever possible, even if Wi-Fi is available.

Unexpected Profile Behavior

If the managed device doesn't seem to be acting the way you expect based on the way you set preferences in profiles, you may have multiple overlapping profiles. It is suggested not to have overlapping profiles that try to manage the same preferences; the results can be unpredictable.

Exercise 11.1
Use Profile Manager for Shared Devices

▶ **Prerequisites**

- ▶ "Exercise 4.2 Configure an Open Directory Certificate Authority" on page 152

- ▶ "Exercise 9.1 Create and Import Network Accounts" on page 292; or use the Server app to create network user Carl Dunn with an account name of carl and a password of net

- ▶ "Exercise 10.1 Turn On Profile Manager" on page 312

It's likely that your organization's needs are more complex than the two sample scenarios in this exercise and the next, but becoming familiar with these workflows will help you determine your own workflow.

In this exercise, you will use the Profile Manager service to manage devices that will be shared by more than user; you'll do this by managing by device group.

First you'll import a set of placeholders that represent devices you have not yet enrolled.

Prepare Profile Manager for Shared Devices

In the scenario for this section, you will create a device group and then create a configuration profile for that device group. You will import placeholders and then add the placeholders to that device group. To help streamline enrolling shared devices with your Profile Manager service, you will create an enrollment profile. It's outside the scope of this course, but you could use this enrollment profile with System Image Utility to streamline enrolling Mac computers or with Apple Configurator to streamline enrolling iOS devices.

Import Placeholders and Assign Them to the Device Group

To represent a lab full of Mac computers, your StudentMaterials folder has a text file in comma-separated value (CSV) format with a list of imaginary serial numbers of devices. Import this list, and then assign the devices to a device group.

1   Perform these exercises on your administrator computer. If you do not already have a connection to your server computer with the Server app on your administrator computer, then connect to it with the following steps: Open the Server app on your administrator computer, choose Manage > Connect to Server, select your server, click Continue, provide administrator credentials (Administrator Name: ladmin, Administrator Password: ladminpw), deselect the "Remember this password" checkbox, and then click Connect.

2   Select Profile Manager in the services sidebar.

3   Click the Open Profile Manager link at the bottom of the pane; this opens https:// server*n*.pretendco.com/profilemanager in your default browser (where *n* is your student number).

> Open Profile Manager ⊙

4   Your administrator computer is configured to trust your server's Open Directory certification authority because of a previous exercise ("Exercise 4.3 Configure Your Administrator Computer to Trust an SSL Certificate" on page 159). If you are using a different computer and see the message that Safari can't verify the identity of the website, click Continue.

5   At the Please Log In pane, provide administrator credentials (User Name: ladmin, Password: ladminpw), deselect the "Keep me logged in" checkbox, and then click Connect.

6   If Safari asks "Would you like to save this password?" then click Never for This Website.

7   In the Profile Manager web app sidebar, select Device Groups.

You could click Add Device Group and then add devices to it, but for this exercise you will import placeholders and then click a button to automatically create a device group with the devices you just imported.

8   In the Profile Manager web app sidebar, select Devices.

9   Click the Add (+) button in the Devices pane, and choose Import Placeholders.

10   In the Open dialog, click Documents in the sidebar, and then navigate to /StudentMa-terials/Lesson11/.

11   Select MacLab.csv, press the Space bar to get a Quick Look preview of the file contents, press the Space bar again to dismiss the preview, and then click Choose.

12   At the success dialog, click Create Device Group.

13   Enter Lab Mac Computers to replace the default name of New Device Group, and then press Tab to stop editing the name.

Note that you imported five placeholders, indicated by the text "5 Members."

14   At the lower-right corner of the Profile Manager web app, click Save.

15   Click the Members tab, and confirm that your five placeholders are listed.

Create a Configuration Profile for the Device Group

Create a configuration profile that can't be removed without an authorization password; for the purposes of this exercise, use profilepw; of course, in a production environment, you should use a secure password.

1   Click the Settings tab.

2   Under Settings for Lab Mac Computers, click Edit.

3   In the Description field, enter Settings for the Mac computers in the lab. Includes Directory, Login Window, and Dock payloads.

Profile Distribution Type
The manner in which the profile is distributed to devices
◉ Automatic Push   ○ Manual Download

Organization
Name of the organization for the profile

Pretendco Project 17

Description
Brief explanation of the content or purpose of the profile

Settings for the Mac computers in the lab. Includes Directory, Login Window, and Dock payloads.|

Security
Controls when the profile can be removed

Always   ⬍

Automatically Remove Profile
Settings for automatic profile removal

Never   ⬍

4   Click the Security pop-up menu, and choose With Authorization.

5   In the Authorization Password field, enter profilepw.

Security
Controls when the profile can be removed

With Authorization   ⬍

Authorization Password

•••••••••

6   In the sidebar, scroll down to the OS X section, select Directory, and then click Configure.

Configure Directory
Use this section to define settings for Directory.

Configure

7 In the Server Hostname field, enter server*n*.pretendco.com (where *n* is your student number).

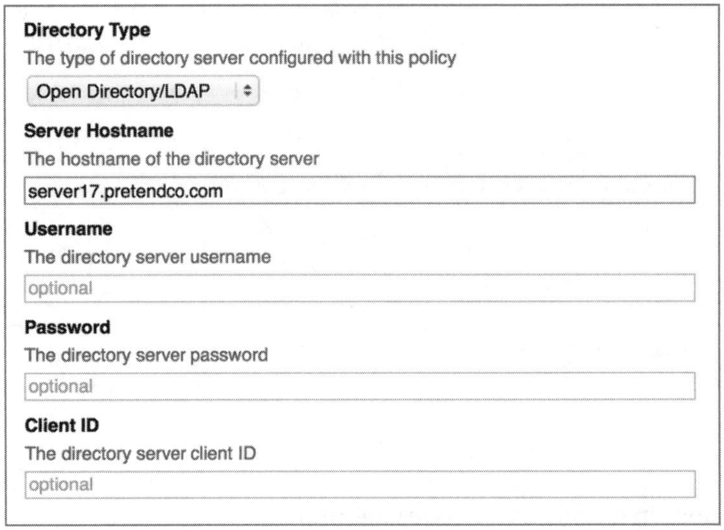

Directory Type
The type of directory server configured with this policy

Open Directory/LDAP ⎪ ⬍

Server Hostname
The hostname of the directory server

server17.pretendco.com

Username
The directory server username

optional

Password
The directory server password

optional

Client ID
The directory server client ID

optional

8 In the sidebar, select Login Window, and then click Configure.

9 Select the checkbox "Show additional information in the menu bar."

10 In the Banner field, enter Property of PretendCo.

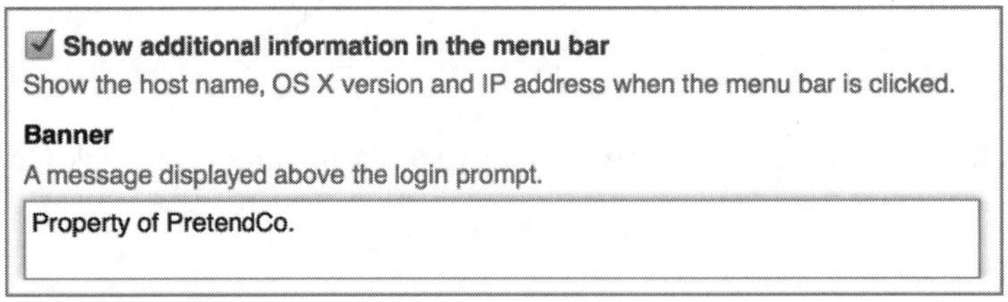

☑ **Show additional information in the menu bar**
Show the host name, OS X version and IP address when the menu bar is clicked.

Banner
A message displayed above the login prompt.

Property of PretendCo.

11 In the sidebar, select Dock, and then click Configure.

12 For Position, select Left.

Display Settings

Settings for Dock behavior and appearance

Dock Size:	6
Magnification:	None
Position:	● Left ○ Bottom ○ Right

13 Click OK to save the change.

14 Confirm that Settings for Lab Mac Computers displays the Directory, Dock, and Login Window payloads.

Settings for Lab Mac Computers

General   Directory   Dock

Login Window

Download   Edit

15 Click Save to save the change.

Test the Configuration Profile

Test by manually downloading and installing the configuration profile. Then use Profiles preferences to remove it.

> **NOTE ▶** If you changed the configuration of your Dock, for the duration of this section of the exercise, set your Dock to display at the bottom of the screen. Open System Preferences, select Dock, and then for "Position on screen," select Bottom.

1 Under Settings for Lab Mac Computers, click Download.

Settings for Lab Mac Computers

General   Directory   Dock

Login Window

Download   Edit

Safari automatically saves the file named Settings_for_Lab_Mac_Computers.mobile-config to your Downloads folder and opens Profiles preferences.

2   Click Show Profile.

3   Inspect the information about this configuration profile.

4   Click Continue.

5   At the Directory Binding pane, leave the optional fields blank, and click Install.

6   You must have administrator credentials to install profiles. Provide administrator credentials, and then click OK.

7   A spinning gear appears with the text "Installing...." Wait a few moments while the profile installs.

8   Confirm that your Dock moved to the left side of your screen.

9   System Preferences is already open; confirm that the profile appears in the list of profiles. Inspect the profile details.

10   Click the Show All (grid of dots) icon in the toolbar.

11   Select Users & Groups, and then select Login Options.

12   Confirm that Network Account Server is set to your server.

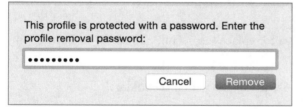

13 Press Command-Shift-Q to log out, if necessary select "Reopen windows when logging back in," and then click Log Out.

14 Confirm that Other is a choice to select for logging in and that the banner message you entered appears.

15 Log in as Local Admin.

16 In System Preferences, click Show All.

17 Select Profiles.

18 Select the Settings for Lab Mac Computers profile.

19 Click the Remove (–) button, and then click Remove.

20 In the profile removal password field, enter profilepw, and then click Remove.

21 If you are prompted with "Profiles wants to make changes. Type your password to allow this." then type your password (since you're logged in as Local Admin, your password is ladminpw), and click OK.

22 Confirm that your Dock moved back to the bottom of the screen.

23 Log out, confirm that Other is no longer displayed, and confirm that your banner message is no longer displayed.

24 Log in as Local Admin.

25 Open Users & Groups preferences, select Login Options, and confirm that your server is no longer listed as the network account server.

Create an Enrollment Profile

When you install an enrollment profile on a Mac computer or an iOS device, it automatically enrolls into the mobile device management (MDM) service specified in the enrollment profile. By default, a new enrollment profile is restricted to be used only by devices that have placeholders; for more flexibility, remove that restriction.

1 If your Profile Manager web app is not open, open https://servern.pretendco.com/profilemanager in your browser (where *n* is your student number), at the Please Log In pane, provide administrator credentials (User Name: ladmin, Password: ladminpw), deselect the "Keep me logged in" checkbox, and then click Connect.

2 At the bottom-left corner of the Profile Manager web app, click the Add (+) button, and choose Enrollment Profile.

3 Enter Unrestricted Enrollment Profile to replace the default name of New Enrollment Profile.

4 Deselect the checkbox "Restrict use to devices with placeholders."

5 Click Save to save the change.

6 Click Download to download Unrestricted_Enrollment_Profile.mobileconfig for future use.

This automatically opens Profiles preferences.

7   Click Cancel to not install the enrollment profile.

8   Quit System Preferences.

You could use this enrollment profile with Apple Configurator to enroll iOS devices or with System Image Utility to create an image that automatically enrolls a newly imaged Mac computer, though both uses are outside the scope of this course.

Clean Up

1   On your administrator computer, open the Downloads folder.

2   Drag Settings_for_Lab_Macs.mobileconfig to the Trash.

3   Leave the enrollment profile for future use.

In this exercise, you imported a set of placeholders, created a device group from those placeholders, and created a sample configuration profile. To test the configuration profile, you manually downloaded the profile and confirmed its effects, and then you removed the profile with Profiles preferences. You also created an unrestricted enrollment profile for future use with organizational-owned computers and devices.

Exercise 11.2
Use Profile Manager for One-to-One Devices

▶ **Prerequisites**

- ▶ "Exercise 4.2 Configure an Open Directory Certificate Authority" on page 152

- ▶ "Exercise 9.1 Create and Import Network Accounts" on page 292; or use the Server app to create network user Carl Dunn with an account name of carl and a password of net

- ▶ "Exercise 10.1 Turn On Profile Manager" on page 312

In this exercise, you'll use the Profile Manager web app to prepare to manage devices that are assigned to a user, perhaps in a bring-your-own-device (BYOD) scenario.

You will use your existing user group and prepare for users to self-enroll using the My Devices portal. You will create a configuration profile for the group and enroll your administrator computer with your Profile Manager service to confirm that the configuration profiles automatically take effect. You can optionally enroll an iOS device as well.

Prepare Profile Manager for One-to-One Devices

1 Perform these exercises on your administrator computer. If you do not already have a connection to your server computer with the Server app on your administrator computer, then connect to it with the following steps: Open the Server app on your administrator computer, choose Manage > Connect to Server, select your server, click Continue, provide administrator credentials (Administrator Name: ladmin, Administrator Password: ladminpw), deselect the "Remember this password" checkbox, and then click Connect.

2 Select Profile Manager in the services sidebar.

3 Click the Open Profile Manager link at the bottom of the pane; this opens https://server*n*.pretendco.com/profilemanager in your default browser (where *n* is your student number).

4 At the Please Log In pane, provide administrator credentials (User Name: ladmin, Password ladminpw), deselect the "Keep me logged in" checkbox, and then click Connect.

5 In the Profile Manager web app sidebar, select Groups.

6 In the Groups column, select Contractors.

7 Click the Settings tab.

8 Under Settings for Contractors, click Edit.

Settings for Contractors

General

Download   Edit

9   In the Description field, enter Settings for the Contractors group. Includes settings to force a passcode, include a web clip, and display the Dock on the right.

Description

Brief explanation of the content or purpose of the profile

Settings for the Contractors group. Includes settings to force a passcode, include a web clip, and display the Dock on the right.

10   Select Passcode in the sidebar, and then click Configure.

11   Click the pop-up menu "Minimum passcode length," and choose 8.

☑ **Allow simple value**
Permit the use of repeating, ascending, and descending character sequences

☐ **Require alphanumeric value**
Requires passcode to contain at least one letter and one number

8 ⬍ **Minimum passcode length**
Smallest number of passcode characters allowed

-- ⬍ **Minimum number of complex characters**
Smallest number of non-alphanumeric characters allowed

12   Select Web Clips in the sidebar, and then click Configure.

13   In the Label field, enter iPad in Business.

14   In the URL field, enter https://www.apple.com/ipad/business/it/.

15   Select Dock in the sidebar, and then click Configure.

16   For the Position, select Right.

Display Settings

Settings for Dock behavior and appearance

Dock Size:	6 ⬍
Magnification:	None ⬍
Position:	◯ Left ◯ Bottom ⦿ Right

17 Click OK.

18 Confirm that Settings for Contractors displays payloads for Passcode, Web Clips, and Dock.

Settings for Contractors ⊖

General   Passcode   Web Clips

Dock

Download   Edit

19 Click Save.

20 At the notice that this may cause settings to be pushed to devices, click Save.

If there were any devices enrolled with your Profile Manager service that were associated with a user who was a member of the Contractors group, that device would automatically have this configuration profile applied to it.

Enroll Using the User Portal

The user portal provides simple access for users to log in, apply profiles, and manage their devices. The portal is accessed via any modern web browser; by simply publishing the website, users anywhere in the world can enroll their devices—whether they be a Mac with OS X or an iOS device. Through the portal, users can lock or wipe their enrolled devices.

In this exercise, you'll create a new administrator user with the same credentials as a local network account. Then you'll log in to your administrator computer with those credentials and use those same credentials to enroll in your server's Profile Manager service.

Create a New Administrator Account

In this scenario, a user would create a new computer account on a Mac computer after taking it out of the box, and that account would be an administrator account. In this exercise, since you don't have a new computer fresh out of the box, you will use System Preferences to create a new account on your administrator computer.

1   Open System Preferences, and then open Users & Groups preferences.

2   Click the lock icon, provide administrator credentials, and click Unlock.

3   Click the Add (+) button.

4   Click the New Account pop-up menu, and choose Administrator.

5   Use the following settings:

> ▶ Full Name: Carl Dunn
> ▶ Account Name: carl
> ▶ Password: Select "Use separate password."
> ▶ Password: net

New Account:	Administrator ⌄
Full Name:	Carl Dunn
Account Name:	carl
	This will be used as the name for your home folder.
Password:	◯ Use iCloud password
	⦿ Use separate password
	••• 🔑
	•••
	Hint (Recommended)
(?)	Cancel Create User

6   Click Create User.

7   Press Shift-Command-Q to log out, and then click Log Out (note that pressing Option-Shift-Command-Q logs you out without the need to confirm by clicking Log Out).

Enroll Your Administrator Computer with Carl Dunn's Credentials

In the BYOD scenario for this exercise, use the same computer account credentials as local network account credentials for Carl Dunn. The constraints of this exercise prevent using an iCloud password instead of a separate password.

> **MORE INFO ▸** The following steps are for enrolling a Mac computer running OS X, but the process for enrolling an iOS device is conceptually and visually similar. The biggest difference is that there is no concept of a local account on an iOS device, which is inherently personal.

1   At the login window, select Carl Dunn, enter the password net, and press Return to log in.

2   If you did not successfully bind your administrator computer to your server's shared directory node, then at the Sign in with Your Apple ID pane, select "Don't sign in," click Continue, and at the confirmation dialog, click Skip.

3   Open Safari, click the Search and Location field, enter https://server*n*.pretendco.com/mydevices (where *n* is your student number), and press Return.

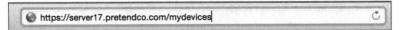

4   Your administrator computer's System keychain is configured to trust your server's Open Directory certification authority (CA) and certificates with a certificate chain that ends with that CA because of a previous exercise ("Exercise 4.3 Configure Your Administrator Computer to Trust an SSL Certificate" on page 159). If you are using a different computer and see the message that Safari can't verify the identity of the website, click Continue.

Enrolling with your server's Profile Manager service automatically configures your computer or device to trust your server's Open Directory certificate authority.

5   Through a series of redirects, Safari displays a Please Log In dialog.

Enter Carl Dunn's user name (carl) and password (net), and then click Log In.

Remember that for the purposes of this exercise, the computer account and local network account credentials are the same.

6 At the dialog about saving the password, click Never for This Website.

The Devices tab displays the device you are using.

7 Click Enroll.

This automatically downloads the file mdm_profile.mobileconfig to your Downloads folder and opens Profiles preferences.

8 In the next pane, you are asked whether you want to install Remote Management, which allows the server to manage that device.

Click Show Profile, and inspect the profile details.

Note that if the System or login keychain on your administrator computer is not configured to trust your server's Open Directory CA, then the profile will be labeled "Unverified" instead of "Verified."

Install "Remote Management"?
This profile will configure your Mac for the following: 2 Certificates, Mobile Device Management, and SCEP Enrollment Request.

Remote Management
Pretendco Project 17 **Verified**

Description Allows the server to manage your device.
Signed server17.pretendco.com Code Signing Certificate
Received Oct 8, 2014, 4:54 PM

Settings SCEP Enrollment Request server17.pretendco.com
Mobile Device Management

Hide Profile   Cancel   Continue

9   Click Continue.

10 You are given a warning asking if you want to continue the installation.
Click Show Details, and review the details.

Are you sure you want to install profile "Remote Management"?
The admin of "https://server17.pretendco.com/devicemanagement/api/device/mdm_connect" will be able to remotely administer this Mac.

MDM
The admin of "https://server17.pretendco.com/devicemanagement/api/device/mdm_connect" will be allowed to remotely administer this Mac. The admin will be able to:

* Erase all data on this computer
* Add or remove configuration profiles
* Add or remove provisioning profiles
* Lock screen
* Change settings
* Application and media management
* Query security information
* Query restrictions

Hide Details   Cancel   Install

11 Click Install.

12 The Username field contains the username of the currently logged-in user, Carl Dunn. In the Password field, enter net, and click OK.

13 Now that the profile has been installed on the computer, note that the Profiles column is updated to include user profiles and device profiles.

Confirm the Administrator Computer Is Enrolled

1 Click the Safari window. If the Safari window does not automatically refresh to display information about your Mac computer, press Command-R to refresh the view in the browser.

Note that your administrator computer is now listed on the Devices pane, with its serial number displayed.

This Mac   Remove

Serial Number: C02M31WBFD57

(Lock)

(Wipe)

From now on, any time you make a change to the configuration profile for the Contractors group and save the change, your Profile Manager automatically uses APNS to notify your Mac that it needs to check in with the Profile Manager service, which results in your Mac downloading the changed configuration profile and applying the changes.

Confirm the Effects of the Profile

1   Note that the Dock is displayed on the right side of the screen.

2   Hover your pointer next to the Trash in the Dock, and confirm that the web clip is displayed.

3   Click the web clip, and confirm that your default browser opens to the specified page.

4   Quit the browser.

Confirm the passcode restriction.

1   Open System Preferences, and then open the Users & Groups preferences.

2   Click Change Password.

3   Enter the following information:

 ▶ Old Password: net
 ▶ New Password: 12345
 ▶ Verify: 12345

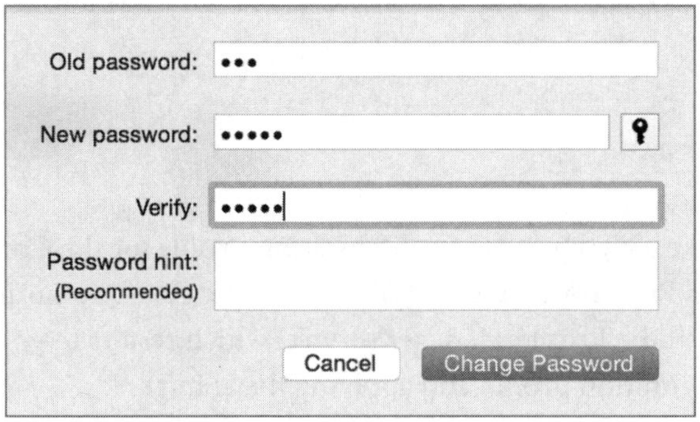

Old password:	•••
New password:	•••••
Verify:	•••••
Password hint: (Recommended)	

Cancel   Change Password

4   Click Change Password.

5   At the notice that your proposed password did not meet the requirements, click OK.

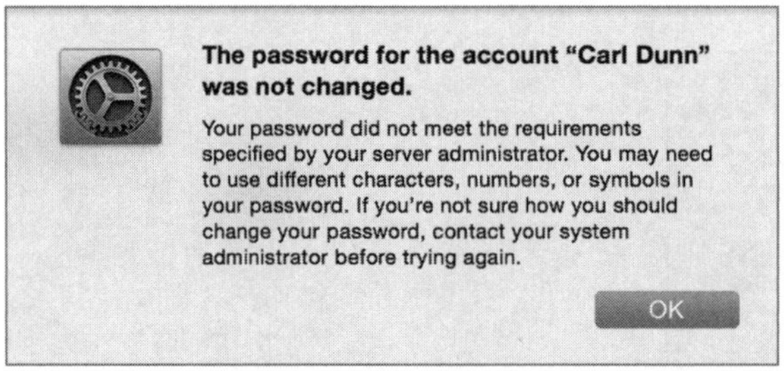

The password for the account "Carl Dunn" was not changed.

Your password did not meet the requirements specified by your server administrator. You may need to use different characters, numbers, or symbols in your password. If you're not sure how you should change your password, contact your system administrator before trying again.

OK

6   Quit System Preferences.

7   Press Command-Shift-Q to log out, and then click Log Out.

Demonstrate Remote Management

In a scenario that a device is lost, use the user portal to remotely lock a device.

> **NOTE ▶** Locking a Mac computer immediately reboots that computer, which can result in unsaved work. Before you lock your administrator computer, make sure you don't have any unsaved work. By contrast, locking an iOS device is the equivalent of pressing its Sleep button to lock the device.

> **NOTE ▶** Do not lose the passcode or you will not be able to get beyond the lock screen on your administrator computer.

1   On a different device, such as your server, open Safari.

    You could use your administrator computer, but using a different device reinforces the concept that a user can remotely manage devices that they enrolled.

2   In Safari open https://servern.pretendco.com/mydevices (where *n* is your student number).

3   At the Please Log In screen, enter Carl Dunn's user name (carl) and password (net), deselect the "Keep me logged in" checkbox, and then click Log In.

4   If you see a dialog about saving the password, click Never for This Website.

5   In the entry for your administrator computer, click the Lock button.

6   Enter a six-digit passcode. For this exercise, use a simple passcode: 123456.

7   Enter the passcode again to confirm you entered it correctly, and then click Lock.

8   At the confirmation dialog, click OK.

9   Click Logout in the Safari window.

    The remote computer reboots.

10 At the dialog to unlock the computer via the passcode, enter the passcode 123456, and
    then click the right arrow.

11 At the login window, log in as Carl Dunn with the password net.

Unenroll from the Profile Manager Service

When it becomes no longer appropriate for their computers and devices to be enrolled
with your server's Profile Manager service, a user can remove the management profile. If,
instead, you as an administrator use the Profile Manager web app to remove the computer
or device, profiles may remain installed.

To remove a management profile from an OS X computer, follow these steps:

1   Open System Preferences, and then open the Profiles preferences.

The various profiles installed on the computer are listed along with their contents and purposes.

2   Select the Remote Management profile, and click the Remove (–) button.

3   In the confirmation dialog box, click Remove.

4   You need to provide administrator credentials; in this case, you're logged in as Carl Dunn, so enter the password net, and click OK.

5   Confirm that the Dock moves back to its original location, the web link disappears from the Dock, and Profiles preferences is no longer displayed.

In this exercise, you created a configuration profile for a user group, enrolled a device using local network user credentials, and confirmed the user group configuration profile was automatically installed and immediately took effect. You demonstrated how you can use the user portal to lock a remote device. You unenrolled the device and confirmed that the effects of the configuration profile disappeared.

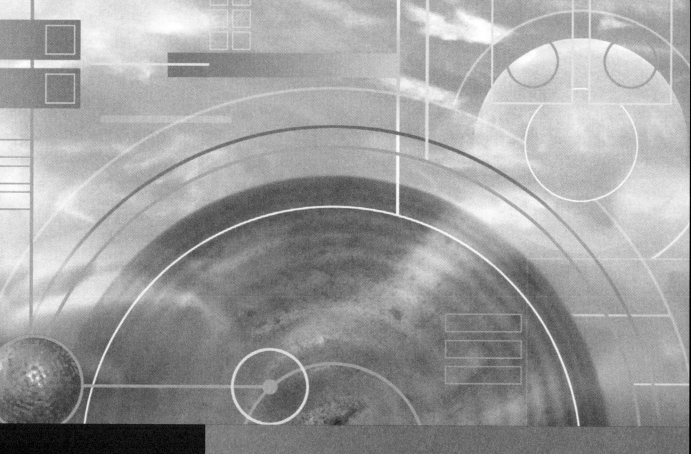

Sharing Files

Lesson 12

Configuring the File Sharing Service

It is simple to use OS X Server to share files across a network for your users, whether they are using OS X, Windows, or iOS. These are the four basic steps:

- Plan.
- Configure accounts.
- Configure the File Sharing service.
- Monitor the server.

GOALS

- Configure OS X Server to share files with iOS, OS X, and Windows clients over the network

- Troubleshoot the File Sharing service on OS X Server

In this lesson, you will explore the challenges associated with file sharing and the issues to consider when setting up file sharing. The main focus of the lesson is on setting up shared folders, also called share points, with appropriate access settings based on standard Portable Operating System Interface (POSIX) permissions and access control lists (ACLs) . This lesson also addresses automatic network mounts, which provide a network destination for home folders for network accounts and general file-sharing troubleshooting issues to consider when turning on the File Sharing service on OS X Server.

You will learn how to use the Server app to add and configure individual share points, and you'll use the Console application while logged in to the server to monitor logs.

Reference 12.1
Addressing the Challenges of File Sharing

When planning to offer file sharing, you need to consider a number of issues. Here are the obvious questions:

▶ What content will you share?

▶ What types of clients will be accessing your file server?

▶ What protocols will the client computers or devices use?

▶ What levels of access do your various users and groups require?

At first glance, these questions might seem relatively easy to answer, but in practice, especially in dynamic organizations, requirements can get complex, and it can be difficult to facilitate your users' access to the things necessary to remain productive without constant intervention from an administrator.

When accessing a file server, you typically have to authenticate, and then you see a choice of valid share points (also known as shares) available to mount. The following figure shows the dialog where you must select one or more share points (which appear as network volumes) to use.

When you navigate inside a mounted share point, folder badges (small icons displayed on the lower-right corner of the folder icon) indicate the access rights for the user account whose credentials you used when you connected to the file service. Folders display a red do-not-enter sign for folders that you are not authorized to access. In the following figure, the connected user does not have access to the Financials folder in the shared folder.

This is a combination of authorization for accessing the File Sharing service and authorization for accessing individual files and folders.

Authorization is a constant occurrence; every time a user accesses a file, the computer checks file permissions against the user's account information to see whether the user is authorized to use the file.

After completing this lesson, you will be in a good position to carefully consider your file-sharing needs before you implement file sharing on your server.

Defining File-Sharing Protocols

OS X Server includes a number of ways to share files. The method you select depends largely on the clients you expect to serve (although security is another factor to consider). You can use the Server app to enable the following file-sharing services:

▶ Server Message Block 3 (SMB3)—SMB3 is the new native file-sharing protocol for Yosemite and offers data protection since the data can be both encrypted and signed. This guide and the Server app use "SMB" to refer to SMB3.

▶ Apple Filing Protocol (AFP)—This protocol was the native file-sharing protocol for Mac computers up until OS X v10.9 Mavericks. OS X and OS X Server fall back to AFP for file sharing for Mac computers running operating systems earlier than OS X Mavericks.

▶ Web-based Distributed Authoring and Versioning (WebDAV)—This protocol is an extension to the web service protocol called Hypertext Transfer Protocol (HTTP), and it enables various clients, including iOS apps, to access files hosted by your server.

▶ File Transfer Protocol (FTP)—This protocol is compatible with many devices and is still widely used, but in most common uses, it doesn't protect the authentication traffic. For this reason, if FTP can be replaced with a more secure protocol, consider doing that. This file-sharing protocol is lightweight in the sense that it is simple and does not have all the features available in the other file-sharing services. FTP allows you to transfer files back and forth between client and server, but you cannot, for example, open a document over an FTP connection. The primary benefit of FTP is that it is ubiquitous. It is hard to find a Transfer Control Protocol (TCP)–capable computer or device that does not support FTP; some copiers and scanners, for example, place files in a shared folder via FTP.

NOTE ▶ The FTP service is separated from the File Sharing service and has its own pane in the Server app Advanced services section.

When Windows clients use NetBIOS to browse for network file servers, a computer running OS X Server with file sharing turned on appears just like a Windows server with file sharing turned on.

If you want to share a folder over WebDAV, you must explicitly turn on that service for that share point by selecting the Share over WebDAV checkbox.

A user with an iOS device can use a share point on your server, but only with apps that support WebDAV and only to share points for which you enable WebDAV by selecting the appropriate checkbox. A user must specify the URL for the WebDAV shared folder, which consists of the following:

▶   http:// or https://

▶   The server's address

▶   Optionally, the shared folder name

Here's an example: https://server17.pretendco.com/Projects.

If you do not provide a specific share point in the uniform resource locator (URL), all WebDAV-enabled share points will appear.

To access the WebDAV service protected with Secure Sockets Layer (SSL), users should supply "https://" instead of "http://" as part of the URL. Even without the benefit of SSL, the traffic for authentication is encrypted via WebDAV digest.

The following figure shows an example of using Keynote on an iOS device to open a connection to a WebDAV share point.

MORE INFO ▸ After signing in to your server's WebDAV service with an app like Keynote on iOS, the app displays the share points available via WebDAV; the user can navigate to a folder in which to open or save a document.

You can share a folder over several different protocols simultaneously. The FTP service is not configured in this manner and will be covered in a later section. When you create a share point in the Server app, the following happens:

▸ The share point is automatically enabled to be shared over SMB.

▸ The share point is automatically enabled to be shared over AFP.

▸ The share point is not automatically enabled for WebDAV.

▸ The share point is not automatically enabled for guest users.

OS X Server also provides file service via Network File System (NFS), which is the traditional method of file sharing for UNIX-based computers. NFS has its heritage in research facilities and academia in the 1980s. Although it can be convenient and flexible and can be used with Kerberos to provide robust security, when used with legacy clients, it can suffer from some security issues that do not affect the other protocols. Since OS X Server v10.7, the primary use for NFS is to facilitate use of the NetInstall service. NFS is also traditionally the way OS X Server provides files to UNIX or Linux computers. NFS is unable to be configured in the user interface of the Server app, and although OS X can use NFS, you should normally use SMB for Yosemite and Mavericks clients and use AFP for clients with earlier versions of OS X.

MORE INFO ▶ The NetInstall service defaults to using HTTP, but when you start the NetInstall service, OS X Server automatically creates the NetBootClients0 share point and makes it available to guest users over NFS. The "Allow guest users to access this share" checkbox for the NetBootClients0 share point has a dash to indicate that the value varies; in this case, guest access is enabled for NFS and AFP but not for SMB.

The configuration and management for NFS are outside the scope of this guide; for additional information, see Apple Support article HT202243, "OS X Server: How to configure NFS exports," and the Server Help menu.

Comparing File-Sharing Protocols

This table provides a short comparison of file-sharing protocols. There really isn't one best protocol. Instead, think of the protocols as different tools at your disposal to give different types of access

	SMB	AFP	WebDAV
Native platform	Multiplatform	OS X versions prior to Mavericks	Multiplatform
Browsable	Bonjour and NetBIOS	Bonjour	Not browsable
Example URL	smb://server17.pretendco.com/Users	afp://server17.pretendco.com/Users	https://server17.pretendco.com/Users

AFP and SMB are both full-featured file-sharing protocols with reasonably good security.

TIP ▶ If you use "https://" instead of "http://" in a WebDAV URL, both the authentication transaction and the payload (the files transferred) are protected from snooping. However, your WebDAV client may warn you or not allow you to access a WebDAV resource via HTTPS if the SSL certificate that the server uses is not valid or is not signed by a certificate authority (CA) that your computer or device trusts.

MORE INFO ▶ To provide WebDAV service to Active Directory accounts, you must configure the WebDAV service to use Basic authentication instead of Digest authentication. In this scenario, it is recommended that you also require SSL for the WebDAV service to protect the authentication. See the Apple Support article in Appendix B, "Additional Resources," appendix available with the guide's downloadable files.

WebDAV is a good alternative for FTP. When authenticating for FTP access, the user name and password are not encrypted at all. If possible, consider other protocols such as WebDAV to use instead of FTP to avoid security problems.

> **MORE INFO** ▶ Secure FTP (SFTP) uses the Secure Shell (SSH) service to securely transfer files using the SSH protocol. SFTP does not use the FTP service, and you must enable the SSH service for your users to use SFTP.

Planning File-Sharing Services

When setting up file-sharing services on OS X Server, proper initial planning can save you time in the long run. Follow these guidelines when you first start planning to implement file-sharing services.

Planning Your File Server Requirements

Determine your organizational requirements:

- ▶ How are your users organized?
- ▶ Is there a logical structure to follow for assigning users to groups that best addresses workflow needs?
- ▶ What types of computers will be used to access your file server?
- ▶ What share points and folder structures will be needed?
- ▶ Who needs what access to various files?
- ▶ How will users interact with one another when accessing these share points?
- ▶ How much storage space do you currently have, how much storage space do your users currently need, and at what rate will their need for storage grow?
- ▶ How will you back up and archive your storage?

These answers will dictate the file-sharing services you configure, as well as how you might organize groups and share points.

Using the Server App to Configure Users and Groups

The main goal is to end up with a group structure that best matches your organizational needs and allows easy maintenance over time. Setting up users and groups at the beginning is trivial. But, setting up users and groups that continue to work as the organization goes through natural changes over time is not as simple as it first appears. Nevertheless, having a logical group structure that can be used to allow and deny access to your server's file system will save you from continually adjusting file-service access later. OS X Server supports groups within groups and setting access control lists on folders.

> **TIP** ▶ For testing of groups, share points, and ACLs, you do not need to have all users entered. You may decide to test with a skeletal set of users and groups that meets the requirements of your organization. After verifying the groups and share points, you can then enter or import the full set of users.

Using the Server App to Start and Configure the File Sharing Service

The Server app is the main application you use to do the following:

▶ Start and stop the File Sharing service

▶ Add new share points

▶ Remove share points

For each share point, you can do the following

▶ Configure ownership, permissions, and the ACL for the share point

▶ Turn on or off SMB for the share point

▶ Turn on or off AFP for the share point

▶ Enable or disable WebDAV for the share point

▶ Allow or disallow guest access to the share point

▶ Make the share point available for network home folders

Performing Regular Maintenance

After you start the file-sharing service, you'll need to perform regular maintenance. You will probably use the Server app to perform the following maintenance tasks as your needs change:

▶ Use the Users pane to add users to groups, groups to users, and groups to groups

▶ Use the Users pane to modify the allowed services for each user

▶ Use the File Sharing pane to add and remove share points

▶ Use the File Sharing pane to modify ownership, permissions, and ACLs for share points

▶ Use the Storage pane to modify ownership, permissions, and ACLs for folders and files

Monitoring Your Server for Problems

Monitoring server usage is a valuable method to keep track of workflow. You can view graphs and watch for usual traffic patterns, usage spikes, and low-usage periods that you could use to plan backups or perform server maintenance.

You can monitor your server in several ways:

▶ Use the Server app Stats pane to monitor processor usage, memory usage, and network traffic

▶ Use the Server app Storage pane to check available disk space

▶ Use the Server app Connected Users tab in the File Sharing pane to monitor the number of connected users (this displays information about users connected via AFP and via SMB)

Be aware that if your server offers services other than file sharing, those other services could also affect resources such as network throughput, so you need to be careful interpreting the graphs.

Reviewing Logs

If you log in at the server, you can use the Console app to view logs, including the following:

▶ /Library/Logs/AppleFileService/AppleFileServiceError.log

▶ /Library/Logs/AppleFileService/AppleFileServiceAccess.log

▶ /Library/Logs/WebDAVSharing.log

▶ /var/log/apache2/access_log

▶ /var/log/apache2/error_log

From a remote computer (or at the server computer), you can use the Server app Logs pane to view logs related to file sharing, including the AFP Error log, and for WebDAV the error and access logs associated with the default and secure websites.

The AFP Error log displays events such as the AFP service stopping. In the Websites logs, you can use the search term "WebDAV" to separate log entries that relate to WebDAV from the log entries that relate to the Websites service in general.

You might use additional software, such as Terminal or third-party software, to monitor your server.

Reference 12.2
Creating Share Points

After determining server and user requirements and entering at least a sample set of users and groups that represents the organizational structure, the next step in sharing files is to configure your share points. A share point can be any folder or any volume that is mounted on the server. When you create a share point, you make that item and its contents available to network clients via the specified protocols. This includes deciding what items you want to give access to and organizing the items logically. It requires using your initial planning and knowledge of your users and their needs. You might decide that everything belongs in a single share point and use permissions to control access within that share point, or you might set up a more complex workflow. For example, you could have one share point for your copywriters and a separate share point for the copyeditors. Perhaps you would also have a third share point where both groups could access common items or share files. Setting up effective share points requires as much knowledge of your users and how they work together as it does the technology of share points.

The Server app File Sharing pane does not allow you to create a new shared folder in a location that you don't have write access to; by default the local administrator does not have write access to the root of the startup disk. In a production environment, you might share files from an external storage unit connected by Thunderbolt, Fibre Channel, Fire-Wire, or Universal Serial Bus (USB).

> **TIP** ▶ OS X Server for OS X Mountain Lion and previous versions automatically created a folder named Shared Items at the root of the startup disk; OS X Server for both Yosemite and Mavericks do not create this folder. See the section "Create a New Location for Shared Folders" on page 396 for a procedure to create that folder.

Exploring File Sharing

The On/Off switch turns the File Sharing service on or off. The Access segment of the File Sharing pane indicates the status of starting or stopping the File Sharing service. A service status indicator dot to the left of the service in the Server app sidebar appears when the service is on and disappears when the service is off.

The Shared Folders segment of the Settings pane is displayed by default, showing the following:

- ▶ The share points
- ▶ Add (+), Delete (–), and Edit (pencil icon) buttons for working with share points
- ▶ A text filter field to limit the share points displayed

NOTE ▶ The Server app displays the File Sharing pane slightly differently depending on whether you run the Server app on the server or on a remote Mac.

Describing the Default Share Points

You don't need OS X Server installed to offer shared folders. You can open System Preferences, open Sharing preferences, and select the File Sharing checkbox. But OS X Server gives you much more flexibility in file sharing than OS X itself offers.

Every time you use Users & Groups preferences in System Preferences to create a new local user account, OS X automatically adds that user's Public folder to the list of folders to share, with a customized folder name (like Local Admin's Public Folder). So when you first install OS X Server and look at the File Sharing pane, you see a list of shared folders that consists of the Public folders for local user accounts.

Although these default share points are convenient, you are free to remove them.

MORE INFO ▶ If you have configured and started the NetInstall service, you will see additional share points named NetBootClients0 and NetBootSP0, which are used for NetInstall. You can find more information about NetInstall in Lesson 14 "Leveraging NetInstall".

Adding and Removing Share Points

It's pretty simple to add a shared folder that allows your users to access the files in the folder using any combination of AFP, SMB, and WebDAV. You can use the Server app to select an existing folder or even to create a new folder to share.

To create a new shared folder, click Add (+) to open a pane that contains your startup volume and any other attached volumes. This pane is different depending on whether you run the Server app directly on your server or you run the Server app remotely. The following figure shows an example of the pane when you run the Server app directly on your server.

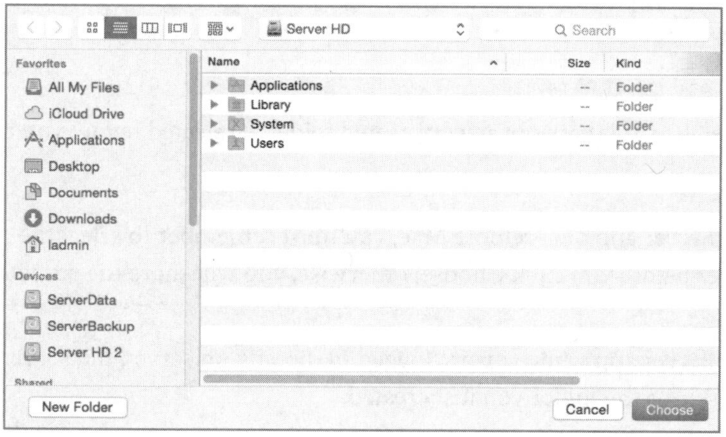

The following figure is what the pane looks like when you run the Server app on a remote Mac.

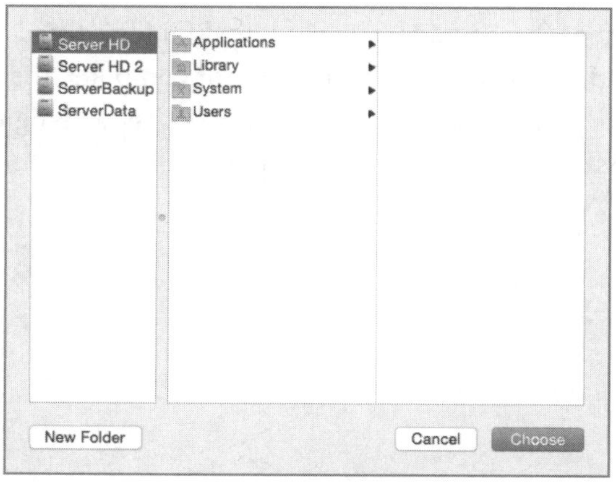

You have two options:

▶ Select an existing folder, and click Choose.

▶ Create a new folder, select the new folder, and click Choose.

If you click New Folder, you'll be asked for the name of the new folder. Assign the folder a name, and click Create.

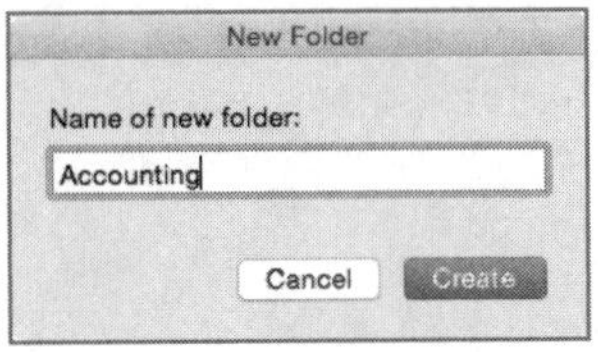

After you create a folder, be sure that your newly created folder is selected before you click Choose:

▶ When you use the Server app on a remote Mac, you must remember to select the newly created folder before you click Choose; otherwise, you will share the parent folder.

▶ When you use the Server app while you are logged in directly on server, the Server app automatically selects the folder you just created.

> **TIP** ▶ If you're using a remote Mac and forget to select the folder you just created and share the parent folder instead, don't worry; you can always remove the accidentally shared parent folder and then add the newly created folder.

The newly shared folder appears in a list of shared folders. Each shared folder is listed. Additionally, when you use the Server app from a remote administrator computer, the Server app displays any nonspecial share point with an icon of a network disk with figures of multiple users (as in the Accounting share point in the following figure).

When you use the Server app while logged in directly on the server computer, the Server app displays any nonspecial share point with an icon of a simple folder. In a remote Server app, the share points will use different icons.

Removing a share point is even easier. Select a share point, and click Remove (–). When you remove a share point, you don't remove the folder or its contents from the file system; you just stop sharing it.

Configuring Individual Share Points

In this section, you will look at what kinds of changes you can make to a share point.

To edit a share point's configuration, you could select a share point and do any of the following:

▶ Double-click the share point

▶ Click Edit (pencil icon)

▶ Press Command–Down Arrow

The editing pane includes the following:

► An icon for the folder

► The full path to the shared folder (such as /Volumes/Data/Projects/).

► The name of the shared folder (which by default is the name of the folder, but you can change it)

► An arrow icon next to View Files; when you click the icon, the Server app opens to that folder in the Storage pane of the Server app

► The Access pane or Permissions area, which includes standard UNIX ownership and permissions and can also include access control list information

► Checkboxes to enable and disable sharing over various protocols

► A checkbox to enable or disable guest access

► The checkbox "Make available for home directories over" (AFP or SMB)

The guest access checkbox affects both AFP and SMB services, so when you use the Server app to enable guest access for AFP, you also enable guest access for SMB. Users from OS X or Windows client computers can access guest-enabled share points without providing any authentication. When users on OS X select your server's computer name in their Finder window sidebar's Shared section, they automatically connect as Guest. In the following figure, notice that the Finder displays the text "Connected as: Guest" below the toolbar and displays the folders accessible to the Guest user.

Making Shared Folders Available for Home Directories

The checkbox "Make available for home directories over" (AFP or SMB) is available only after your server is configured as an Open Directory master or replica. This concept is also referred to as a network home directory or a network home folder.

A network home folder makes it easy for a user to move from one shared computer to another shared computer because when they log in, their computer automatically mounts their network home folder; files they save are stored on the server. Of course, the shared computers must be configured properly (a Mac must be bound to the shared directory) for this to work. Keep in mind that a local home folder (a home folder stored on the startup disk of the computer they use) may offer better performance than a network home folder and may be more appropriate for users who do not share computers.

> **NOTE ▶** A network home folder is not a backup system; be sure to back up network home folders, as well as local home folders. Keep in mind that OS X Server offers the Time Machine service, and there are plenty of third-party backup services as well.

After you make one or more shared folders "available for home directories," when you create and edit user accounts, you will see these shared folders available in the Home Folder pop-up menu, as shown in the following figure.

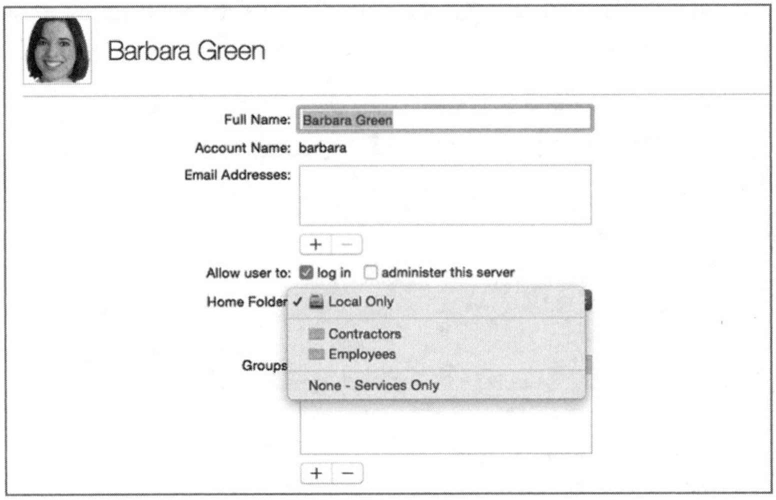

NOTE ▶ When you create a new user account, if there is no Home Folder pop-up menu, this indicates you do not have any folders configured to be available as network home folders.

Configuring a Group Folder

When you edit a group and select the checkbox "Give this group a shared folder," the Server app performs the following actions:

▶ Creates a Groups shared folder if necessary (creates a folder named Groups at the root of your startup disk if necessary and configures it as a shared folder)

▶ Creates a folder with that group's account name in the Groups share point

▶ Creates an access control entry (ACE) in the Groups folder ACL that gives the members of the group full access over their group folder so they can use their group folder for collaboration

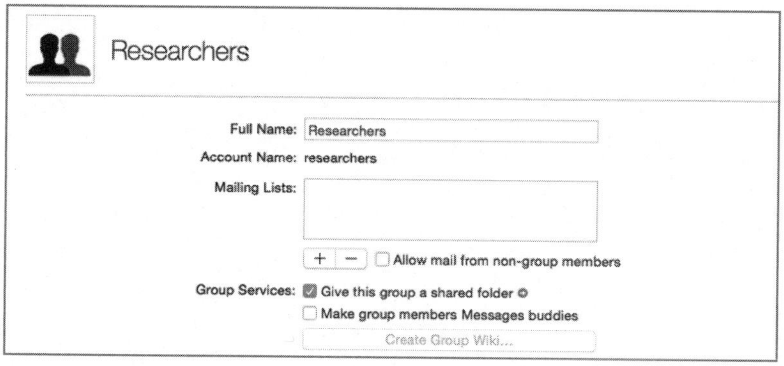

NOTE ▶ The behavior of the arrow icon next to the "Give this group a shared folder" checkbox depends on where you are running the Server app. If you click the icon while logged in on your server, the Finder opens to the Groups folder. If you click the icon while using the Server app on an administrator computer, it attempts to open an AFP connection for the Groups folder on your server. If the group folder does not yet exist, be sure to select the checkbox "Give this group a shared folder" and then click OK before you click the arrow icon.

Using the Connected Users Pane

The Connected Users pane displays information about the users who are currently connected via AFP or SMB (it does not include WebDAV and FTP connections).

The tab displays the number of connected users.

After you click the Connected Users tab, you see a list of connected users, including the following information:

▶ User name

▶ Address

▶ Idle time

▶ Type (AFP or SMB)

You can press Command-R (or choose View > Refresh) to refresh the list of currently connected users.

If you select a user currently connected, you can click the Disconnect button to forcibly disconnect that client's file-sharing connection, without any warning to the client.

Reference 12.3
Troubleshooting File-Sharing Services

Whether you're using AFP, SMB, or WebDAV, troubleshooting file-sharing services on OS X Server typically involves the following considerations:

▶ Service availability—Is the service turned on? For Time Machine, the File Sharing service must be turned on.

▶ User access—What users or groups should have access to the specific files and folders on the server, and are their appropriate permissions set correctly?

▶ Platform and protocol access—From which clients, such as Mac computers, Windows computers, or iOS devices, are users trying to access the server? What protocols are they using when accessing the server?

▶ Special needs—Are there any special circumstances, such as users needing access to files in a format not native to the system they are using?

► Concurrent access—Is there a possibility that in your users' workflow, there could be multiple clients simultaneously accessing the same files, regardless of the file-sharing protocols being used?

Although the different sharing protocols (AFP, SMB, WebDAV) support multiple platforms, it can be tricky to provide concurrent access to the same files, especially with the Auto Save and Versions document management features in OS X. Concurrent access means that multiple users are trying to access or modify the same files at the same time. Many times this is dependent on the specific cross-platform applications knowing how to allow multiple users to access the same file. OS X Server includes support for ACLs, and these ACLs are compatible with those from the Windows platform, so permissions mapping between Windows clients will be in line with what Windows users expect to see.

Reference 12.4
Providing FTP Service

You use the File Sharing service to serve files via AFP, SMB, and WebDAV (and NFS, but you don't use the Server app to configure NFS), and you use the FTP service to serve files via FTP. As stated earlier, in most cases, the FTP service leaves everything including the user name, password, and data in the files being transferred in clear text, so the FTP service might not be appropriate except for certain circumstances.

The FTP pane offers the On switch, the Share pop-up menu to choose the parent folder (the folder that contains the files you make available via FTP), a basic access pane, and a View Files link to open the parent folder in the Storage pane.

By default, if you simply turn on the FTP service, users who successfully authenticate see contents of the default Websites folder (see Lesson 20 "Hosting Websites" for more information).

However, you can click the Share pop-up menu to change the parent folder.

You can choose any share point configured on your server or configure another folder to be the parent folder and then choose it. If you configure a custom parent folder, the FTP pane offers the View Files link to open the folder in the Storage pane, and the Server app displays the Access section (you'll learn more about controlling access to files in Lesson 13 "Defining File Access").

In the following figure, the parent folder is a folder named FTPStuff, which is not other-wise a shared folder.

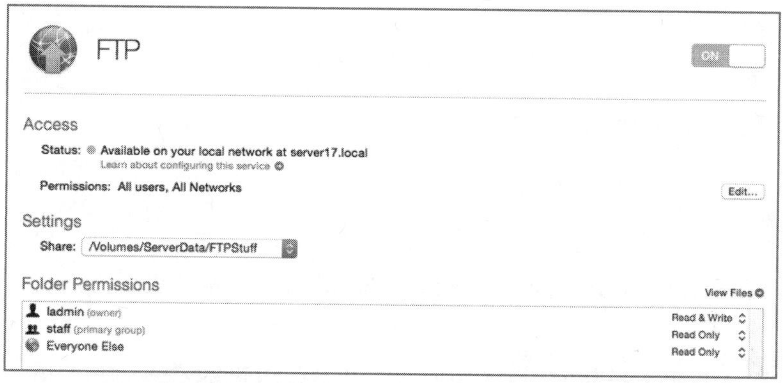

If, instead, you choose a parent folder that's configured as a file-sharing share point (regardless of whether your file-sharing service is started), the FTP pane offers the Edit Share Point link to open the share point in the File Sharing pane.

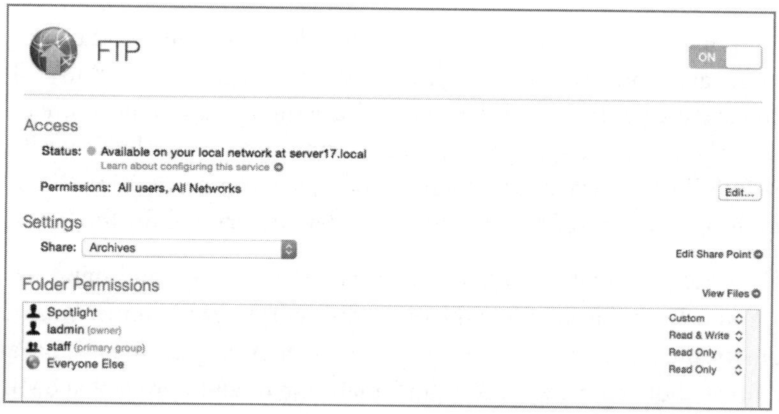

You can use the OS X command-line environment or third-party software to access the FTP service with read and write capabilities. In the Finder, you can connect to the FTP service by choosing Go > Connect to Server, entering ftp://*<your server's host name>*, providing credentials, and clicking Connect, but the Finder is a read-only FTP client.

> **MORE INFO** ▶ If someone attempts to connect anonymously, he will appear to make a successful connection but will see no files or folders available.

Because the FTP service normally does not encrypt the user name or password, it's recommended to leave the FTP service off unless there is no other alternative to meet your organization's needs to provide file service.

Exercise 12.1
Explore the File Sharing Service

▶ **Prerequisites**

- ▶ "Exercise 4.2 Configure an Open Directory Certificate Authority" on page 152

- ▶ "Exercise 9.1 Create and Import Network Accounts" on page 292; or use the Server app to create users Barbara Green and Todd Porter, each with an account name that is the same as their first name in lowercase, with a password of net, and each a member of a group named Contractors

In this exercise, you'll use the Server app to view the default shared folders, their respective protocols, and the available free space on your server's storage devices. You will create a new folder, make it available for file sharing, and use the Groups pane to create a shared folder for members of a group. You'll use the Connected Users tab to monitor connections to the File Sharing service and then disconnect a user connection. Finally, you'll stop sharing the default shared folder and the folder you created for this exercise.

A new feature of OS X Server for OS X Yosemite is the ability to encrypt and sign SMB connections. You will see that enabling the option to encrypt SMB connections for a shared folder automatically makes the AFP and WebDAV file-sharing protocols unavailable for that shared folder, but capturing packets and analyzing them to prove that SMB connections are encrypted is outside the scope of this guide.

1   Perform these exercises on your administrator computer. If you do not already have a connection to your server computer with the Server app on your administrator com-

puter, then connect to it with the following steps: Open the Server app on your administrator computer, choose Manage > Connect to Server, select your server, click Continue, provide administrator credentials (Administrator Name: ladmin, Administrator Password: ladminpw), deselect the "Remember this password" checkbox, and then click Connect.

2   In the Server app sidebar, click File Sharing. By default, you should have Local Admin's Public Folder as the only shared folder at this time.

Shared Folders

📁 **Local Admin's Public Folder** guest accessible

---

3   In the Shared Folders field, double-click Local Admin's Public Folder to edit that share point.

4   Confirm that the "Allow guest users to access this share" checkbox is already selected; select it if it is not selected.

NOTE ▶ When you turn on guest access, you turn it on for both the AFP and SMB protocols. Of course, for guests to access the share point using a given protocol, that protocol must be enabled for that share point; in other words, turning on guest access does not automatically turn on any specific protocol.

5   Select the checkbox "Encrypt connections."

6   Note that the checkboxes for AFP and WebDAV are automatically deselected and dimmed.

```
Share over:  ☑ SMB      ☐ AFP      ☐ WebDAV
Settings:  ☑ Encrypt connections
```

7   Deselect the checkbox "Encrypt connections."

8   Select the checkbox AFP.

9   Click OK to return from the Local Admin's Public Folder detail view to the File Sharing overview.

Stop and Start the File Sharing Service

Use the Server app to stop and start the File Sharing service and to verify that it is working properly. Regardless of how your File Sharing service is currently configured, start this exercise by making sure that "Enable screen sharing and remote management" is selected and that the File Sharing service is off.

1   In the Server app, select your server in the sidebar, and then click Settings.

2   Ensure that the checkbox "Enable screen sharing and remote management" is selected.

3   In the Server app sidebar, select the File Sharing service.

4   Click Off to turn off the service.

5   Confirm that the Status field displays that the service is Offline.

```
Access
    Status: ◎ Offline - Turn on service to share files
            Learn about configuring devices for this service ◎
```

On your administrator computer, observe how browsing for services with the Finder behaves before and after the File Sharing service is started.

1   On your administrator computer, in the Finder, press Command-N to open a new Finder window.

2   If your server appears in the Finder window sidebar, select your server.

> Shared
>   ⬜ server17

Otherwise, if there are enough computers on your network that your server does not appear in the Shared section of the Finder sidebar, click All, and then select your server.

Your server's File Sharing service is off, so Finder displays only the Share Screen button, not the Connect As button.

3   Close the Finder window.

NOTE ▶ Be sure to close the Finder window; otherwise, the rest of this section will not work as expected.

4   In the Server app, in the File Sharing pane, click On to turn on the service.

Once the File Sharing service has started, its service status indicator dot in the Server app sidebar reappears, and as shown in the following figure, the Status field displays information about connecting to the service.

> Access
>
> Status: ● "server17" is available on your local network in the Finder sidebar
>   Learn about configuring devices for this service ⊙

5   In the Finder, press Command-N to open a new Finder window.

6   If your server appears in the Finder window sidebar, select your server; otherwise, click All, and then select your server.

7   In the Finder, observe the change in your administrator computer's Finder: You are automatically connected as the Guest user, a Connect As button appears, and any shared folders identified as "guest accessible" in the Server app list of share points are listed in the Finder window (in this case, it is just Local Admin's Public Folder).

🖥 server17	
🔡 ☰ ⫘ ⫙ ▦ ⌄ ✱ ⌄ ⬆ ⬭	Q Search
Connected as: Guest	Share Screen... Connect As...
📁 Local Admin's Public Folder	

When you turned on the File Sharing service, your server used Bonjour to broadcast the availability of the File Sharing service to the local subnet. Your administrator computer's Finder received the broadcast and updated the Finder window sidebar accordingly.

Create a New Location for Shared Folders

For the purposes of the exercises, to create a new folder in which you will create new shared folders, you will do the following:

► Create a folder named Shared Items at the root of your startup disk
► Change the ownership of that folder

Although you use the Finder while logged in on the server, you will use the Storage pane of the Server app to become more familiar with that functionality.

You will learn more about permissions in Lesson 13 "Defining File Access".

1   On your administrator computer, in the Server app, select your server in the sidebar, and then click Storage.

2   In the Storage pane, click the List View button if it is not already selected.

3 Click the disclosure triangle to reveal the contents of your startup disk if necessary.

4 Select your server computer's startup disk.

5 Click the Action (gear icon) pop-up menu, and choose New Folder.

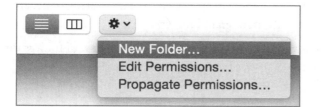

6 Enter Shared Items in the "Name of new folder" field, and then click Create.

7 Select the Shared Items folder.

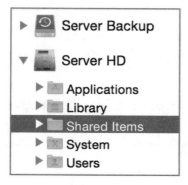

8 Click the Action (gear icon) pop-up menu, and choose Edit Permissions.

9   Double-click the name "root" in the User or Group column to edit it.

10 Enter ladmin, and then choose Local Admin (ladmin).

11 Click OK to save the change.

Create a New Shared Folder

A folder has to exist on the server to be used as a shared folder. One way to create a new folder is to log in on the server and create a new folder with the Finder. However, you can also use the Server app to make new folders on your server.

1   On your administrator computer, in the Server app, click the File Sharing pane, and then click the Add (+) button to add a new shared folder.

The Server app displays a list of volumes on the left and a column view of folders for the selected volume on the right.

NOTE ▶ If you create the new shared folder using your server computer rather than your administrator computer, the Server app displays files similar to what you would see in the Finder. Be sure to perform these steps from your administrator computer so your experience matches the steps in this exercise.

Although the contents look similar to that of the Finder, there is a significant difference: You are looking at the file system of the server, not the local file system of your administrator computer. Any folders you create or choose are ones that exist on your server's storage devices.

2   Select your server's startup volume, and then select the Shared Items folder.

3 Click the New Folder button to create a new folder on the server.

The Server app prompts you for the folder name.

4 Enter the name **Pending Projects**, and click Create.

5 Select the new Pending Projects folder.

6 Click Choose.

The new shared folder appears in the list of shared folders and is immediately available for file-sharing clients to use.

Note that if you use the Server app on your server instead of on your administrator computer, the Pending Projects shared folder appears with a blue folder icon instead of a special shared volume icon.

On your administrator computer, you're currently connected via SMB as the Guest user. Connect to the new folder as the user Barbara Green.

1   On your administrator computer, in the Finder, press Command-N to open a new Finder window if necessary, and select your server in the Finder window sidebar (or click All and select your server).

2   Click Connect As in the upper-right corner of the Finder window.

3   Provide Barbara Green's credentials (Name: barbara, Password: net), and click Connect.

    You see a list of shared folders you can access.

4   Open the Pending Projects folder.

5   Choose View > Show Status Bar.

    Note the pencil icon with a slash through it in the lower-left corner of the Finder window, indicating that you do not have write access to this folder. You will learn more about this in Lesson 13 "Defining File Access".

6   Close the Finder window.

It is easy to use the Server app to create a new shared folder, but you need to update the permissions in order to allow users to create files and folders in that folder. One big time-saver is the feature in the Server app to create a shared folder for a group, which you will use next.

Give a Group a Shared Folder

Use the Server app to give the Contractors group a shared folder. One of the great things about this feature is that you do not need to perform any additional configuration to give users shared read and write access to the resources they create in this shared folder.

You'll give the Contractors group a shared folder and then confirm that members of the group have read and write access to resources in the folder.

1   In the Server app sidebar, select Groups.

2   Click the pop-up menu, and choose Local Network Groups.

3   If the lock at the bottom of the pane is locked, click it, provide directory administrator credentials (Administrator Name: diradmin, Administrator password: diradminpw), leave the "Remember this password in my keychain" checkbox unselected, and click Authenticate.

4   Double-click the Contractors group to edit that group.

5   Select the checkbox "Give this group a shared folder."

Group Services: ☑ Give this group a shared folder ⊙
                ☐ Make group members Messages buddies
                    Create Group Wiki...

Members: Gary Pine
          Lucy Sanchez
          Maria Miller
          Sue Wu
          Todd Porter
          + −

Keywords:
Notes:
                            Cancel   OK

6   Click OK to create the shared folder in the Groups folder.

This creates a folder named Groups at the root of your startup disk if it did not previously exist and configures it as a shared folder.

7   In the Server app sidebar, select File Sharing to return to that pane.

Use the following steps to confirm that a member of the Contractors group can edit files in the Contractors group folder. You should still be connected to the server as the user Barbara Green, who is a member of the Contractors group.

Confirm that you are still connected as Barbara Green.

1   On your administrator computer, in the Finder, press Command-N to open a new Finder window.

2   In the Finder window sidebar, select your server, or click All and select your server.

3   If you do not see "Connected as: barbara" under the Finder window toolbar, click Connect As, provide barbara's credentials (Name: barbara, Password: net), and click Connect.

4   Open the Groups folder.

5   Open the contractors folder.

Note that the folder's name is based on the short name of the group.

6   Create a new folder by pressing Command-Shift-N, enter Barbara Created This as the folder name, and press Return to save the name change.

Note that when you view the contractors folder in the Finder, no icon appears in the lower-left corner of the Finder window. This means you have read and write access to this folder (because the Server app automatically configures read and write access for members of the group).

Connect as Todd Porter, another member of the Contractors group, and confirm that you can edit the resources Barbara Green placed into the folder.

1   In the Finder window, click the Eject icon next to your server sidebar to eject the volume.

Shared

　　⬚ server17　　　　　　　　　⏏

2   Click Connect As, provide user credentials for a different user in the group (Name: todd, Password net), and click Connect.

3   Open the Groups folder, and then open the contractors folder.

4   Press Command-Shift-N to create a new folder, enter Todd Created This as the folder name, and press Return to save the name change.

5   While you are still connected as Todd Porter, drag the folder the other user created (named Barbara Created This) to the Trash to demonstrate that you can modify a resource a different user created.

When you are asked if you are sure, click Delete.

View and Disconnect Connected Users

Use the Connected Users tab to view the users who are currently using your server's File Sharing service.

1 In the File Sharing pane, click the Connected Users tab.

2 Choose View > Refresh (or press Command-R) to refresh the number of connected users.

3 Select the connected user; the user with the short name of todd should still be connected from the steps of the previous section.

4 Click Disconnect.

5 At the confirmation dialog, click Disconnect.

6 In the Finder, confirm that you are no longer connected to your server's shared folder; confirm that the Eject button is no longer next to the name of your server in a Finder window sidebar.

Clean Up

You will remove the Pending Projects and the Local Admin's Shared Folder shared folders since you will not use them for any other exercises.

1 On your administrator computer, in the Server app sidebar, select File Sharing.

2 Click the Settings tab.

3 Select the Pending Projects shared folder.

4 Click Remove (–), and at the confirmation dialog, click Remove.

Note that the contents of the shared folder will not be deleted.

5 Select the Local Admin's Public Folder shared folder.

6   Click Remove (–), and at the confirmation dialog, click Remove.

You made the Finder status bar visible; hide it so that the figures in the rest of the exercises are consistent with what you see on your screen.

1   In Finder, choose View > Hide Status Bar.

You used the Server app to view the default shared folders, their respective protocols, and the available free space on your server's storage devices. Then you created a folder at the root of your startup disk as a location for new shared folders, created a new folder there, and made it available for file sharing. You created a group folder and saw that you do not need to take any extra steps to grant write access to this folder for members of the group. You used the Connected Users tab to monitor and disconnect user connections.

You will learn more about how OS X Server controls access to files, so you have the ability to modify resources other users create, in Lesson 13 "Defining File Access".

Exercise 12.2
Use Logs to Troubleshoot Problems with File Sharing

▶ **Prerequisite**

   ▶   "Exercise 12.1 Explore the File Sharing Service" on page 392

Inspect the AFP Access Log

The AFP Access Log keeps track of AFP activity.

1   On your administrator computer, if you are not already connected to your server, open the Server app, connect to your server, and authenticate as a local administrator.

2   In the Server app sidebar, select Logs.

3   Click the pop-up menu, and choose AFP Access Log.

4   Note that you see activity that includes connecting to, disconnecting from, and creating files in shared folders.

Note that SMB is the default file-sharing protocol for OS X Mavericks and later, so the folders you created in this exercise were created via SMB and are not included in the AFP Access Log.

Inspect the AFP Error Log

Given the classroom nature of the course, there may be few or no error messages within the logs. However, you should practice locating the logs and viewing their contents when you are experiencing no issues.

1   In the Server app sidebar, select Logs.

2   Click the pop-up menu, and choose AFP Error Log.

There shouldn't be much here under normal operation.

3   Click the pop-up menu, and choose one of the logs in the Websites section.

If you haven't accessed the File Sharing service via WebDAV, you will not see any WebDAV information in any of the Websites logs.

You used the Server app to inspect various logs. Remember that even though the logs are stored on the server, you can use the Server app remotely to inspect the logs.

Lesson 13
Defining File Access

Now that Lesson 12 "Configuring the File Sharing Service" has familiarized you with the file-sharing protocols you can enable, as well as the basics of creating, removing, and editing share points, it's time to configure access to files. For access to files and folders, OS X Server uses basic file permissions in addition to optional access control lists (ACLs) to make authorization decisions about access to files and folders. In OS X, every file and every folder has a single user account assigned as its "owner," a single group associated with it, and an optional ACL. Access permissions are assigned for the owner, for the group, and for everyone else, and the optional ACL adds additional permissions information.

When a file-sharing client uses the File Sharing service, she must authenticate as a user (or as a guest if you turned on guest access for the share point). A remote user has the same access to files over file sharing that she would have if she logged in locally with the same user credentials she provided to mount the share point.

This lesson covers how to use the Server app to configure access to files.

Reference 13.1
Configuring Access to Share Points and Folders

Once you've created a share point and determined the protocols you will use, you can begin to address levels of access within that share point. You need to consider POSIX privileges (UNIX-based ownership and permissions) as well as file system ACLs. Using this flexible system, you can apply complex access settings to any folder or file.

You can configure access for your shared folders with the Server app File Sharing pane, and you can configure access for any folder or file with the Server app Storage pane. Be aware that these two panes behave differently, and they display information differently. This guide first addresses the File Sharing pane; then it addresses the Storage pane.

Configuring Basic Access with the Server App File Sharing Pane

To configure access settings for a share point, use the Permissions window when viewing that share point. The standard POSIX settings are listed with the owner's full name, followed by the word "owner" in parentheses; the full name of the group associated with the folder, followed by the words "primary group" in parentheses; and Everyone Else.

In the following figure, the local user Local Admin is the owner, and the local group named Staff is the primary group associated with this sample share point.

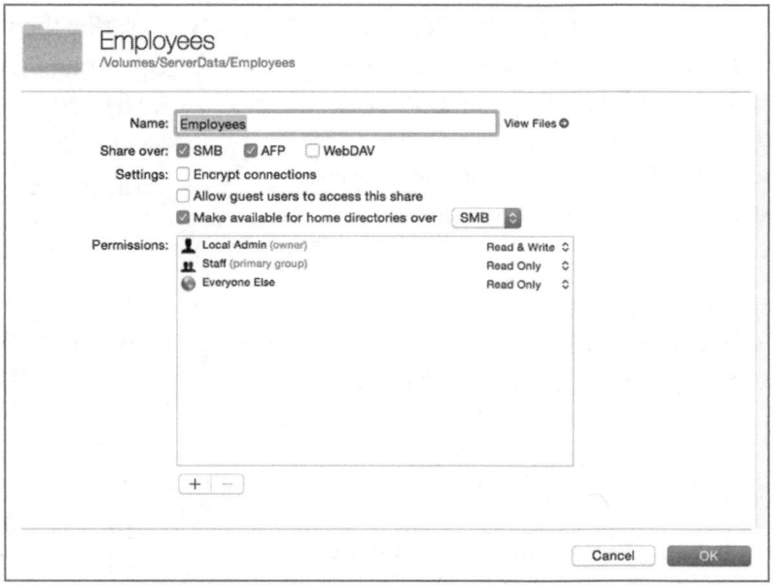

If there are any access control entries in that folder's ACL, these ACEs will appear above the POSIX entries. In the following figure, the first entry in the Access field is an ACE for the local network group ProjectAdmins, and the second is an ACE for the local network group Developers.

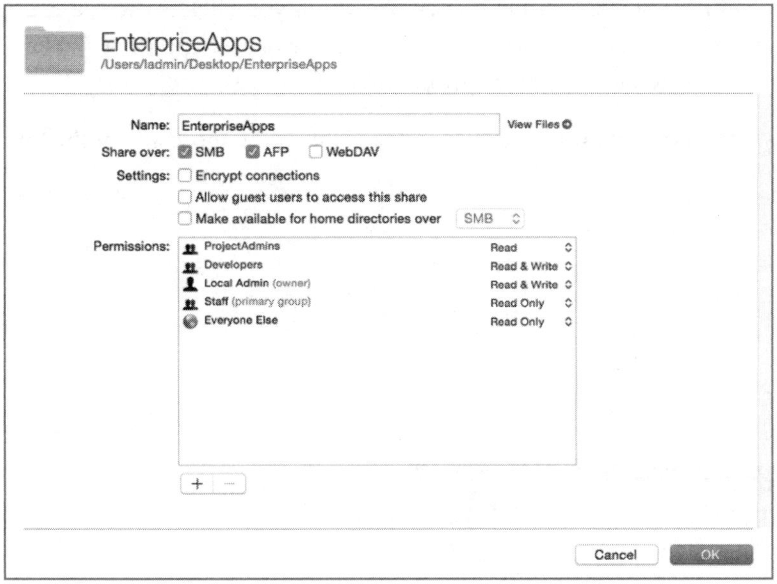

To change the standard POSIX owner of a share point, double-click the name of the current owner; to change the group, double-click the name of the current primary group. Once you start typing, a menu with names that match what you have typed appears. The following figure illustrates the process of changing the POSIX owner.

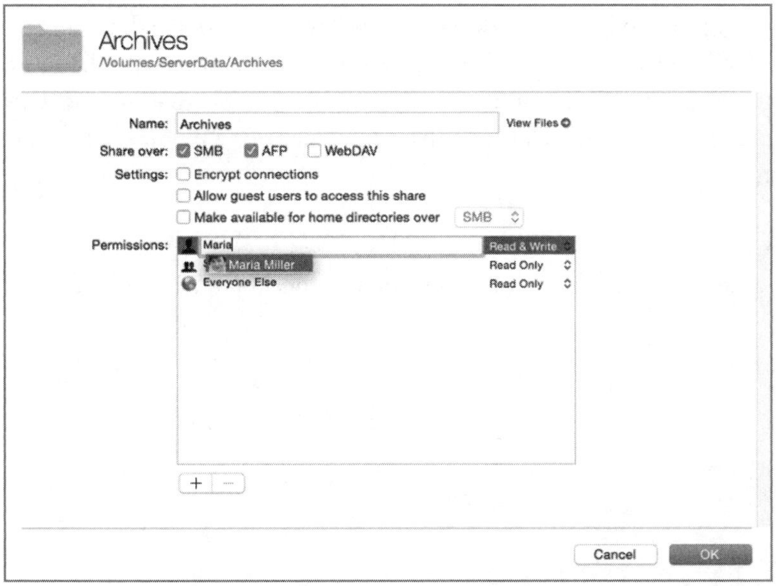

From there, you can either choose a name or click Browse. If you click Browse, a dialog of accounts appears; choose an account, and then click OK. The Server app then displays the account's full name in the owner or primary group field.

To change permissions, click the pop-up menu on the right, and choose any of the four options:

- ▶ Read & Write
- ▶ Read Only
- ▶ Write Only
- ▶ No Access

After making permissions changes, be sure to click OK to save your changes. If you select a different pane in the Server app or quit the Server app, your changes might not get saved. Permissions can be propagated to the files and folders enclosed; you'll learn more about propagation later in the lesson.

Once the user is authenticated, file permissions control access to the files and folders on your server. One setting should be called out with respect to permissions: the Others permissions, which is displayed as Everyone Else when editing permissions with the File Sharing pane. When you set Others permissions, those permissions apply to everyone who can see the item (either a file or a folder) who is neither the owner nor a member of the group assigned to the item.

Allowing Guest Access

You turn on guest access for a share point by selecting the checkbox "Allow guest users to access this share."

Guest access can be useful, but before you enable it, be sure you understand its implications in your permissions scheme. As the name implies, guest access lets anyone who can connect to your server use its share points. A user who authenticates as Guest is given Others permissions for file and folder access. If you give read-only access to Others on a share point that allows guest access, everyone on your network (and, if your server has a public IP address and is not protected by a firewall, the entire Internet) can see and mount that share point, a situation you might not intend to allow.

If a user creates an item on an Apple Filing Protocol (AFP) share point while connected as Guest, the AFP client sets the owner of that item to "nobody."

If a folder is buried deep within a file hierarchy where guests can't go (because the enclosing folders don't grant access to Others), guests can't browse to that folder.

TIP▶ The best way to validate permissions is by connecting to the File Sharing service from a client computer, providing valid credentials (or connecting as Guest), and testing access.

Configure Access with the Server App Storage Pane
In contrast to the File Sharing pane, where you can configure access to share points, you can use the Server app Storage pane to configure permissions for individual files and folders; additionally, you have more granular control.

One way to get to the Storage pane is by selecting your server in the Server app sidebar and then clicking the Storage pane. You can then navigate to a specific file or folder.

The other way to get to the Storage pane is via this shortcut: In the File Sharing pane, when you edit a share point and click the arrow next to the words "View Files," the Server app opens the share point's folder in the Storage pane.

In the Storage pane, when you select a file or folder and click the Action (gear icon) pop-up menu, you see three choices:

▶ New Folder

▶ Edit Permissions

▶ Propagate Permissions

You'll learn more about Propagate Permissions later in this lesson. If you choose Edit Permissions, the Server app opens a permissions dialog that's similar to the File Sharing pane's permissions field, but the Storage pane's permissions dialog offers you more configuration options.

Using the Storage Pane's Permissions Dialog

In the Storage pane's permissions dialog in the following figure, each ACE has a disclosure triangle to hide or reveal more information about the ACE; additionally, some information, such as the Spotlight ACE, which is hidden in the File Sharing pane, is displayed in the permissions dialog.

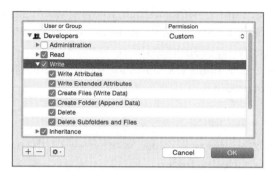

NOTE ▶ The inherited ACE for Spotlight allows Spotlight to maintain an index of the files on your server. Do not modify or remove this ACE or you may experience unexpected behavior.

You'll learn more about modifying an item's ACL in the next section.

Reference 13.2
POSIX Permissions Compared to ACL Settings

The Server app is a powerful tool with many options to configure file access. It is important to understand how the POSIX permissions model and the file system ACLs behave, and how they behave together, to accurately configure share points to behave as you intend. This section starts with a quick review of POSIX ownership and permissions and then considers ACLs.

Explaining POSIX Ownership and Permissions

The OS X standard file system permissions structure is based on decades-old UNIX-style permissions. This system is also sometimes referred to as POSIX-style permissions. In the POSIX permissions model, which OS X and OS X Server use, each file and each folder is associated with exactly one "owner" and exactly one "group." As an administrator, you can change the POSIX owner and the POSIX group, but keep in mind that every file must have one and only one owner and one and only one group as part of the POSIX ownership. This limits your flexibility, so you may choose to use ACLs to add flexibility in managing access to files, but it is important for you to understand the basics of POSIX ownership and permissions. For more information, see "File System Permissions" in Lesson 11 "Managing with Profile Manager" in *Apple Pro Training Series: OS X Support Essentials 10.10*.

When you move an item from one folder to another *within* a single volume, that item always retains its original ownership and permissions. In contrast, when you create a new item on a network volume via AFP, Server Message Block (SMB), or WebDAV or when you copy an item from one volume to another volume, OS X uses the following rules for ownership and permissions for the new file or folder:

▶   The owner of the new item is the user who created or copied the item.

▶   The group is the group associated with the enclosing folder; in other words, the newly copied item inherits its group from the enclosing folder.

▶   The owner is assigned read and write permissions.

▶   The group is assigned read-only permissions.

▶   Others (also displayed as Everyone Else) is assigned read-only permissions.

Under this model, if you create an item in a folder in which the group has read/write permission, the new item will not inherit that group permission, so other users are not able to edit that item (but because they have read/write permission to the folder, they can remove the item from the folder).

Without using ACLs, if a user wants to grant other group members write access to the new item, she must modify its permissions manually, using the Finder's Get Info command, chmod in the command line, or some third-party tool. This would be required for every new item; instead, you can use ACLs to prevent the need for users to add this step of manually modifying permissions to their workflow.

> **MORE INFO** ▶ The variable that controls the POSIX permissions for newly created files is called the umask. Changing the umask from the default value is not recommended and is outside the scope of this guide. When a user creates files on the server via AFP or SMB, the user's umask on the client computer affects the permissions for the newly created items; however, the umask on the server computer affects the permissions for files created via WebDAV.

Defining Access Control Lists

Because of the limitations of the POSIX permissions model, consider using ACLs to help control access to folders and files. The Apple ACL model maps to the Windows ACL model, so Windows users experience the same permissions for folders and files that OS X users do.

In this section, you'll learn about applying ACLs with the Server app File Sharing pane, which presents a simplified interface, and with the Storage pane's permissions dialog, which offers more flexibility. You'll learn how ACL inheritance works and why it is so powerful.

NOTE ▶ You can apply ACLs only on Mac OS Extended volumes.

In OS X Server, you use the Server app to configure ACLs. An ACL consists of one or more ACEs. Each ACE includes the following:

▶ The globally unique ID (GUID) or universally unique ID (UUID) of the one user or group for which this ACE applies

▶ Whether the ACE allows access or denies access (you can use the Server app to create only Allow entries; though you cannot use the Server app to create Deny entries, it displays a selected Deny checkbox to indicate that a rule specifies *either* Allow or Deny, as further explained in the text after this list)

▶ The permission the ACE allows or denies (see the section "Configuring Complex Permissions for an ACE" on page 419)

▶ The inheritance rules for the ACE (see the section "Defining ACL Inheritance" on page 421)

▶ The folder or file to which the ACE applies

The Server app does not visually distinguish between Allow and Deny. You simply see a checkbox. When you assign a new ACE, it is assumed you are assigning an Allow rule. However, when you use the Server app to inspect an ACE that has a Deny rule, there is no indication whether this rule is an Allow rule or a Deny rule. For example, OS X automatically applies a Deny ACE to some items in each user's home folder to prevent accidental removal, as shown in the following figure.

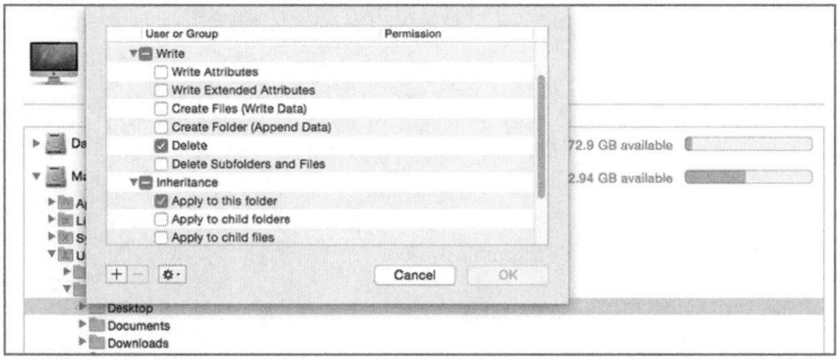

You can add as many ACEs for an item as you like, and you have a much larger range of permission types available than with standard POSIX permissions, which you'll learn about in the section "Configuring Complex Permissions for an ACE" on page 419.

Describe How File System ACLs Work

When you use the Server app to define ACLs, you are creating individual ACEs.

The order of entries is important because OS X evaluates lists top to bottom.

Allow and Deny matches work differently for ACLs. When evaluating ACLs, the operating system starts with the first ACE and moves downward, stopping at the ACE that applies to the user, and matches the operation, such as reading, being performed. The permission (either to allow or to deny) for the ACE is then applied. Any ACEs farther down in the list are then ignored. Any matching Allow or Deny ACE overrides standard POSIX permissions. In cases where there is Allow in both the ACLs and POSIX, the effective access is cumulative. If User1 has write access in an ACE and Everyone has read in POSIX, User1 will effectively have read and write.

Configuring ACLs with the Server App File Sharing Pane

In the Server app File Sharing pane, when editing a share point, you add a new ACE for a share point with the following general steps.

> **NOTE** ▸ This is an example workflow and not part of this lesson's exercise.

1   Click Add (+).

2   Specify the user or group. You must choose the account from the list, or you must choose Browse and choose the account from the list.

3   Specify the access to allow. Note that you can specify Read & Write, Read, or Write.

4   Repeat steps 1 through 3 for additional ACEs, and then click OK to save the changes.

Configuring ACLs with the Server App Storage Pane

The Storage pane of the Server app offers a little more flexibility than the File Sharing pane for configuring ACLs, particularly the ability to do the following:

▶ Configure complex permissions for an ACE, more than just Read & Write, Read, or Write

▶ Configure the inheritance for ACLs

▶ Configure POSIX ownership and permissions and the ACL for an individual file, not just for folders

▶ Configure POSIX ownership and permissions for files that are not shared (the File Sharing pane allows you to configure share points only)

To access the Storage pane, select your server in the Server app sidebar, and click the Storage tab. You can select an existing folder or create a new folder. To access the permissions dialog for a file or folder, select a file or folder, click the Action (gear icon) pop-up menu, and choose Edit Permissions.

Once you are viewing the permissions dialog, you can click Add (+) to create a new ACE. Unlike in the File Sharing pane, there is no Browse option; you need to start typing and choose a user or group that matches what you have entered from the list.

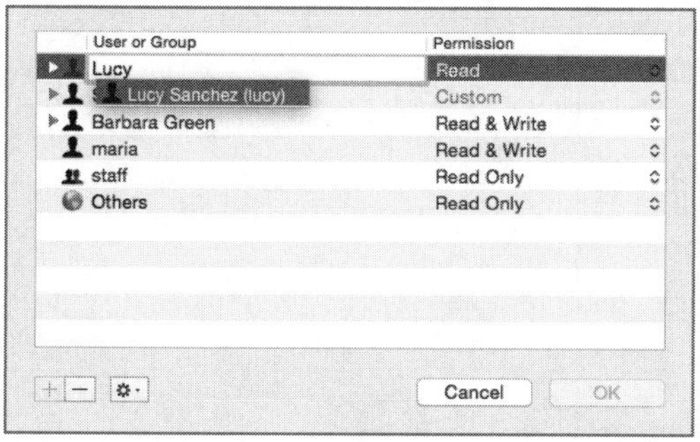

After you specify the user or group for the ACE, you can click the permissions pop-up menu and choose Full Control, Read & Write, Read, or Write.

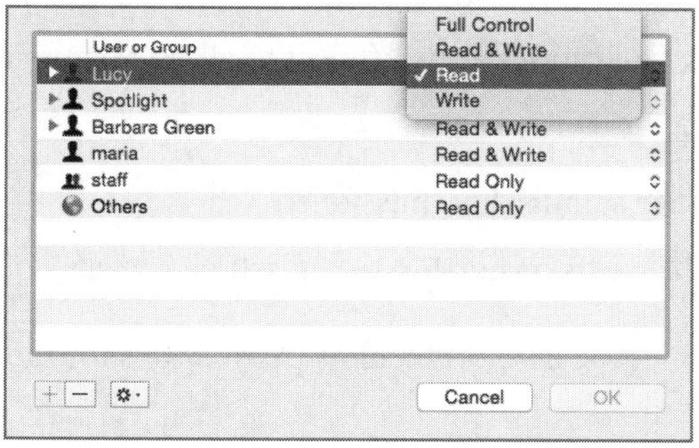

Of course, your permissions choice is just a starting point; you can fine-tune the permissions, as you'll see in the next section.

Configuring Complex Permissions for an ACE

When you edit an ACE with the Storage pane's permissions dialog, you can use the disclosure triangles to show the details for the ACE. You have four broad categories for which you can apply Allow rules:

▶   Administration

▶   Read

▶   Write

▶   Inheritance

User or Group	Permission	
▼ 👤 Lucy	Read	⊗
▶ ☐ Administration		
▶ ☑ Read		
▶ ☐ Write		
▶ ☑ Inheritance		
▶ 👤 Spotlight	Custom	⇅
▶ 👤 Barbara Green	Read & Write	⇅
👤 maria	Read & Write	⇅
👥 staff	Read Only	⇅
🌐 Others	Read Only	⇅

| + | − | ⚙ · | | Cancel | OK |

For the first three (Administration, Read, and Write), selecting a checkbox allows access for the user or group in the ACE. Deselecting a checkbox does not deny access; it just doesn't explicitly allow access.

For the Administration set of permissions, you can select or deselect to allow permissions for the following:

▶ Change Permissions—A user can change standard permissions.

▶ Change Owner—A user can change the item's ownership to himself or herself.

For the Read set of permissions, you can select or deselect to allow permissions for the following:

▶ Read Attributes—A user can view the item's attributes, such as name, size, and date modified.

▶ Read Extended Attributes—A user can view additional attributes, including ACL and attributes added by third-party software.

▶ List Folder Contents (Read Data)—A user can read files and see the contents of a folder.

▶ Traverse Folder (Execute File)—A user can open files or traverse a folder.

▶ Read Permissions—A user can read the POSIX permissions.

For the Write set of permissions, you can select or deselect to allow permissions for the following:

▶ Write Attributes—A user can change POSIX permissions.

▶ Write Extended Attributes—A user can change ACL or other extended attributes.

► Create Files (Write Data)—A user can create files, including changing files for most applications.

► Create Folder (Append Data)—A user can create new folders and append data to files.

► Delete—A user can delete files or folders.

► Delete Subfolders and Files—A user can delete subfolders and files.

With just these 13 checkboxes, you have a large amount of flexibility to allow additional permissions beyond what you can configure with just POSIX permissions.

Because the Server app does not allow you to create Deny rules, the best strategy is to set the standard POSIX permissions for Others to No Access and then configure an ACL to build up rules to allow appropriate access for various groups.

Defining ACL Inheritance

One powerful feature of ACLs is inheritance: When you create an ACE for a folder, from that point on when a user creates a new item in that folder, the operating system assigns that same ACE to the new item. In other words, the ACE is inherited. For each ACE in the folder's ACL, you can control how that ACE is inherited; when you edit an ACE, you can select or deselect each of the following checkboxes (by default, all four "Apply to" checkboxes are selected):

► Apply to this folder—This ACE applies to this folder.

► Apply to child folders—This ACE will be assigned to new folders inside this folder but not necessarily to new folders that are created inside the child folders of this folder, unless "Apply to all descendants" is also selected.

► Apply to child files—This ACE will be assigned to new files inside this folder but not necessarily to files that are inside the child folders of this folder, unless "Apply to all descendants" is also selected.

► Apply to all descendants—This makes the two preceding options apply to items in an infinite level of nested folders and files in this folder.

When an ACE is inherited from a folder, its permissions appear dimmed, as in the following figure (you can remove or inspect an inherited ACE, but you cannot otherwise change it as long as it is inherited).

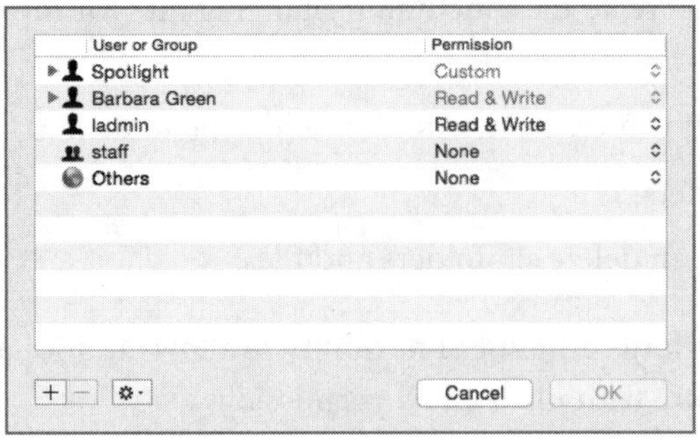

If an inherited ACL doesn't meet your needs, first consider why the ACL model didn't work in this case: Do you need a different share point, a different group, or maybe a different set of ACEs in the ACL? In any event, you can click the Action (gear icon) pop-up menu and choose one of these two actions to change the inherited entries:

▶ Remove Inherited Entries

▶ Make Inherited Entries Explicit

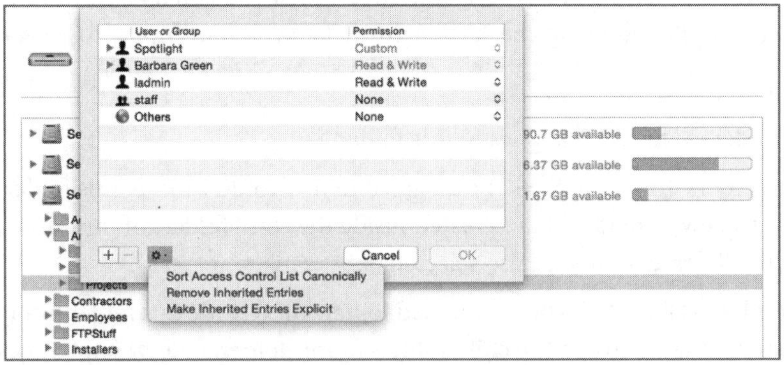

Remove Inherited Entries removes all the inherited ACEs, not just one ACE that you might have selected. The inherited ACL could be an aggregation of inherited ACEs from more than one parent folder.

Make Inherited Entries Explicit applies all the inherited ACEs as if they were applied directly to the ACL on the current file or folder. Once you perform this action, you can edit the ACEs, including editing or removing individual ACEs that were previously dimmed. The following figure illustrates what happens if you choose Make Inherited Entries

Explicit: The ACEs are no longer dimmed, and you can remove them or modify them. The ACE for Spotlight is automatically created—do not modify that ACE.

When you use the Server app's File Sharing pane to update a folder's ACL that has inheritance rules, the Server app automatically updates the ACL for items in the folder that have already inherited the ACL (this is not the case if you update the ACL using the Storage pane).

Sorting ACLs Canonically

The order in which each ACE is listed in an ACL is important and can possibly change the behavior of an ACL, especially if a Deny rule is involved. Although the Server app does *not* allow you to create ACEs to deny access, some ACLs do contain one or more Deny ACEs. In the Storage pane's permissions dialog, you can click the Action (gear icon) pop-up menu and choose Sort Access Control List Canonically. This reorders the ACEs into a standard order for applying ACLs. If you don't have Deny rules in your ACL, it isn't crucial to use this command.

Applying ACL Portability

ACLs are applied when a file or folder is created, so note the following:

▶   If you move an item from one location to another on the same volume, the ACL for that item (if one exists) does not change and is still associated with the item.

▶   If you copy an item from one location to another, the item's ACL does not get copied; the copied item will inherit, from its enclosing folder, any ACEs that are appropriately configured to be inherited.

However, what happens if you update an existing ACL, or create a new ACL, *after* files have already been created? You'll need to propagate the ACL.

Propagating Permissions

When you use the File Sharing pane to update a share point's ACL or POSIX permissions, the Server app automatically propagates the ACL but not the POSIX. When you propagate the ACL, the Server app adds each ACE of the current folder to the ACL of each child object (folders and files inside the parent folder) as an inherited ACE. Don't worry about overwriting explicitly defined ACEs for child objects because propagating an ACL does not remove any explicitly defined ACEs.

In contrast, when you use the Storage pane's permissions dialog to create or update an ACL for an item, your actions affect only that item and do not affect existing child objects. In the Storage permissions dialog, to propagate the ACL changes to existing child objects, you must do so manually. Click the Action (gear icon) pop-up menu, and choose Propagate Permissions. The following figure illustrates that by default the Access Control List checkbox is selected, but you can select additional checkboxes to also update different combinations of standard POSIX ownership and permissions to existing child objects.

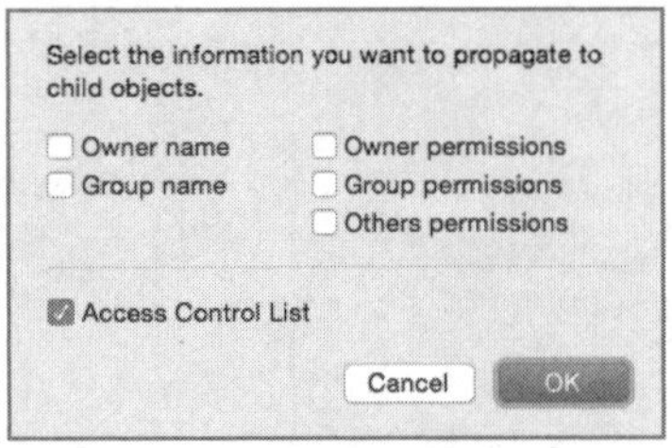

Features Common to POSIX and ACLs

Now that you have a better understanding of POSIX ownership and permissions, as well as ACLs and ACEs, this section covers how the two models work together to affect access to files.

Distinguishing Between the Uses of UID, GID, and GUID

POSIX owners and groups are determined by user and group IDs (UIDs and GIDs). UIDs and GIDs are simple integers, so it is possible (but not recommended) for users to have duplicate user IDs. Usually this is an error, but sometimes an administrator will want the POSIX UID to be identical on two separate users. From a permissions perspective, this will grant these users identical access rights.

ACLs are much more complex and require a unique identification of a user or group. For this purpose, every user and group has a globally unique ID (GUID). In Accounts preferences, when you Control-click (or secondary-click) a user account and choose Advanced Options, the GUID is labeled UUID; it is also referred to as a generated UID.

An account's GUID is not exposed in the Server app because there should be no reason to change it. Every time a user or group is created, a new 128-bit string is randomly generated for that user or group. In this way, users and groups are virtually guaranteed unique identification in ACLs.

When you create an ACE for a user or group, the ACE uses the GUID of that user or group, rather than the user name, user ID, group name, or group ID. When displaying an ACL, if the server computer cannot match an ACE's GUID to an account, the Server app displays the GUID instead of the account name in the ACL. Some reasons for this include that the account associated with the ACE:

► Has been deleted

► Belongs to a directory node that the server is bound to but is unavailable

► Belongs to a directory node that is unavailable because the volume was connected to a different server when the ACE was created

Here's an example of an exposed GUID in the Server app. In the following figure, an ACE was created for a local network user, and then an administrator deleted the local network user with the Server app; the ACE was not automatically removed.

If you see this, without knowing what account corresponds to the GUID, you could either leave the entry in place or remove the entry. If you happen to import the account in a way that also imports its GUID, that entry will be associated with the user or group again.

However, if the account associated with the GUID is truly gone forever, you can remove the ACE; highlight the ACE, and click the Delete (–) button.

Describing Group Membership and ACLs

When working with ACLs, it is important that you plan your setup properly to avoid conflicting permissions settings, such as having a user be a member of two groups, one with read permissions on a folder and one with no access permissions on the same folder. These types of conflicts can occur if you do not plan your ACL permissions models well.

Using ACLs to control access to server resources can be extremely valuable, as long as you take care up front to organize your user and group accounts appropriately. The recommended way to approach this management is to take advantage of using smaller groups to correctly reflect the needs of your organization, including nesting groups within groups. Use these group accounts to manage access on a more granular basis.

Impact of Multiple Groups

The standard POSIX permissions work well in a single desktop model such as OS X. Yet when the system becomes more complex, the standard POSIX permissions model does not scale well.

Complex workflows might require more than just the User, Group, and Others classes available with the standard POSIX permissions model. In particular, having a single group is limiting. The POSIX owner must be an individual user account (it can't be a group), and granting permission to Others (Everyone Else) usually opens up the files to a wider audience than you want. Adding an ACL permits you to assign multiple groups to a folder and assign each a unique permissions setting. ACLs can assign different permissions to multiple groups, so you must carefully plan what your group structure is going to look like to avoid any confusion. This is a common requirement in any environment that has multiple groups collaborating on a single project.

Behavior of Nested Groups

In addition to assigning multiple groups to a single folder, OS X Server allows groups to contain other groups. Breaking down groups into subgroups can make your access easier to understand as an administrator. You can use nested groups to reflect the structure of your organization.

Although nested groups are powerful, they should be used with care. If you build a deep, complex hierarchy, you may find that access is harder—rather than easier—to understand.

Mirroring your organizational structure is usually safe and useful. However, be wary of ad hoc groups that don't relate to any external structure. They may be a quick way to give access to some users but later may make it more difficult to understand your access.

Describing POSIX and ACL Rules of Precedence

When a user attempts to perform an action that requires authorization (read a file or create a folder), OS X will allow this action only if the user has permission for that action. Here is how OS X combines POSIX and ACLs when there is a request for a specific action:

1. If there is no ACL, POSIX rules apply.

2. If there is an ACL, the order of the ACEs matters. You can sort the ACEs in an ACL in a consistent and predictable way: In the Server app Storage pane, select an ACL, and then from the Action (gear icon) pop-up menu, choose Sort Access Control List Canonically. This is especially important if you add an ACE to an ACL containing an ACE that denies access.

3. When evaluating an ACL, OS X evaluates the first ACE in the list and continues to the next ACE until it finds an ACE that matches the permission required for the requested action, whether that permission is Allow or Deny. Even if a Deny ACE exists in an ACL, if a similar Allow ACE is listed first, the Allow ACE is the one that is used because it is listed first. This is why it is so important to choose Sort Access Control List Canonically.

4. A POSIX permission that is restrictive does not override an ACE that specifically allows a permission.

5. If no ACE applies to the permission required for the requested action, the POSIX permissions apply.

For example, if Barbara Green attempts to create a folder, the requested permission is Create Folder. Each ACE is evaluated until there is an ACE that either allows or denies Create Folder for Barbara Green or a group that Barbara Green belongs to.

Even though this is an unlikely scenario, it illustrates the combination of an ACL and POSIX permissions: If a folder has an ACE that allows Barbara Green (short name: barbara) full control, but the POSIX permission defines Barbara Green as the owner with access set to None, Barbara Green effectively has full control. The ACE is evaluated before the POSIX permissions.

As another example, consider a folder with an ACL that has a single ACE that allows Carl Dunn to have read permission, and the folder's POSIX permission defines Carl Dunn as the owner with read and write permission. When Carl Dunn attempts to create a file in that folder, there is no ACE that specifically addresses the Create Files (Write Data) request, so no ACE applies to that request. Therefore, the POSIX permissions apply, and Carl Dunn can create the file.

In this lesson, you learned about POSIX ownership and permissions, file ACLs, and how you can configure share points and files to control access to files.

Exercise 13.1
Configure Access Control

▶ **Prerequisites**

- ▶ You must have the File Sharing service turned on.

- ▶ "Exercise 4.2 Configure an Open Directory Certificate Authority" on page 152 and "Exercise 9.1 Create and Import Network Accounts" on page 292; or, use the Server app to create users Maria Miller, Gary Pine, Lucy Sanchez, Enrico Baker, and Todd Porter, each with an account name that is the same as their first name in lowercase and with a password of net.

- ▶ "Exercise 12.1 Explore the File Sharing Service" on page 392; or, use the Storage pane to create at the root of the startup disk a folder named Shared Items that is owned by the user Local Admin.

In this exercise, you will create a folder hierarchy and a means of controlling access to facilitate the workflow of the users and groups on your server, using standard POSIX permissions and file system ACLs. You will discover that the ability to manipulate a file can be determined by where the file is located in the system, rather than by who created or owns the specific file.

To properly configure your server, you need to understand the intended workflow of your users. Here is the scenario: Your group needs a share point for a secret project, ProjectZ. The two people in the project, Maria Miller and Gary Pine, need to be able to read and write documents in the share point, including documents that the other person created. It is expected that more people will be added to the project later. No one else in the organization should see the folder for the project, except the vice president (VP) of sales, Lucy Sanchez, who needs only read access to the files.

You can't just use the Server app to create the folder for the group in the Groups folder because this folder would be visible to other people, and even though other people would not be able to browse the contents of the folder, other people would start asking questions about it.

You could start by creating a group, configuring that group as the primary group for a folder, and assigning read/write permissions for the group to the folder, but that's not enough because any new items created will automatically have a permission of read-only for the primary group. In addition, you need to create an ACE for the ProjectZ group to allow them read/write access. You will also need to create an ACE for Lucy Sanchez, the VP of sales, to allow read access.

As part of this scenario, after you get the users, groups, and share points configured, be prepared for management to assign another request, which you will cheerfully fulfill.

Configure a Group and a Shared Folder

1   Perform these exercises on your administrator computer. If you do not already have a connection to your server computer with the Server app on your administrator computer, then connect to it with the following steps: Open the Server app on your administrator computer, choose Manage > Connect to Server, select your server, click Continue, provide administrator credentials (Administrator Name: ladmin, Administrator Password: ladminpw), deselect the "Remember this password" checkbox, and then click Connect.

Create the ProjectZ Group and Add the Two Users to the Group

1   In the Server app sidebar, select Groups.

2   If a pop-up menu is visible, set the pop-up menu to Local Network Groups.

3   If the lock icon at the bottom of the pane is locked, unlock it: Click the lock icon at the bottom of the pane, provide directory administrator credentials (Administrator Name: diradmin, Administrator Password: diradminpw), and click Authenticate.

4   Click the Add (+) button to create a new group, and enter the following information:

▶   Full Name: ProjectZ

▶   Group Name: projectz

5   Click Create to create the group.

6   Double-click the ProjectZ group to edit it.

7   Press Command-B to show the accounts browser.

8   Drag Gary Pine and Maria Miller to the Members list.

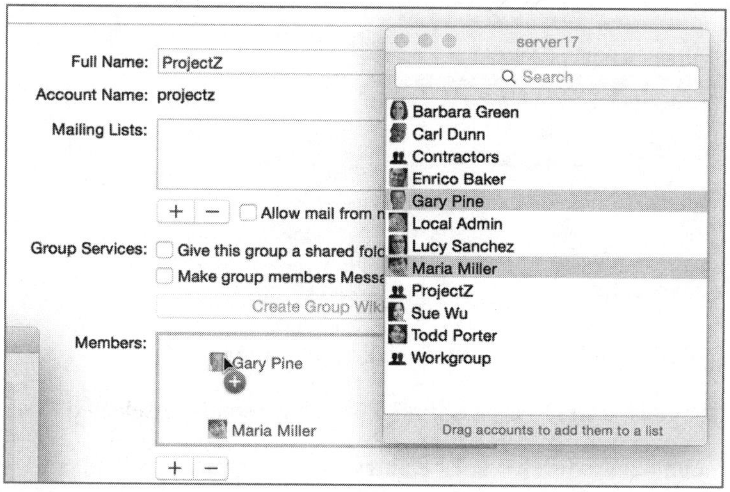

9   Press Command-B to hide the accounts browser.

10 Click OK to save the changes.

Create and Configure the Shared Folder

Create a shared folder for the ProjectZ group, and configure its permissions as follows:

▶   No one else can see the share point or its contents.

▶   Members of the ProjectZ group have read/write access to all items.

▶   Lucy Sanchez, the VP of sales, has read-only access to all items.

Start by creating the share point.

1   In the Server app sidebar, select File Sharing.

2   Click the Settings tab if necessary.

3   Click the Add (+) button.

4   Navigate to the Shared Items folder on your server's startup volume.

5   Click New Folder.

6   Name the folder ProjectZ, and then click Create.

7   Select the new ProjectZ folder you just created.

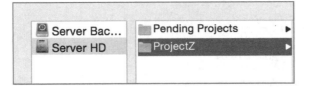

8   Click Choose.

Configure access to the share point.

1   In the File Sharing pane, double-click the ProjectZ share point.

2   Make sure the "Allow guest users to access this share" checkbox is unselected.

3   Click the pop-up menu for the Everyone Else entry in the Permissions field, and choose No Access.

Name:	ProjectZ View Files ⊙
Share over:	☑ SMB ☑ AFP ☐ WebDAV
Settings:	☐ Encrypt connections
	☐ Allow guest users to access this share
	☐ Make available for home directories over SMB ⌄
Permissions:	👤 Local Admin (owner) Read & Write ⌄
	👥 System Group (primary group) Read Only ⌄
	👤 Everyone Else No Access ⌄

Note that the owner and primary group are inherited from the enclosing folder (Shared Items). Don't worry about that; the owner of new items will be the user who creates the items (explained in detail in "Reference 13.2 POSIX Permissions Compared to ACL Settings" on page 413) over AFP and SMB, and newly created items will get read-only access applied to the primary group, so you need to use an ACL to provide read/write access to the ProjectZ group.

4   Click the Add (+) button.

5   Start typing ProjectZ, and then choose ProjectZ.

Permissions:	Pro	Read & Write ⟡
	ProjectZ er)	Read & Write ⟡
	System Group (primary group)	Read Only ⟡
	Everyone Else	No Access ⟡

Confirm that the permission is automatically set to Read & Write for the ProjectZ group.

Create an ACE that allows Lucy Sanchez, the VP of sales, read-only access.

1   Click the Add (+) button, start typing Lucy, and choose Lucy Sanchez.

2   Set the permissions for Lucy Sanchez to Read.

Permissions:	Lucy Sanchez	Read ⟡
	ProjectZ	Read & Write ⟡
	Local Admin (owner)	Read & Write ⟡
	System Group (primary group)	Read Only ⟡
	Everyone Else	No Access ⟡

3   Click OK to save these settings.

Start the File Sharing Service If Necessary

1   In the Server app sidebar, select File Sharing.

2   If the File Sharing service is not already on, click On to turn on the service.

Confirm Permissions Allow Desired Access

Confirm that Maria Miller and Gary Pine can create and edit items in the ProjectZ share point and that the VP of sales (Lucy Sanchez) cannot create, edit, or remove items.

1   On your administrator computer, in the Finder, choose File > New Finder Window.

2   If there is an Eject button next to your server in the Finder sidebar, click it to eject any mounted volumes from that server.

3   If your server appears in the Finder sidebar, select your server.

Otherwise, if there are so many computers on your network that your server does not appear in the Shared section of the Finder sidebar, click All, and then select your server.

If Guest access is enabled for any share point, you are automatically connected as Guest.

4   In the Finder window, click Connect As.

5   At the authentication window, provide credentials for Maria Miller (Name: maria, Password: net).

Leave the checkbox to remember the password unselected.

NOTE ▶ Do not select the checkbox to remember the password; otherwise, you will need to use Keychain Access to remove the password before you can connect as a different user.

6   Click Connect.

After you successfully authenticate, you see all the share points that the user Maria Miler has access to read.

7 Open the ProjectZ folder.

8 Press Command-Shift-N to create a new folder, and enter the name Folder created by Maria.

9 Press Return to stop editing the folder name.

You won't do anything else with this folder in the exercise, but you confirmed that Maria Miller has permission to create a folder.

Create a text file as Maria Miller; you will eventually confirm the following:

▶ Gary Pine can also edit that document.

▶ Lucy Sanchez can read, but cannot change, that document.

▶ Other users cannot see that the ProjectZ share point exists.

1 Use a Spotlight search to open TextEdit.

2 If you do not see a new blank document, create a new blank document by pressing Command-N or choosing File > New.

3 Enter the following text: This is a file started by Maria.

4 Save the TextEdit document by pressing Command-S or choosing File > Save.

5 If necessary, click the disclosure button next to the Save As field to reveal more options.

In the Shared section of the Save As window sidebar, select your server, and then open the folder ProjectZ.

6 In the Save As field, name the file Maria Text File.

7 Click Save.

8 Close the TextEdit document by pressing Command-W or choosing File > Close.

9 If no Finder window is still open, in the Finder, press Command-N to open one.

10 In the Finder sidebar, click the Eject button next to your server (if your Finder window is configured with the Icon view, click Disconnect).

Shared

server17   ⏏

Connect as the other project member, Gary Pine, and confirm that you can edit files with his credentials.

1 If your server appears in the Finder sidebar, select your server.

Otherwise, if there are so many computers on your network that your server does not appear in the Shared section of the Finder sidebar, click All, and then select your server.

2 In the Finder window, click Connect As.

3 At the authentication window, provide credentials for Gary Pine (Name: gary, Password: net).

Leave the checkbox to remember the password unselected.

4 Click Connect.

5 Open the ProjectZ folder.

6 Open the file named Maria Text File.

7 Add another line at the end of the text file: This was added by Gary.

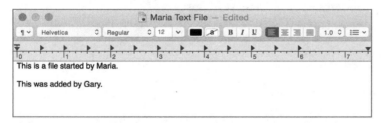

8 Close the TextEdit document by pressing Command-W or choosing File > Close.

When you see the dialog that the document is on a volume that does not support permanent version storage and that you will not be able to access older versions of the document once you close it, click OK.

This automatically saves the change you just made to the file.

> **The document "Maria Text File" is on a volume that does not support permanent version storage.**
>
> Your changes have been saved and you will not be able to access older versions of this document once you close it. To undo your changes, click Revert.
>
> ☐ Do not show this message again
>
> Revert   Cancel   OK

NOTE ▶ For more information about version storage, see Lesson 18.3, "Auto Save and Versions," in *Apple Pro Training Series: OS X Support Essentials 10.10.*

9 In the Finder window sidebar, click the Eject button next to your server.

Confirm that you can see, but not edit, a file in the ProjectZ folder when connected as the VP of sales, Lucy Sanchez.

1 If your server appears in the Finder sidebar, select your server.

Otherwise, if there are so many computers on your network that your server does not appear in the Shared section of the Finder sidebar, click All, and then select your server.

2 In the Finder window, click Connect As.

3 At the authentication window, provide credentials for Lucy Sanchez (Name: lucy, Password: net).

Leave the checkbox to remember the password unselected.

4 Click Connect.

5 Open the ProjectZ folder.

6 Open the file named Maria Text File.

7 Confirm that you can read the text and that the toolbar contains the text "Locked," indicating that you cannot save changes to this file.

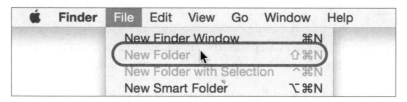

8   Attempt to edit the file by appending text, and note that you see a dialog stating the file is locked.

9   Click Cancel.

10 Close the TextEdit document by pressing Command-W or choosing File > Close.

Confirm that you cannot create a new folder in the ProjectZ folder as the Lucy Sanchez user.

1   In the Finder window, confirm that you are viewing the ProjectZ folder.

2   Click the File menu, and confirm that New Folder is dimmed.

You are not able to create a new folder on the network volume because the user Lucy Sanchez has only read permissions.

Confirm that you cannot delete an item in the ProjectZ folder as the Lucy Sanchez user.

1   Select Maria Text File, and choose File > Move to Trash.

2   At the "Are you sure" dialog, click Delete.

3 Because you effectively have read-only permission, you see a dialog that you don't have permission. Click OK to close the dialog.

Confirm that a different user (Todd Porter, who isn't a member of the ProjectZ group) cannot view items in the ProjectZ folder.

1 In the Finder sidebar, click the Eject button next to your server.

2 If your server appears in the Finder sidebar, select your server.

Otherwise, if there are so many computers on your network that your server does not appear in the Shared section of the Finder sidebar, click All, and then select your server.

3 In the Finder window, click Connect As.

4 At the authentication window, provide credentials for Todd Porter (Name: todd, Password: net).

Do not select the checkbox to remember the password.

5 Click Connect.

6 Confirm that the ProjectZ folder is not visible.

7 In the upper-right corner of the Finder window, click Disconnect, or if you selected a shared folder, click the Eject button next to your server in the Finder sidebar.

You have successfully managed users and groups, created a share point, and managed the POSIX permissions and ACL for the share point to provide the access that management requested.

Update Permissions Because of Evolving Needs

However, the company just promoted a new vice president of marketing, Enrico Baker, who also wants read access to the files.

Rather than adding another individual user to the ACL, at this point in the scenario it makes more sense to create a group for vice presidents, add appropriate users to that group, and then add an ACE to allow read access for that group. To prevent confusion in the future, you will also remove the original ACE for Lucy Sanchez; her ACE is unnecessary because her user account is part of a group that has an ACE.

Create a New Group and Update Permissions

Create the Vice Presidents group, and add the two users to the group.

1   In the Server app sidebar, select Groups.

2   If there's a pop-up menu visible, set the pop-up menu to Local Network Groups.

3   If the lock icon at the bottom of the pane is locked, unlock it: Click the lock at the bottom of the pane, provide directory administrator credentials (Administrator Name: diradmin, Administrator Password: diradminpw), and click Authenticate.

4   Click the Add (+) button to create the following group:

▶   Full Name: Vice Presidents

▶   Group Name: vicepresidents

5   Click Create to create the group.

6   Double-click the Vice Presidents group.

7   Press Command-B to show the accounts browser.

8   Drag Lucy Sanchez and Enrico Baker to the Members list.

Members:	Enrico Baker
	Lucy Sanchez

+ −

9   Press Command-B to hide the accounts browser.

10 Click OK to finish editing the group.

Update the ACL for the ProjectZ folder using the File Sharing pane .

1   In the Server app sidebar, select File Sharing.

2   Double-click the ProjectZ share point.

3   Click the Add (+) button, start typing vicepresidents, and choose Vice Presidents from the list.

4   Click the permissions pop-up menu for Vice Presidents, and choose Read.

5   Select the ACE for Lucy Sanchez, and click the Delete (–) button.

The Permissions section of the Server app should appear like the following figure (the positions of the Vice Presidents ACE and the ProjectZ ACE relative to each other do not matter for the purposes of this exercise).

Permissions:	Vice Presidents	Read
	ProjectZ	Read & Write
	Local Admin (owner)	Read & Write
	System Group (primary group)	Read Only
	Everyone Else	No Access

6   Click OK to save the changes to the ACL.

The Server app automatically propagates the updated ACL to items in the share point.

Confirm Permissions

Confirm that Enrico Baker, a member of the Vice Presidents group, can read files in the ProjectZ folder.

1   On your administrator computer, in the Finder, if there is no Finder window visible, choose New > New Finder Window.

2   If your server appears in the Finder sidebar, select your server.

Otherwise, if there are so many computers on your network that your server does not appear in the Shared section of the Finder sidebar, click All, and then select your server.

3   In the Finder window, click Connect As.

4   Enter credentials for Enrico Baker (Name: enrico, Password: net).

Do not select the checkbox to remember the password.

5   Click Connect.

After you authenticate, you see a list of share points you can access.

1   Open the ProjectZ folder, and open Maria Text File.

2   Confirm that the toolbar contains the text "Locked" to indicate that you cannot make changes to the file.

3   Press Command-W to close the file.

Compare Views of Permissions

View the permissions to see the contrasting ways in which the File Sharing pane and the Storage pane's permissions dialog display permissions information for this share point.

1   In the Server app sidebar, select File Sharing if it is not already displayed.

2   Double-click the ProjectZ share point.

3   Make a note of how the Permissions field is displayed in the File Sharing pane.

4   Click the View Files link.

Name: [ProjectZ   ]   View Files⊚

The Storage pane opens, and the ProjectZ folder is automatically selected.

5   Click the Action (gear icon) menu, and choose Edit Permissions.

> New Folder...
> **Edit Permissions...**
> Propagate Permissions...

6   Inspect how the permissions information is displayed in the Storage pane's permissions dialog.

User or Group	Permission	
▶ 👤 Spotlight	Custom	⇕
▶ 👥 ProjectZ	Read & Write	⇕
▶ 👥 Vice Presidents	Read	⇕
👤 ladmin	Read & Write	⇕
👥 wheel	Read Only	⇕
🌐 Others	None	⇕

Note that in the Storage pane's permissions dialog, you see there is an ACE for Spotlight, but the File Sharing pane simplifies your view and hides that particular ACE. In the Storage pane's permissions dialog, you can use the disclosure triangles to configure a custom set of access settings, as well as configure that ACE's inheritance rules; the File Sharing pane offers a pop-up menu with Read & Write, Read, and Write options for an ACE. The

File Sharing pane can also display "Custom" for an ACE, but you cannot modify the custom access in the File Sharing pane. Both panes offer Read & Write, Read Only, Write Only, and No Access options for POSIX permissions. The Storage pane permissions dialog lists the POSIX owner and group account names (ladmin and wheel), but in the File Sharing pane, the full names are used (Local Admin and System Group). Additionally, in the File Sharing pane, the name Everyone Else is used instead of the name Others.

Use the Server app Storage pane's permissions dialog to inspect the ACL for the share point.

1   Click the disclosure triangle for ProjectZ to reveal the permissions allowed for the ProjectZ group.

2   Click the disclosure triangle for the Write set of permissions.

The permissions dialog should look like the following figure.

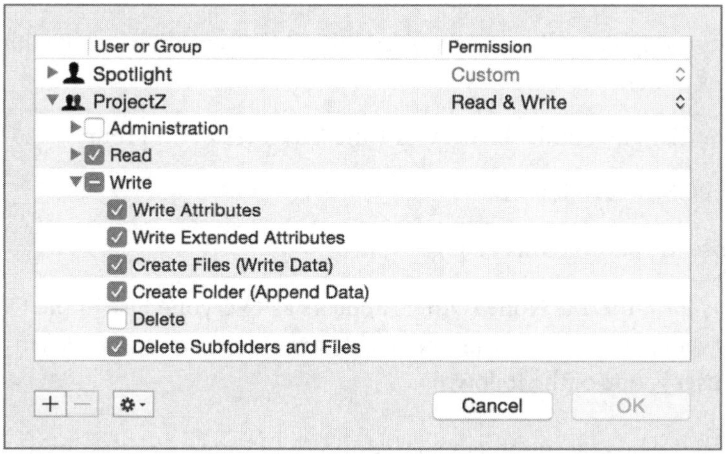

The ProjectZ group has full read access and partial write access (the ACE does not specify to allow delete permission, but Delete Subfolders and Files is selected, so anyone in the ProjectZ group can effectively delete any item except the ProjectZ share point).

Inspect the permissions for the Vice Presidents group.

1   Click the disclosure triangle to hide the detail for the ProjectZ group.

2   Click the disclosure triangle to reveal the permissions for the Vice Presidents group.

3 Click the disclosure triangle for the Read permissions allowed for the Vice Presidents group.

User or Group	Permission	
▼ 👥 Vice Presidents	Read	⇕
▶ ☐ Administration		
▼ ☑ Read		
⟶ ☑ Read Attributes		
⟶ ☑ Read Extended Attributes		
⟶ ☑ List Folder Contents (Read Data)		
⟶ ☑ Traverse Folder (Execute File)		
⟶ ☑ Read Permissions		
▶ ☐ Write		
▶ ☑ Inheritance		
👤 ladmin	Read & Write	⇕

`[ + ]` `[ − ]` `[ ✿ ▾ ]` `[ Cancel ]` `[ OK ]`

The Vice Presidents group has full read access, and this ACE gets inherited to all new items created in this folder.

4 Click the disclosure triangle to hide the detail for the Vice Presidents group.

5 View the standard POSIX permissions.

6 Click Cancel to close the permissions dialog.

The POSIX permissions for Others is None (Others appears as Everyone Else in the File Sharing pane of the Server app), so a user will not be able to access or examine files in this share point unless the user is one of the following:

▶ The local user account whose account name is ladmin (Full Name: Local Admin)

▶ In the local group whose group name is wheel (a legacy group)

▶ A member of the ProjectZ group or the Vice Presidents group

As long as you don't share any of the shared folder's ancestor folders (in this case, /Shared Items/, or the root of the startup volume), no other users will see the ProjectZ folder (although skilled users could inspect the attributes for a user and see that they are a member of the ProjectZ group).

Inspect the ACL for a folder inside the ProjectZ folder to see that when you updated the ACL for ProjectZ, the Server app automatically propagated the change. For the ProjectZ folder, you started with an ACE for Lucy Sanchez, but after you created the "Folder created by Maria" folder, you removed that ACE for Lucy Sanchez and added an ACE for the Vice Presidents group.

1   Select the "Folder created by Maria" folder.

2   Click the Action (gear icon) pop-up menu, and choose Edit Permissions.

Note in the following figure that there is no ACE for Lucy Sanchez, but there is an inherited ACE for Vice Presidents. It was automatically inherited from the ProjectZ folder's ACL when you used the Server app's File Sharing pane to update the share point's ACL.

User or Group	Permission	
▶ 👤 Spotlight	Custom	↕
▶ 👥 ProjectZ	Read & Write	↕
▶ 👥 Vice Presidents	Read	↕
👤 maria	Read & Write	↕
👥 wheel	Read Only	↕
🌐 Others	Read Only	↕

3   Click Cancel to close the permissions dialog for the folder.

Clean Up

Remove the ProjectZ folder; it is not necessary for any other exercises.

1   In the Finder sidebar, click the Eject button next to your server.

2   In the Server app sidebar, select File Sharing.

3   Select the ProjectZ share point, click the Remove (–) button, and at the confirmation dialog, click Remove.

Remove the Vice Presidents and ProjectZ groups, which are not necessary for any other exercises.

1   In the Server app sidebar, select Groups.

2   If a pop-up menu is visible, set the pop-up menu to Local Network Groups.

3   If the lock icon at the bottom of the pane is locked, unlock it: Click the lock at the bottom of the pane, provide directory administrator credentials (Administrator Name: diradmin, Administrator Password: diradminpw), and click Authenticate.

4   Select the Vice Presidents group.

5   Click the Remove (–) button, and at the confirmation dialog, click Remove.

6   Select the ProjectZ group.

7   Click the Remove (–) button, and at the confirmation dialog, click Remove.

In this exercise, you used POSIX permissions and an ACL to control access to a shared folder and a text file. You assigned No Access for Everyone Else to prevent all users from accessing the shared folder and then added an ACE to grant read/write access to a group. You also created an ACE for a particular user, but as the situation evolved, you replaced that ACE with an ACE for yet another group and noted that this change you made with the File Sharing pane was automatically propagated to existing items. You saw that the File Sharing and Storage panes offer different views of POSIX ownership and permissions and an item's ACL; the File Sharing pane offers a simple summary and options, and the Storage pane offers more advanced information and options. Finally, you proved that the Server app automatically propagates the share point's ACL whenever you use the File Sharing pane to make a change to the share point's ACL or POSIX permissions.

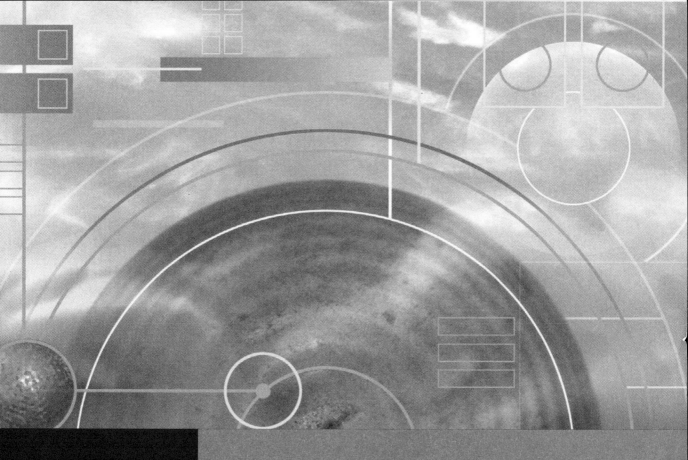

Implementing
Deployment Solutions

Lesson 14

Leveraging NetInstall

One significant challenge for OS X administrators today is deploying software to multiple computers. Whether it is operating system (OS) releases and updates or commercial applications, installing the software manually is a labor-intensive process. OS X Server provides services and technologies to aid in this deployment. The NetInstall service simplifies OS rollout and upgrades.

Knowing how to use time efficiently is an important aspect of an administrator's job. When managing several hundred OS X computers, an administrator needs a solution that is both speedy and flexible for performing day-to-day management of computers. When computers need to be set up for the first time, what software should be installed? Should they have the latest software updates? Should they have a full complement of non-Apple software, such as Adobe Creative Cloud or Microsoft Office? What about shareware programs and the necessary work-related files? Safety videos? Mandatory PDFs? Trust and enrollment profiles for Profile Manager?

Before you can push out data to a computer, you must decide *how* to push out that data and in what state. Though there are several third-party tools that complete the tasks of image creation and deployment, Apple has several applications to assist you with this process. These helpful applications include System Image Utility, Apple Software Restore (ASR), Apple Remote Desktop (ARD)

With the advantage of these deployment software tools, you can build an automated system that needs little user interaction to function. This lesson focuses primarily on the NetInstall service provided by OS X Server.

Creating NetInstall images can be a lengthy process, but most of the time is spent waiting for the image to be processed. Review the exercise, and plan your time.

Reference 14.1
Managing Computers with NetInstall

Think about the ways in which you start up your computer. Most often, your computer starts up from system software located on the local hard disk. This local startup provides you with a typical computer experience of running applications, accessing information, and accomplishing tasks. When you perform an OS installation for versions of OS X prior to Lion, you could start up from a CD-ROM or DVD-ROM disc.

Managing a single standalone computer isn't much of an inconvenience. However, imagine managing a lab of computers. Every time you need to upgrade the operating system or install a clean version of OS X, you would need to boot each computer in the lab from OS X Recovery. That isn't practical.

OS X Server provides the NetInstall service, which simplifies the management of operating systems on multiple computers. With NetInstall, client computers start up using system software they access from a server instead of from the client's local hard disk. Once started from the server-based operating system, the computer can be used much like a normal computer (NetBoot), have an OS or other software installed on it (NetInstall), or have a clone of another computer copied to it (NetRestore). These three techniques make deployment and management of OS X computers convenient and efficient.

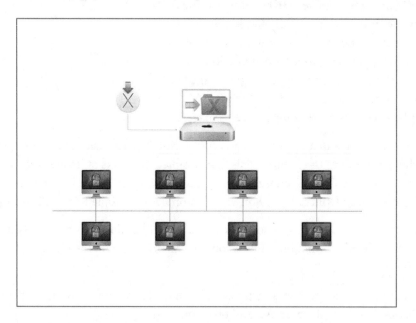

NetInstall is most effective in situations in which there is a high frequency of user turnover and in which a large number of computers are being deployed with a common configuration. The ability to deploy standard configurations across multiple computers makes NetInstall ideal for computing environments such as the following:

▶   Configuring groups of computers—The NetInstall service makes it easy to configure multiple identical desktop systems quickly.

▶   Updating computers—Using NetInstall to install system software allows you to update workstations quickly. Also, because installation is done over the network, it can even be done in place at the user's desk.

▶   When using kiosks and in libraries—With the NetInstall service, you can set up protected computing environments for customers or visitors. For example, you can configure an information station with an Internet browser that connects only to a specific website, or you can set up a visitor kiosk that runs only a database for collecting feedback. If a system is altered, a simple restart restores it to its original condition.

▶   Repurposing computers—You can use NetInstall to quickly repurpose computers with different software including operating systems and applications simply by deploying from a different image.

▶   Creating an emergency boot disk—You can use the NetInstall service to troubleshoot, restore, and maintain client computers. The NetInstall service can also help access computers whose boot drives have failed and whose recovery partition is not available. A creative way to take advantage of this technology is to create a NetInstall service image with various computer diagnosis and disk recovery software. Booting into a rescue image at a user's desk could save a lot of time for a frustrated user.

Hardware Requirements

For NetInstall to function properly, certain minimum hardware requirements must be met:

▶   2 GB RAM on the client computer

▶   100Base-T switched Ethernet (up to 50 clients)

▶   1000Base-T switched Ethernet (beyond 50 clients)

Although there are some Mac computers that can use NetInstall over Wi-Fi, it is best to use Ethernet for NetInstall when possible. NetInstall over Wi-Fi is neither supported by Apple nor recommended. For computers shipped without an Ethernet port, such as the

MacBook Air, using a Universal Serial Bus (USB) to Ethernet or Apple Thunderbolt to Gigabit Ethernet adapter is recommended.

Defining NetInstall Image Types

There are three NetInstall image types:

▶ A NetBoot startup (using a NetBoot boot image) uses an operating system accessed from a server. To the user it behaves just like a regular operating system but allows the client computer's internal drive not to be used for startup. Multiple network clients can use each disk image at once. You are setting up a centralized source of system software, so you need to configure, test, and deploy only once.

▶ A Network Install, also known as NetInstall, startup sequence (using a NetInstall image) enables you to quickly perform fresh installations of your operating system. It also allows you to install applications or updates. To the user, starting up with NetInstall looks just like a familiar installer environment. The terms "Network Install" and "NetInstall" are used interchangeably in this lesson.

▶ NetRestore is aimed at deploying full system images. A typical situation is where you make a clean install of the operating system on a computer, install any additional software needed, configure the settings, and then make a NetRestore image from it. This is called a monolithic image. A version of this is when instead of including all of the software in the "golden master" image, you just make an image of the computer and build installer packages of the other software. This gives you a more modular approach to imaging computers. The system image is embedded by default in the NetRestore folder, or you can define a custom workflow that uses an image hosted on a file share on a server. This makes NetRestore a powerful tool in your deployment arsenal.

Keep these three types of NetInstall images in mind while you read the remainder of this lesson.

When you start up from a NetInstall, NetBoot, or NetRestore image, the startup volume is read-only. When a client needs to write anything back to its startup volume, the NetInstall service automatically redirects the written data to the client's shadow files (which are discussed later in this lesson, in the section "Reference 14.3 Describing Shadow Files" on page 461). Data in shadow files is kept for the duration of a NetInstall service session. The startup volume is read-only, so you always start from a clean image.

Stepping Through the NetInstall Client Startup Process

When a client computer boots from a NetInstall image, it performs a number of steps to start up successfully:

1   The client places a request for an IP address.

When a NetInstall client is turned on or restarted, it requests an IP address from a Dynamic Host Control Protocol (DHCP) server. While the server providing the address can be the same server providing the NetInstall service, the two services do not have to be provided by the same computer.

NOTE ▶ DHCP available on the network is a requirement for NetInstall to work.

2   After receiving an Internet Protocol (IP) address, the NetInstall client sends out a request via the Boot Service Discovery Protocol (BSDP) for startup software. The NetInstall server then delivers the core system files (booter and kernel files) to the client using Trivial File Transfer Protocol (TFTP) via its default port, 69.

3   Once the client has the core system files, it initiates a mount and loads the images for the NetBoot network disk image.

The images can be served using Hypertext Transfer Protocol (HTTP) or Network File System (NFS) with HTTP being the default.

4   After booting from the NetInstall image, the NetInstall client requests an IP address from the DHCP server.

Depending on the type of DHCP server used, the NetInstall client might receive an IP address different from the one received in step 1.

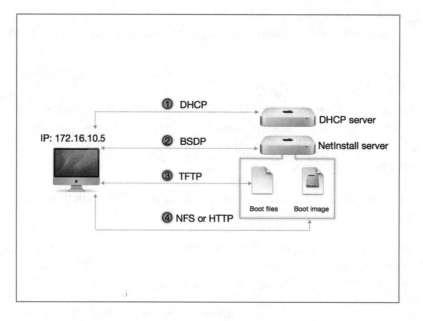

Reference 14.2
Creating Images with System Image Utility

System Image Utility is the tool you use to create all three types of NetInstall images. Available from the Tools menu in the Server app, System Image Utility uses files from a mounted volume, disk image, or the Install OS X Yosemite application to create a NetInstall image. The application is located in /System/Library/Core Services/Applications/.

NOTE ▶ For more information, refer to the System Image Utility Help, https://help.apple.com/systemimageutility/mac/10.10.

Each image requires an image ID, or index, which client computers use to identify similar images. If, when a client lists the available NetInstall images in the Startup Disk pane of System Preferences, two images have the same index, the client assumes that the images are identical and displays only one entry. If only one server will serve an image, assign it a value between 1 and 4095. If multiple servers will serve the same image, assign it a value between 4096 and 65535. By default, System Image Utility generates a semirandom index between 1 and 4095, but you can change it if you customize the image during creation or after using the Server app.

When creating an image, you specify where to store it. For the NetInstall service to recognize the image, it must be stored in /<volume>/Library/NetBoot/NetBootSP*n*/*imagename*.nbi, where *n* is the volume number and *imagename* is the image name you entered when you created the image. If you have already configured the NetInstall service, the Save dialog includes a pop-up menu listing the available volumes. If you choose a volume from that pop-up menu, the save location changes to the NetBootSP*n* share point on that volume.

> **TIP** ▶ In a NetInstall environment, many clients booting from the same NetInstall server can place high demands on the server and slow down performance. To improve performance, you can set up additional NetInstall servers to serve the same images. NetInstall is also sensitive to disk speed, with faster disk storage helping increase performance.

System Image Utility also enables you to customize your NetBoot, NetRestore, or Network Install configurations by adding any of the following Automator workflow items:

▶ Add Configuration Profiles—Allows embedding profiles in the image for device management.

▶ Add Packages and Post-Install Scripts—Allows you to add third-party software or make virtually any customization you desire automatically.

▶ Add User Account—Includes additional users in your image. These users could include system administrator accounts or user accounts.

▶ Apply System Configuration Settings—Allows you to automatically bind computers to LDAP directory servers, along with applying basic preferences such as the computer's host name.

▶ Bless NetBoot Image Folder—Defines a network disk image as bootable.

▶ Create Image—Acts as the basis for all image building.

▶ Customize Package Selection—Defines which packages are usable and visible.

▶ Define Image Source—Allows the user to pick the source for the image.

▶ Define Multi-Volume NetRestore—Allows restoration of multiboot systems.

▶ Define NetRestore Source—Defines the network location of the NetRestore image.

▶ Enable Automated Installation—Assists in doing speedy deployments in which you're dealing with identical configurations and want to do hands-off installation.

▶ Filter Clients by MAC Address—Restricts which clients can use the network-based images.

▶ Filter Computer Models—Restricts which model computers can use the network-based images.

▶ Partition Support—Comes built-in to System Image Utility so you can add a partition automatically in your deployments.

Using NetInstall

NetInstall is a convenient way to reinstall the OS, applications, or other software onto local hard disks. For system administrators deploying large numbers of computers with the same version of OS X, NetInstall can be useful. All startup and installation information is delivered over the network. You can perform software installations with NetInstall using a collection of packages or an entire disk image (depending on the source used to create the image).

> **TIP** ▶ For installing small packages rather than entire disks, it might be easier to use ARD because not all packages require a restart. If NetInstall is used to deploy a package, the client will need to be rebooted whether or not the package requires it.

When creating an install image with System Image Utility, you have the option to automate the installation process to limit the amount of interaction from anyone at the client computer. Keep in mind that responsibility comes with this automation. An automatic network installation can be configured to erase the contents of the local hard disk before installation, so data loss can occur. You must control access to this type of Network Install disk image, and you must communicate to users the implications of using these images. Always instruct users to back up critical data before using automatic network installations. When configuring your NetInstall server, you will be warned about this even if you aren't doing automated installs.

> **NOTE** ▶ Set the default NetInstall image on every server. You can also turn off the NetInstall service when you don't need it.

When creating NetInstall images, specify a source for the image in System Image Utility. You should use System Image Utility only to build images of like versions of OS X. You can use OS X Server to serve images of any version of OS X, but if you want to make images of earlier OS X versions, you should use the respective version of OS X and its version of System Image Utility to build the image. You can create images from the following sources:

▶ Install OS X Yosemite—You can download this from the Mac App Store.

▶ Disk images—Instead of using a configured hard disk as a source, you can use Disk Utility to create a disk image of a configured hard disk and then use the disk image as a source for creating NetBoot images.

▶ Mounted volumes—When you select a mounted volume as a source, the entire contents of the volume, including the operating system, configuration files, and applications, are copied to the image. When a client computer starts up from an image created from a mounted volume, the boot experience is similar to that of starting up from the original source volume. A copy of the source volume is written to the client computer's hard disk. A benefit of using volumes for image sources is that the image creation is much faster than when using discs. In addition, installations that use images created from volumes are faster than installations that use disc-created images.

Additional features are available, including external image sources such as a network share or ASR multicast streams, by choosing Customize and the Define NetRestore Source Automator action. This is where you can define that a network share with a disk image made from an existing volume is available.

Use the latest version of the operating system when creating NetBoot images. If you are creating OS X 10.9 images, use the imaging tools from OS X 10.9. If you are creating OS X 10.10 images, use the imaging tools on OS X 10.10 or OS X Server for Yosemite 10.10. Be aware that there is the possibility that a particular model of computer might be limited to a specific version of OS X, and as a result you would need to match the startup operating system with the hardware.

When adding new computers to the NetInstall environment, you may need to update the NetInstall image to support them. Check the OS software version that accompanied the new computer.

Using NetRestore

NetRestore places the contents of a disk image onto the startup volume of a Mac. The disk image can be created from a Mac that has already been configured with the settings and software that you want, or you can make an image of a never started Mac. This gives you flexibility in customizing the disk image that gets placed, and you can deploy that image to as many Mac systems as you need.

Creating an image requires mounting the volume you want to image on the Mac you will run System Image Utility on. If you have created a master image using a Mac that has all the configurations and software you need, you can start the Mac in Target Mode and use Thunderbolt or FireWire to connect it to the Mac running System Image Utility. The volume from the Mac in Target Mode will show up as an option in System Image Utility where it can be picked and a disk image made. In this method, the disk image of the Mac will be embedded in the .nbi file that results. The .nbi file contains all the necessary files to start up the remote computer and the disk image payload that will be copied down to the Mac being imaged.

You can also use Disk Utility to make a disk image that can be deployed from a file server. You can find directions on how to do this in Apple Support article HT202841, "OS X: Creating a software deployment image with a recovery partition." The resulting image is hosted on a file server that can be reached by the Mac computers being imaged. System Image Utility is used to create a custom workflow that includes the location of the file server hosting the image.

> **NOTE** ▶ See System Image Utility Help for details on creating the external NetRestore volume workflow at https://help.apple.com/systemimageutility/mac/10.10/index.html?localePath=en.lproj#/sysma045230a.

Reference 14.3
Describing Shadow Files

Many clients can read from the same NetBoot image, but when a client needs to write anything (such as print jobs and other temporary files) to its startup volume, NetInstall automatically redirects the written data to the client's shadow files, which are separate from regular system and application software files. These shadow files preserve the unique identity of each client during the entire time the client is running off a NetInstall image. NetInstall also transparently maintains changed user data in the shadow files, while reading unchanged data from the shared system image. The shadow files are re-created at boot time, so any changes that the user makes to the startup volume are lost at restart.

This behavior has important implications. For example, if a user saves a document to the startup volume, the document will be gone after restart. This preserves the condition of the environment the administrator set up, but it also means you should configure each network user account to have a network home folder if you want users to be able to save their documents.

For each image, you can specify where the shadow file is stored using the Diskless checkbox in the NetBoot image configuration in the Server app. When the Diskless option for an image is deselected, the shadow file is stored on the client computer's local hard disk at /private/var/netboot/.com.apple.NetBootX/Shadow/. When the Diskless option is enabled, the shadow file is stored in a share point on the server named NetBootClients$n$ in /<volume>/Library/NetBoot/, where n is the number of the volume that stores the shadow file. With the Diskless option enabled, a NetBoot image enables you to operate client computers that are literally diskless.

> **TIP** ▶ Make sure you consider the storage need for shadow files when configuring your server. When running diskless, users may experience delays since writes to the shadow files take place via the network and not locally.

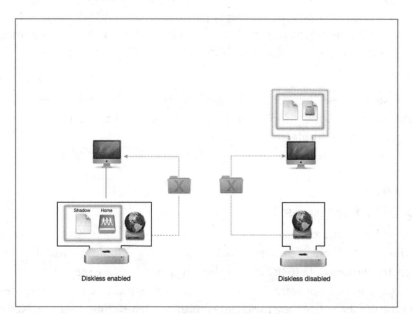

Diskless enabled   Diskless disabled

Reference 14.4
Troubleshooting NetInstall

NetInstall is a fairly straightforward process. If a client does not successfully start up from a NetInstall server, you can troubleshoot the issue by looking into the following areas:

▶ Check the network. The client must have an IP address obtained through DHCP.

▶ Check the server logs for bootpd messages, since the underlying process that serves NetInstall is bootpd. These logs can also identify if you mistyped an Ethernet hardware address or selected the wrong type of hardware for a filter.

▶ Press and hold the Option key as you boot the client, which will indicate whether you have a firmware password configured for the computer. A firmware password requires that a password be entered before any alternate boot sources are used, such as a NetInstall image. A firmware password is applied if a lock command was ever sent to an OS X computer.

▶ Check the disk space on the server. Shadow files and disk images may be filling the server's disk space. You may want to add disks with larger capacity or more of them to accommodate these files.

▶ Check for server filters. Do you have filters enabled for IP address, hardware address, and model type? If so, you should disable the filters to allow all computers on the network to start up using the NetInstall service.

▶ Check firewall configurations. NetInstall requires that a combination of the DHCP/ BOOTP, TFTP, NFS, AFP, and HTTP ports be open. Temporarily disabling the firewall or adding a rule to allow all traffic from the subnet you're starting up with NetInstall will indicate whether you have a firewall configuration problem.

Exercise 14.1
Prepare the NetInstall Service

▶ **Prerequisite**

▶ Your server needs a wired Ethernet connection.

In this exercise, you will specify the disk on which to store NetInstall service images and client data. This automatically creates the folder structure for the NetInstall service, which makes it easy for you save NetInstall images in the right place when you create them in the next exercise. You can't turn on the NetInstall service without a valid image, so you will not turn it on in this exercise yet.

In a production environment, you can use multiple disks and combine multiple Ethernet ports (using link aggregation, which is outside the scope of this guide) to increase the performance of the NetInstall service. To keep things simple for this exercise, use your server's startup volume.

1   Perform these exercises on your administrator computer. If you do not already have a connection to your server computer with the Server app on your administrator computer, then connect to it with the following steps: Open the Server app on your administrator computer, choose Manage > Connect to Server, select your server, click Continue, provide administrator credentials (Administrator Name: ladmin, Administrator Password: ladminpw), deselect the "Remember this password" checkbox, and then click Connect.

2   In the Server app sidebar, in the Advanced section, select NetInstall.

3   Next to the "Enable NetInstall on" field, click Edit.

4   Confirm that an Ethernet port (either a built-in one or an Ethernet port from an adapter) is selected.

The NetInstall service is not supported over Wi-Fi.

5   Click OK to dismiss the Network Interfaces pane.

6   In the lower-left corner of the NetInstall pane, click Edit Storage Settings.

7   For the purposes of this exercise, select your server's startup volume.

8   Click the Stored Data column for your server's startup volume, and choose Images & Client Data.

9   Click OK to dismiss the Storage Settings pane.

In this exercise, you specified your server's startup disk to be used for the NetInstall images and client data. This automatically created /Library/NetBoot/NetBootSP0/ and /Library/NetBoot/NetBootClients0/. Because you have not yet created any NetInstall images, you cannot start the service.

Exercise 14.2
Create a Customized NetInstall Image

▶ **Prerequisites**

▶   "Exercise 4.2 Configure an Open Directory Certificate Authority" on page 152

▶   "Exercise 10.1 Turn On Profile Manager" on page 312

▶   "Exercise 14.1 Prepare the NetInstall Service" on page 463

In this exercise, you will create a NetInstall image; after you create the image, in "Exercise 14.4 Start Up from a NetInstall Image" on page 478 you will confirm that you can start up from it, and then in "Exercise 14.5 Monitor the NetInstall Service" on page 480 you will confirm that you can monitor the client and the service.

In a production environment you may find that it takes more time to perform an installation of OS X Yosemite using a NetInstall image than it does to restore a NetRestore image of the Install OS X Yosemite app. For the purposes of the exercises in this lesson, you will take advantage of the fact that it takes less time to create a NetInstall image than it does to create a NetRestore image of the Install OS X Yosemite app.

Even though you can create NetInstall, NetRestore, and NetBoot images using any Mac computer with Yosemite, in this exercise you will create the image directly on your server computer so you do not need to spend time copying the image to your server computer from another Mac computer.

In this exercise, you will customize the NetInstall image to install the trust profile for your Profile Manager service in addition to installing OS X. Using the image to actually install OS X on your administrator computer is outside the scope of this exercise, so you will examine the resulting NetInstall image and confirm the trust profile is included. If you were to use this customized NetInstall image to install OS X on a Mac, you could hand that Mac to a user; after the user turns it on and goes through the Setup Assistant to create a computer account, she can go to your server's Profile Manager service and enroll without a warning that Safari cannot verify the identity of the server because the trust profile will have been automatically installed.

> **NOTE ▶** The amount of time it takes to create an image depends on the speed of your disk. It could take less than two minutes to create your NetInstall image with a solid-state drive (SSD) or flash storage or longer with a disk that physically spins.

Download the Trust Profile

If you already have your server's Open Directory trust profile handy, skip this section, and continue with "Create the Customized NetInstall Image" on page 467.

Otherwise, use these steps to download it now.

1   On your server, open your Profile Manager web app; in Safari, open https://server*n*.pretendco.com/profilemanager (where *n* is your student number).

2   At the Please Log In pane, provide administrator credentials (User Name: ladmin, Password: ladminpw), deselect the "Keep me logged in" checkbox, and then click Connect.

3 In the upper-right corner of the Profile Manager web app, click your login name, and then choose Download Trust Profile.

4 At the dialog, click Download.

5 When Profiles preferences opens and asks if you want to install the profile, click Cancel.

6 Quit System Preferences.

7 Close the Safari window that displays your Profile Manager web app.

The trust profile is now in your Downloads folder; you are ready to continue.

Create the Customized NetInstall Image

1 On your server computer, copy the Install OS X Yosemite application into the Applications folder of the server if it isn't already there.

If you are in an instructor-led environment, the installer is available in the /StudentMaterials/Lesson14/ folder. If you are performing these exercises on your own, you can download the installer from the Mac App Store.

2 Use Spotlight to open System Image Utility.

> If Spotlight cannot find the application, in the Finder, choose Go > Go to Folder,
> enter /System/Library/CoreServices/Applications, click Go, and then open System Image
> Utility from that folder.

3   Click the pop-up menu, and then choose Install OS X Yosemite.

4   Select NetInstall Image.

5   Click Customize.

6   Read the software license agreements, and then click Agree.

7   In the first step of the System Image Utility workflow, confirm that Source is set to
Install OS X Yosemite.

If it is not, click the Source pop-up menu, and choose Install OS X Yosemite.

8   From the Automator Library window, drag Add Configuration Profiles between the
Define Image Source and Create Image workflow steps.

9   In the Add Configuration Profiles workflow step, click the Add (+) button.

10   In the sidebar of the Open file dialog, select Downloads, select your server's trust pro-
     file, and then click Open.

11   In the Create Image workflow step, ensure that the Save To pop-up menu is set to
     NetBootSP0.

     If NetBootSP0 is not in the pop-up menu, choose Other in the pop-up menu, press
     Command-Shift-G, enter **/Library/NetBoot/NetBootSP0/**, click Go, and then click
     Choose.

12 In the Image Name and Network Disk fields, enter Server *n* NetInstall of Install OS X
Yosemite with Trust Profile (where *n* is your student number).

13 In the Description field, append with Trust Profile to the existing text.

By default the OS build information is included in parentheses. You can use this information to keep track of which version of OS X the image contains, which is useful
when there are updates. The Description field is visible when you double-click an
image in the NetInstall pane in the Server app.

▼ 🛠 **Create Image**			×
Type:	○ NetBoot		
	◉ NetInstall		
	○ NetRestore	☑ Include Recovery partition	
Installed Volume:			
Save To:	▦ NetBootSP0	○	
Image Name:	Server 17 NetInstall of Install OS X Yose		
Network Disk:	Server 17 NetInstall of Install OS X Yosemite with Trust Profile	Image Index:	1006
Description:	NetInstall of OS X 10.10 (14A389) Install (7.84 GB) with Trust Profile		
Results Options			
Back		Save	Run

14 Click Run.

15 Authenticate as ladmin when prompted.

16 Press Command-L to display the log, and then scroll through its contents.

```
Create NetInstall Image
Initiating NetInstall from OS X install source.
created: /Library/NetBoot/NetBootSP0/Server 17 NetInstall of Install OS X Yosemite with Trust Profile.nbi/
NetInstall.dmg
pkgbuild: Adding top-level postinstall script
pkgbuild: Wrote package to /tmp/niutemp.KobnyYLt/netInstallConfigurationProfiles.sh.inner.pkg
productbuild: Wrote product to /tmp/niutemp.KobnyYLt/netInstallConfigurationProfiles.sh.pkg
chmod: /tmp/mnt.hg6N0r9Q/Packages/Extras/Setup: No such file or directory
"disk4" unmounted.
"disk4" ejected.
"disk3" unmounted.
```

After System Image Utility completes creating the image, you'll see the following:

▶ You'll see a green checkmark at the bottom-left corner of the Create Image workflow step.

▶ The button in the lower-right corner changes from Stop to Run.

▶ The log states "Workflow Finished" and includes the date and time (you can scroll to the top of the log to see the time the workflow started to calculate the amount of time it took to create the image).

Save the Workflow

Save the workflow so you can run it again after the OS X Installer is updated.

1 Click Save.

2 In the Save As field, enter **Server *n* NetInstall of Install OS X Yosemite with Trust Pro-file** (where *n* is your student number).

3 If the Where pop-up menu is displayed, click it, and choose Documents.

Otherwise, select Documents in the Save dialog sidebar.

4 Click Save.

5 Quit System Image Utility.

In the future, after you download an update to the Install OS X Yosemite app, you would remove your existing NetInstall image from /Library/NetBoot/NetBootSP0/ and then open the workflow, update the build number in the Description field, and click Run to create an updated NetInstall image.

Inspect the Customized NetInstall Image

Use the Finder on your server to confirm that the trust profile was included in the NetInstall image you just created.

1 On your server, in the Finder, choose Go > Go to Folder.

2 Enter **/Library/NetBoot/NetBootSP0**, and click Go.

3 Open Server *n* NetInstall of Install OS X Yosemite with Trust Profile.nbi (where *n* is your student number).

4 Open NetInstall.dmg.

5 Select the NetInstall volume in the Finder window sidebar.

6 Open the Packages folder.

7 In the Finder toolbar, click the Column View icon.

8 Navigate to the /Packages/Extras/ConfigurationProfiles/ folder.

9   Confirm that your server's trust profile is in the ConfigurationProfiles folder.

10 Next to the NetInstall volume in your Finder window sidebar, click Eject.

11 Close any extra open Finder windows, if there are any.

When a Mac computer starts up from your customized NetInstall image and uses it to install OS X, your server's trust profile is also automatically installed.

You just created and inspected a NetInstall image of an OS X installer with your server's trust profile.

Exercise 14.3
Start the NetInstall Service

Prerequisite

▶ "Exercise 14.2 Create a Customized NetInstall Image" on page 465

Now that you have a valid image, you can configure a few settings for that image and then start the NetInstall service.

For each image, you can specify which protocol, NFS or HTTP, to use to serve the image. For the purposes of this exercise, you will configure the image to be served using NFS instead of HTTP. HTTP is now the default because it enables you to serve disk images without having to reconfigure any firewall to allow NFS traffic. The NetInstall service does not require the Websites service to be turned on to service images over HTTP.

You will configure your NetInstall image to be the default image.

Finally, you will use the File Sharing pane to inspect the folders associated with the NetInstall service.

Configure the NetInstall Image Protocol

Start by configuring your NetInstall image to be served using NFS instead of HTTP.

1   Perform the rest of this lesson's exercises on your administrator computer. If you do not already have a connection to your server computer with the Server app on your administrator computer, then connect to it with the following steps: Open the Server app on your administrator computer, choose Manage > Connect to Server, select your server, click Continue, provide administrator credentials (Administrator Name: ladmin, Administrator: Password ladminpw), deselect the "Remember this password" checkbox, and then click Connect.

2   If you performed the previous exercise on your server as directed, you have a NetBoot image (NBI) in /Library/NetBoot/NetBootSP0/ on your server.

    If you created the image on another computer, copy the image to your server at that location, providing your local administrator credentials if necessary.

3   In the NetInstall pane, click the Settings tab, and select your NetInstall image.

    If the image does not appear, choose View > Refresh.

4   Double-click the NetInstall image to edit it.

5   Note that the description of the image is displayed under the name of the image.

6   Under Availability, click the pop-up menu, and choose NFS.

7   Under Access, click the pop-up menu, and choose "only some Mac models."

8   Scroll through the list, and note the variety of models of Mac computers.

9   Click Cancel.

10 Select the checkbox to restrict access.

11 Click the Add (+) button, and note that you can enter a MAC address.

12 Click Cancel.

13 Confirm that the image is available over NFS.

Availability

☑ Make available over   NFS ⇕

14 Click OK to save your changes and return to the main NetInstall pane.

15 Click On to turn on the NetInstall service.

The only change you made was to make the image available over NFS instead of HTTP.

Specify a Default Image

Within the Server app, the Images pane lists the available NetInstall images on the server, which can host up to 25 different NetInstall images. If you deselect the checkbox "Make available over" for an image, then clients cannot use that image.

If you can have several images, you can specify one of them to be the default image, which is the image that your NetInstall service will serve to a NetInstall client that has not otherwise chosen a specific image. For a Mac that has never started up from your NetInstall service, when you turn it on and hold down the N key, your server will provide the default image to that Mac, and the Mac will use that image as a default in the future. However, on that Mac you can hold down Option-N to use the current default, regardless of what image was the default the first time that Mac used your server's NetInstall service.

1 In the NetInstall pane, click the Settings tab.

2 Select your NetInstall image.

3 From the Action (gear icon) menu, choose Use as Default Boot Image.

The image is now noted as "(default)" on the right side of the pane.

> **TIP** ▶ Remember that image files can be large and take up a significant amount of disk space on the server. Consider using a second volume to hold the images and keep them off your server's startup volume.

Inspect the Shared Folders Related to the NetInstall Service

Your NetInstall service is now configured. Use the File Sharing pane to review that the File Sharing service offers the following:

▶ NetBootClients0 via the Apple Filing Protocol (AFP) so diskless clients can store shadow files

▶ NetBootSP0 via NFS so clients can quickly mount the NetInstall image

Do not attempt to modify these shared folders; otherwise, you may inhibit your ability to use the NetInstall service.

1 In the Server app sidebar, select File Sharing.

2 Review the Shared Folders field.

3 Double-click the NetBootClients0 shared folder.

4 Confirm that AFP is selected.

```
Name:  NetBootClients0
Share over:  ☐ SMB   ☑ AFP   ☐ WebDAV
```

5 Click Cancel.

6 Double-click the NetBootSP0 shared folder.

7 Confirm that neither AFP, SMB, nor WebDAV are selected.

```
Name:  NetBootSP0
Share over:  ☐ SMB   ☐ AFP   ☐ WebDAV
```

There is no interface to select NFS; the NetInstall service automatically configures a shared folder to be available via NFS.

8 Click Cancel.

In this exercise, you configured your NetInstall image to be served over NFS instead of HTTP, you specified a default NetInstall image, and you inspected the shared folders associated with the NetInstall service.

Exercise 14.4
Start Up from a NetInstall Image

▶ **Prerequisites**

- ▶ DHCP must be available on your network.

- ▶ "Exercise 14.3 Start the NetInstall Service" on page 473

- ▶ Your server and your administrator computer each needs a wired Ethernet connection.

As long as your client computer has the latest version of its firmware and is a supported client computer, you don't need to install any other special software. The Extensible Firmware Interface (EFI) (Intel) boot code contains the software used to boot a computer using a NetInstall image.

There are at least three ways to cause a computer to use NetInstall at startup:

- ▶ Hold down the N key until the blinking NetInstall globe appears in the center of the screen. This method allows you to use NetInstall for a single startup. Subsequent reboots return the computer to the previous startup state. Your client computer will then boot from the default NetInstall image hosted by the NetInstall server.

- ▶ Select the desired network disk image from the Startup Disk pane in System Preferences. The version of the Startup Disk pane included with OS X v10.2 and later presents all available network disk images on the local network. Notice that each type of NetInstall image maintains a unique icon to help users differentiate between the types of images. With the desired network disk image selected, you can reboot the computer. The computer then attempts to use the NetInstall service on every subsequent startup.

- ▶ Hold down the Option key during startup. This invokes the Startup Manager, which presents a list of available system folders as well as a globe icon for NetInstall. Click the globe icon, and click the advance arrow to begin the NetInstall process. This option doesn't allow you to pick which image you want to boot from. As when holding down the N key, you will get the default image.

It is important to note a couple of things that can upset the NetInstall process:

▶ If no network connection exists, a NetInstall client will eventually time out and look to a local disk to start up. You can prevent this by keeping local hard disks free of system software and denying users physical access to the Ethernet ports on a computer so they cannot disconnect the network connection.

▶ Resetting the parameter random-access memory (PRAM) resets the configured startup disk, requiring you to reselect the NetInstall volume in the Startup Disk pane of System Preferences.

You'll try starting up your client computer with NetInstall now.

1   On your administrator computer, quit the Server app.

2   On your administrator computer, open System Preferences, and then open the Startup Disk preferences.

3   Select the NetInstall image hosted by your server.

If you are in an instructor-led environment, hover your pointer over a NetInstall image until you see an image for your server.

If you are performing these exercises on your own on an isolated network, your server's NetInstall image should be the only NetInstall image that appears.

4   Click Restart.

Your administrator computer starts the OS X Installer from the NetInstall image you just created and enabled.

5   Do not reinstall OS X on your administrator computer, but leave your administrator computer started up from the NetInstall image so you can explore the monitoring options with the NetInstall service on your server.

Exercise 14.5
Monitor the NetInstall Service

> **Prerequisite**
>
> ▶   "Exercise 14.4 Start Up from a NetInstall Image" on page 478

In this exercise, you will monitor your NetInstall clients. The Connections pane provides a list of client computers that are started up from images hosted by your server's NetInstall service. It reports the computer's host name and IP address, its progress, and its status.

Monitor the NetInstall Service Log

1   On your server, open the Server app, and connect to your server if you are not already connected.

2   In the Server app sidebar, select Logs.

3   Click the pop-up menu, and in the NetInstall section, choose Service Log.

4   In the Search field, enter INFORM, and then press Return.

```
Oct 14 14:34:23 server17.pretendco.com bootpd[6272]: BSDP INFORM [en0] 1,40:6c:8f:3d:e7:b NetBoot001 arch=i386
sysid=MacBookPro11,3
Oct 14 14:34:23 server17.pretendco.com bootpd[6272]: NetBoot: [1,40:6c:8f:3d:e7:b] BSDP ACK[LIST] sent 10.0.0.186 pktsize
353
```

| Service Log | ⬦ | | Q- INFORM | ⊗ | ? |

An INFORM packet is sent from the NetInstall service to a Mac and contains information about the available NetInstall images and service.

Use the NetInstall Connections Tab

Once a NetInstall client has successfully started from a NetInstall image, the Connections tab of the NetInstall pane contains information about the client.

1   In the Server app sidebar, select NetInstall.

2   Click the Connections tab.

3   Note that your administrator computer is listed with the status of NetInstall.

	Settings	Connections		
Host Name	IP Address		Status	Progress
MacBookPro\03218479371773395...	10.0.0.186		NetInstall	0%

Clean Up

Restart your administrator computer from its usual startup disk, and turn off the NetInstall service.

Restart Your Mac

1   On your administrator computer, from the Apple menu, choose Startup Disk.

2   Select your normal startup volume (Macintosh HD unless you changed it).

3   Click Restart, and then at the confirmation dialog, click Restart.

Turn Off the NetInstall Service

1   On your server computer, in the NetInstall pane, click Off to turn off the NetInstall service.

2   In the Server app sidebar, select File Sharing.

3   Confirm that the NetBootClients0 and NetBootSP0 shared folders no longer appear.

4   Quit the Server app.

You learned how to configure NetInstall and leverage it for imaging and startup.

Lesson 15

Caching Content from Apple

The Caching service speeds up the download and distribution of software and other content distributed by Apple. It caches the first download of various items distributed by Apple and then makes these items available to devices and computers on your local network. This means you can offer fast downloads of items distributed by Apple to clients on your network.

This allows you to save time as well as Internet bandwidth use.

> **MORE INFO** ► One significant new feature in the Caching service for OS X Server for Yosemite is that it can be configured to work even if the server has a public address and is not behind network address translation (NAT). This is covered in the configuration section of this lesson.

Reference 15.1
Describing the Caching Service

For eligible computers and devices, the Caching service transparently caches many items, including the following:

► Software updates

► App Store purchases and downloads

► Mac App Store purchases and downloads

► iBooks Store purchases and downloads

GOALS

► Describing the Caching service

► Configure and maintain the Caching service

► Review Caching service clients

► Compare and contrast the Caching service and the Software Update service

► Troubleshoot the Caching service

▶   iTunes U items

▶   Internet Recovery

The Caching service supports Mac computers with OS X 10.8.2 or later and iOS 7 or later. It also supports iTunes content for Mac and Windows computers with iTunes 11.0.2 or later.

The network requirements to use the Caching service are as follows:

▶   Be on an Ethernet network with a network device that performs network address translation to and from the Internet

▶   Have the same public Internet Protocol version 4 (IPv4) source address on the Internet side of the NAT device as on the Caching server for outgoing traffic (in simpler terms, have the same public IP address as the server behind NAT)

▶   If not behind NAT (not on the same private network as clients where the same public IPv4 address is being used), have a Domain Name System (DNS) TXT record configured to allow the clients to find it

To use the Caching service with the Mac App Store, a Mac must:

▶   Have OS X version 10.8.2 or later

▶   Not be configured to use the OS X Server Software Update service

In the most common configuration, the key is that your clients and the Caching servers must share the same Internet connection behind a NAT device, and their traffic from your network to the Internet must have the same source IPv4 address. (This applies even if the client and the Caching server are on different subnets, as long as they have the same public IPv4 source address.) With OS X Server for Yosemite, it is now possible to configure Caching even if the hosting OS X Server is not behind NAT.

Eligible clients will automatically use the appropriate Caching server. Otherwise, the client will use servers operated by Apple or a content distribution network partner (just like they did before the Caching service was introduced as a feature).

In the following figure, a network device performs NAT, and the organization has two subnets. The clients and the Caching servers in both subnets have the same public IPv4 source address on the public Internet side of the NAT device, even though they are in different subnets. The clients in both subnets automatically use one of the Caching servers in their organization's network (in the figure, one subnet has two servers to illustrate that you don't need a Caching service for each subnet behind NAT). Once the clients leave the local network, they automatically use servers controlled by Apple.

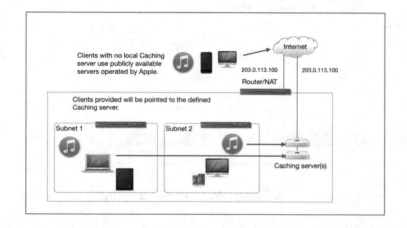

In the following figure, the Caching service is using an external IP address that is not the same as the clients. Clients will be pointed to the external Caching service.

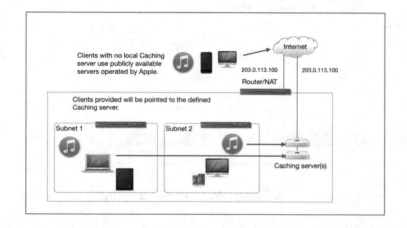

The Caching server automatically registers its public IPv4 address and local network information with Apple servers. When a client communicates with Apple servers to download an item, if the client's public IPv4 address matches your Caching server's public IPv4 address, the Apple servers instruct the client to get the content from the local Caching server. If the client cannot communicate with its local Caching server, it automatically downloads the content from servers controlled by Apple on the Internet.

The Caching service caches only items distributed by servers that are under Apple's control (including items from a content distribution network partner); it does not cache content from random third parties.

Be sure to read the "Provide a Caching server" topic in Help Center for the Server app; it is an informative and up-to-date reference. Click the link on the Caching server pane; or, in the Server app, from the Help menu, enter Provide a Caching server in the search field.

Reference 15.2
Configuring and Maintaining the Caching Service

It's simple to configure the Caching service. You could click the On switch to turn the service on and be done configuring.

The Server app allows a few configuration features. You can do the following:

▶ Click the link next to Status to learn more about configuring this service

▶ Click Permissions to set which network segments can use the service

▶ Click Edit to select a volume for caching

▶ Use the slider to set the cache size

▶ Deselect the checkbox "Only cache content for local networks" to serve only clients on subnets that your server is not directly connected to (for complex networks)

▶   Click Reset to erase the existing cached content

The volume you select to use for the Caching service must have at least 50 GB free (even if you set the Cache Size slider to 25 GB). If you select a volume that doesn't have enough space, the Server app alerts you, and the Choose button becomes unavailable. Simply select a different volume.

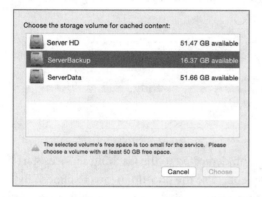

By default, the Caching service uses the startup volume for the cached content. Even though the slider is labeled "Unlimited," the Caching service is smart enough to not fill up the entire volume; when only 25 GB is left on the volume you're using for the Caching service, your server deletes the least recently used cached content (not necessarily the oldest content) to make space for new content. If your users download a large variety of different content, consider using a volume large enough to cache as much content as you can; otherwise, the Caching service may constantly delete items that it will end up downloading again, after deleting yet more items to make room for the newly requested items.

If you change the volume used for the Caching service, the existing cached content will be copied to the newly selected volume.

> **MORE INFO** ▶ See the "Configure advanced cache settings" section of the OS X Server: Advanced Administration guide (https://help.apple.com/advancedserveradmin/mac/4.0/) for more advanced options, such as limiting the network interfaces on which the service listens and limiting the number of concurrent client connections.

The Caching service will not start unless your server has a wired Ethernet connection. Wireless connections are not supported for the server itself.

If your organization has a number of subnets with a Caching server that are all behind the same network device that performs NAT and they all have the same public IPv4 address but the internal subnets have slow links between them, you may want to select the check-box "Only cache content for local networks" so that each subnet has its own local copy of items. This way, clients on each subnet can download cached content quickly from a local Caching server, as opposed to using up the slow link between subnets. Caching servers will download content from their peers, if available, rather than from the Internet.

The Usage section shows you at a glance the kind of content your Caching server has downloaded.

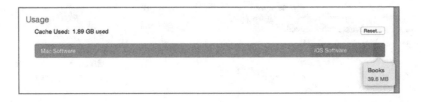

The Stats pane of the Server app has one graph dedicated to the Caching service. Start by selecting the Stats pane in the Server app sidebar. Use the pop-up menus to choose Bytes Served as the type of activity, and then choose a time period. The graph shows how much data the Caching service has downloaded from the Internet and from other peer servers and how much it has served to clients from its cache.

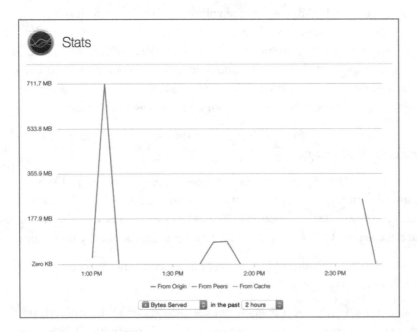

If you need to configure a server that has a public IP address rather than a local area network (LAN) IP address behind your router, there is an additional configuration needed. In the Permissions dialog, define that all networks will have content cached and will serve clients on other networks. Define a new network by giving it a name and range of IPs.

Caching
Configure how devices use this caching server.

Cache content for clients connecting from: all networks

Serve clients with public addresses: on other networks

Labs (10.1.0.1 - 10.1.0.254)

+ −   Client Configuration...

Additional configuration is required for clients in the specified IP address ranges to use this caching server. Click Client Configuration to view these settings.

?   Cancel   OK

You need to copy the content displayed by clicking the Client Configuration button and save it for the manual configuration of DNS.

Copy the TXT record below and enter it into your network DNS configuration.

_aaplcache._tcp   259200 IN TXT "prs=10.1.0.1-10.1.0.254"

?   Done

+ −   Client Configuration...

Additional configuration is required for clients in the specified IP address ranges to use this caching server. Click Client Configuration to view these settings.

?   Cancel   OK

Set up a new DNS domain called caching.apple.com and create a machine record for www with an IP address of 127.0.0.1.

Records

Primary Zone: caching.apple.com

www.caching.apple.com machine

www.caching.apple.com nameserver

In /Library/Server/named/, edit the db.caching.apple.com file, and add the line you copied from the Client Configuration dialog. With DNS running and client computers and devices using your DNS service, they will be able to use your Caching server even though the server is not behind NAT but exposed with a different public IP address.

```
●○○                        ↑ ladmin → nano — 107×26
  GNU nano 2.0.6          File: /Library/Server/named/db.caching.apple.com           Modified

caching.apple.com.              10800 IN SOA     caching.apple.com. admin.caching.apple.com. (
                                                 2014100703 ; serial
                                                 3600       ; refresh (1 hour)
                                                 900        ; retry (15 minutes)
                                                 1209600    ; expire (2 weeks)
                                                 86400      ; minimum (1 day)
                                                 )
                                10800 IN NS      www.caching.apple.com.
www.caching.apple.com.          10800 IN A       127.0.0.1
_aaplcache._tcp                 259200 IN TXT    "prs=10.1.0.1-10.1.0.254"




  ^G Get Help    ^O WriteOut    ^R Read File    ^Y Prev Page    ^K Cut Text     ^C Cur Pos
  ^X Exit        ^J Justify     ^W Where Is     ^V Next Page    ^U UnCut Text   ^T To Spell
```

Reference 15.3
Comparing the Software Update and Caching Services

The current and several previous versions of OS X Server have offered the Software Update service (see Lesson 16 "Implementing the Software Update Service"). This service allows you to limit the software updates available to your Mac clients. However, because OS X clients cannot simultaneously use the Software Update service and the Caching service of OS X Server, you must choose which service is more appropriate for your needs.

If a Mac is already configured to use the Software Update service, it will not use the Caching service; to use a Caching server, you must reconfigure such a Mac to *not* use the Software Update service.

Here are the main differences between the two services:

▶ The Caching service caches many different kinds of content, but the Software Update service caches software updates only.

▶ The Caching service caches an item only after the first client requests it, but the Software Update service allows you to automatically download software updates before the first Mac client needs them.

▶ The Caching service makes all appropriate items available to clients automatically, but with the Software Update service, you can allow clients to download only the updates you have approved (for instance, if you are required to confirm that each software update is compatible with your other software and workflows).

▶ Eligible computers with OS X automatically use an appropriate Caching server, but you must configure a computer with OS X to use a specific Software Update server.

▶ The Caching service provides no ability to manage what clients can download, but the Software Update service does.

▶ The Caching service is great for mobile clients whether or not they are inside your local network. In contrast, if a client that is configured to use your server's Software Update server cannot contact it once the client leaves your local network, then the client cannot use Software Update or the Mac App Store to install software updates until it returns to your local network.

▶ The Software Update service does not provide any service at all to iOS devices.

Table 15-1 summarizes the differences between the Caching service and the Software Update service.

TABLE 15.1   Differences Between Caching Service and Software Update Service

Category	Caching Service	Software Update Service
Type of content cached	OS X and iOS software updates; App Store, Mac App Store, and iBooks Store items; iTunes U items; Internet Recovery; Apple TV updates; Siri voices and language dictionaries; GarageBand content (refer to Apple Support article HT6018, "Content types supported by the Caching service," for more details.)	OS X software updates only
Specify content to serve	Not applicable	Automatic or manual
Download trigger	Client requests item from Apple	Immediate or manual

Category	Caching Service	Software Update Service
Client configuration	None	defaults command, managed preferences, or configuration profile

Even though it is possible to use the same server to provide Software Update and Caching services, be aware that this may require a large amount of storage space, and a single client cannot use both services.

Unless you need to prevent Mac clients from installing specific software updates via Software Update or the Mac App Store, it is recommended that you use the Caching service instead of the Software Update service.

Reference 15.4
Troubleshooting the Caching Service

The Caching service is transparent, so there isn't much troubleshooting necessary. The first time a client downloads an item that isn't already cached, that initial download isn't any faster. However, subsequent downloads of the same item, whether from the same client or from a different client, are limited only by the speed of the disks of the client and server or the bandwidth of the local network.

Deleting Items to Test the Caching Service

To test downloading items, you can use a computer that's an eligible client of the Caching server to download an item from iTunes (11.0.2 or later), the Mac App Store, or the App Store and then delete it, download it again (or download the same item from multiple eligible clients), and confirm that the subsequent download speeds are appropriate for downloading items locally as opposed to across the Internet.

> **TIP** You can use your server that's running the Caching service to perform the first download of an item; it is automatically a Caching service client as well as a server.

Confirming the Basics

If you suspect problems with the Caching service, you can do the following:

▶ For iTunes, confirm that iTunes is version 11.0.2 or later. On a Mac, choose iTunes > About iTunes. On a PC with Windows and iTunes, choose Help > About iTunes.

▶ Confirm that the Caching service is turned on in the Server app. The Caching service status indicator in the Server app sidebar list of services is green when the service is turned on.

▶ Confirm that the client and the server have the same public IPv4 source address on the Internet side of a NAT device or confirm that clients are looking at a DNS server with TXT records defining the location of the Caching server if the Caching server is not on the same private network.

▶ Confirm that the Mac clients are not configured to use a Software Update server.

▶ Confirm that iOS devices are using the same network as your Caching service. In other words, confirm that the iOS device is using Wi-Fi and is not using *only* a cellular network.

▶ Check the Cache Used field. If the value is None, perhaps no eligible client has downloaded any eligible content.

Use Activity Monitor to confirm that your server is downloading items from the Internet and then serving items to clients. On your server, open Activity Monitor, choose View > All Processes, click the Network tab, set the pop-up menu to Data, and monitor the graph. When the Caching service downloads an item from the Internet to cache it, this is reflected in a purple "Data received/sec" line. When the Caching service sends a cached item to a local client, this is reflected in a red "Data sent/sec" line.

Using the Caching Service Logs

You can use the Logs pane of the Server app to check the service log for the basics. In the Logs pop-up menu, choose Service Log under the Caching menu item. If the system log has been automatically rotated as part of daily system maintenance tasks, the Logs field may simply contain "No contents to display." This view filters out any line in the generic system log that does not contain the "AssetCache" string.

For more detailed information, use the Console app on your server. Choose File > Open, navigate to /Library/Server/Caching/Logs/, select Debug.log, and click Open. You can click

Hide Log List in the Console app toolbar to devote more room to displaying the log contents.

Logs

```
downloaded from origin, 0 bytes from peers
Oct  7 13:45:25 server17.local AssetCache[45017]: Since server start: 1.85 GB returned to clients, 1.85 GB requested
from servers (1.85 GB from origin, 0 bytes from peers)
Oct  7 13:45:35 server17.local AssetCache[45017]: #KK/uwHFExOUw Request by "itunesstored/1.0" for http://
a1599.phobos.apple.com/us/r30/Publication3/v4/a2/b0/dc/a2b0dc48-fd1c-8d08-363c-01f244264593/
_mzbf_streamable_5448192056620173495.d2.dlv.epub?a=357316318
Oct  7 13:45:35 server17.local AssetCache[45017]: Since server start: 1.85 GB returned to clients, 1.85 GB requested
from servers (1.85 GB from origin, 0 bytes from peers)
Oct  7 13:45:40 server17.local AssetCache[45017]: #DBGJWW2my/+L Request by "itunesstored/1.0" for http://
a1599.phobos.apple.com/us/r30/Publication3/v4/a2/b0/dc/a2b0dc48-fd1c-8d08-363c-01f244264593/
_mzbf_streamable_5448192056620173495.d2.dlv.epub?a=357316318
Oct  7 13:45:41 server17.local AssetCache[45017]: #DBGJWW2my/+L 4.9 MB of 4.9 MB served, 0 bytes from cache, 4.9 MB
downloaded from origin, 0 bytes from peers
Oct  7 13:45:41 server17.local AssetCache[45017]: Since server start: 1.86 GB returned to clients, 1.86 GB requested
from servers (1.86 GB from origin, 0 bytes from peers)
Oct  7 13:45:52 server17.local AssetCache[45017]: #gZWthP9Uxkap Request by "itunesstored/1.0" for http://
a1656.phobos.apple.com/us/r30/Publication3/v4/ff/d4/49/ffd449fe-3dee-7959-26f0-55ec806dcd15/
mzbf_zlrozdjf_.d2.dlv.epub?a=376229549
Oct  7 13:45:57 server17.local AssetCache[45017]: #gZWthP9Uxkap 17.1 MB of 17.1 MB served, 0 bytes from cache, 17.1 MB
downloaded from origin, 0 bytes from peers
Oct  7 13:45:57 server17.local AssetCache[45017]: Since server start: 1.88 GB returned to clients, 1.88 GB requested
from servers (1.88 GB from origin, 0 bytes from peers)
Oct  7 13:46:06 server17.local AssetCache[45017]: #nytOmKNiEij7 Request by "itunesstored/1.0" for http://
a1395.phobos.apple.com/us/r30/Publication1/v4/c4/3f/a0/c43fa0d3-f66e-c51e-8ba9-c953c94856b9/
_mzbf_streamable_47697418491408844.d2.dlv.epub?a=412379804
Oct  7 13:46:11 server17.local AssetCache[45017]: #nytOmKNiEij7 17.6 MB of 17.6 MB served, 0 bytes from cache, 17.6 MB
downloaded from origin, 0 bytes from peers
Oct  7 13:46:11 server17.local AssetCache[45017]: Since server start: 1.89 GB returned to clients, 1.89 GB requested
from servers (1.89 GB from origin, 0 bytes from peers)
Oct  7 14:36:12 server17.local AssetCache[185]: Caching Server started
Oct  7 14:36:12 server17.local AssetCache[185]: Request for configuration from http://suconfig.apple.com/resource/
registration/v1/config.plist failed: The Internet connection appears to be offline.
Oct  7 14:36:12 server17.local AssetCache[185]: Reverting to last accepted configuration
Oct  7 14:36:13 server17.local AssetCache[185]: Request for blacklist from http://suconfig.apple.com/resource/
registration/v1/blacklist.plist failed: The Internet connection appears to be offline.
Oct  7 14:36:13 server17.local AssetCache[185]: 1 consecutive cleanup failure(s).  Will retry in 16 seconds.
Oct  7 14:36:25 server17.local AssetCache[185]: Registration succeeded.  Resuming server.
```

Service Log | ◇ | Q Search | ?

Here are some strings in Debug.log that might help you understand what is happening:

▶ "Issuing outgoing full request" when the Caching service downloads an item from public servers

▶ "Data already cached for asset" when the Caching service already has an item cached locally

Some items in the log have human-recognizable names, but other items have names that might seem random. Reviewing the content and context of the logs when there are no known problems will help you be able to parse them when troubleshooting.

Recognizing Performance Bottlenecks

A single Caching server can handle hundreds of clients simultaneously and can saturate a Gigabit Ethernet network interface. To determine whether your server (as opposed to local network capacity) is the bottleneck, open Activity Monitor on your server, click the CPU tab, and monitor the CPU Usage graph. If your server's CPU usage is near its maximum, consider additional servers for the Caching service.

Moving the Caching Service Data Volume

If you attach a new volume to your server after you've started the Server app and connected to your server, choose View > Refresh (or press Command-R) to select the newly attached volume as the destination for the Caching service. After you choose a new location, the Server app automatically moves the cached content to the new volume.

Lesson 16

Implementing the Software Update Service

Once you have deployed computers, the question of how to keep the software on them up to date will arise. Built into OS X Server is the ability to mirror the Apple software updates that exist on the Apple Software Update servers onto your local server.

Reference 16.1
Managing Software Updates

With OS X Server, you have the option of mirroring the Apple Software Update servers on your local server. This has two distinct advantages. The first is that you can save Internet bandwidth, and the second is that you can control the updates available to your users.

GOALS

▶ Describe the concepts of the Software Update service (SUS)

▶ Configure the server to provide software updates

▶ Configure a client to use the Software Update service

▶ Configure which updates are provided to the clients

▶ Learn to troubleshoot the Software Update service

Only software updates to Apple-supplied software can be served by the update services. Third-party software or modified Apple updates can't be added to the service. Refer to Apple Support article HT200117, "OS X Server: Software Update Service compatibility."

When using the Software Update service, all of your client computers will retrieve their software updates from the server on your local network rather than over the Internet, which will also result in faster downloads for your users. You can configure the service to automatically download and make the update available, or you can do the updates manually.

The process of manually controlling which updates can be downloaded and made available to your users can be particularly useful when a software update might be incompatible with some software you're using or the update hasn't gone through testing in your environment.

If you have set the service to automatically download and make updates available, the service will remove obsolete updates automatically. If you set the service to Manual, you will need to cull outdated updates manually.

You can configure clients to use the update service by making a manual change to a preference list, by setting managed preferences, or by using a configuration profile. Configuration profiles with a software update payload are available only for devices and device groups.

Settings for Pretendco Mac Lab
2 Payloads Configured - Created 10/07/14 at 5:30 PM

For situations in which multiple Software Update service implementations are appropriate to use, such as for load balancing across a large number of client computers, you can create a cascade of servers. You create one main server and point others at it to get their updates. This prevents having many Software Update servers from using additional network bandwidth. Refer to Apple Support article HT201962, "OS X Server: How to cascade Software Update Servers from a Central Software Update Server."

Reference 16.2
Troubleshooting the Software Update Service

If the Software Update service doesn't work as expected, you can troubleshoot the issue by looking into the following areas:

▶ Check the network. The client must be able to contact your Software Update service and be able to communicate with it. The default port the service uses is 8088.

▶ Are the updates listed in SUS? If the updates haven't been downloaded, they won't be available to the client devices. The Software Update service can't work through an authenticated proxy if you are using one.

▶ Is space available on the server's disk? Logs will indicate that Software Update will stop synchronizing if the server's volume has less than 20 percent of its total storage space available.

▶ Is the Software Update service profile installed on the device? If the computer doesn't have a profile containing the Software Update service information, it won't know to look for your Software Update service.

▶ Is the specific update enabled? Check in the list of updates.

▶ Check the Software Update logs (Service, Access, and Error logs).

▶ Does the client computer have a profile pointing it to the right Software Update service?

Providing Network
Services

Lesson 17

Offering Time Machine Network Backup

A powerful feature of Time Machine is its ability to use network-based share points as a backup location. You can use OS X Server to provide a centralized destination for backups and to quickly monitor your users' backups, including information about how large each backup is, the progress of a backup, and the last time a backup was successfully completed.

To use your server as a Time Machine backup destination, users simply select your server's Time Machine destination from a list; your server uses Bonjour to advertise the shared folder or folders it offers for the Time Machine service. It is a simple process.

GOALS

▶ Turn on the Time Machine service

▶ Configure OS X Server to offer Time Machine services

Reference 17.1
Configuring Time Machine as a Network Service

Time Machine is a powerful backup and restore service available to users of OS X (OS X Yosemite, OS X Mavericks, OS X Mountain Lion, Mac OS X Lion, Mac OS X Snow Leopard, and Mac OS X Leopard); you can use the Time Machine service with OS X Server to provide a backup destination on your server to Time Machine users.

You can now configure a limit to the size of each client backup, but only a Mac running OS X Mavericks or newer will obey this limit. Apart from this limitation, Time Machine will by design eventually fill up the destination volume with backup files, so it's a good idea to use a volume (or volumes) that you dedicate to Time Machine only.

It is also a good idea to use the exclusions in Time Machine on the computer being backed up to limit the amount of data being backed up to a manageable level. You might decide to back up only the user home folder and documents to save space.

You must turn on the File Sharing service for clients to use the Time Machine service. The destination you define in the Time Machine service will appear as a share point in the File Sharing list.

TIP The Server app provides no warning that if you turn off the File Sharing service, you will interrupt active Time Machine backups or restores; so, if you offer the Time Machine service, be sure not to turn off the File Sharing service until you have confirmed that no client computers are actively backing up or restoring with the Time Machine service.

After you use the Server app to choose a destination for Time Machine backups, click the On switch to turn on the Time Machine service.

On the Time Machine destination, each client computer gets its own sparse disk image (a sparse disk image can grow in size), and there is an automatically configured access control list (ACL) to prevent anyone from accessing or deleting Time Machine files from the sparse disk image. The Backups pane shows a list of the backups done and their status.

If you later change the backup volume, users who use your server's Time Machine service will automatically use the new volume. However, OS X Server does not automatically migrate existing backup files. The next time a client's Mac runs a Time Machine backup, the user sees a warning that the identity of the backup disk has changed since the previous backup. After the user agrees to use the disk, OS X uses Time Machine to back up all the nonexcluded files, not just the files that have changed since the last time a successful Time Machine backup completed, so it may take a long time, depending on how much data is backed up.

Remember that you can use the Permissions edit functionality to configure user and group access to the Time Machine service.

Exercise 17.1
Configure and Use the Time Machine Service

> **Prerequisites**

> ▶ "Exercise 9.1 Create and Import Network Accounts" on page 292; or, create a user with a full name of Barbara Green, an account name of barbara, and a password of net.

> ▶ You must have a folder named Shared Items, owned by the Local Admin user and located at the root of the startup disk; you can use the section "Create a New Location for Shared Folders" on page 396 in Exercise 12.1 to create that folder and modify its ownership. Alternatively, you can use an extra disk if you have one available.

You will configure your server to be a network destination for Time Machine backups so client computers can keep a Time Machine backup in a centralized location.

In a production environment, you should use a disk other than your startup disk as a Time Machine backup destination. In this exercise, you will create a new folder to use on the startup disk for testing purposes. Be sure to follow the instructions to stop the Time Machine service at the end of the exercise; otherwise, your server's startup disk might become filled with backup files.

1   Perform these exercises on your administrator computer. If you do not already have a connection to your server computer with the Server app on your administrator computer, then connect to it with the following steps: Open the Server app on your administrator computer, choose Manage > Connect to Server, select your server, click Continue, provide administrator credentials (Administrator Name: ladmin, Administrator Password: ladminpw), deselect the "Remember this password" checkbox, and then click Connect.

2   In the Server app sidebar, select Time Machine.

3   Below the Destinations field, click the Add (+) button.

4   Next to the "Store backups in" field, click Choose.

5   Select your startup disk, and then select the Shared Items folder.

6   Click New Folder.

7   Enter the name Time Machine Backups, and click Create to create the new folder.

8   Select the folder you just created.

9   Click Choose.

10 Confirm the details of the shared folder you are about to create.

11 Click Create.

Note that the Server app displays which volume is used as the backup destination, as well as how much space is available on that volume.

12 Click On to start the service.

When you turn on the Time Machine service, the Server app automatically starts the File Sharing service if it is not already running.

Configure an OS X Computer to Use the Time Machine Destination

Verify that network-based Time Machine works as expected. Configure your administrator computer to use the Time Machine service.

Configure Time Machine to Exclude Most Files

Since this is a learning environment, you can reduce the amount of space required for a Time Machine backup by excluding your Documents folder, as well as system files such as the system applications and UNIX tools. Configure this before setting a Time Machine destination to ensure that you don't back up files that are unnecessary for the exercise.

1 On your administrator computer, open System Preferences, and then open Time Machine Preferences.

2 Select the checkbox "Show Time Machine in menu bar."

☑ Show Time Machine in menu bar   Options...   ?

3 Click Options.

4 Click Add (+) to add a folder to be excluded.

5 In the sidebar, select Documents, and then click Exclude.

6 Click Add (+).

7 Click the pop-up menu in the center of the top of the window, and choose your startup disk.

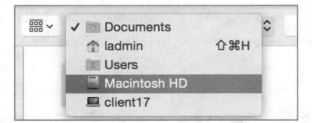

8   Hold the Command key and select each of the visible folders except the Users folder.

9   Click Exclude.

10   At the notice that you've excluded the System folder, click Exclude All System Files.

11   If you have any other disks or volumes on your administrator computer, add those to the list of excluded items.

12   Review the list of exclusions.

Note that the "Back up while on battery power" option appears only on portable Mac computers.

13   Click Save.

Configure Time Machine to Use Your Server's Time Machine Service

Now that you've configured your administrator computer's Time Machine preferences to exclude most files, select your server's Time Machine network volume.

1   In Time Machine preferences, click Select Backup Disk.

NOTE ▸ If you are in a classroom environment, do not select another student's server because this will create unexpected results when their Time Machine service stops.

2   Select the item named Time Machine Backups with your server's computer name.

For the sake of keeping things simple for this exercise, leave the "Encrypt backups" checkbox unselected.

3   Click Use Disk.

4   Provide credentials for a user on the server, and click Connect. Use Barbara Green's user name (barbara) and password (net).

5   Click Connect.

Time Machine preferences displays the server name, how much space is available, and information about backup dates.

6   From the Time Machine status menu, choose Back Up Now.

7   Once the backup has completed, click Close at the notification.

Inspect the Status of the Backup at the Server

The Time Machine service allows you to monitor the status of the backups.

1   On your administrator computer, in the Server app, connect to your server.

2   In the Server app sidebar, select Time Machine.

3   Click the Backups tab.

4   Double-click the entry for the backup of your administrator computer, or select it and click Edit (pencil icon).

5   Note all the information displayed, and then click View Share Point.

The Server app opens the File Sharing pane, with details about the Time Machine Backups shared folder.

MORE INFO ▶ In the Permissions field, Everyone Else is set to No Access. A user account has access to the Time Machine service if it's a member of the com.apple.access_backup group. This group is normally not visible; you add members to this group when you use the Users pane or Groups pane to manage access to services for an account.

6   Click View Files.

The Server app opens the Storage pane, and the disk image's name uses the client's computer name.

7   Click File Sharing in the Server app sidebar.

8   Note that the Time Machine destination is listed with a special icon.

Clean Up

Since this is a test environment, stop using Time Machine from your server.

1   On your administrator computer, from the Time Machine status menu, choose Open
     Time Machine Preferences.

2   Click Select Disk.

3   Under Backup Disks, select the Time Machine destination you just used, and click
     Remove Disk.

4   At the message asking if you are sure, click Stop Using This Disk.

5   To stop automatic backups, click Off.

6   Quit System Preferences.

Configure the Time Machine service to stop offering your server's volume.

1   In the Server app sidebar, select Time Machine.

2   Click the Settings tab.

3   In the Destinations field, select Time Machine Backups, and then click the Remove (−)
     button.

4   At the message asking if you are sure, click Remove.

The Server app automatically turns off the Time Machine service (but it does not turn off
the File Sharing service).

In this exercise, you configured your server to be a network destination for Time Machine
backups so client computers can keep a Time Machine backup in a centralized location.
You made a limited backup and then used the Server app to view information about that
backup. In a production environment, be sure to periodically test to verify that you can
restore items from your backups using the Time Machine service.

Lesson 18
Providing Security via the VPN Service

A virtual private network connection is like having an impossibly long Ethernet cable from a user's computer or device somewhere else in the world to your organization's internal network; your users can use the VPN to encrypt all traffic between their computers or devices and the computers inside your organization's internal network.

Don't confuse a firewall and a VPN; a firewall can block network traffic based on several possible criteria—such as the port number and source or destination address—and there is no authentication involved, but a user must authenticate to use the VPN service.

GOALS

► Identify the benefits of a virtual private network (VPN)

► Configure the VPN service

Your organization may already have a network device that provides VPN service, but if you don't, consider using the OS X Server VPN service, which is both powerful and convenient, especially considering its tight integration with AirPort devices.

Reference 18.1
Describing VPNs

Even though your server can offer many of its services using Secure Sockets Layer (SSL) to secure the content of data being transferred, some services, such as the AFP service, do not use SSL. In general, for services offered by OS X Server, authentication is almost always secure and encrypted over the network, but the payloads may not be. For example, without a virtual private network connection to encrypt traffic, the contents of files transferred over the Apple Filing Protocol (AFP) are not encrypted. So if an eavesdropper can capture unencrypted network traffic, he might not be able to reassemble credentials, but he can reassemble information to which you probably don't want him to have access.

If your organization does not have a dedicated network device that provides VPN service, you can use OS X Server to provide VPN service using the Layer 2 Tunneling Protocol (L2TP) or using L2TP and the Point to Point Tunneling Protocol (PPTP). PPTP is considered less secure, but it is more compatible with older versions of Mac and Windows operating systems.

Regardless of what you use for virtual private networking, you can configure your users' computers and devices to use a VPN so that when they are outside of your organization's internal network, they have a secure connection to your internal network. If you provide VPN service for your users, you can use a firewall to allow services that you provide to all users, such as the Web and Wiki services, but configure your firewall to block outside access to Mail and File Sharing services. When your users are on the other side of the firewall from your server, they can use the VPN service to establish a connection as if they were on your internal network, and the firewall will not affect them; they can access all the services as if they were not remote.

The most difficult part of establishing a VPN connection falls outside the scope of this guide; you need to be sure that the router passes the appropriate traffic from outside your network to your server so that VPN clients can establish and maintain a VPN connection. See Apple Support article HT202944, "TCP and UDP ports used by Apple software products," for more information about well-known ports.

Reference 18.2
Configuring the VPN Service with the Server App

The VPN service is configured and ready for you to start with the default options; just click the On button. This lesson explains the configuration options.

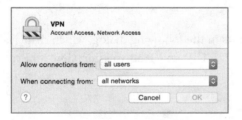

If you have older clients that aren't compatible with L2TP, click the "Configure VPN for" pop-up menu, and choose L2TP and PPTP

You can edit the permissions to define where incoming VPN connection requests will be honored from.

To allow you the flexibility of using an alternate Domain Name System (DNS) host name that clients use to access your server's VPN service, you can change the VPN Host Name field. When you modify the field, the status indicator is red if your server has no DNS record available for the host name your enter, and the status indicator is green to indicate the existence of a DNS record. Keep in mind that the host name you specify here will likely be used by people who are external to your local network; the host name you specify should have DNS records available outside of your local network as well.

For example, if your server is behind an AirPort device that provides Dynamic Host Control Protocol (DHCP) and network address translation (NAT), make sure that the host name you specify in the VPN Host Name field has a publicly accessible DNS record that matches the public Internet Protocol version 4 (IPv4) address of the AirPort device. The following figure from the AirPort Utility Network tab illustrates that the VPN service appears if you use the Server app to manage your AirPort device and make the VPN service available.

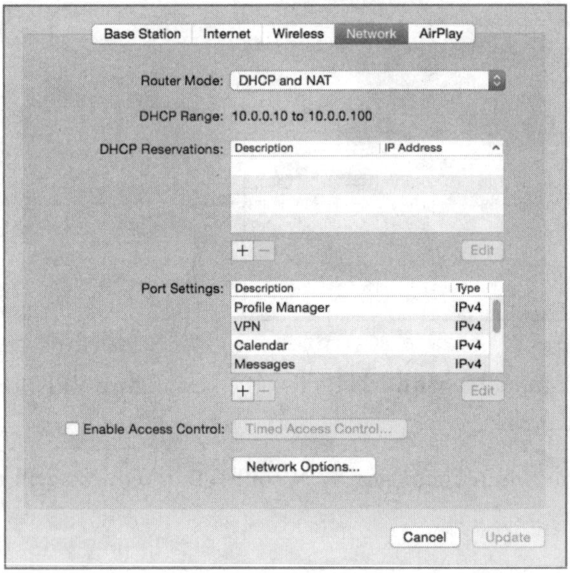

Selecting the VPN entry and clicking Edit results in the following dialog, which displays the VPN-related public User Datagram Protocol (UDP) and Transmission Control Protocol (TCP) ports that are sent to your server.

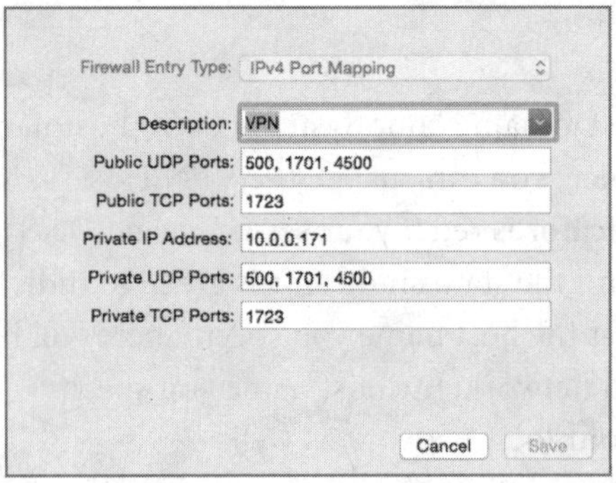

To ensure confidentiality, authentication, and communications integrity, both the OS X Server VPN service and the VPN clients must use the same shared secret, which is like a passphrase. To establish a VPN connection, a user must still authenticate with her user name and password. By default, the Server app generates a random string of characters for the shared secret. You can change the string to something else, but it's best if this is a random string. This shared secret is included if you create a configuration profile to distribute to users. If you change the shared secret later, each of your users needs to update their VPN client configuration. Here are some ways of accomplishing this:

▶ Save the configuration profile again, distribute it to your users, and have them install the new configuration profile.

▶ Use the Profile Manager service to distribute a configuration profile that includes VPN configuration, which automatically updates the shared secret in the configuration profile when it is installed or reinstalled.

▶ Instruct your users to manually enter the new shared secret at their VPN client.

Settings

Configure VPN for: L2TP

VPN Host Name: server17.pretendco.com

Clients configured using profiles will access the VPN service from the Internet using this hostname or IP address.

Shared Secret: -d.F5T>]liu5LH3\syf^

☑ Show shared secret

Using Advanced Configuration Options

You could simply turn on the VPN service without configuring these advanced options, but if you have more than a few networked devices on your local network, you should at least review the configuration of the Client Addresses field to ensure that local clients and VPN clients never accidentally get assigned the same IPv4 address.

The Client Addresses field shows the number of IPv4 addresses the VPN service hands out to VPN clients; click Edit to configure the range. If you've enabled both L2TP and PPTP, you can use a slider to distribute the number of clients available for each protocol.

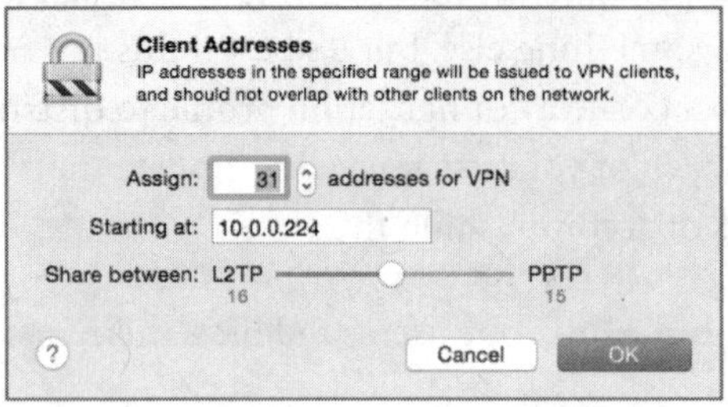

When you hover the pointer over the "Starting at" field, the Server app displays the effective IPv4 address range for each protocol, as shown in the following figure.

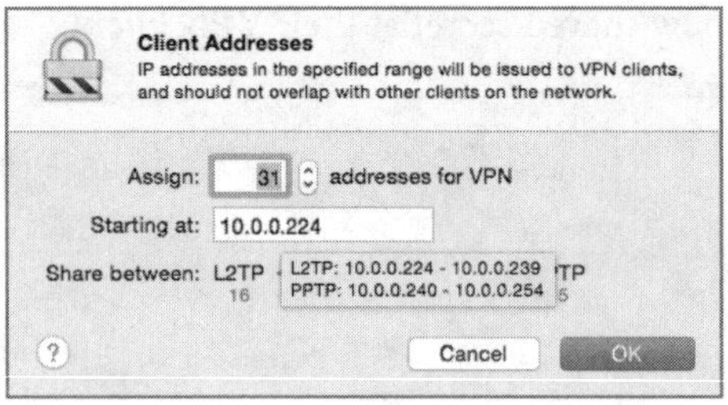

When a VPN client successfully connects to your server's VPN service, the VPN service assigns the VPN client an IPv4 address for your local network. Be sure that no other devices on your local network use an IPv4 address in the range that the VPN service issues to clients; you should configure your local network's DHCP service to not offer IPv4 addresses in the same range and ensure that there are no devices with manually assigned IPv4 addresses in the same range.

Similarly, you can assign one or more default search domains that are appropriate for clients on your internal network.

By default, the VPN service configures VPN clients to use the same DNS server or servers, and the same search domain or search domains, that your server uses. This means that VPN clients have access to DNS records that are available for clients on your internal network only.

Click Edit next to the DNS Settings field to confirm that the DNS settings are valid.

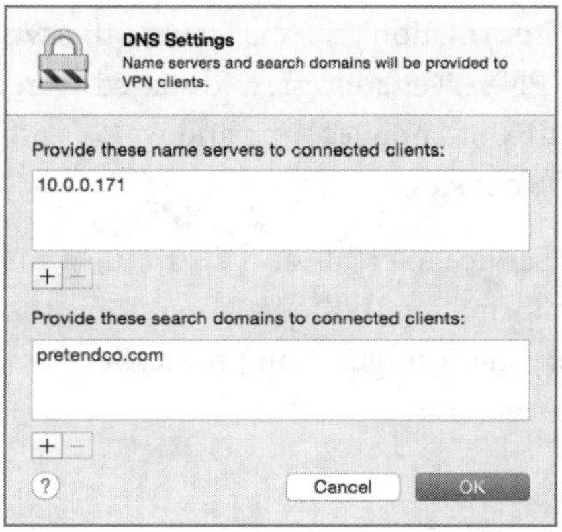

For example, for clients in your local network, server17.pretendco.com should resolve to 10.0.0.171, but clients not on your local network should have server17.pretendco.com resolve to a publicly accessible IPv4 address. Of course, pretendco.com is a domain intended for training purposes, and you should use a domain that you control instead of pretendco.com.

If you have a complex network configuration, you can specify additional routes and whether they are private or public. One example would be if you have multiple private subnets, as shown in the following figure.

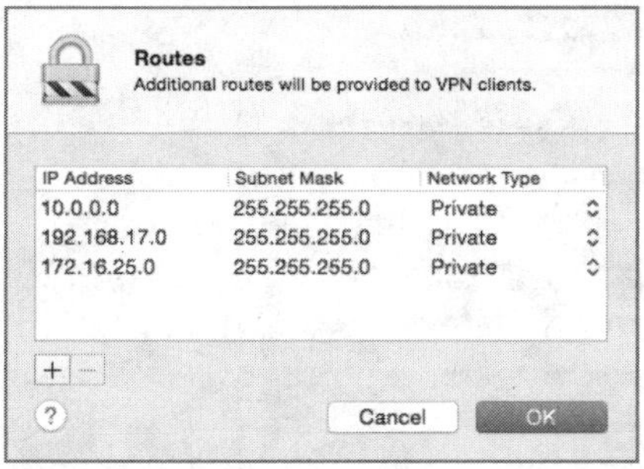

Saving a Configuration Profile

After you've configured your VPN settings, you can create a configuration profile for your users; just click the Save Configuration Profile button in the VPN pane.

The configuration profile uses the VPN host name that you specify in the Server app's main configuration pane for the VPN service.

Having a configuration profile for a computer (a Mac with OS X v10.7 Lion or later) or an iOS device makes it easy to set up a VPN connection; a user needs to provide only a user name and password and doesn't need to enter the information that she would otherwise need to manually enter, such as the service type, VPN server address, and shared secret. By default, the configuration profile filename has a suffix of .mobileconfig and works with both Mac computers (OS X Lion and later) and iOS devices.

You can also use the OS X Server Profile Manager service to create and distribute a configuration profile that contains VPN configuration information. If the VPN service is started, it is automatically included in the Settings for Everyone configuration profile. See Lesson 11 "Managing with Profile Manager" for more information.

Reference 18.3
Troubleshooting

The VPN service writes log messages to /private/var/log/ppp/vpnd.log, but when you use the Server app to view the logs, you don't need to know the log locations; just open the Logs pane, and choose Service Log in the VPN section of the pop-up menu.

You might not understand all the information, but you might compare information about a trouble-free connection with information related to someone experiencing problems. In general, it is a good idea to keep examples of "known good" logs so that you can use them as a reference when you are using logs to troubleshoot problems.

Exercise 18.1
Configure the VPN Service

▶ **Prerequisite**

- ▶ "Exercise 9.1 Create and Import Network Accounts" on page 292; or create a user (Full Name: Barbara Green, Account Name: barbara, Password: net)

The VPN service is easy to configure and turn on. You will configure the VPN service on the server, save a profile with that configuration information, install the profile on your administrator computer, and start a VPN connection. In the instructor-led environment, the instructor does not have the ability to configure the classroom router to allow VPN service for each student's server, so you will make a VPN connection from inside the classroom network, which is still a valid connection.

Once a VPN client connects and successfully authenticates, the VPN service needs to assign the client an IPv4 address on a local network. For the purposes of this exercise, you will configure addresses between 10.0.0.n6 and 10.0.0.n9, where n is your student number. For example, student 1's range is 10.0.0.16 through 10.0.0.19, and student 16's range is 10.0.0.166 through 10.0.0.169.

You will use your administrator computer to make a VPN connection; then you'll use the Server app Logs pane to look at what gets logged for a successful connection.

Configure and Start the VPN Service

1   Perform these exercises on your administrator computer. If you do not already have a connection to your server computer with the Server app on your administrator computer, then connect to it with the following steps: Open the Server app on your administrator computer, choose Manage > Connect to Server, select your server, click Continue, provide administrator credentials (Administrator Name: ladmin, Administrator Password: ladminpw), deselect the "Remember this password" checkbox, and then click Connect.

Be sure you are using your administrator computer so that you can install the configuration profile in the next exercise.

2   In the Server app sidebar, select VPN.

3   In the instructor-led environment, confirm that VPN Host Name is set to your server's host name.

If you are performing the exercises independently and your router forwards all traffic, or all traffic on VPN-related ports, to your server's IPv4 address, you could configure VPN Host Name to be a host name that maps to your server's publicly available IPv4 address.

4   Select the "Show shared secret" checkbox to view the shared secret.

Shared Secret: %bFg}CN+UUg?9b8F09YV
☑ Show shared secret

Assign the range of client addresses.

1   Next to Client Addresses, click the Edit button.

2   Enter 4 in the "Assign addresses for VPN" field.

3   Enter 10.0.0.n6 (where n is your student number) in the "Starting at" field.

4   Press Tab to save the change to the "Starting at" field.

5   Hover your pointer over the "Starting at" field until the range of IP addresses appears.

Client Addresses
IP addresses in the specified range will be issued to VPN clients, and should not overlap with other clients on the network.

Assign: [4 ⌄]   addresses for VPN

Starting at: [10.0.0.176]

L2TP: 10.0.0.176 - 10.0.0.179
Cancel   OK

Confirm that the range is what you expect.

6   Click OK to save the changes.

Update the DNS settings.

1 Next to DNS Settings, click Edit.

2 Select the default value in the first field (10.0.0.1).

3 Click Remove (–).

4 Click Add (+).

5 Enter 10.0.0.*n*1 (where *n* is your student number), and then press Return to save the change.

6 Confirm your settings, and then click OK.

Turn on the VPN service.

1 Click On to turn on the service.

Save the configuration profile.

1 Click Save Configuration Profile.

2 Press Command-D to change the destination folder to your desktop.

3 Click Save.

The VPN shared secret was automatically generated. In addition to user credentials, a VPN client needs to provide the shared secret to the VPN service, so if you modify the shared secret with the Server app, you need to resave the configuration profile and redistribute it to clients, or VPN clients need to manually modify the shared secret.

See Lesson 11 "Managing with Profile Manager" for more information about distributing configuration profiles to computers and devices.

Install and Use the VPN Profile

On your administrator computer, open and install the VPN configuration profile, and then open a VPN connection.

1   On your administrator computer, from the desktop, open the mobileconfig file (the default name is VPN.mobileconfig).

2   When System Preferences opens the mobileconfig file, click Show Profile.

3   Scroll through the profile, and inspect its settings.

There are two things to note in the following figure (you may need to resize the pane in order to display all the information without scrolling): The configuration profile is not signed, and if you have configured your server to provide device management in the Profile Manager pane of the Server app, the configuration profile's Description field reflects the organization name you specified, rather than the server's host name.

4   Click Continue, and when asked to confirm, click Continue.

5   In the "Enter settings for 'VPN'" pane, leave Username blank so that each user of this computer will be required to enter his own user name, and click Install.

6   When prompted, provide local administrator credentials, and click OK.

The profile appears in Profiles preferences' list of profiles.

NOTE ▶ If you have already completed "Exercise 8.1 Inspect Your Open Directory Master" on page 273, then the Description field will contain "VPN settings for Pretendco Project *n*" (where *n* is your student number).

Configure the VPN icon to appear in the menu bar so that users can start a VPN connection without opening System Preferences.

1   Click Show All to return to the list of all preferences.

2   Open Network preferences.

3   In the list of interfaces, select the newly installed VPN entry.

4   Select the "Show VPN status in menu bar" option.

5   From the VPN menu item, choose Connect VPN.

6   At the VPN Connection pane, provide credentials for a local user or a local network user on your server, and click OK.

You can use the user name barbara and a password of net.

If you successfully authenticate and make a VPN connection, Status is shown as Connected, and you see connection information (Connect Time, IP Address, and Sent and Received traffic meters). As a reminder, in the following figure, the Account Name field is blank so that each user of this Mac must provide both a user name and a password.

Status:	**Connected**
Connect Time: 00:00:13	Sent: ▯▯▯▯▯▯▯▯▯▯
IP Address: 10.0.0.177	Received: ▯▯▯▯▯▯▯▯▯▯

Configuration: Default

Server Address: server17.pretendco.com

Account Name:

Authentication Settings...

Disconnect

7   If you are not in an instructor-led environment and your Mac is outside your local network, confirm that you can access internal resources. For example, if your server's Websites service is not already on, then on the server computer, use the Server app Websites pane to turn on the service. Then on your administrator computer, open Safari, and in the Location field, enter your server's private IPv4 address. Confirm that the page opens as expected.

8   Click Disconnect.

Examine Logs

Use the Server app to inspect information related to the VPN service. You'll examine the information for a successful connection.

1   On your administrator computer, if you are not already connected to your server, open the Server app, connect to your server, and authenticate as a local administrator.

2   In the Server app sidebar, select Logs.

3   In the pop-up menu, choose Service Log under the VPN section.

4   In the Search field, enter barbara (the name of the user you specified when making a
VPN connection earlier), and then press Return.

5   Press Return to go to the next instance of your search term.

In this exercise, you configured the VPN service with the Server app, used a configuration
profile to quickly configure a VPN client, used System Preferences to quickly establish a
VPN connection, and used the logs to view the VPN service log.

Exercise 18.2
Clean Up

On your administrator computer, remove the VPN profile to prepare for the
other exercises.

1   In Network preferences, deselect the "Show VPN status in menu bar" checkbox.

2   Click Show All.

3   Open Profiles.

4   Select the VPN profile.

5   Click the Remove (–) button, then click Remove to remove the profile.

6   If asked, provide your local administrator credentials, and click OK.

Note that when there are no profiles, Profiles is not displayed in the available preferences.

7   Quit System Preferences.

8   In the Server app, in the VPN pane, click Off to turn the service off.

9   In the Finder, drag VPN.mobileconfig to the Trash, choose Finder > Empty Trash, and click Empty Trash.

Lesson 19

Configuring DHCP

You can use the OS X Server Dynamic Host Configuration Protocol (DHCP) service to dynamically configure network settings for computers and devices so that you don't have to manually configure them. The word "Host" in "Dynamic Host Configuration Protocol" refers to the computers and devices that are DHCP clients. Although many networks now provide Domain Name System (DNS) service and DHCP service as part of their basic infrastructure, you may want to use the OS X Server DHCP service because it is easier and more convenient to administer DHCP with the Server app than it is to administer with your network router's interface. Additionally, you can dedicate one or more of your server's network interfaces to providing DHCP, DNS, and NetInstall services to an isolated or dedicated NetInstall subnet (as Lesson 14 "Leveraging NetInstall" explains, NetInstall clients require DHCP service on the network to successfully start up from a network image).

Warning: If your network's infrastructure already provides DHCP service, *do not* turn on the OS X Server DHCP service; otherwise, client computers on your local network may no longer be able to function on the network (for instance,

GOALS

▶ Describe how DHCP functions and its use

▶ Use the Server app to configure and manage the DHCP service

▶ Describe static addresses and their use

▶ Identify current clients of OS X Server DHCP services

▶ Display the log files for the DHCP service

they may obtain an Internet Protocol version 4 [IPv4] address from your server's DHCP service that another DHCP service has already assigned, or they may start using a DNS server that isn't configured properly). You should not have more than one DHCP service active on the same network. Of course, it is possible for multiple DHCP servers to coordinate with each other, but the OS X Server DHCP service is designed as a standalone service.

Reference 19.1
Describing How DHCP Works

The process followed by a DHCP server granting an address to a client is well documented. The interaction occurs in this order:

1. A computer or device (host) on the network is configured to obtain network configuration information via DHCP. It broadcasts a request over its local network to see whether a valid DHCP service is available.

2. A DHCP server receives the request from the host and responds with the appropriate information. In this example, the DHCP server proposes that the host use an IPv4 address of 172.16.16.5, along with some other network settings, including a valid subnet mask, router, DNS servers, and default search domain.

3. The host replies to the first DHCP offer it sees on the network; it sends a request for the IPv4 address of 172.16.16.5, the setting that the DHCP server just offered it.

4. The DHCP server formally acknowledges that the host can use the settings it requested. At this time, the host has a valid IPv4 address and can start using the network.

A key benefit provided by the DHCP server in this example is the assignment of configuration information to each host on the network. This negates the need to manually configure the information on each computer or device. When the DHCP server provides this configuration information, you are guaranteed that users will not enter incorrect information when configuring their network settings. If a network has been engineered properly, a new user can take a new Mac out of the box, connect to either a wired or wireless network, and automatically configure the computer with appropriate networking information. The user can then access network services without any manual intervention. This capability provides a simple way to set up and administer computers.

Using DHCP Networks

You can use OS X Server to offer DHCP service on multiple network interfaces. It is likely that each network interface will have different network settings and that you will want to offer a different set of information to DHCP clients depending on what network they are on.

OS X Server uses the term "network" to describe a set of DHCP settings; a network includes the network interface on which you offer DHCP service, the range of IPv4 addresses you offer on that interface, and the network information to offer, including lease time, subnet mask, router, DNS server, and search domain. For clarity, this guide refers to this kind of network as a DHCP network. The DHCP network is the foundation of the DHCP service in OS X Server.

If you need to offer multiple ranges of IPv4 addresses per network interface, you can create multiple DHCP networks per network interface.

MORE INFO ▶ Other DHCP services use the word "scope" to describe DHCP networks.

As part of your planning process, you should decide whether you need multiple DHCP networks or whether a single DHCP network will suffice.

Defining Leases

A DHCP server leases an IPv4 address to a client for a temporary period, the lease time. The DHCP service guarantees that the DHCP client can use its leased IPv4 address for the duration of the lease. Halfway through the lease time, the host requests to renew its lease. The host relinquishes the address when the network interface is no longer in use, such as when the computer or device is shut down, and the DHCP service can assign that IPv4 address to another host if necessary. In the Server app, you specify a lease time of 1 hour, 1 day, 7 days, or 30 days.

If mobile computers and devices use your network, it's likely that they don't all need to be on your network at the same time. Leasing allows an organization to support a larger number of network devices than there are available IPv4 addresses by reusing IPv4 addresses over time. If this is the case for you, the lease time is one of the key options to consider when implementing a DHCP service; if network devices come and go often, consider a short lease time so that once a network device leaves the network, its IPv4 address becomes available for a different network device more quickly.

Even if you have more available IPv4 addresses than devices, the fact that hosts need to periodically renew their DHCP leases means that you can make a change to the DHCP information you hand out, and hosts will eventually receive updated information when they renew their lease. If it is a big change, like an entirely different set of network settings, you can force a lease update by rebooting clients or by briefly disconnecting and then reconnecting their network connections.

Comparing Static and Dynamic Address Assignments

You can use the DHCP service to dynamically or statically assign an IPv4 address to individual computers and devices. Each computer or device's network interface has a unique Media Access Control (MAC) address, which is a physical attribute that cannot be easily changed; it uniquely identifies the network interface. The DHCP service associates a lease with a MAC address. The MAC address is also known as a physical or network address; an example of a MAC address is c8:2a:14:34:92:10. Understand the difference between a dynamic and a static address:

▶ Dynamic address—An IPv4 address is automatically assigned to a computer or device on a network. The address is typically "leased" to the computer or device for a specific period of time, after which the DHCP server either renews the lease of the address to that computer or device or makes the address available to other computers and devices on the network.

▶ Static address—You assign an IPv4 address to a specific computer or device on the network and rarely change it. Static addresses can be applied to a computer or device manually. Nonchanging addresses can be assigned by configuring the DHCP server to provide to a MAC address the same IPv4 address every time the computer or device with that MAC address connects to the network. This is called a reservation, and although technically it is a dynamic address, the result is the same as a static one.

It is possible that you will have a combination of statically and dynamically assigned addresses on your network. One of the determining factors as to which address type is most appropriate is the use of the computer or device. For example, if the computer or device is a server, network appliance, or printer, you should consider a static address, whereas mobile computers and devices that come and go on your network would likely be assigned dynamic IPv4 addresses.

Serving Multiple Subnets

The location of the DHCP server has a direct impact on the viability of a DHCP implementation. When a network client asks for DHCP service, it uses the Bootstrap Protocol (BootP) network protocol. By default, most routers do not forward BootP traffic beyond network borders, whether physically separate subnets or programmatically separated virtual local area networks (VLANs). For network clients to receive DHCP service, the DHCP server must be providing DHCP service on the subnet via a network interface on that subnet, or the router must be configured to relay BootP traffic between subnets; this is sometimes referred to as configuring a helper address or a DHCP relay agent.

Reference 19.2
Configuring DHCP Service

This section details the necessary steps for using the Server app to configure OS X Server.

NOTE ▶ Do not turn on the DHCP service at this time; refer to the optional exercise for complete instructions.

The process for configuring DHCP with the Server app involves the following steps:

1. Configuring your server's network interfaces
2. Editing and creating networks
3. Starting the DHCP service
4. Monitoring the DHCP service

NOTE ▶ You have to show the Advanced section of the Server app sidebar to select the DHCP service (or you could choose DHCP from the View menu).

Configuring Your Server's Network Interface

Before you can offer any services on a network interface, you need to configure the interface and make it active. Use Network preferences on your server to configure each network interface on which you intend to serve DHCP. The following figure shows a Mac configured with extra Apple Thunderbolt to Gigabit Ethernet adapter and a USB to Ethernet adapter so it can offer DHCP service on multiple networks.

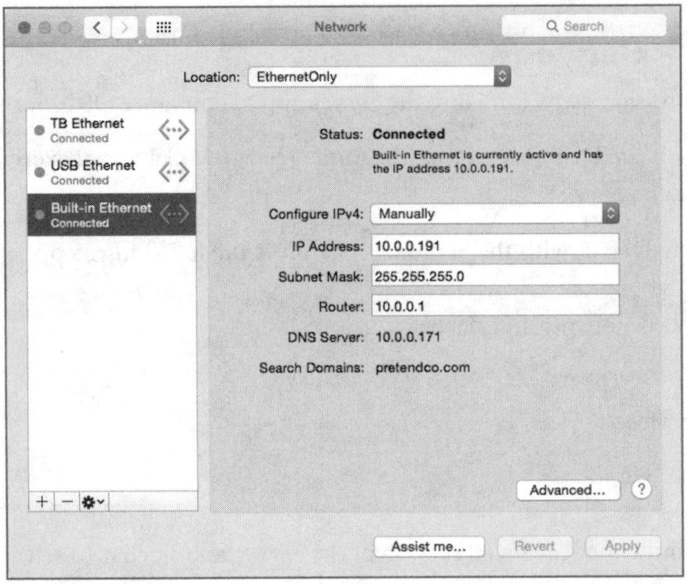

Editing a Subnet

Your next step is to edit one or more subnets. This process includes the configuration of any optional settings, such as DNS information.

By default, when you open the DHCP pane in the Server app, the Networks tab displays one DHCP network, based on your server's primary network interface.

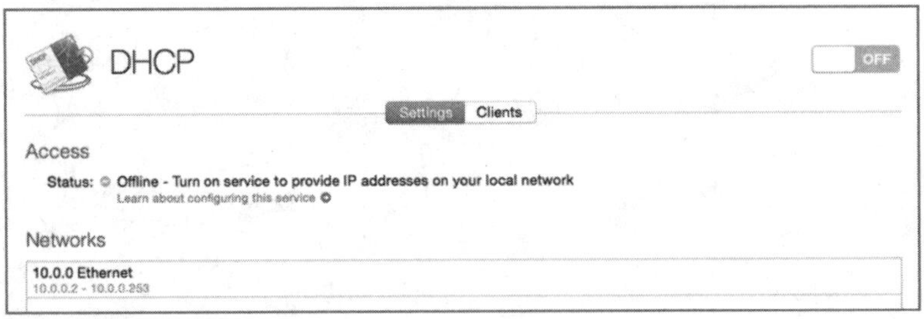

If you double-click this default DHCP network to edit it, you'll see that the name is based on the IPv4 address of your server's primary network interface, and the starting IPv4 address and ending IPv4 address are just starting points. You need to edit the range of IPv4 addresses that DHCP service offers; your server's own IPv4 address is included in the range, and you do not want to hand out your server's IPv4 address to a client for the client to use. One default DHCP network's settings are shown in the following figure.

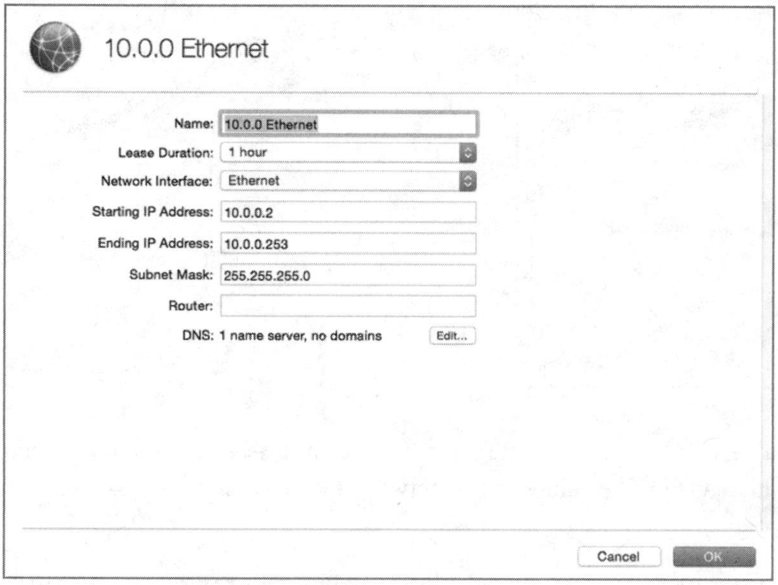

As you can see, the information you can specify for a DHCP network includes the following:

- ▶ Name
- ▶ Lease duration
- ▶ Network interface
- ▶ Starting IP address
- ▶ Ending IP address
- ▶ Subnet mask
- ▶ Router

Also, if you click the Edit button next to DNS, you can specify the following:

- ▶ DNS name servers
- ▶ Search domains

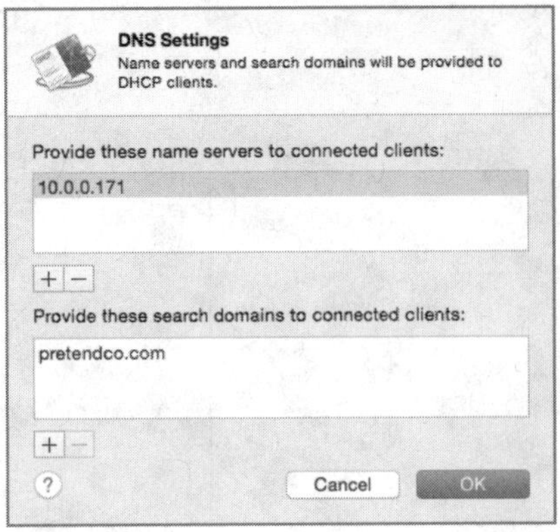

When you create a new network, the Router, name server, and search domain fields are automatically populated from the values of the network interface that the new network uses.

> **NOTE ▶** If you specify your server's IPv4 address to be a name server, be sure to configure your DNS service to perform lookups for all appropriate networks. Also note that OS X Server does not perform routing; it will not pass traffic from an otherwise isolated network to the Internet.

In the Networks pane, you can configure multiple subnet ranges. For example, you can add an additional subnet range for a second range on an existing network interface or for a range on a different network interface. When you create a new DHCP network, the Server app will not allow you to specify a range of IPv4 addresses that another DHCP network already includes.

Click Add (+) to create a new DHCP network, and click Remove (–) to remove an existing DHCP network. The following figure shows an example of the Server app displaying three DHCP networks, with two on the same subnet.

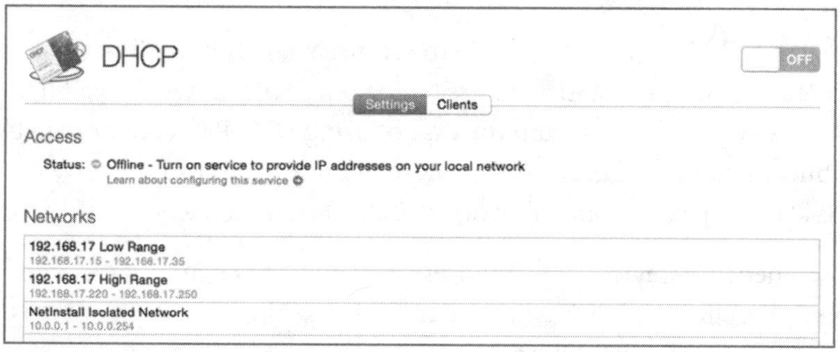

Starting the DHCP Service

To start the DHCP service, click On to turn on the service.

> **NOTE** ▶ Do not turn on the DHCP service at this time; refer to the optional exercise for complete instructions.

Monitoring and Configuring the DHCP Service

You can use the Server app to view information about the DHCP clients associated with the DHCP service. To view the DHCP client information, click the Clients tab.

> **TIP** ▶ You can change the size of the columns in the Server app window to display more information for a particular column.

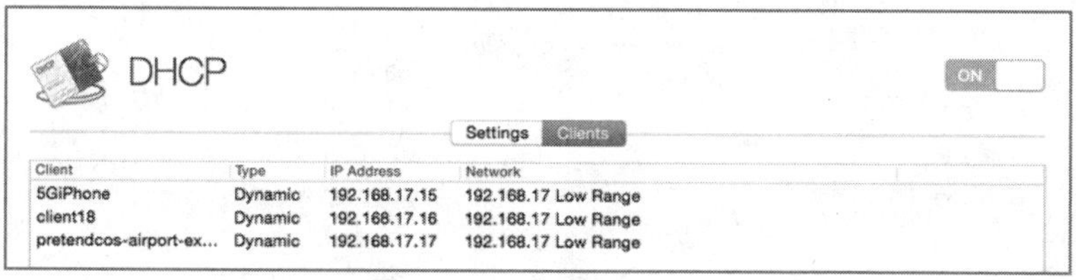

The Clients pane provides the following information:

▶ Client (for Mac computers, this is the client's computer name)

▶ Type (Dynamic or Static)

▶ IP address

▶ Network (DHCP network)

Assigning Static Addresses

In the Clients pane, the DHCP service allows you to create a static IPv4 address for a client; the Server app refers to this as a static address (some other DHCP servers call this a reservation). This allows you to benefit from the ease of using DHCP to configure network settings such as subnet mask and DNS servers, while assigning static IPv4 addresses to key equipment (such as servers, printers, and network switches) automatically.

If you already know a network device's MAC address, it's simple to create a static address for it. In the Clients pane, click Add (+), assign a name, choose the DHCP network, assign an IPv4 address, and specify the MAC address.

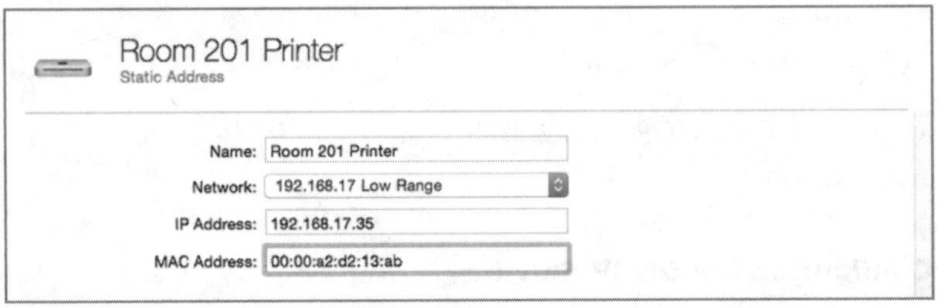

But what if you don't know the MAC address? You can create a static address for a DHCP client that already has a lease. In the Clients pane, select the client in the list, click the Action (gear icon) pop-up menu, and choose Create Static Address. The following figure shows, the pretendcos-airport-ex entry that is an AirPort Extreme we want to be able to manage at a known IP address.

After you choose Create Static Address, you can specify the Name, Network, and IP Address settings; MAC Address is prepopulated.

Reference 19.3
Troubleshooting DHCP

Like with many network services, it is sometimes difficult to locate the cause of a DHCP problem. At times, configuration errors will be present on client systems. Other times, problems with the network infrastructure will prevent the computers and devices on the network from communicating with the DHCP server. On occasion, issues arise when the DHCP server has not been configured correctly or is not behaving in an expected manner.

To think through the troubleshooting process, imagine that a specific computer or device on your network is unable to obtain a DHCP address from your server. First troubleshoot the client, and then troubleshoot the server.

Ask the following questions when you are troubleshooting DHCP issues for OS X:

▶ Is the computer or device configured correctly on the network? Check physical network issues, such as cabling, broken routers or switches, and limitations of the physical subnet. Ensure that the appropriate network interfaces are active.

▶ Can you establish any network connection? Can you ping another host? Can you see another host over Bonjour?

▶ Is the configuration properly set up? Are you using addresses dynamically assigned via DHCP or manually assigned static address? If the problem is with DHCP, would a static address work?

▶ Is an IPv4 address assigned via DHCP, or is the address self-assigned (169.254.x.x range)? Can you ping another host via both IPv4 address and host name? Can you perform a DNS lookup?

In this imaginary situation, you were able to connect to an external website by manually configuring the network interface with a static address, so you have concluded that the issue must be with the server.

Ask the following questions when you are troubleshooting DHCP issues for OS X Server:

▶ Is the DHCP server configured correctly on the local network? Is the server reachable on the network via ping? Does the server have the proper IPv4 address?

▶ Is the DHCP service configured properly? Is the DHCP service turned on?

▶ Does the Server app show the expected DHCP client activity?

▶ Do the DHCP log entries match the expected DHCP client activity?

Examining the Logs

DHCP log entries are contained in the main System log file. You can view the System log using other utilities such as the Console app, but if you use the Server app Logs pane to view the DHCP service log, only the DHCP entries will be displayed.

> **TIP** You can change the size of the Server app window to display log entries on a single line.

Apple's implementation of DHCP relies on BootP `bootpd` process.

You can look for specific events by entering them in the search box at the top right of the pane. Note the specific DHCP entries and the general flow of the events for DHCP:

▶ DHCP DISCOVER—A DHCP client sends a discover message to look for DHCP servers.

▶ OFFER—A DHCP server responds to a client DHCP DISCOVER message.

▶ DHCP REQUEST—A DHCP client requests DHCP configuration information from the DHCP server.

▶ ACK—A DHCP server responds with DHCP configuration information for the DHCP client.

You can remember this chain of events with the acronym DORA: Discover, Offer, Request, Acknowledge.

You can also determine whether a client has received an IPv4 address from a DHCP server. If the DHCP server has run out of available network addresses or no DHCP service is available, the client will automatically generate a self-assigned link-local address. Link-local addresses are always in the IPv4 address range of 169.254.x.x and have a subnet mask of 255.255.0.0. The network client will automatically generate a random link-local address and then check the local network to make sure no other network device is using that address. Once a unique link-local address is established, the network client will be able to establish connections only with other network devices on the local network.

Exercise 19.1
Configure the DHCP Service (Optional)

▶ **Prerequisites**

▶ An additional isolated network

▶ An additional network interface for your server

▶ An additional network interface for your administrator computer

NOTE ▶ Skip this exercise if you do not have an additional isolated network and an additional network interface or if you cannot turn off DHCP on the router for the isolated network you are using with this guide.

Do not turn on the DHCP service on a network that already has DHCP service.

Follow along with the steps in this exercise to configure an additional network interface on your server computer, turn off the default DHCP network, and create a new DHCP network for an additional isolated network.

You will use your administrator computer as a DHCP client on an isolated network.

Start by making sure your extra isolated network is ready.

1   If you have a Mac Pro with multiple Ethernet ports, you can use the Ethernet port you are not already using. Otherwise, connect the Apple USB to Ethernet Adapter or the Apple Thunderbolt to Gigabit Ethernet Adapter to your server computer.

2   Use an Ethernet cable to connect the Ethernet adapter (or your server's network port) to an isolated network Ethernet switch.

Now that your server computer's other network interface is connected to an Ethernet switch, configure that network interface.

1   On your server computer, log in as a local administrator if you are not already logged in as a local administrator.

2   Open System Preferences, then open Network.

3   Select the newly added, or unconfigured, network interface.

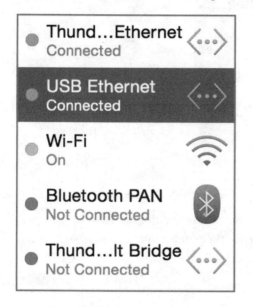

4   Click the Configure IPv4 pop-up menu, and choose Manually.

5   Enter the following information:

IP Address: 192.168.*n*.1 (where *n* is your student number)

Subnet Mask: 255.255.255.0

Router: 192.168.*n*.1 (where *n* is your student number)

6   Click Advanced to set the DNS server and search domains.

7   Click the DNS tab.

8   For the DNS Server field, click Add (+), and enter 192.168.*n*.1 (where *n* is your student number).

9   For the Search Domains field, click Add (+), and enter pretendco.com.

10 Click OK to return to Network preferences.

11 Review your settings.

Status:	**Connected**
	USB Ethernet is currently active and has the IP address 192.168.17.1.
Configure IPv4:	Manually
IP Address:	192.168.17.1
Subnet Mask:	255.255.255.0
Router:	192.168.17.1
DNS Server:	192.168.17.1
Search Domains:	pretendco.com

12 Click Apply.

Configure the DHCP service.

1 In the Server app sidebar, select DHCP. If the Server app does not display the Advanced services in the sidebar, then hover the pointer over the word "Advanced," and click Show.

2 Select the default DHCP network, which is based on your server's primary network interface.

3 Click the Delete (–) button, and then click Delete.

4 Click the Add (+) button to create a new DHCP network.

5 Enter Extra Net in the Name field.

6 Click the Lease Duration pop-up menu, and choose 1 hour.

7 Click the Network Interface pop-up menu, and choose the network interface you just configured at the beginning of this exercise.

Name:	Extra Net
Lease Duration	1 hour
	Ethernet
Network Interface	✓ USB Ethernet
	Wi-Fi
Starting IP Address	

8 Enter the following information:

Starting IP Address: 192.168.*n*.50 (where *n* is your student number)

Ending IP Address: 192.168.*n*.55 (where *n* is your student number)

9 If necessary, enter the following information:

Subnet Mask: 255.255.255.0

Router: 192.168.*n*.1 (where *n* is your student number)

10 For DNS, click Edit, and enter the following information, if necessary:

Provide these name servers to connected clients: 192.168.*n*.1 (where *n* is your student number).

Provide these search domains to connected clients: pretendco.com.

11 Click OK to dismiss the DNS Settings pane.

12 Review the settings.

Name:	Extra Net
Lease Duration:	1 hour
Network Interface:	USB Ethernet
Starting IP Address:	192.168.17.50
Ending IP Address:	192.168.17.55
Subnet Mask:	255.255.255.0
Router:	192.168.17.1
DNS:	1 name server, 1 domain Edit...

13 Click Create to save the changes.

Start the DHCP service.

1 Click On to start the DHCP service.

Use the following steps to connect your administrator computer to the extra isolated network and allow it to obtain a DHCP address. Create a new network location for your administrator computer to use DHCP, and prepare to switch networks. A network location is a collection of all the settings for all your network interfaces, and switching between network locations allows you to quickly change network settings. See Lesson 21, Advanced

Network Configuration, in *Apple Pro Training Series: OS X Support Essentials 10.10* for more information on network locations.

1   On your administrator server, quit the Server app if it is open.

2   In the Finder, press Command-N to open a new Finder window.

3   If there are any eject icons for network volumes in the Finder window sidebar, click them to eject all network volumes.

4   Connect your administrator computer's Ethernet cable to the isolated network's Ethernet switch.

Preserve your current network location so you can quickly return to it.

1   On your administrator computer, open System Preferences.

2   Choose View > Network.

3   If the current network location already has an appropriate name, move on to the next steps.

     If your current network location is still named Automatic, click the Location pop-up menu, choose Edit Locations, double-click Automatic, enter Server Essentials, press Return to save the name change, click Done, and then click Apply.

Create a new network location.

1   Click the Location pop-up menu, and choose Edit Locations.

2   Click Add (+).

3   Enter DHCP Exercise as the new location name, and then click Done.

4   In the Location pop-up menu, choose the location named DHCP.

5   Confirm that the Location pop-up menu is set to DHCP.

6   Click Apply.

7   Select the Ethernet connection that's connected to the isolated network's Ethernet switch to display its details.

```
Status:  Connected
         Thunderbolt Ethernet is currently active and
         has the IP address 192.168.17.50.

Configure IPv4:  Using DHCP

    IP Address:  192.168.17.50

  Subnet Mask:  255.255.255.0

       Router:  192.168.17.1

   DNS Server:  192.168.17.1

Search Domains:  pretendco.com
```

8 Leave the Network pane open so you can change locations again at the end of this exercise.

Without any configuration of your new location, each network interface is set to use DHCP. Wait for your administrator computer's Ethernet interface to receive a new IPv4 address assigned by DHCP.

Monitor the service and view the logs.

1 On your server computer, in the DHCP pane, click Clients.

2 From the View menu, choose Refresh (or press Command-R).

Confirm that your administrator computer is listed.

DHCP

Settings | Clients

Client	Type	IP Address	Network
client17	Dynamic	192.168.17.50	Extra Net

3 In the Server app sidebar, select Logs.

4 Click the Logs pop-up menu, and choose Service Log under the DHCP section.

```
        Logs

Oct 10 12:27:32 server17.pretendco.com bootpd[8756]: server name server17.pretendco.com
Oct 10 12:27:32 server17.pretendco.com bootpd[8756]: interface en0: ip 10.0.0.171 mask 255.255.255.0
Oct 10 12:27:32 server17.pretendco.com bootpd[8756]: interface en4: ip 192.168.17.1 mask 255.255.255.0
Oct 10 12:27:32 server17.pretendco.com bootpd[8756]: dhcp: re-reading lease list
Oct 10 12:27:32 server17.pretendco.com bootpd[8756]: bsdpd: re-reading configuration
Oct 10 12:27:32 server17.pretendco.com bootpd[8756]: bsdpd: shadow file size will be set to 48 megabytes
Oct 10 12:27:32 server17.pretendco.com bootpd[8756]: bsdpd: age time 00:15:00
Oct 10 12:27:32 server17.pretendco.com bootpd[8756]: DHCP DISCOVER [en4]: 1,40:6c:8f:3d:e7:b <client17>
Oct 10 12:27:32 server17.pretendco.com bootpd[8756]: OFFER sent <no hostname> 192.168.17.50 pktsize 306
Oct 10 12:27:33 server17.pretendco.com bootpd[8756]: DHCP REQUEST [en4]: 1,40:6c:8f:3d:e7:b <client17>
Oct 10 12:27:33 server17.pretendco.com bootpd[8756]: ACK sent <no hostname> 192.168.17.50 pktsize 306
```

Confirm that you can see the Discover, Offer, Request, and Acknowledge (Ack) log entries.

Clean Up

Change back your administrator computer's network location, reconnect to the network for the rest of the exercises, and turn off the DHCP service.

1   On your administrator computer, click the Location pop-up menu, and choose Server Essentials.

2   Click Apply, and then quit System Preferences.

3   Disconnect your administrator computer's Ethernet cable from the isolated network switch.

4   Connect your administrator computer's Ethernet cable to the network switch you were using before this lesson.

5   In the Server app sidebar, select DHCP, and click Off to turn off the service.

     Confirm that the status indicator next to DHCP in the Server app sidebar disappears, indicating that the service is off.

6   On your server, open System Preferences, and then open Network preferences.

7   Select the Ethernet interface from which you served DHCP, click the Action (gear icon) menu, and choose Make Service Inactive.

8   Click Apply, and then quit System Preferences.

You enabled the DHCP service on a network interface that's connected to an isolated network. You confirmed that a client (your administrator computer) can obtain an IPv4 address from your server's DHCP service, and you viewed the DHCP service logs.

Lesson 20
Hosting Websites

OS X Server provides a straightforward, intuitive interface for providing web hosting services. Based on open source, popular, and well-understood Apache, the OS X Server hosting facilities allow even a new administrator to bring a website online.

Reference 20.1
Identifying the Web Service Software

This lesson helps you understand, manage, and secure the various aspects of the Apple web services, including managing high-bandwidth connections, sharing files, and locating log files for access, viewing, and troubleshooting.

Even with the Websites server not running, you might reach a webpage hosted by OS X Server. This is because the httpd process that serves webpages may be running because it is used by Profile Manager for its management console, by NetInstall to host images, and by the Calendar and Contact services. If any of those services are running, httpd will be also.

GOALS

▶ Define the OS X Server web engine

▶ Describe how to manage the Websites service

▶ Control access to websites

▶ Configure multiple websites and locate site files

▶ Examine website log files

▶ Locate and use secure certificates for websites

The OS X Server web service is based on Apache, open source software commonly used in a variety of operating systems. It is a well-accepted and well-understood web server that is serving more than 50 percent of all the websites on the Internet.

As of this writing, the version installed in OS X Server is Apache 2.4.9.

To provide web hosting that is available to users on the Internet, proper Domain Name System (DNS) entries for external hosts must be registered, and the server on which OS X Server is installed must be exposed to the Internet via a demilitarized zone (DMZ), also known as perimeter networking or port forwarding.

Reference 20.2
Describing Basic Website Structure

Before you manage any websites, it is important to know where critical Apache and website files are stored. Commonly used Apache and Apple configuration files for web services are located in /Library/Server/Web/.

Configuration files still exist at /private/etc/apache2/, which is normally hidden from view in the Finder, but they should not be manipulated. Apache modules—including Apple-specific modules (pieces of code that perform Apple-specific functions in Apache)—are located in /usr/libexec/apache2/, which is also normally hidden from view in the Finder. Apache modules will not be covered in this guide, but you can find additional information in Apache documentation. The default location for the OS X Server website is in /Library/ Server/Web/Data/Sites/.

All website files and the folders in which they normally reside must be at least read-only for Everybody or the _www user or group; otherwise, users won't be able to access the files with their web browsers when they visit your site.

Turning Websites On and Off

When managing websites on OS X Server, you use the Server app. You also use the Server app to manage file and folder permissions, thus allowing or restricting access to folders that are to be seen by web browsers, such as Safari.

Because OS X Server has preconfigured web services for the default website, all you need to do to start exploring is turn on the web service.

To create a new website, simply click Add (+) at the bottom of the window, enter the appropriate information, and click OK. The default set of files will be created if you did not define an existing directory containing your website. Make sure that DNS is configured properly.

To turn off a website, you simply remove it from the list of websites in the Server app. This does not remove the site files, just the reference to the site in the web service configuration files.

Managing Websites

To allow multiple websites to be hosted on one server, a domain name, an Internet Protocol (IP) address, and a port are used to separate sites from one another.

For example, you can have two sites on the same IP address as long as their ports are different. You can also have two sites with the same IP address and different domain names. By editing and ensuring that one of these three parameters is unique, you are logically separating your sites. The uniform resource locator (URL) to reach a server's webpage is its IP address or fully qualified domain name (FQDN), such as the following:

► http://10.0.0.171

  or

► http://www.pretendco.com

This can be modified by adding a port definition, such as the following:

► http://www.pretendco.com:8080

  or

► http://www.pretendco:16080

Domain Name: www.pretendco.com
IP Address: Any   Port: 16080

Users visiting the site may need to be told the port value to access the site. Ports 80 (http://) and 443 (https://) are known by most browsers and do not require additional typing when entering the address.

You can define the site to use a Secure Sockets Layer (SSL) certificate to protect the transfer of data between the requesting client and your server.

Make sure that the common name used in the certificate matches that of the site's domain.

SSL Certificate ✓ None
Store Site Files In   server17.pretendco.com - server17.pretendco.com OD Intermediate CA
Who Can Access   www.pretendco.com - Self-signed

You can set permissions to access the Websites service globally and by individual sites. The global permissions are based on which network the request comes across.

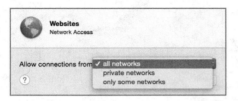

Individual site permissions are set by defining what groups you allow to access them.

If you want your website to answer to alternate domain names, you can define these in the Additional Domains dialog.

You can allow folder listings using the alias functionality.

You can set up redirects to point users to a desired location or another site. This is a useful tool if you need to protect the data and you want to force the use of an SSL-protected version of your site. You can make a standard Hypertext Transfer Protocol (HTTP) site that redirects to an SSL version so the user doesn't have to remember to preface the site address with "https." This is useful when setting up wikis or any other password-protected site.

Reference 20.3
Monitoring Web Services

Apache has excellent logging capabilities and uses two main files when logging website information: the Access log and the Error log. The log files can store all kinds of information, such as the address of the requesting computer, the amount of data sent, the date and time of transaction, the page requested by the visitor, and a web server response code.

Log files, named access_log and error_log, are located inside /var/log/apache2/ and are readable via the Server app. The Apache logs are parsed to display the Access and Error logs per site. While the logs are also viewable in the Console app, they are not parsed, and they will need to be filtered to find entries for specific sites.

Reference 20.4
Troubleshooting

To troubleshoot web services, it helps to understand how the service works and what pieces control what aspects of the service. Here are some areas to investigate:

▶ Check whether the Websites service is running by verifying that a green status indicator dot appears next to the service in the Server app.

▶ Check that the website is pointing to the location where the website files are stored.

▶ Verify that the website files and directory can be read by the _www user or group or by the group Everybody.

▶ Check whether there are site restrictions as to who can access the site.

▶ Check that the appropriate networking ports aren't blocked to the server (80 for http, 443 for https, and any others that may have been defined for a specific website).

▶ Check that the proper IP address has been set for the website.

▶ Use Network Utility to check that DNS resolves properly for the website's FQDN.

Exercise 20.1
Turn On Web Services

▶ **Prerequisites**

▶ "Exercise 2.1 Create DNS Zones and Records" on page 71

▶ "Exercise 9.1 Create and Import Network Accounts" on page 292

In this exercise, you will see what happens when you use a web browser to open your server's default website when the Websites service is off.

Then you'll turn on the Websites service and confirm that when you open your server's default website, you are automatically redirected to the HTTP Secure (HTTPS) version of the website.

Explore Response When the Websites Service Is Off

1   Perform these exercises on your administrator computer. If you do not already have a connection to your server computer with the Server app on your administrator computer, then connect to it with the following steps: Open the Server app on your administrator computer, choose Manage > Connect to Server, select your server, click Continue, provide administrator credentials (Administrator Name: ladmin, Administrator Password: ladminpw), deselect the "Remember this password" checkbox, and then click Connect.

2   In the Server app, select Websites in the sidebar.

3   If the service is already on, click Off to turn off the service.

Visit Your Server's Website When the Websites Service Is Off

To prevent Safari from automatically entering the uniform resource locator (URL) for your server's Profile Manager service, you will clear your history and website data.

1   On your administrator computer, open Safari.

2   Choose Safari > Clear History and Website Data.

3   Click the Clear pop-up menu, choose "all history," and click Clear History.

4   In the address and search field, enter http://servern.pretendco.com (where *n* is your student number), and then press Return.

5   Confirm that you see a page that the Websites service is off.

> Websites are turned off.
> An administrator can turn them on using the Server application.

6   Close the Safari window.

View Default Website Parameters

The default website is named "Server Website" and has an automatic redirect to the default website protected by Secure Sockets Layer (SSL).

1   In the Websites pane, select the default website (Server Website).

2   Click the Edit (pencil icon) button below the Websites field.

3 Note that the Server app displays the path to the folder that contains the files for the website (/Library/Server/Web/Data/Sites/Default/).

4 Note that the information available for you to edit includes the following:

▶ Store Site Files In—The location of the files served up by the selected website. When you use the Server app on your server, it displays an arrow next to the pop-up menu that opens a Finder window at the location where the website files are stored.

▶ Who Can Access—Allows the website to require authentication for access.

▶ Additional Domains—Alternate domain names for the website.

▶ Redirects—Redirects requests to other URLs.

▶ Aliases—Makes folders accessible via multiple URLs.

▶ Index Files—The index files used when a request arrives for a folder instead of a file.

▶ Edit Advanced Settings—Gives access to advanced website preferences, including CGI and web apps.

5 Next to Redirects, click Edit.

6 Note that the existing redirect automatically redirects all requests for this website to https://%{SERVER_NAME}. %{SERVER_NAME} is a variable that's replaced by your server's name.

Source	Destination	Status
This Website	https://%{SERVER_NAME}	Not Applicable

7   Click Cancel to dismiss the Redirects pane.

8   Click Cancel to return to the list of websites.

Explore the Default Websites

When you turn on your server's Websites service, two websites are automatically created. The first default website responds to all HyperText Transfer Protocol (HTTP) requests that use your server's IP addresses and host names on port 80. The other default website responds to all HTTPS Secure (HTTPS) requests that use your server's IP addresses and host names on port 443.

Turn on the Websites service, open the default website, and confirm that you are automatically redirected to the secure website.

Turn On the Websites Service

To use the Websites service, you must first turn it on as a service in the Server app.

1   On your administrator computer, in the Websites pane, click On turn on the service.

2   Wait until the Status field displays a green status indicator.

3   Note that the Permissions field indicates who has access to the Websites service.

Inspect the Automatic Redirect Settings

1   Click the View Server Website link at the bottom of the Websites pane.

2   Confirm that in the Safari address and search field, there is a lock icon in front of your server's host name.

This indicates that this information was sent via HTTPS instead of via HTTP.

3   Click the lock icon.

4   Click Show Certificate.

5   Confirm that the sheet displays information about your server's SSL certificate that was issued by your Open Directory intermediate certificate authority (CA).

6   Click OK to close the certificate information pane.

> **NOTE ▶** To explore the change password service, refer to the "Exercise 20.1 Supplement" available with this guide's downloadable lesson files.

In this exercise, you inspected the page that your server returned when you used a web browser to open your server's default website when the Websites service was off. You turned the Websites service on and confirmed that you were automatically redirected to the secure version of the website.

Exercise 20.2
Modify the Default Websites

▶ **Prerequisite**

▶   "Exercise 20.1 Turn On Web Services" on page 559

In this exercise, you will change the contents of the default websites and then create a new website at a different host name and Internet Protocol version 4 (IPv4) address.

Customize the Content of the Default Websites

The default website contains basic information about OS X Server and offers links to your server's Profile Manager, Xcode, Wiki, and Change Password services, but you may want to offer different information to visitors to your website.

Don't attempt to remove the default website. Instead, you could do one of the following:

▶   Add a new index file and content to the default folder
▶   Change the folder that the default website uses

In this exercise, you will specify a different folder, share that folder via the File Sharing service with read/write permissions members for the Contractors group, make a file-sharing connection with Barbara Green credentials, and then copy new website files from your administrator computer to the new folder.

Change the Folder That the Default Webite Uses

1   On your administrator computer, if you are not already connected to your server, open the Server app, connect to your server, and authenticate as a local administrator.

2   If necessary, in the Server app sidebar, select Websites.

3   In the Websites pane, double-click Server Website.

4   Click the pop-up menu for Store Site Files In, and choose Other.

Store Site Files In ✓ Default
Who Can Access   Other...

5   Select your server's startup disk, and then navigate to /Library/Server/Web/Data/Sites/.

| Server Bac... | Sites | ▶ | Default | ▶ |
| Server HD | WebApps | ▶ | | |

6   Click New Folder.

7   In the New Folder dialog, enter servern.pretendco.com (where *n* is your student number), and then click Create.

8   Select the folder you just created, and then click Choose.

9   Confirm that the path updates beneath the Server Website title.

 Server Website
/Library/Server/Web/Data/Sites/server17.pretendco.com

If the path is /Library/Server/Web/Data/Sites/, instead of /Library/Server/Web/Data/
Sites/servern.pretendco.com (where *n* is your student number), then click Cancel, and
start again with step 1 of this section.

10   Click OK.

Once you click OK, the Server app creates a new folder and then in that folder creates
aliases to the Server.png graphic file and basic index files for various languages.

Change the Folder That the Default Secure Website Uses

You might want to have your non-SSL website and your SSL website display different content, which is why changing the folder for the default website doesn't automatically change
the folder for the SSL website. Update the folder that the Server Website (SSL) website
uses.

1   Double-click Server Website (SSL).

2   Click the Store Site Files In pop-up menu, and choose Other.

3   Select your server's startup disk, and then navigate to /Library/Server/Web/Data/
Sites/.

4   Select the servern.pretendco.com (where *n* is your student number) folder, and click
Choose.

5   Click OK to save the change.

NOTE ▶ Even though your replacement page does not have links to Change Password or Profile Manager, for instance, you can still reach those services (as long as those services are available). For example, the URL for the Change Password feature is https://server*n*.pretendco.com/changepassword, and the user portal is https://server*n*.pretendco.com/mydevices (where *n* is your student number).

Share the New Website Folder via File Sharing

Share the new website folder so that members of the Contractors group can update its contents, and confirm that the Everyone group has read access to the contents.

When you copy files via Server Message Block (SMB) or the Apple Filing Protocol (AFP) to a network volume, those files automatically inherit the access control list (ACL) of the destination parent folder.

1   In the Server app sidebar, select File Sharing.

2   Click Add (+).

3   Select your server's startup disk, and then navigate to /Library/Server/Web/Data/Sites/.

4   Select the new folder you recently created (server*n*.pretendco.com, where *n* is your student number).

5   Click Choose.

6   Double-click the server*n*.pretendco.com (where *n* is your student number) shared folder.

7   Press Command-B to show the accounts browser.

8   Drag Contractors into the Permissions field.

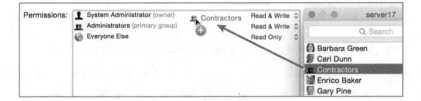

9   Press Command-B to hide the accounts browser.

10 Confirm that the permissions for Everyone Else is Read Only and that Contractors is set to Read & Write.

11 Leave the other permissions at their defaults.

12 Click OK.

13 If the File Sharing service is not on yet, click On to turn on the File Sharing service, and then wait until the green status indicator is displayed.

Copy New Contents to the New Website Folder

1   On your administrator computer, in the Finder, press Command-N to open a new Finder window.

2   Select Documents in the Finder window sidebar, and then navigate to the Lesson20 folder in your StudentMaterials folder.

3   Open the Lesson20 folder.

4   Drag the Finder window that displays the contents of Lesson20 to the left side of your screen.

5   Press Command-N to open a second new Finder window.

6   Drag this second folder to the right side of your screen.

7   In the Finder window on the right side of your screen, select your server in the Finder sidebar (or if there are too many entries in the Shared section of the Finder sidebar for your server to appear, select All, and then double-click your server).

8   Click Connect As.

9   In the connection dialog, enter the following information, and then click Connect:

▶   Name: **barbara**

▶   Password: **net**

10   Open the server*n*.pretendco.com (where *n* is your student number) folder.

Note that the Server app automatically added a number of files, including aliases of default index.html files for various languages. You can ignore the existing files.

11   Click the Finder window with the Lesson20 folder open, and press Command-A to select all files.

12   Drag the selected files to the server*n*.pretendco.com (where *n* is your student number) folder.

13   In a Finder sidebar, click Eject next to your server.

> **Shared**
>
> 🖳 server17   ⏏

14   Close any remaining Finder windows that are still open.

Confirm the Default Webite Uses the New Content

1   In the Server app sidebar, select Websites.

2   In the Websites pane, click the View Server Website link at the bottom of the Websites pane.

3   Confirm that Safari displays the new content.

If the new content is not displayed, press Command-R to refresh the content.

4   Click your server's address in the Safari search and location field, and confirm that the URL starts with "https://," which indicates that you were automatically redirected to the website protected by SSL.

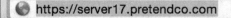

🌐 https://server17.pretendco.com

5   Close the Safari window.

Stop Sharing the Webite via File Sharing

To prevent confusion in the future, stop sharing the websites folder.

1 In the Server app sidebar, select File Sharing.

2 Select the server*n*.pretendco.com (where *n* is your student number) shared folder.

3 Click Remove (–).

4 At the confirmation dialog, click Remove.

In this exercise, you created a different folder for the default websites to use, shared that folder via the File Sharing service, and used SMB to copy new files to the folder. You used the Server app to confirm the files have the correct permissions to allow the World Wide Web Server user or group to read the files. You confirmed that the Websites service uses your new content.

Exercise 20.3
Create and Remove a New Website

> **Prerequisites**
>
> ► "Exercise 20.1 Turn On Web Services" on page 559
> ► "Exercise 4.2 Configure an Open Directory Certificate Authority" on page 152

You can create many additional websites, as long as each new website has a unique combination of the following attributes:

► Host name
► IPv4 address
► Port number

This leaves you with a nearly infinite amount of flexibility with a limited set of hardware.

You can use alternative ports, such as 8080 instead of 80. You can have multiple websites use the same folder of content.

NOTE ▶ Do not create a website that uses port 8008 or 8443 if you plan to configure your server to provide the Calendar or Contacts services.

In this scenario, your organization will host a website at the host name new$n$.pretendco.com at IPv4 address 10.0.0.n4 (where n is your student number), and your server will host that website temporarily.

In this exercise, you will create a new Domain Name System (DNS) record. You can configure the same physical network port to use multiple IPv4 addresses, so you will configure your server to use an additional interface for 10.0.0.n4 (where n is your student number). To secure the new website, you will use your Open Directory (OD) intermediate CA to issue a certificate for the website.

Create a New DNS Record

1   On your administrator computer, in the Server app sidebar, select DNS.

2   Click the Action (gear icon) pop-up menu.

3   If Show All Records displays a checkmark, choose Show All Records to remove the checkmark.

4   Click Add (+).

5   In the Host field, enter new$n$.pretendco.com (where n is your student number).

6   In the IP Addresses field, enter 10.0.0.n4 (where n is your student number).

Host Name:	new17.pretendco.com
IP Addresses:	10.0.0.174

7   Click Create.

8   Quit the Server app.

Configure Your Server to Use an Additional IPv4 Address

1   On your server, open System Preferencesand then open Network preferences.

2   Select your primary network interface.

3   Click the Action (gear icon) pop-up menu, and choose Duplicate Service.

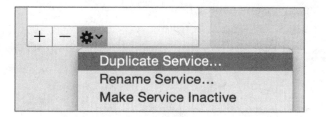

4   In the Name field, enter Interface for extra website.

5   Click Duplicate.

6   Select the new interface, click the Configure IPv4 pop-up menu, and choose Manually.

7   In the IP Address field, enter 10.0.0.n4 (where n is your student number).

Configure IPv4:	Manually
IP Address:	10.0.0.174

8   Leave the other settings at their defaults, and then click Apply.

9   Quit System Preferences.

Issue a New SSL Certificate

Because you do not have the necessary information in your System keychain on your administrator computer, you must perform the following steps on your server computer.

1   On your server, open the Server app, select your server, click Continue, provide administrator credentials (Administrator Name: ladmin, Administrator Password: ladminpw), deselect the "Remember this password" checkbox, and then click Connect.

2   In the Server app sidebar, select Certificates.

3   Click the Action (gear icon) pop-up menu.

4   If Show All Certificates does not display a checkmark, choose Show All Certificates to select it.

5   Click Add (+), and choose Create a Certificate Identity.

6   In the Name field, enter new$n$.pretendco.com (where n is your student number).

7 Click the Identity Type pop-up menu, and choose Leaf.

> | Name: | new17.pretendco.com |
> |---|---|
> | Identity Type: | Leaf |
> | Certificate Type: | SSL Server |

8 Click Create.

9 In the Choose An Issuer field, in the Identity column, select your intermediate CA.

> **Choose An Issuer**
>
> Please choose an issuer for the certificate. An issuer signs the certificate you are going to create.
>
> | Identity | Keychain |
> |---|---|
> | IntermediateCA_SERVER17.PRETENDCO | System.keychain |
>
> **Pretendco Project 17 Open Directory Certificate Authority**
> Root certificate authority
> Expires: Thursday, October 31, 2019 at 12:34:07 PM Central Daylight Time
> ○ This certificate has custom trust settings
>
> Learn More...
>
> Create

10 Confirm that your intermediate OD CA is displayed in both fields.

11 Click Create.

12 If you are prompted to allow use of the System keychain, provide local administrator credentials, and then click Allow.

13 At the Conclusion pane, click Done.

14 So that the Server app can add the certificate to your System keychain, enter your local administrator credentials, and click Allow.

15 Confirm that your new certificate appears in the Certificates list.

16 Quit the Server app.

Create the New Website

1 If you do not already have a connection to your server computer with the Server app on your administrator computer, then connect to it with the following steps: Open the Server app on your administrator computer, choose Manage > Connect to Server, select your server, click Continue, provide administrator credentials (Administrator Name: ladmin, Administrator Password: ladminpw), deselect the "Remember this password" checkbox, and then click Connect.

2   In the Server app sidebar, select Websites.

3   Click the Add (+) button to create a new website.

4   In the Domain Name field, enter newn.pretendco.com (where *n* is your student number).

5   Click the IP Address pop-up menu, and choose 10.0.0.n4 (where *n* is your student number).

6   Click the SSL Certificate pop-up menu, and choose newn.pretendco.com (where *n* is your student number).

7   Confirm that the Port field automatically changed to 443.

8   Leave the Store Site Files In pop-up menu at "Automatically create new folder."

9   Click Create.

Inspect the Service Certificates

1   In the Server app sidebar, select Certificates.

2   Click the pop-up menu "Secure services using," and choose Custom.

3   Confirm that the new website is listed as using the new certificate.

4   Click Cancel to close the Service Certificates pane without making any changes.

Confirm the New Website Is Active

You don't have to populate the new website folder with files; the Server app automatically adds placeholder files. You've already demonstrated how to copy new files to a website folder, so you will just use these placeholder files for the purposes of this exercise.

1   On your administrator computer, in the Safari address and search field, enter
    http://new*n*.pretendco.com (where *n* is your student number), and press Return to contact the website.

    Note that you do not need to use "https"; you will automatically be redirected to the secure website.

2   Click the lock icon in the address and search field, and then click Show Certificate.

3   Confirm that the certificate is signed by your server's intermediate OD CA.

4   Click OK to close the certificate information pane.

Remove a Website

In this scenario, a new computer has arrived to host the website, and it is ready to be configured at the IPv4 address you configured, so your server no longer needs to host the website. Remove the website, confirm that the files are still there but are no longer being served, and remove the extra IPv4 address.

There is no button or checkbox to turn off a website. You must remove the website from the Websites service , but when you do that, it leaves the files in place.

1   Open your administrator computer, and in the Websites pane, select the new*n*.pretendco.private (where *n* is your student number) website.

2   Click the Delete (–) button at the bottom of the pane.

3   Click Delete to confirm.

Confirm the Files for the Removed Website Still Exists

1   On your administrator computer, in the Server app sidebar, select your server.

2   Click the Storage pane.

3   Select your server's startup volume, and then navigate to /Library/Server/Web/Data/Sites/.

4   Confirm that the folder new*n*.pretendco.private (where *n* is your student number) still exists.

5   Open the folder new*n*.pretendco.private (where *n* is your student number).

6   Confirm that files are still in the folder.

Confirm the Website Is No Longer Available

Your server's default website is still configured to respond to web requests on all interfaces, so it will respond to the request at 10.0.0.*n*4 (where *n* is your student number).

1   On your administrator computer, open Safari.

2   Choose Safari > Clear History and Website Data.

3   Leave the Clear pop-up menu set to "all history," and click Clear History.

4   In the address and search field, enter http://new*n*.pretendco.com (where *n* is your student number), and press Return to contact the website.

5   At the certificate message, click Show Certificate.

6   Confirm that the web page uses the certificate for your server's host name, and then click Continue.

> **Safari can't verify the identity of the website "new17.pretendco.com".**
>
> The certificate for this website is invalid. You might be connecting to a website that is pretending to be "new17.pretendco.com", which could put your confidential information at risk. Would you like to connect to the website anyway?
>
> ☐ Always trust "server17.pretendco.com" when connecting to "new17.pretendco.com"
>
> 🔲 Pretendco Project 17 Open Directory Certificate Authority
> ↳ 🔲 IntermediateCA_SERVER17.PRETENDCO.COM_1
> ↳ 🔲 server17.pretendco.com
>
> **server17.pretendco.com**
> Issued by: IntermediateCA_SERVER17.PRETENDCO.COM_1
> Expires: Sunday, October 30, 2016 at 12:34:08 PM Central Daylight Time
> ⊗ This certificate is not valid (host name mismatch)
>
> ▶ Trust
> ▶ Details
>
> (?)   Hide Certificate   Cancel   Continue

7 Confirm that Safari displays the content for your default website.

8 Quit Safari.

Remove the Additional IPv4 Address

You no longer need your server to use the additional IPv4 address, so you can remove it now.

NOTE ▶ Be careful to delete the correct network interface. When you use Network preferences to delete a network interface, there is no opportunity to confirm the deletion. However, you can click Revert instead of Apply if you remove the wrong interface.

1 On your server, open System Preferences.

2 Open Network preferences.

3 Select "Interface for extra website."

4 Click Delete (–).

5 Click Apply.

6   Quit System Preferences.

In this exercise, you created and removed a new website. Even though you could have used any combination of host name, IPv4 address, and port, the scenario for this exercise required you to configure your server to temporarily use a different IPv4 address and host name. To support that requirement, you created a new DNS record, used your OD CA to issue an SSL certificate, and configured your server to temporarily use the new IPv4 address.

Exercise 20.4
Restrict Access to a Website

▶ **Prerequisite**

▶   "Exercise 20.2 Modify the Default Websites" on page 563

In this exercise, you restrict access to a portion of a website to a group.

Manage Website Access

OS X Server provides a mechanism to control access to a whole website or portions of the website that can be accessed only by certain users or groups.

Controlling access can be incredibly useful when dealing with websites that contain sensitive information or sections of a website that should be accessible to only one person or group. For example, you could set up a website so that only those users in a given group can access the website. You could also set up a portion of the website so that only a department has access to those particular pages. In most cases, access limitations are set up after users and groups are created because the access to certain web directories is based on users, groups, or both.

Configure your website to require credentials of someone in the Contractors group to access a portion of the information in the website.

Restrict Access for the Default Website and the Default Website (SSL)

1   On your administrator computer, in the Server app sidebar, select Websites if it is not already selected.

2   Double-click Server Website.

3   Click the Who Can Access pop-up menu, and choose "Limit access by folder."

4   Select new_product.

5   Double-click in the new_product's Group column.

6   Start typing Contractors, and then choose Contractors from the list that appears.

7   Click OK.

Repeat for the SSL website.

1   Double-click the Server Website (SSL).

2   Click the Who Can Access pop-up menu, and choose "Limit access by folder."

3   Select new_product.

4   Double-click in the new_product's Group column.

5   Start typing Contractors, and then choose Contractors from the list that appears.

6   Click OK.

Confirm Access Is Restricted

1   On your administrator computer, open Safari, and in the address and search field, enter http://servern.pretendco.com/new_product (where *n* is your student number), and then press Return.

Note that you are notified that you must log in. Safari displays a realm ID that is automatically generated.

To view this page, you must log in to this area on
server17.pretendco.com:443:

Realm ID 24288378

Your login information will be sent securely.

Name:

Password:

☐ Remember this password in my keychain

Cancel   Log In

2   In the Name field, enter barbara, and in the Password field, enter net.

3   Click Log In.

4   Confirm that Safari displays the page.

5   Quit Safari.

In this exercise, you required a user to authenticate to access a portion of your website.

Exercise 20.5
Monitor Web Services

▶ **Prerequisite**

► "Exercise 20.1 Turn On Web Services" on page 559

OS X Server keeps two logs related to the Websites service (access_log and error_log
in /var/log/apache2/), but the Server app parses these logs and makes them available in the
Logs pane.

In this exercise, you will use the Logs pane to inspect logs related to changing your password in "Exercise 20.1 Turn On Web Services" on page 559, then request a page that
doesn't exist, and then search for that request in the logs.

View the Server Website Access Log

Use Safari to request a website that does not exist, and then view the request in the access log. The default website redirects requests to the SSL website, so the request appears in both the Server Website and Server Website – SSL views of the log.

1   On your administrator computer, in the Server app sidebar, select Logs.

2   Click the pop-up menu, and scroll to the Websites section.

3   Choose Access Log (Server Website – SSL).

4   In the Search field, enter new_product, and press Return.

The log displays the search term and highlights all instances of the search term in yellow.

5   At the left side of the Search field, click the down arrow, and choose Filter.

This filters out any log entry that does not include the search term.

Request a Page That Doesn't Exist

Use Safari to request a page that doesn't exist so you can later look for it in the logs.

1   On your administrator computer, open Safari, and in the address and search field, enter http://server*n*.pretendco.com/bogus.html (where *n* is your student number), and then press Return.

That URL does not exist, so the Websites service informs your browser to return a 404 code, and Safari displays a "Not Found" page.

2   Quit Safari.

Find the Request in the Logs

1   In the Server app, in the Search field, enter bogus, and press Return.

The log displays the search term and highlights all instances of the search term in yellow.

In this exercise, you used the Logs pane to inspect the logs related to the Websites service.

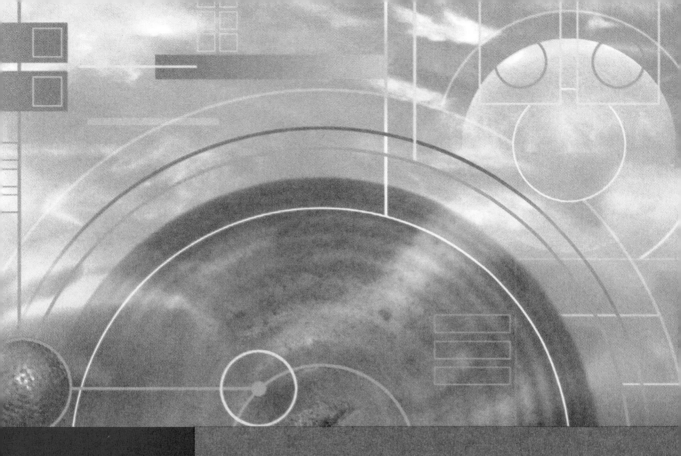

Using Collaborative Services

Lesson 21
Providing Mail Service

OS X Server provides a simple interface for setting up a capable and standards-based email service. The configuration of this service in OS X Server for Yosemite has been simplified yet still allows administration of the deeper details.

Reference 21.1
Hosting Mail Services

Email is one of the fundamental services on the Internet. OS X Server includes a feature-rich email service you can use to send, receive, and store email for your organization. Aside from the obvious reason of hosting an email server to gain an Internet identity, a number of other factors make hosting your own mail service advantageous. If you have a small office with a slow Internet connection, you may find that keeping all of your email within the building rather than using external email servers makes better use of your network bandwidth. This is especially true if typical messages within your organization include large attachments. Additionally, many organizations are required to keep the information in their email messages secure for regulatory or competitive reasons. Hosting your own email server in-house can keep confidential data from falling into the wrong hands. You may also find that various third-party email services don't offer the exact services you want. By running your own mail servers, you can customize various options to meet the needs of your organization.

The Mail service in OS X Server is based on two open source email packages:

▸ Postfix handles acceptance and delivery of individual messages.

▸ Dovecot accepts connections from individual users downloading their messages to their mail client. Dovecot is a replacement for Cyrus, found in Mac OS X v10.5 and earlier versions.

In addition to these programs, the Mail service in OS X Server uses a number of other packages to provide features, such as spam and virus scanning. Push notification of email is offered and leverages the Apple Push Notification service (APNs). Each of these is discussed in this lesson, but first you must learn how email works.

Defining Mail Services

Although email is one of the oldest and simplest systems on the Internet, it is composed of a number of different protocols. The primary protocol is Simple Mail Transfer Protocol (SMTP), which is responsible for delivering a message from the sender to the sender's email server and between email servers. When a message is sent, the outgoing mail server first looks up the address of the destination's Mail eXchange (MX) server using DNS. A given Internet domain can have multiple MX servers to help balance the load and provide redundant services. Each MX server is assigned a priority. The highest-priority servers are assigned the lowest number and are tried first when delivering mail via SMTP. In the following image, the priority number follows right after the record type (for example, the first MX record has a priority of 10 in the example for apple.com).

To look up information about a domain's MX servers, you can enter dig –t MX <DOMAIN> in the Terminal app.

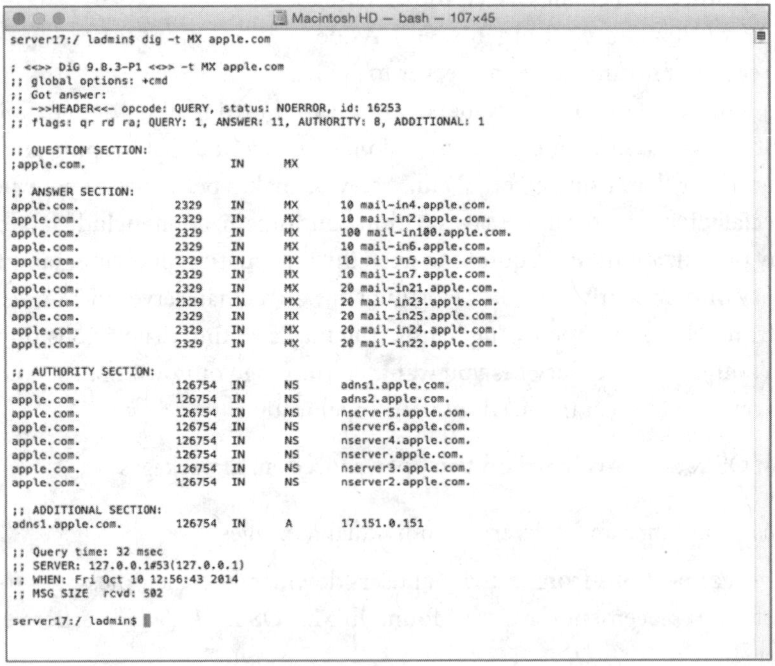

```
server17:/ ladmin$ dig -t MX apple.com

; <<>> DiG 9.8.3-P1 <<>> -t MX apple.com
;; global options: +cmd
;; Got answer:
;; ->>HEADER<<- opcode: QUERY, status: NOERROR, id: 16253
;; flags: qr rd ra; QUERY: 1, ANSWER: 11, AUTHORITY: 8, ADDITIONAL: 1

;; QUESTION SECTION:
;apple.com.                     IN     MX

;; ANSWER SECTION:
apple.com.            2329     IN     MX     10 mail-in4.apple.com.
apple.com.            2329     IN     MX     10 mail-in2.apple.com.
apple.com.            2329     IN     MX     100 mail-in100.apple.com.
apple.com.            2329     IN     MX     10 mail-in6.apple.com.
apple.com.            2329     IN     MX     10 mail-in5.apple.com.
apple.com.            2329     IN     MX     10 mail-in7.apple.com.
apple.com.            2329     IN     MX     20 mail-in21.apple.com.
apple.com.            2329     IN     MX     20 mail-in23.apple.com.
apple.com.            2329     IN     MX     20 mail-in25.apple.com.
apple.com.            2329     IN     MX     20 mail-in24.apple.com.
apple.com.            2329     IN     MX     20 mail-in22.apple.com.

;; AUTHORITY SECTION:
apple.com.            126754   IN     NS     adns1.apple.com.
apple.com.            126754   IN     NS     adns2.apple.com.
apple.com.            126754   IN     NS     nserver5.apple.com.
apple.com.            126754   IN     NS     nserver6.apple.com.
apple.com.            126754   IN     NS     nserver4.apple.com.
apple.com.            126754   IN     NS     nserver.apple.com.
apple.com.            126754   IN     NS     nserver3.apple.com.
apple.com.            126754   IN     NS     nserver2.apple.com.

;; ADDITIONAL SECTION:
adns1.apple.com.      126754   IN     A      17.151.0.151

;; Query time: 32 msec
;; SERVER: 127.0.0.1#53(127.0.0.1)
;; WHEN: Fri Oct 10 12:56:43 2014
;; MSG SIZE  rcvd: 502

server17:/ ladmin$
```

An individual email message may travel through many servers while en route to its final destination. Each server that a message passes through will tag the message with the name of the server and the time it was processed. This provides a history of which servers handled a given message. To examine this trail using the Mail application, you can choose View > Message > Long Headers while viewing the message.

```
Received: from cooper ([127.0.0.1]) by localhost (cooper.pretendco.com [127.0.0.1]) (amavisd-new, port
          10024) with ESMTP id 09379-03 for <david.pugh@pretendco.com>; Sat, 21 Sep 2002
          15:31:32 -0400 (EDT)
Received: from mail-out4.apple.com (mail-out4.apple.com [17.254.13.23]) by cooper (Postfix) with
          ESMTP id 5D5B9B7C672 for <david.pugh@pretendco.com>; Sat, 21 Sep 2002 15:31:32
          -0400 (EDT)
Received: from relay14.apple.com (relay14.apple.com [17.128.113.52]) by mail-out4.apple.com (Postfix)
          with ESMTP id 292BD251CA2; Sat, 21 Sep 2002 15:31:31 -0700 (PDT)
Received: from relay14.apple.com (unknown [127.0.0.1]) by relay14.apple.com (Symantec Mail Security)
          with ESMTP id 0E96B20A4C; Sat, 21 Sep 2002 15:31:31 -0700 (PDT)
Received: from [17.09.21.02] (sep21-2002.apple.com [17.09.21.02]) (using TLSv1 with cipher AES128-
          SHA (128/128 bits)) (No client certificate requested) by relay14.apple.com (Apple SCV relay)
          with ESMTP id E1B20A24685; Sat, 21 Sep 2002 15:31:30 -0700 (PDT)
```

Once the email message is delivered to the recipient's mail server, it will be stored there for the recipient to receive the message using either of the two available protocols:

▶ Post Office Protocol (POP) is a common email retrieval protocol used on mail servers where disk space and network connections are at a premium. POP is preferred in these environments because a mail client connects to the server, downloads the email, removes it from the server, and disconnects quickly. Although good for the server, POP mail servers are typically less user-friendly because they don't support server-side folders and may cause difficulties for a user connecting from multiple devices. As time goes on, the use of POP has been decreasing because of the need for people to have equal access to their mail across multiple devices and POP is not friendly to this goal.

▶ Internet Message Access Protocol (IMAP) is commonly used by mail services that want to provide more features to the user. IMAP allows the storage of all email and email folders on the server, where they can be backed up. Additionally, a mail client will often remain connected to the mail server for the duration of the user session. This can result in quicker notification of new messages. The downside to using IMAP is that it puts more load on the resources of the mail server. IMAP is the most practical choice when users have multiple devices they need to see their mail on.

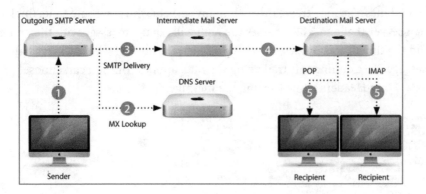

Configuring DNS for Mail

When you send an email, you'll need to ensure that the Domain Name System (DNS) is configured for your domain so that mail can be delivered to the proper address. DNS can be provided by a DNS hosting company or by using your own DNS servers. Although the examples here will rely on the basic DNS service provided by OS X Server, you would need an additional DNS service for a "real-life" email server setup accessible from the Internet.

Specifically, you will need to set up an MX record for the domain. The MX record is how the sending email server knows where to send the email. You can set up multiple MX records with different priority levels. The lower the priority number, the higher the preference for use. An MX record with a 10 priority will be used before one with a 20 priority unless the 10 priority mail server is not responding.

Without an MX record, the server will utilize an A record for the domain listed. Considering that often the email server will be a different server than that used for hosting a domain's website, this may not be a good situation because the mail might be delivered to the wrong location.

Configuring Access Permissions and Authentication Methods

You can set up limits to who can connect to the mail service based on users and the networks they are accessing from. You can define individual users or groups of users. Network access is granted by defining the network range allowed. Note that this is not the same as blacklisting, greylisting, or spam or virus filtering; it's taking control of network usage via client devices.

You can define authentication methods as automatic in which case the client device and the server will check a list of available methods and use a common one. You can also define specific authentication methods based on local and network directory services or define custom configurations of the standard email authentication choices.

Relaying Outgoing Mail

The OS X Server email service has the option to relay outgoing email through another SMTP server. This can be important if you don't want to run your own SMTP service with the attendant issues with blacklists or if the Internet service provider (ISP) you use doesn't allow you to host your own SMTP server.

Most likely you'll need user credentials to connect to the ISP's SMTP server. If your ISP allows nonauthenticated connections to the SMTP server, it will most likely be tagged an open relay at some point in the blacklists. If your ISP doesn't require credentials to connect, find a new SMTP service that does to prevent problems later.

By setting up the relay, your server can submit alert emails to the outside world with less likelihood of them being caught in spam filters. In this case, just configure the relay; you don't need to turn on the service if you are not using the full mail service.

Setting Mail Quotas for Users

To set a mail storage quota for a user, the Server app provides a simplified management tool as compared to earlier versions of OS X Server. One difference with OS X Server is that the same quota is applied to all users when set in the Mail service pane.

Individual users can have a mail quote set specifically for them by selecting the user and in the Action menu using the mail options to set a quota.

A quota can be helpful to manage the amount of mail users can retain on the email server, but it can also limit them if they exceed their limit and they miss email because of full mailbox errors.

Turning On Incoming Virus Scanning, Mail Blacklists, Greylists, and Junk Filtering

A common concern when running a mail server is how to protect your users from viruses. The OS X email service uses the ClamAV and Amavis virus-scanning packages for this purpose. The virus definitions are updated on a regular basis using a process called `fresh clam`. Any email that has been identified as containing a virus is stored in the /Library/ Server/Mail/Data/scanner/virusmails/ folder and is deleted after a period of time. The virusmails folder is created once virus filtering is turned on and the mail service is started. An alert is sent to the defined recipients in the Server app Alert notifications.

Blacklists are lists of domains known to host junk mail or other unwanted email servers. By subscribing to a blacklist, your email server will scan the incoming email, compare the host Internet Protocol (IP) address from where it came, and allow it to pass or not based on whether that host IP is listed. By default, the OS X Server email service utilizes the blacklist hosted by the Spamhaus Project, but you can change this to any other blacklist.

The danger of using a blacklist is that sometimes innocent hosts can get listed, and thus proper and desired emails can get blocked from delivery to your users. Getting off black-lists can be daunting and may result in lost email.

Greylists are a method of spam control that tosses out the initial attempt of a sender to send an email to an email server. A legitimate email sender will try sending the message again, whereas a spam producer usually tries only once.

The OS X Server email service can also use the SpamAssassin software package to scan incoming email and rank its likelihood of being spam. The text of the message is analyzed using a complex algorithm given a number that reflects how likely it is to be spam. This can be remarkably accurate unless the email contains terms and words commonly applied to spam. To counteract this, you can manage the service by adjusting what score is consid-ered spam. Certain types of organizations, such as a school, might need to use higher scores, while others, such as a medical office, might use a lower score.

The levels of score are as follows:

▶ Aggressive—The filter tolerates few signs of being junk mail.

▶ Moderate—The filter tolerates some signs of being junk mail.

▶ Cautious—The filter tolerates many signs of being junk mail.

Messages that are tagged as spam have the subject line appended by ***JUNK MAIL*** and are sent to the recipient. The recipient can then either delete the mail, open it, or pos-sibly configure a filter in the mail client to move it to a junk folder.

Mail Domains

The Mail service can host email for multiple domains. This might happen if an organiza-tion has two or more Internet domains it uses. In the following figure, there are two domains that can have users assigned to for email accounts.

Setup is simple; define the domain, and add users. The users must have an account prior to being added. Repeat for additional domains. The rest of the configuration choices work across all hosted domains.

Reference 21.2
Troubleshooting Mail Services

To troubleshoot the Mail service as provided by OS X Server, it helps to have a good understanding of how email works in general. Review the previous sections to make sure you understand each working piece.

Here are some common problems and suggestions for rectifying them:

▶ DNS problems—If the domain doesn't have proper MX records associated with it, other email servers may not be able to locate your email server to deliver the messages. You can utilize Network Utility to do a DNS lookup of your domain.

▶ Service issues—Utilize the Logs tab in the Server app to review the Mail log for clues as to why the service might not start or work properly.

▶ Can't send or receive email—Review the SMTP log for problems with users not being able to send mail, and review the POP and IMAP logs for problems with users not being able to receive mail.

▶ Too much spam being sent to the users—Increase the spam filtering rating in the filtering preferences in the Mail service in the Server app.

▶ Too many real emails being marked as spam—Decrease the spam filtering rating in the filtering preferences in the Mail service in the Server app.

Exercise 21.1
Turn On the Mail Service

▶ **Prerequisites**

▶ "Exercise 2.1 Create DNS Zones and Records" on page 71

▶ "Exercise 9.1 Create and Import Network Accounts" on page 292

The OS X Server email service is easy to configure using the Server app. In this exercise, you will start the service, examine the configuration options, create two domains, turn on the Mail service for user and group accounts, and set quotas.

Start and Configure the Mail Service

Start the Mail service right away so the virus definitions can start downloading, and then continue configuring the Mail service.

Turn On the Mail Service to Start Downloading the Virus Definitions

1   Perform these exercises on your administrator computer. If you do not already have a connection to your server computer with the Server app on your administrator com-

puter, then connect to it with the following steps: Open the Server app on your administrator computer, choose Manage > Connect to Server, select your server, click Continue, provide administrator credentials (Administrator Name: ladmin, Administrator Password: ladminpw), deselect the "Remember this password" checkbox, and then click Connect.

2   In the Server app sidebar, select Mail.

3   Click On to turn on the Mail service.

4   Confirm that the Status field indicates "Downloading virus definitions...."

5   In the Server app sidebar, select Logs.

6   Click the pop-up menu, and choose Anti-Virus Database Update Log.

     A number of virus definition files need to download, including main.cvd, daily.cvd, and bytecode.cvd.

7   Click the pop-up menu, and choose Anti-Virus Service Log.

     Note that entries in the beginning of the log indicate that it is waiting for the previously mentioned files to download.

8   In the Server app sidebar, select Mail.

9   In the Permissions field, note which users and networks are allowed.

Confirm the SSL Certificate

1   In the Server app sidebar, select Certificates.

2   If the "Secure services using" pop-up menu is set to "Custom configuration," click the pop-up menu, choose Custom, confirm that the two entries for Mail use the certificate "server*n*.pretendco.com - server*n*.pretendco.com OD Intermediate CA" (where *n* is your student number), and then click Cancel.

     If the "Secure services using" pop-up menu is set to "server*n*.pretendco.com - server*n*.pretendco.com OD Intermediate CA" (where *n* is your student number), then all your server's services use that certificate.

> **TIP** ▶ When providing the Mail service in a production environment, ensure that the common name (CN) of the SSL certificate that you use to protect the Mail service matches the fully qualified domain name (host name) of your server.

Inspect Authentication Methods

1   In the Server app sidebar, select Mail.

2   Next to the Authentication field, click Edit.

3   Click the pop-up menu, and note the various options available.

4   Leave the pop-up menu set to Automatic.

5   Click Cancel.

Configure Filtering Options

1   Next to the Filtering field, click Edit.

2   Leave the checkbox "Enable virus filtering" selected.

3   Select the checkbox "Enable blacklist filtering," and leave the blacklist server field at its default.

4   Leave the "Enable greylist filtering" checkbox unselected because you will use the Mail app on your administrator computer to send mail using your server's Mail service, and greylist filtering will initially reject delivery attempts for the first minute.

5   Leave the "Enable junk mail filtering" checkbox selected, and leave the slider at its default setting.

6   Click OK.

Inspect the Relay Options

1   Select the checkbox "Relay outgoing mail through ISP."

2   Note that you can specify the host name or IPv4 address of another server to relay mail from your server's mail service.

3   Note that you can select the checkbox "Enable SMTP relay authentication" and provide a username and password.

4 If you have a valid SMTP server and credentials to use for this exercise, enter them now, and click OK.

Otherwise, click Cancel to return to the main Mail pane.

Set Mail Quotas

Set the default quota for all users to be 200 MB, but allow Barbara Green to keep 700 MB of mail on the server. Verifying these limits is outside the scope of this guide.

1 Select the checkbox "Limit mail to."

> ☑ Limit mail to   200   MB per user

2 Note that the default value is 200 MB.

3 In the Server app sidebar, select Users.

4 Click the pop-up menu, and choose Local Network Users.

5 Select Barbara Green, click the Action (gear icon) menu, and choose Edit Mail Options.

6 Select the "Limit mail to" checkbox.

7 Select the existing limit, 200, and enter **700** to replace the original value.

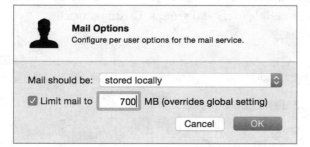

8 Click OK.

Turn On Mail for Domains and Accounts

By default, the Mail service doesn't accept mail for anyone until you add at least one domain and specify an email address for that domain.

Add an Email Domain

1 In the Server app sidebar, select Mail.

2 Click Add (+) to add a new domain.

3 In the Domain field, enter server*n*.pretendco.com (where *n* is your student number).

server17.pretendco.com

Domain: server17.pretendco.com

Members	Email

4 Click Create.

Specify an Email Address for Each of Your Local Network Accounts

After you start the Mail service and enable mail service for a domain, when you use the Users pane to create a new user, the Server app automatically populates the Email Addresses field for the new user based on the user's account name and the domain or domains that are enabled for mail service on your server.

Since you created the users before configuring the Mail service, you need to manually specify an email address for users. Configure an email address for one user, and then demonstrate that you can configure multiple users and groups. Use the shortcut.

1 Double-click your domain.

2 Click Add (+) to create a new email address.

3 Start entering Barbara Green, and then choose Barbara Green.

Domain: server17.pretendco.com

Members	Email
bar	@server17.pretendco.com
Barbara Green	

4 Note that the Email field is automatically populated with an appropriate email address based on Barbara Green's account name, barbara: barbara@server*n*.pretendco.com (where *n* is your student number).

5 If the accounts browser is not already visible, choose Window > Show Accounts Browser.

6 If you see system accounts, choose View > Hide System Accounts.

7 Click the accounts browser window, and then press Command-A to select all the accounts.

8 Command-click Barbara Green to deselect her account.

9 Drag the user and group accounts from the accounts browser to the list of members and their email addresses.

   If you accidentally drag Barbara Green to the list and she already has an email address defined, she will get an additional email address, based on her account name, followed by the number 1. If this happens, you can select this extra email address and then click Remove (–).

10 Press Command-B to hide the accounts browser.

11 Confirm that your local network users and groups have appropriate email addresses assigned; the left part of the email address is based on the account name, and the right part of the email address is server*n*.pretendco.com (where *n* is your student number).

Domain:	server17.pretendco.com
Members	**Email**
Barbara Green	barbara@server17.pretendco.com
Carl Dunn	carl@server17.pretendco.com
Contractors	contractors@server17.pretendco.com
Enrico Baker	enrico@server17.pretendco.com
Gary Pine	gary@server17.pretendco.com
Local Admin	ladmin@server17.pretendco.com
Lucy Sanchez	lucy@server17.pretendco.com
Maria Miller	maria@server17.pretendco.com
Sue Wu	sue@server17.pretendco.com
Todd Porter	todd@server17.pretendco.com
Workgroup	workgroup@server17.pretendco.com

12 Click OK to save the change and return to the main Mail pane.

Configure an Additional Email Domain

Previously you created a domain and then went back and added email addresses for that domain. Now you will create a domain and add email addresses at the same time.

In a production environment, you should not have multiple Mac computers with OS X Server that host the same domain; it is only for demonstration purposes that you will configure your server to host the domain pretendco.com in addition to the domain server*n*.pretendco.com (where *n* is your student number). In an instructor-led environment, you could send mail to users at another student's server using an email address that ends in @server*x*.pretendco.com (where *x* is your classmate's student number). If you send mail to an address that ends in @pretendco.com, MX records will determine the server to which your Mail client attempts to deliver the message.

1   Click Add (+) to add another domain.

2   In the Domain field, enter pretendco.com.

3   Press Command-B to show the accounts browser.

4   Click the Accounts browser, and then press Command-A to select all the accounts.

5   Drag the accounts to the list of members and email addresses.

6   Press Command-B to hide the accounts browser.

7   Confirm that each email address has been automatically configured based on the account name and ends with @pretendco.com.

8   Click Create.

Inspect a User Account

1   In the Server app sidebar, select Users.

2   Double-click Barbara Green.

3   Confirm that there are two email addresses in the Email Addresses field.

Full Name:	Barbara Green
Account Name:	barbara
Email Addresses:	barbara@server17.pretendco.com
	barbara@pretendco.com

+ —

4   Click Cancel.

Inspect a Group Account

1   In the Server app sidebar, select Groups.

2   Double-click Contractors.

3   Confirm that there are two email addresses in the Mailing Lists field.

4   Note that if you leave unselected the checkbox "Allow mail from non-group members, " the Mail service will not accept mail for a group's mailing list unless it is from a group member. Assuming that Todd is a member of the Contractors group, this means that if you configure your Mail client address to be todd@pretendco.com, mail you send to contractors@server$n$.pretendco.com will be rejected; similarly, mail from todd@server$n$.pretendco.com to contractors@pretendco.com will be rejected (where n is your student number).

5   Click Cancel to not make any changes.

Confirm Mail Is Running

Confirm that the Mail service is running.

1   In the Server app sidebar, select Mail.

2   Confirm that the status indicator Status field indicates "Available on your local network at server$n$.local" (where n is your student number).

In this exercise, you configured the Mail service with two domains, server$n$.pretendco.com (where n is your student number) and pretendco.com. It's not enough to just add a domain, so you also added user and group accounts to each domain and saw that the Server app automatically created an appropriate mail address for each account.

Exercise 21.2
Send and Receive Mail

▶ **Prerequisite**

- ▶ "Exercise 21.1 Turn On the Mail Service" on page 594

In this exercise, you'll use Internet Accounts preferences to configure the Mail app for Todd Porter on your administrator computer, and since you don't have an extra client Mac computer, you'll use your server to configure Mail for Sue Wu. You'll see how easy it is to send mail and reply to it.

Set Up the Mail Application with Internet Accounts Preferences

On your administrator computer, you will use Internet Accounts preferences for Todd Porter at the @pretendco.com domain. On your server, you will do the same for Sue Wu.

Set Up Mail for Todd Porter on Your Administrator Computer

1   On your administrator computer, open System Preferences.

2   Open Internet Accounts.

3   Scroll down in the right column, and select Add Other Account.

4   In the account type pane, select "Add a Mail account," and click Create.

5   Provide the following information:

- ▶ Full Name: Todd Porter
- ▶ Email Address: todd@pretendco.com
- ▶ Password: net

6   Click Create.

7   At the message that the account must be manually configured, click Next.

8   In the Incoming Mail Server Info pane, use the following settings:

▶   Account Type: IMAP

▶   Mail Server: server*n*.pretendco.com (where *n* is your student number)

▶   User Name: todd (this is automatically entered from the previous pane)

▶   Password: net (this is automatically entered from the previous pane)

9   Click Next.

10 If you receive a warning that the identity of your server cannot be verified, click Show Certificate, select the checkbox "Always trust...," click Connect, provide your local administrator credentials, and click Update Settings.

11 In the Outgoing Mail Server Info pane, enter the following information, and then click Create:

▶   SMTP Server: server*n*.pretendco.com (where *n* is your student number)

▶   User Name: todd

▶   Password: net

12 Click Create.

13 Confirm that todd@pretendco.com appears in the left column of Internet Accounts preferences.

14 Quit System Preferences.

Set Up Mail for Sue Wu on Your Server Computer

1   On your server computer, open System Preferences.

2   Open Internet Accounts.

3   Scroll down in the right column, and select Add Other Account.

4   In the account type pane, select "Add a Mail account," and click Create.

5   Provide the following information:

  ▶ Full Name: Sue Wu

  ▶ Email Address: sue@pretendco.com

  ▶ Password: net

6   Click Create.

7   At the message that the account must be manually configured, click Next.

8   In the Incoming Mail Server Info pane, use the following settings:

  ▶ Account Type: IMAP

  ▶ Mail Server: server*n*.pretendco.com (where *n* is your student number)

  ▶ User Name: sue (this is automatically entered from the previous pane)

  ▶ Password: net (this is automatically entered from the previous pane)

9   Click Next.

10   In the Outgoing Mail Server Info pane, enter the following information, and then click Create:

  ▶ SMTP Server: server*n*.pretendco.com (where *n* is your student number)

  ▶ User Name: sue

  ▶ Password: net

11   Confirm that sue@pretendco.com appears in the left column of Internet Accounts preferences.

12   Quit Internet Accounts.

Send Mail to a Group as Todd Porter

Use the Mail application as Todd Porter to send mail to the Contractors group. Remember that because you configured Todd Porter to use the pretendco.com domain, you must use the pretendco.com domain for the group message.

1   On your administrator computer, open Mail by clicking it in your Dock.

2   In the toolbar, click the "Compose new message" (pencil-and-paper icon) button.

3   In the To field, enter Contractors@pretendco.com.

4   In the Subject field, enter Looking forward to this next project.

5   In the Main mail window, enter text similar to the text shown in the following figure.

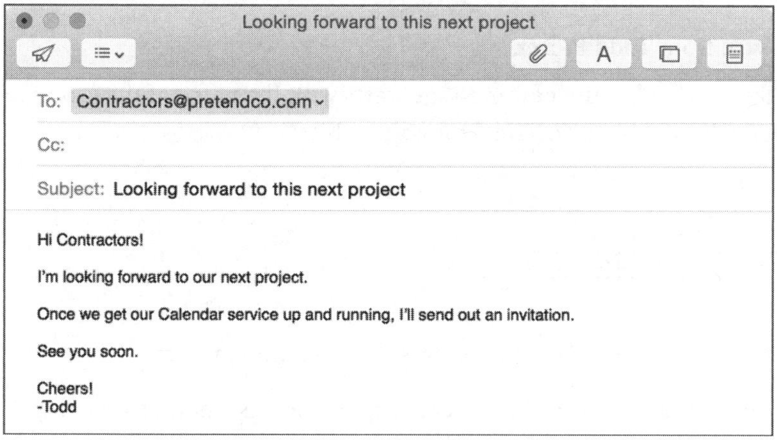

6   Click the "Send message" button in the upper-left corner of the message window.

7   If you are asked for the password for todd@pretendco.com, enter net, and then click OK.

8   Close the main Mail window, but leave Mail running.

Reply to the Mail Message as Sue Wu

Use Mail as Sue Wu to read and reply to the mail message from Todd Porter.

Confirm the Message Was Scanned for Viruses

1   On your server computer, open Mail by clicking it in your Dock.

2   Confirm that the message from Todd is in the Inbox.

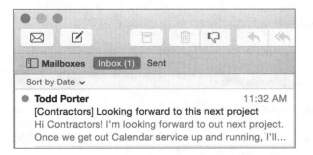

3   Select the message from Todd Porter.

Note that the Subject field of the new message starts with the name of the group in square brackets, followed by the original message subject.

☆ **Todd Porter**
To: Contractors@pretendco.com
[Contractors] Looking forward to this next project

4   Choose View > Message > All Headers (or press Shift-Command-H).

5   Confirm that one of the headers is "X-Virus-Scanned: amavisd-new at server*n*.pretendco.com," where *n* is your student number.

Reply to the message.

1   With the message from Todd still selected, choose Message > Reply All.

2   Note that this replies to both the sender and the group addresses.

3   In the main body of the message, enter the message Thanks, looking forward to it! -Sue.

4   Click the "Send message" button.

5   If you are asked for the password for sue@pretendco.com, enter net, and then click OK.

Check the Reply as Todd Porter
On your administrator computer, since Mail is already running, look for a notification banner. As soon as the Mail app receives the message, a banner appears in the upper-right corner of your screen for a short period of time and then slides offscreen to the right unless you hover your pointer over it or click it. Additionally, the Mail icon in the Dock

has a red badge with a "2" in it to indicate that you have two new Mail messages (the same message is actually delivered twice; one message is to Todd Porter directly, and the other message is addressed to the Contractors group).

1   On your administrator computer, click the banner to read the message.

2   If you miss the banner before it slides off the screen, click the Notification Center icon in the upper-right corner of the screen, then click Notifications, and finally select the message.

Alternatively, you could click Mail in the Dock and then select the new message to read it.

Test the Spam Filter

Send a message with an attachment that contains the text of GTUBE (which stands for the "Generic Test for Unsolicited Bulk Email"), and confirm that it is marked as Junk.

Send a Sample Message

1   On your administrator computer, in Mail, in the toolbar, click the "Compose new message" (pencil-and-paper icon) button.

2   In the To field, enter sue@pretendco.com.

3   In the Subject field, enter Just a test.

4   In the toolbar, click the Attachment (paperclip icon) button.

5   In the open file dialog, select Documents in the sidebar, and then open /StudentMaterials/Lesson21/.

6   Select the Sample A text file.

7   Press the Space bar to preview the contents.

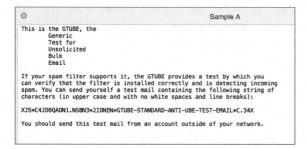

8   Press the Space bar again to close the preview.

9   Click Choose File.

10   Click the "Send message" button.

11   Quit Mail.

Confirm the Message Was Flagged as Junk

1   On your server computer, select the new message.

2   Confirm that ***JUNK MAIL*** was automatically added to the beginning of the subject.

3   Select the "Just a test" message.

4   Choose View > Message > All Headers (or press Shift-Command-H).

5   Confirm that one of the headers is "X-Spam-Flag: YES."

6   Quit Mail.

In this exercise, you confirmed that you can use the Mail service to send a mail message to individuals and groups and to reply as well. Additionally, you confirmed that the junk mail filter successfully detected the sample incoming junk mail.

Exercise 21.3
Examine Mail Service Logs

► **Prerequisite**

► "Exercise 21.2 Send and Receive Mail" on page 602

In this exercise, you will take a quick look at the logs related to your server's Mail service. Detailed information about using the information in the logs to troubleshoot problems is outside the scope of this guide.

Examine Mail Service Logs

1   On your administrator computer, in the Server app sidebar, select Logs.

2   Click the pop-up menu, and choose SMTP Log.

3   Browse the contents of the log, which is related to your server's Mail service accepting and delivering mail.

4   Click the pop-up menu, and choose IMAP Log.

5   Scroll through the contents of the log, which is related to users checking their mail.

6   Click the pop-up menu, and choose List Server Log.

    This contains information about attempts to deliver mail to groups with a mail account set up and turned on.

In this exercise, you took a quick look at a few of the logs for the Mail service.

Lesson 22

Configuring the Wiki Service

OS X Server provides a simple interface for configuring the Wiki service. Wikis are growing in popularity because they offer an easy, cross-platform method to share information with many users.

Reference 22.1
Configuring and Managing a Wiki

A wiki is a collaborative web-based tool that allows users and groups to post information in a manner that promotes the logical progression of an idea, project, theme, or any other focal point of discussion within an organization.

Wikis are central to the idea of all users within a given group being able to post, edit, review, and discuss material without interference from other groups or departments within an organization. This can benefit the group whose wiki is hosting a confidential project or sensitive information. OS X Server wikis also keep a detailed history of a group's posts, so you can retrieve older information if necessary.

Wikis have a few layers of access control. You can administratively control the users and groups you allow to create wikis. Once a user creates a wiki, she can specify who can read it and who can edit it, all without any intervention from an administrator.

The user who creates the wiki becomes the default administrator for that wiki. That user can then assign administration rights to other nonserver administrator users. Existing server administrators already have administration rights.

Once users have access to a wiki, they can post articles, images, and files for downloading; link pages together; and format the pages to their liking. Media files such as images, movies, and audio are presented right on the webpage and do not need to be downloaded by the user.

Similar to wikis are blogs. Blogs permit users and groups to catalog their experiences surrounding a project or theme. Whereas wikis are collaborative, blogs tend to be singular in nature and organized in a chronological format; however, with group blogging, shared experiences may be posted together.

The files for the Wiki service are stored at /Library/Server/Wiki/.

The wiki calendar feature is reliant on the Calendar service being turned on. If you plan on having a group calendar, make sure Calendar is turned on.

Since a wiki is a web service and can be used across the Internet, it is wise to protect the wiki with Secure Sockets Layer (SSL). This will prevent the content from being readable as it passes across networks.

iOS users can be granted access to the files in the wiki via WebDAV for use in iWork.

Files that are hosted in a wiki or blog can be viewed by the wiki users directly in the wiki courtesy of the Quick Look functionality of OS X Server. This is handy because not all users will have the appropriate applications installed on their computers to view files.

Reference 22.2
Troubleshooting the Wiki Service

Here are some common suggestions for rectifying issues with the Wiki service:

▶   If your users can't connect to the Wiki service, check that the clients are using a Domain Name System (DNS) server that is providing the proper name resolution for the server.

▶   If users can't connect to the wiki, check that ports 80 and 443 are open to the server. Check that the Wiki service is running.

▶   If users can't authenticate to the Wiki service, check that the users are using proper passwords. Reset if needed. Check that the users are allowed access to the service as per the access controls.

For additional information on troubleshooting web issues, refer to Lesson 20 "Hosting Websites".

Exercise 22.1
Turn On the Wiki Service

▶ **Prerequisites**

- ▶ "Exercise 2.1 Create DNS Zones and Records" on page 71
- ▶ "Exercise 9.1 Create and Import Network Accounts" on page 292; or use the Server app to create a user with a full name of Carl Dunn, an account name of carl, and a password of net, who is a member of a group named Contractors

Most of the configuration of the Wiki service is done within a wiki itself via a web browser. You can use the Server app to do the following:

- ▶ Start and stop the Wiki service
- ▶ Configure the list of users who have access to the Wiki service
- ▶ Turn on or off WebDAV access to the wiki files (mainly for iOS devices)

In this exercise, you will turn on the Wiki service and then limit who can create wikis. You will ensure that your site uses SSL to protect it.

Use the Server App to Turn On and Configure the Wiki Service

1 Perform these exercises on your administrator computer. If you do not already have a connection to your server computer with the Server app on your administrator computer, then connect to it with the following steps: Open the Server app on your administrator computer, choose Manage > Connect to Server, select your server, click Continue, provide administrator credentials (Administrator Name: ladmin, Administrator Password: ladminpw), deselect the "Remember this password" checkbox, and then click Connect.

2 In the Server app sidebar, select Wiki.

3 Click On to turn on the service.

4 Confirm that the Status field displays a green status indicator, along with reachability information.

Configure Who Can Create a Wiki

By default, as soon as you turn on the Wiki service, any user defined on your server can create a wiki.

To become more familiar with controlling who can create a wiki, limit it to members of the Contractors group.

1   Next to the Permissions field, click Edit.

2   Click the "Allow wiki creation for" pop-up menu, and choose "only some users."

3   Press Command-B to show the accounts browser.

4   Drag Contractors from the accounts browser to the list of accounts.

5   Click OK to save the change.

6   Confirm that the Permissions field indicates "2 groups can create wikis."

Turn On WebDAV for iOS Users Using iWork

Although using an iOS device with iWork is outside the scope of this guide, turn on WebDAV for iWork; if you have an iOS device with iWork, feel free to try this feature on your own.

1   Select the checkbox "Enable WebDAV access to Wiki files."

Create a Wiki

Users who you authorized to create wikis can begin the process of creating a wiki. Wikis are web-based, so you can use any browser on any platform to authenticate users to start the process of wiki creation.

In this exercise, you will create a wiki as Carl Dunn (a member of the Contractors group) and configure it at the time of creation so that members of the Contractors group can read and write the wiki, other logged-in users can read the wiki, and unauthenticated users cannot access the wiki.

1   Click the View Wiki link at the bottom of the Wiki pane in the Server app.

2   In the upper-right corner of the Safari window, click Log in.

3   At the Please Log In pane, in the User Name field, enter carl, and in the Password field enter net.

4 Click Log In.

5 Note that the Log Out (unlocked lock icon) button appears in the upper-right corner after you successfully log in.

6 Like the instructions on the page indicate, click the Add (+) button, and choose New Wiki.

7 Give the wiki a name, such as Demo wiki, and a description, such as Just testing things out.

8 Click Continue.

9 In the "Set permissions" pane, start entering Contractors into the Permissions field, and then choose Contractors from the list that appears.

10 For the Contractors group, click the pop-up menu, and choose Read & Write.

11 For "All logged-in users," set permissions to "Read only."

12 For "All unauthenticated users," leave permissions at "No access."

Set permissions (step 2 of 3)		
Permissions	Type a user or group name here	
	Contractors	Read & write
	All logged in users	Read only
	All unauthenticated users	No access

Cancel   Go back   Continue

13 Click Continue.

14 In the "Set appearance" pane, select one of the color schemes.

15 Click Create.

16 Click Go to Wiki at the "Setup complete" pane.

17 Note that the wiki offers some welcome text, along with instructions how to edit it.

   Review the various menus, buttons, and links in the wiki to get used to the interface.

In this exercise, you used the Server app to perform the initial configuration of the Wiki service and then used Safari to log in and create a wiki.

Exercise 22.2
Edit a Wiki

Prerequisite

► "Exercise 22.1 Turn On the Wiki Service" on page 615

Now that you have created a wiki, you can edit and configure it. In this exercise, you'll use network user credentials to edit the wiki, attach a file, manage access to the wiki, configure the wiki to provide a blog, create some content, and then delete the wiki.

Edit Wiki Text and Upload Documents

1 You should still be logged in as Carl Dunn and viewing the wiki you just created. If you aren't, use the steps in the previous exercise to log in with his credentials. If this doesn't automatically display the wiki you just created, click the icon in the upper-left corner, choose All Wikis, and then select the wiki you just created.

2 Click the Edit (pencil icon) button.

3 Note that this changes the set of available tools.

4   At the end of the existing text, press Return for a new line, and then click the Attachment (paperclip icon) button in the upper-left corner.

5   Click Choose File, select your Documents folder in the sidebar, and then navigate to /StudentMaterials/Lesson22/.

6   Select Planets.numbers, and then click Choose.

7   Click Upload to attach the file.

8   Click Save to save the edits to the page.

9   View the results of the edit.

10 Click the Quick Look (eye icon) button next to the filename to view the attachment without downloading it.

11 Click Close (X) to close the Quick Look window.

Users can upload additional media using the appropriate buttons in the toolbar. The media will be presented on the webpage and won't require downloading for use by the user.

Upload a Document to the Wiki
You just added a document to the text of a wiki, but you can also upload a document separately.

1   Click the Add (+) button, and choose Upload File to Demo Wiki.

2   Click Choose File.

3   In the Lesson22 folder, select the Sample Pages document.

4   Click Choose.

5   In the Upload File dialog, click Upload.

6   Click Documents in the toolbar.

7   Confirm that list of documents includes the Demo wiki page and the Sample Pages document.

Configure Wiki Settings

Add a blog for the wiki, review the appearance options for the wiki, and update the per-missions for the wiki so that unauthenticated users can access the wiki.

1   Click the Action (gear icon) pop-up menu, and choose Wiki Settings.

2   While viewing the wiki settings, with General selected in the sidebar, select the Blog checkbox.

3   In the Wiki Settings sidebar, select Appearance, and then review the available appearance options.

4   In the Wiki Settings sidebar, select Permissions, click the permissions pop-up menu for "All unauthenticated users," and choose "Read only."

5   Click Save.

Add a Blog for the Wiki

1   Click the Add (+) button, and choose New Blog Post in "Demo wiki."

2   Give your blog post a name like Demo blog post, and then click Add.

3   Note that the default text entry for the blog post contains information about editing it.

4 Click the blog entry text, press Command-A to select all the text, and then press Delete.

5 Enter some text, such as Learned about the Wiki service today.

6 Click Save.

View the Wiki and Blog as an Anonymous User

1 Click the Log Out (unlocked lock icon) button, and then at the Log Out pane, click Log Out.

2 Note that even though you are no longer authenticated to the wiki, because you configured the wiki to allow unauthenticated users to read the content, you still see the blog entry.

Log In and Delete the Wiki

Since this wiki was just for testing, delete it.

1 Click the Log In (lock icon) button in the toolbar.

2 In the Please Log In pane, provide credentials (User Name: carl, Password: net), and click Log In.

3 If you are not already viewing the wiki, click Wikis in the toolbar, and then select the wiki.

4 Click the Action (gear icon) button, and choose Delete Main Page.

If you didn't upload any documents, choose Delete Wiki.

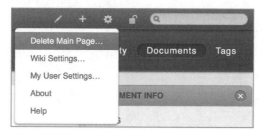

5 At the confirmation dialog, click Delete.

6 Click the Log Out (unlocked lock icon) button in the toolbar.

7   At the Log Out pane, click Log Out, and then quit Safari.

In this exercise, you used Safari to edit the wiki settings and to edit the wiki content.

Lesson 23

Implementing the Calendar Service

As one of the core collaboration services, Calendar provides a standards-based method of scheduling tasks and resources.

Reference 23.1
Describing Calendar Service Data Locations

Like most other services, the data repository for the Calendar service is located at /Library/Server/. Within that directory is a folder containing data specific to the Calendar service at /Library/Server/Calendar and Contacts/.

Within that folder is a Config folder that has the main configuration file, caldavd-system.plist, for the caldav daemon.

Logs are also stored in the /Library/Server/Calendar and Contacts/ directory, which is a change from previous versions.

Reference 23.2
Using the Calendar Service

OS X Server contains a calendaring service based on several open source initiatives, mainly the Calendar Server Extensions for WebDAV (CalDAV) calendaring protocol. The Calendar service uses Hypertext Transfer Protocol (HTTP) and HTTP Secure (HTTPS) for access to all of its files. Users who want to use the calendaring service can take advantage of several handy features:

► Scheduling rooms or items that can be checked out, such as projectors

► Enabling access control for the delegation of scheduling and restricted viewing of your calendar (or calendars)

► Allowing multiple calendars per user

► Permitting the attachment of files to events

► Sending invitations to events, regardless of whether the recipient is a user on the Calendar server

► Checking to see whether users or meeting locations are available for a certain event

► Privately annotating an event with comments that only they and the event organizer can access

► Using push notifications to support immediate updates for computers and mobile devices

And these under-the-hood features should make administrators happy:

▶ Integration with Open Directory in OS X Server, Microsoft's Active Directory, and Lightweight Directory Access Protocol (LDAP) directory services requires no modification to user records.

▶ Service discovery makes it easy for users to set up Calendar when you choose Create Users and Groups or Import Users and Groups during your initial server setup.

▶ Server-side scheduling frees up client resources for better client performance and more consistent scheduling results.

Once the Calendar service is started, users can create and manipulate their events and schedules with Calendar (v4.0 or higher), Calendar for iPhone and iPod touch, and wiki calendar pages. A number of third-party applications also work with the Calendar service; you can locate them by doing a web search for CalDAV support.

You can set permissions based on users, groups, and what networks they are connecting from in a similar manner as the other services. This is configured under Permissions of the Access section of the Calendar service pane.

When allowing email invitations, you can define an email account to handle that duty, but most of the time simply using the default local email account created by the Server app for the task is the easiest path to take. Either way, it needs to be a dedicated account and not one that is used for any other purpose. It will also configure the local email server settings to be used with that email address.

The Calendar service provides a way to create and use resources (such as a projector or a set of speakers) and locations (such as a building or a meeting room). You add locations and resources with the Server app in the Calendar pane. If no delegate has been set, the Calendar service automatically accepts the invitation for the location or resource if it is free and makes the free/busy information available to users. You can also define a delegate to moderate the availability of the resource or location. A useful feature is the automatic lookup of addresses and pin placement on a map.

Conference Room A

Type:	Location
Name:	Conference Room A
Address:	Apple Inc., 1 Infinite Loop, Cupertino, CA 9...
	37.331863, -122.029524
Delegate:	Barbara Green
	Delegates can view and manage resources using Calendar
Scheduling:	Accept If Free, Decline If Busy
Accept Group:	Employees
	Invitations from members of this group will always be accepted

Cancel   Create

Projector 1

Name:	Projector 1
Delegate:	Carl Dunn
	Delegates can view and manage resources using Calendar
Scheduling:	Accept If Free, Decline If Busy
Accept Group:	Contractors
	Invitations from members of this group will always be accepted

Cancel   OK

Delegates can have two functions based on whether you set Automatic or With Delegate Approval. If you set Automatic, the resource will automatically accept the invitation, but the delegate can view and modify the resource's calendar. If With Delegate Approval has been selected, the delegate must accept or deny the invitation. The delegate can also view and modify the resource's calendar.

Reference 23.3
Troubleshooting the Calendar Service

To troubleshoot the Calendar service provided by OS X Server, it helps to have a good understanding of how the Calendar service works in general. Review the preceding sections to make sure you understand each working piece.

Here are some common problems and potential solutions:

▶ If your users can't connect to the Calendar service on the server, check that the clients are using a Domain Name System (DNS) server that is providing the proper name resolution for the server.

▶ If users can't connect to the Calendar service, check that ports 8008 and 8443 are open to the server.

▶ If users can't authenticate to the Calendar service, check that the users are using proper passwords. Reset if needed. Check that the users are allowed access to the service as per the service access controls.

Exercise 23.1
Configure and Start the Calendar Service

► **Prerequisites**

- ► "Exercise 2.1 Create DNS Zones and Records" on page 71
- ► "Exercise 9.1 Create and Import Network Accounts" on page 292
- ► "Exercise 21.1 Turn On the Mail Service" on page 594

You use the Server app to start and manage the Calendar service. The parameters you can adjust are limited to the following:

- ► Secure Sockets Layer (SSL) certificate (in the Server app Certificates pane)
- ► Turning on and off email invitations and various related settings
- ► Locations and resources

Starting the Calendar service with the Server app is simple, but you will want to gather the email server information you'll use with email invitations.

Review Certificates
Confirm that the Calendar service uses an SSL certificate to secure communications between the service and its clients.

1   Perform these exercises on your administrator computer. If you do not already have a connection to your server computer with the Server app on your administrator computer, then connect to it with the following steps: Open the Server app on your administrator computer, choose Manage > Connect to Server, select your server, click Continue, provide administrator credentials (Administrator Name: ladmin, Administrator Password: ladminpw), deselect the "Remember this password" checkbox, and then click Connect.

2   In the Server app sidebar, select Certificates.

3   If all services use the same certificate, that certificate will be displayed next to "Secure services using."

Otherwise, click the pop-up menu, choose Custom, confirm that Calendar and Contacts is set to use a certificate, and click OK to close the certificates pane.

Inspect Email Invitation Settings

NOTE ▶ Be sure that you use an email account that is dedicated to the Calendar service. The following steps illustrate an email account that is automatically created for you to use.

1   In the Server app sidebar, select Calendar.

2   Select the "Enable invitations by email" checkbox.

There should be an email address, com.apple.calendarserver@server*n*.pretendco.com (where *n* is your student number), already populating the field. This default email account for the user com.apple.calendarserver, a system account, is filled in for you. If you like, you may use another account, but don't use an email account that is used for normal email transactions. Still, it is suggested you use the default email account.

3   Click Next.

4   The incoming mail server information should be filled in for you, but if it isn't, enter the mail server information for the account you entered in the previous step, and click Next.

Configure Server Email Address

Enter account information for the incoming mail account.

Mail Server Type:	IMAP
Incoming Mail Server:	server17.pretendco.com
Port:	993 ☑ Use SSL
User Name:	com.apple.calendarserver
Password:	•••••••••••••••

5   The outgoing mail server information should be filled in for you, but if it isn't, enter the mail server information for the account you entered in step 4, and click Next.

```
Configure Server Email Address

    Enter account information for the outgoing mail account.

     Outgoing Mail Server:  [ server17.pretendco.com              ]
                     Port:  [ 587   ]  ☑ Use SSL
       Authentication Type: [ Login                        ⬍ ]
                User Name:  [ com.apple.calendarserver          ]
                 Password:  [ ••••••••••••••••                  ]
```

6   Review the Mail Account Summary page. If you made any changes, click Finish; otherwise, click Cancel.

Start the Calendar Service

1   Click On to start the Calendar service.

2   Confirm that the Status field displays a green status indicator along with information about the availability of the service.

3   Review the Permissions field.

In this exercise, you inspected the SSL certificate the service uses and the settings related to the "Enable invitations by email" option, and you started the service.

Exercise 23.2
Use the Server App to Add Resources and Locations

▶ **Prerequisite**

   ▶   "Exercise 23.1 Configure and Start the Calendar Service" on page 629

In the scenario for this exercise, to prevent double-booking locations and resources for events, your organization decided that everyone in the organization should use the Calendar service. In this exercise, you will create a location and a resource and configure each to automatically accept an invitation if it is not already scheduled and to decline it if it is already scheduled. You will assign Enrico Baker as the delegate so he can view and modify the schedule of each resource.

Create a Location

Create a location over which your organization has control of the free/busy status, such as a conference room. Configure it so that the delegate, Enrico Baker, can view and edit the calendar for the location.

1   In the Server app sidebar, select the Calendar service.

2   Under the Locations and Resources section, click the Add (+) button.

3   Leave the Type pop-up menu set to Location.

4   In the Name field, enter Conference Room A.

5   For the purposes of this exercise, leave the Address field blank.

    In a production environment, you could enter the real address of the location and then choose it from the list that appears.

6   In the Delegate field, start typing Enrico Baker, and then choose Enrico Baker.

7   Leave the Scheduling pop-up menu at Accept If Free, Decline If Busy.

8   Leave the Accept Group field blank.

9   Click Create.

You added a location that you can use with events for a calendar hosted by the Calendar service.

Create a Resource

Creating a resource is similar to creating a location. Create a resource for the organization's 3D printer, and add Enrico Baker as the delegate.

1   Click the Add (+) button, and then choose Resource from the pop-up menu.

2   In the Name field, enter 3D Printer 1.

3   In the Delegate field, start typing Enrico Baker, and then choose Enrico Baker.

4   Leave the Scheduling pop-up menu set to Accept If Free, Decline If Busy.

5   Leave the Accept Group field blank.

The image shows an indoor setting.

6 Click Create.

7 Confirm that the new resource is in the list of locations and resources.

Locations and Resources
🖨 3D Printer 1
🔎 Conference Room A

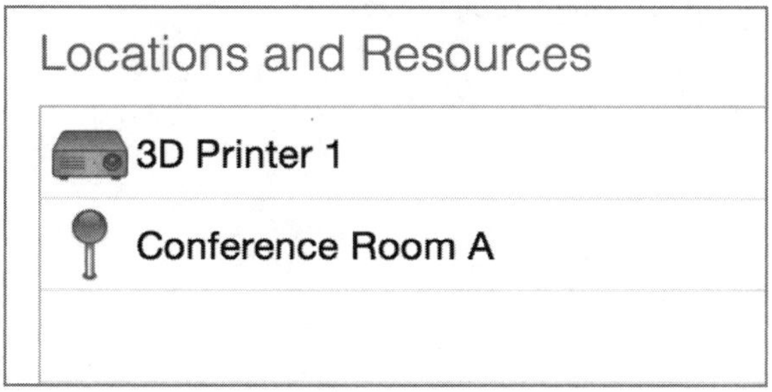

You just created a location and a resource and configured Enrico Baker to be the delegate for each. You will use these in the next exercise.

Exercise 23.3
Use the Calendar Service

A triangular arrow marker.

▶ **Prerequisites**

   ▶ "Exercise 23.2 Use the Server App to Add Resources and Locations" on page 631

   ▶ "Exercise 21.2 Send and Receive Mail" on page 602

Users can create and modify events with the Calendar app, a web browser, and mobile devices. In this exercise, as Gary Pine, you will use the Calendar app to create an event invitation. On your server computer, as Sue Wu, you'll use the Calendar app to accept the invitation.

Configure the Calendar App and Send an Invitation

Start out by using Internet Accounts preferences to add a CalDAV account.

Add a CalDAV Account

On your administrator computer, configure the Calendar app for Gary Pine.

1   On your administrator computer, open System Preferences.

2   Open Internet Accounts.

3   There may be other accounts in the left column, which you can ignore for this exercise.

4   In the right column, scroll to the bottom of the list, and select Add Other Account.

5   Select "Add a CalDAV account."

6   Click Create.

7   Use the following settings:

▶ Account Type: Automatic

▶ Email Address: gary@servern.pretendco.com (where *n* is your student number)

▶ Password: net

8   Click Create to add the account.

9   If your user account on your administrator computer is not configured to trust your server's Open Directory (OD) certificate authority (CA) and a message appears that Calendar can't verify the identity of the server, click Show Certificate, select your server's OD CA, select the checkbox to always trust, click Continue, provide credentials for the currently logged-in user, and click Update Settings.

10   In the left column of Internet Accounts, select the new entry for Calendars.

11 In the right column, confirm that the Description field is set to your server's host name.

If it is set to OS X Server, enter server*n*.pretendco.com (where *n* is your student number) in the Description field.

12 Click Configure in Calendar.

This opens the Calendar app and opens Accounts preferences for the Calendar app.

13 Confirm that the Description field is set to your server's host name.

14 Close the Accounts window.

Send an Invitation

Send an invitation involving a location, a resource, and another local network user. This exercise uses "tomorrow," which appears as December 3, 2014, for various figures in this section. Of course, the date of your event likely will not match this date.

1   Choose File > New Event, or click the Create Event (+) button, to create a quick event.

2   Enter an event name, date, and time, such as Project update tomorrow at 9, and press Return to choose the automatically selected suggestion.

3   Click Add Location, and then wait a few moments.

4   At the dialog that says "Calendar would like to use your current location," click OK.

   NOTE ▶ You will be asked two more times for permission for Calendar to use your current location. You will click OK each time.

5   In the Add Location field, start typing the first few characters of Conference Room A. Select Conference Room A when it appears, and then press Return.

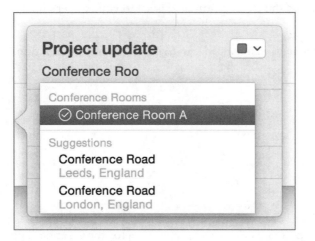

6   At the "Calendar would like to use your current location" dialog, click OK.

7   At the "Calendar would like to use your current location" dialog, click OK.

8   Click Add Invitees, and then enter only the first few characters of Sue Wu. Select "Sue Wu <sue@server17.pretendco.com>" when it appears.

   Sue Wu has more than one email address associated with her user account; it does not matter which one you use, so if only sue@pretendco.com appears, you can select that address.

9   With "Sue Wu <sue@server17.pretendco.com>" selected in the list that appears, press Return to choose it.

10 While still in the invitees field, start typing 3D Printer 1.

   Note that you need to type at least the first three letters of the name.

11 Select 3D Printer 1 from the list that appears, and then press Return.

12 Click Send to save the changes to this event and send the invitation.

The Calendar service sends an invitation to Conference Room A, 3D Printer 1, and Sue Wu.

13 Double-click the event you just created.

You configured the Conference Room A location and the 3D Printer 1 resource to automatically accept invitations if they are free, so after a few moments, the Calendar service automatically accepts the invitation for the location and for the resource.

14 Wait a few moments until the checkmark next to the location and the checkmark next to the resource change from black to green.

15 Choose File > Close to close the details of the event (or just click anywhere else in the Calendar).

16 Quit Calendar on your administrator computer.

Reply to the Invitation

Use your server computer to simulate using the Calendar service on Sue Wu's Mac computer.

Configure Calendar for Sue Wu on Your Server

You can use Internet Accounts preferences or the Calendar app preferences to add CalDAV accounts. On your administrator computer, you used Internet Accounts preferences; for this section of the exercise, use the Calendar app preferences on your server.

1 On your server, open the Calendar app.

2 On your administrator computer, open Calendar.

3 Choose Calendar > Add Account.

4 Select Add CalDAV Account, and click Continue.

5 Use the following settings:

   ▶ Account Type: Automatic

   ▶ Email Address: sue@server*n*.pretendco.com (where *n* is your student number)

   ▶ Password: net

6 Click Create to add the account.

7   Close the Accounts window.

Reply to the Invitation

1   Note the Notifications button indicates that there is an invitation you have not replied to.

2   Click the Notifications button.

3   For the 9 AM invitation, click Accept.

4   Quit Calendar on your server.

> **NOTE ▶** To explore how to resolve scheduling conflicts and use the web interface of the Calendar service, refer to "Exercise 23.3 Supplement" available with this guide's downloadable lesson files.

> **MORE INFO ▶** You can also add a calendar to a wiki: While logged in to the wiki as a user with Owner permissions, click the Action (gear icon) menu, choose Wiki Settings, and then in the General settings, select the Calendar checkbox.

Since the Calendar service relies on HTTP or HTTPS to transfer data from server to client and vice versa, standard web troubleshooting applies, such as checking for open and available ports. On a client, the Calendar app discovers the Calendar server via DNS lookup, so DNS problems could prevent Calendar from working as expected.

In this exercise, you used Mac computers, but the Calendar service also works with the Calendar app on iOS devices (choose Settings > Mail, Contacts, Calendars > Add Account > Other > Add CalDAV account).

Lesson 24

Managing the Contacts Service

With OS X Server you can easily provide Contacts services. Contacts provides central storage and makes the stored information available to clients.

GOALS

▶ Configure the Contacts service

▶ Identify associated protocols

▶ Connect to the Contacts service

Reference 24.1
Introducing the Contacts Service

The Contacts service lets users store contacts on the server and access those contacts via multiple computers and devices. In addition to any app that can use CardDAV, the following Apple apps are compatible with the Contacts service:

▶ Contacts and Address Book

▶ Mail

▶ Messages

You can set up a Contacts server that provides a centralized address book for your users. This way, your users can access the same pool of contact information. You can also set up Contacts to provide Lightweight Directory Access Protocol (LDAP) searches of the directory service your server is bound to. This way, your users don't have to configure their Contacts preferences to include LDAP servers.

NOTE ▶ You can't configure this option if your server isn't bound to another directory service.

The Contacts service uses open source technologies, including CardDAV (an extension to WebDAV), Hypertext Transfer Protocol (HTTP), and HTTP Secure (HTTPS), as well as vCard (a file format for contact information).

The data repository for the Calendar service is located at /Library/Server/. Within that directory is a folder containing data specific to the Contacts service at /Library/Server/ Calendar and Contacts/.

You can set permissions based on users, groups, and what networks they are connecting from in a similar manner as the other services. This is configured under Permissions of the Access section of the Contacts service pane.

When you create a contact with the Contacts service, you use CardDAV, not LDAP, to copy the changes to the server.

Reference 24.2
Troubleshooting the Contacts Service

Here are some common problems with the Contacts service and how they might be rectified:

▶ If your users can't connect to the Contacts service on the server, check that the clients are using a Domain Name System (DNS) server that is providing the proper name resolution for the server.

▶ If users can't connect to the Contacts service, check that ports 8800 and 8843 are open to the server.

▶ If users can't authenticate to the Contacts service, check that the users are using proper passwords. Reset if needed. Also check that the users are allowed to use the service based on the service access controls.

Exercise 24.1
Configure the Contacts Service

▶ **Prerequisites**

▶ "Exercise 2.1 Create DNS Zones and Records" on page 71

▶ "Exercise 9.1 Create and Import Network Accounts" on page 292

There is little to configure in the Contacts service. The Server app allows you to do the following:

▶ Turn the service on and off

▶ Set up directory contacts for search

Before you start the Contacts service, confirm that the service uses a Secure Sockets Layer (SSL) certificate.

Confirm the SSL Certificate

1   Perform these exercises on your administrator computer. If you do not already have a connection to your server computer with the Server app on your administrator computer, then connect to it with the following steps: Open the Server app on your administrator computer, choose Manage > Connect to Server, select your server, click Continue, provide administrator credentials (Administrator Name: ladmin, Administrator Password: ladminpw), deselect the "Remember this password" checkbox, and then click Connect.

2   In the Server app sidebar, select Certificates.

3   If all the services use the same certificate, then the pop-up menu is set to the certificate that all the services use; confirm that the certificate is the certificate that is signed by your server's Open Directory (OD) intermediate certificate authority (CA), and then skip to the next exercise.

4   If the pop-up menu is set to "Custom configuration," then click the pop-up menu and choose Custom.

5   Confirm that the Calendar and Contacts entry is set to the certificate that is signed by your server's OD intermediate CA, and then click Cancel to return to the Certificates pane.

Configure the Contacts Service

1   In the Server app, select the Contacts service.

2   Select "Allow users to search the directory using the Contacts application."

> **NOTE** ▶ The "Allow users to search the directory using the Contacts application" option is unavailable if the server is not bound to another directory service or is not an Open Directory master. If it is dimmed, you can still use the Contacts service to store contacts and make them accessible to multiple computers and devices that you own.

3   Click On to turn on the Contacts service.

4   Confirm that there is a green status indicator in the Status field.

5   Review the permissions for the service.

Exercise 24.2
Configure OS X to Use the Contacts Service

▶ **Prerequisite**

   ▶ "Exercise 24.1 Configure the Contacts Service" on page 641

The Contacts app for OS X and the Contacts app for iOS are designed to work with the services that use CardDAV or LDAP; this includes the Contacts service from OS X Server.

In this exercise, you will configure the Contacts app to access the Contacts service, create a new contact, and confirm it is accessible from the Contacts app on another Mac computer. You will also confirm that you can use the Contacts app to search your server's directory using the Contacts app.

Configure the Contacts App to Access the Contacts Service

Use the Contacts app on your administrator computer.

Set Up Contacts to Access Your CalDAV on Your Administrator Computer

You can use Internet Accounts preferences or the Contacts app preferences to add a Cal-DAV account. For the purposes of this exercise, use the Contacts app.

1   On your administrator computer, open Contacts, which is in the Dock by default.

2   Choose Contacts > Preferences (or press Command-Comma).

3   Select Accounts in the Contacts preferences toolbar.

4   Click the Add (+) button, select "Other contacts account," and click Continue.

5   Leave the account type as CardDAV because the Contacts service implements Card-DAV.

6   In the User Name field, enter gary.

    You must use the user's Account Name attribute (as opposed to their full name).

7   In the Password field, enter the password net.

8   In the Server Address field, enter servern.pretendco.com (where *n* is your student number).

9   Click Create.

10   Select the General tab.

11   Confirm that Default Account is set to your server (instead of On My Mac) so that new contacts you create are stored with the Contacts service.

12   Close the General pane.

13   Note that the sidebar consists of four sections:

   ▶   All Contacts

   ▶   server*n*.pretendco.com (where *n* is your student number) because you just added the CardDAV account

   ▶   On My Mac

   ▶   Directories (because you selected "Include directory contacts in search")

Create a New Contact

1   Select All Contacts in the sidebar.

2   Click the Add (+) button, and choose New Contact.

3   Enter sample name information for a user, such as the following:

▶   First: Yuri

▶   Last: Ishikura

▶   mobile: 773-555-1212

▶   home (email): yuri@example.com

4   Click Done to save your changes.

The contact you just created is stored locally on your OS X computer for offline use, and it is also stored with the Contacts service, so you can access it from other computers and devices.

5   In the sidebar, select "All server*n*.pretendco.com" (where *n* is your student number).

6   Confirm that your new contact appears in the middle column; this is currently the only contact you have stored with your CardDAV account.

The contacts you create with your Contacts service account are available to you on other OS X computers and iOS devices, as long as you configure Contacts with your Contacts service account. You can also access your contacts with any application that uses CardDAV.

Confirm Your Contacts Are Accessible on Multiple Devices

To verify that the Contacts service is allowing you to access the information from multiple devices, create a contact on one Mac computer, and confirm that you can access it from another Mac computer.

Set Up Contacts on a Second Mac Computer

To simulate using Contacts on another Mac computer, use your server computer for the purposes of this exercise.

1   On your server, open Contacts.

2   Choose Contacts > Preferences.

3   Select Accounts in the preferences toolbar.

4   Click the Add (+) button, select "Other contacts account," and click Continue.

5   Leave the account type as CardDAV because the Contacts service implements Card-DAV.

6   In the User Name field, enter gary.

    You must use the user's account name (as opposed to their full name).

7   In the Password field, enter the proper password, net.

8   In the Server Address field, enter servern.pretendco.com (where *n* is your student number).

9   Click Create.

10 Close the Accounts window if it does not automatically close.

11 In the Contacts app sidebar, select "All server*n*.pretendco.com" (where *n* is your student number).

12 Confirm that the contact you created appears in the middle column.

13 Quit Contacts on your server.

Confirm Directory Searches

NOTE ▶ At the time of this writing, the Contacts app does not return records for contacts that have more than one email address.

Create a New Local Network Account

Create a new local network account in the shared directory so that you can search for it with the Contacts app to verify that your Contacts service allows users to search the directory.

1   In the Server app sidebar, select Users.

2   Click the pop-up menu, and choose Local Network Users.

3   If the lock icon at the bottom of the Users pane is locked, click it to authenticate.

4   Deselect the checkbox "Remember this password in my keychain."

5   If necessary, enter your directory administrator credentials (Administrator Name: dir-admin, Administrator Password: diradminpw).

6   Leave the checkbox "Remember this password in my keychain" unselected.

7   Click Authenticate.

8   Click the Add (+) button.

9   Leave the Type field set to Local Network User.

> **NOTE ▸** For the next step, configure the Account Name field first because the full name that you enter is used to automatically generate a suggestion for the account name as well as the Email Addresses values.

10   In the Account Name field, enter trudy.

11   In the Full Name field, enter Trudy Phan, and then press Tab.

12   In the Email Addresses field, select trudy@pretendco.com.

13   Click the Remove (–) button.

14   If the Email Addresses field does not include trudy@server*n*.pretendco.com (where *n* is your student number), then click the Add (+) button and enter it.

15   In the Password and Verify fields, enter net.

16 Click Create.

Search for a Local Network User

1 In the Contacts app sidebar, in the All Contacts column, under Directories, select server*n*.pretendco.com (where *n* is your student number).

2 In the Search field, enter trudy.

The entry from the search result, Trudy Phan, is automatically selected.

3 Confirm that the email address you configured for Trudy Phan appears in the right column.

4 Quit Contacts on your administrator computer.

In this exercise, you confirmed that the contacts you create and store with your server's Contacts service are accessible from multiple devices. You also confirmed that you can use the Contacts app to search your directory of local network users.

Lesson 25

Providing the Messages Service

As one of the common collaboration services, Messages provides a standards-based method of communicating with one or many other users.

Reference 25.1
Managing the Messages Service

The Messages service, previously known as iChat, allows users to collaborate in real time. Messages users can use the following features to quickly share information without the delay associated with email messages and wiki posts:

► Exchange text messages instantly

► Send files to each other

► Set up an instant audio conference (using either the microphone built into many Mac computers or an external unit)

► Initiate a face-to-face video conference using video cameras (including the iSight or FaceTime camera built into many Mac computers and iOS devices)

► Allow another Messages user to take control of a Mac (using screen sharing)

► Use a persistent chat (called a room) with a group of people to keep a conversation going

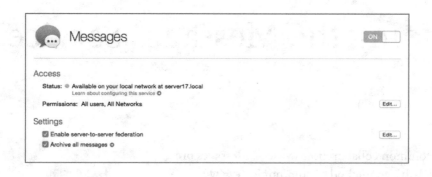

Unlike a telephone call, which you must either answer immediately or allow to go to voicemail, you can accept an instant text message but answer it when you are ready to process it.

You can set permissions based on users, groups, and what networks they are connecting from in a similar manner as the other services. This is configured under Permissions of the Access section of the Messages service pane.

By running your own Messages service, you gain these advantages, plus others such as chat transcript archives and the ability to keep all messages secure and private.

Users who chat with each other can use the Messages service to keep those chats within their organization. Like many other services on OS X Server, the Messages service can be restricted to certain users or groups, permitting chats to be private and controlled. Chats can also be secured through encryption and logged, permitting them to be searched later. The Messages service is based on the open source Jabber project. The technical name for the protocol used is the Extensible Messaging and Presence Protocol (XMPP).

Configuring Messages Service Users

After the Messages service has been set up, you can permit users to join the Messages service (called Jabber in the Messages app interface). A full Messages service account consists of the following:

- ▶ A user's account name (also known as the short name)
- ▶ The @ symbol
- ▶ A Messages service's host domain

For example, a user with a full name of Chat User1 and an account name of chatuser1 on server17.pretendco.com would configure the Messages application with a Jabber account name of chatuser1@server17.pretendco.com.

There are at least three ways to configure the Messages app, including the following:

▶ Using a configuration profile

▶ Using Internet Accounts preferences and selecting "Add an OS X Server account"

▶ Specifying a Jabber account in the Messages app

Defining Messages Network Ports

Various ports are used for the Messages service, depending on whether the service is used internal to your network or exposed to other networks. Refer to Table 25-1 for port usage information.

TABLE 25.1 Messages Port Usage

Port	Description
1080	SOCKS5 protocol, used for file transfers.
5060	iChat Session Initiation Protocol (SIP), used for audio or video chats.
5190	Only required for basic instant messenging (IM) use.
5222 TCP	Used only for Transport Layer Security (TLS) connections if a Secure Sockets Layer (SSL) certificate is enabled. If no SSL certificate is used, this port is used for nonencrypted connections. TLS encryption is preferred to legacy SSL connections because it is more secure.
5223 TCP	Used for legacy SSL connections when an SSL certificate is used.
5269 TCP	Used for encrypted TLS server-to-server connections, as well as nonencrypted connections. TLS encryption is preferred to legacy SSL connections because it is more secure.
5678	UDP port used by Messages to determine the user's external Internet Protocol (IP) address.

Port	Description
5297, 5298	Used by Messages versions older than Mac OS X 10.5 for Bonjour IM. Mac OS X 10.5 and later use dynamic ports.
7777	Used by the Jabber Proxy65 module for server file transfer proxy.
16402	Used for Session Initiation Protocol (SIP) signaling in Mac OS X 10.5 and later.
16384–16403	These ports are used by Mac OS X 10.4 and earlier for audio or video chat using Real-time Transport Protocol (RTP) and RTP Control Protocol (RTCP). Traffic was exchanged in .Mac (MobileMe) to determine the user's external port information.

Illustrating Messages Logging

The Messages service can meet the need to review the chat archive of a conversation, perhaps for auditing or administrative purposes. In addition to archiving all messages, any user can configure the Messages app to archive personal chats for review.

The archives are kept in plain text, even if the communications between the Messages users are encrypted. The Messages service does not archive audio or video content or files transferred using the service.

The Messages service can log all chat messages. The default folder for the archive is on the service storage volume in /Library/Server/Messages/Data/message_archives/. The archive file is jabberd_user_messages.log, and it contains all the messages your users have exchanged using your server's Messages service.

The ownership and permissions of the jabberd_user_messages.log file allow only a hidden service account (named _jabberd) or the root user to access its contents.

Although it is possible to change permissions on the message_archives folder and the log it contains so you can use a graphical user interface (GUI) text editor to view the file, it is safer and more secure to use the command-line tools in Terminal to view the file; you can use the sudo command in Terminal to obtain the temporary root access you need to access and view the contents of the file. If you do want to use a GUI editor, an app such as Pages that can deal with parsing delimited files would be useful.

Configuring Messages Federation

Your organization may have more than one computer running OS X Server. If both of those servers use the Messages service, it is possible to join them together, allowing users and groups in both Open Directory masters to engage each other in instant messaging. The process of joining different Messages service servers is called federation. Not only does federation allow two servers running Messages services to join, but it also allows any other XMPP chat service, such as Google Talk, to join. The Messages service federation is turned on by default.

NOTE ▶ You can use secure encryption for the federation if you are already using an SSL certificate. This forces all communications between the servers to be encrypted, similar to the way in which the communications between Messages and the Messages server are encrypted when using that certificate. For archiving purposes, messages are always decrypted on the server.

Reference 25.2
Troubleshooting the Messages Service

To troubleshoot the Messages service provided by OS X Server, it helps to have a good understanding of how the Messages service works in general. Review the preceding sections to make sure you understand each working piece.

Here are some common problems and suggestions for rectifying them:

▶   If your users can't connect to the Messages service on the server, check that the clients are using a DNS server that is providing the proper name resolution for the server.

▶   If users can't connect to the Messages service, check that the appropriate ports are open to the server, as listed in Table 25-1 earlier in the lesson.

▶   If users can't authenticate to the Messages service, check that the users are using proper passwords. Reset if needed. Check that the users are allowed access to the service as per the service access controls.

Exercise 25.1
Set Up the Messages Service

▶ **Prerequisite**

  ▶   "Exercise 2.1 Create DNS Zones and Records" on page 71

  ▶   "Exercise 9.1 Create and Import Network Accounts" on page 292

You use the Server app to turn on the Messages service like most of the other services of OS X Server. Once you've turned it on, you manage the service in a fashion similar to that of the other services.

Confirm the SSL Certificate

1   Perform these exercises on your administrator computer. If you do not already have a connection to your server computer with the Server app on your administrator computer, then connect to it with the following steps: Open the Server app on your administrator computer, choose Manage > Connect to Server, select your server, click

Continue, provide administrator credentials (Administrator Name: ladmin, Administrator Password: ladminpw), deselect the "Remember this password" checkbox, and then click Connect.

2   To confirm that Messages is configured to use SSL, select Certificates in the Server app sidebar.

NOTE ▶ If you haven't yet configured your server to be an Open Directory master, you will see a self-signed SSL certificate instead of the certificate signed by the Open Directory (OD) intermediate certificate authority (CA).

3   If all the services use the same certificate, then the pop-up menu is set to the certificate that all the services use; confirm that the certificate is the certificate that is signed by your server's OD intermediate CA, and then skip to the next exercise.

4   If the pop-up menu is set to "Custom configuration," click the pop-up menu, and choose Custom.

5   Confirm that the Messages entry is set to the certificate that is signed by your server's OD intermediate CA, and then click Cancel to return to the Certificates pane.

Start the Messages Service

1   In the Server app, select the Messages service, and then click On to turn the service on.

2   Once the service is turned on, confirm that the green status indicator is displayed and there is a link for help about Messages service beneath the Status field.

3   Note the contents of the Permissions field.

Turn On Messages Service Archiving
You will turn on Messages service logging.

1   Select the "Archive all messages" checkbox.

2   To view the location of the Messages archives, click the link next to the "Archive all messages" checkbox.

☑ Archive all messages ❍

The Server's Storage pane opens and displays the folder that contains the text file with the log in clear text, jabberd_user_messages.log.

NOTE ▶ If you click the link next to the "Archive all messages" checkbox while using the Server app on the server, as opposed to from an administrator computer, instead of the Server app opening the folder in the Storage pane, it opens the folder in a new Finder window.

In this exercise, you started the Messages service and configured it to archive all messages. In the next exercise, you will use the service and view the logged messages.

Exercise 25.2
Use the Messages Service

▶ **Prerequisite**

  ▶ "Exercise 25.1 Set Up the Messages Service" on page 654

Now that you've set up the service, use your administrator computer to access the service and then view the logged messages.

Configure Messages on Your Administrator Computer

Verify that you can connect to the service.

You will enable a Messages account to use the Messages (Jabber) service.

1   On your administrator computer, open the Messages app by clicking the Messages icon in your Dock.

2   At the iMessage Setup pane, click Not Now, and then at the confirmation dialog, click Skip.

The Messages window appears, and then an Account Setup pane appears.

3   At the Account Setup pane, select "Other messages account" from the menu, and click Continue.

4   In the Account Type pop-up menu, choose Jabber.

5   Enter sue@servern.pretendco.com (where *n* is your student number) in the Account Name field.

> **NOTE ▶** As of the current writing, after you enter information in the Account Name field, pressing Tab will not advance to the next field; click the Password field to enter information in the Password field.

6   Click the Password field, and then enter the password net.

7   In the Server Options section, leave the Server and Port fields blank, and leave the checkboxes unselected. Messages automatically uses the appropriate server and port.

8   Click Create.

The Messages (Jabber) service Buddies window for Sue Wu automatically opens.

> **MORE INFO ▶** In the header at the top of the Buddies window, Messages displays the full name of the user logged in on OS X, not the full name of the account you used to authenticate to the Messages service. You can change this by opening Contacts, choosing Card > Go to My Card, and editing the full name.

> **TIP ▶** If you close your Buddies window, you can display it again by choosing Window > Buddies (or by pressing Command-1).

Configure the Messages App on Your Server Computer

Now that you have the Messages app configured on your administrator computer with the Sue Wu user account, configure the Messages app on your server computer as another user, Carl Dunn, so you can use Messages to communicate between the two computers.

1   On your server computer, if you aren't already logged in with the Local Admin account, log in now (Name: Local Admin, Password: ladminpw).

2 On your server computer, open the Messages app by clicking the Messages icon in your Dock.

3 At the iMessage Setup pane, click Not Now, and then at the confirmation dialog, click Skip.

4 At the Account Setup pane, select "Other messages account," and then click Continue.

5 In the Account Type pop-up menu, choose Jabber.

6 Enter the following information:

▶ Account Name: carl@server*n*.pretendco.com (where *n* is your student number)

▶ Password: net

7 In the Server Options section, leave the Server and Port fields blank, and leave the checkboxes unselected.

Messages automatically uses the appropriate server and port.

8 Click Create.

The Messages (Jabber) service buddy list for Carl Dunn automatically opens.

MORE INFO ▶ You can use your buddy lists to see the availability status of AIM, Jabber, Google Talk, or Yahoo! buddies. iMessage doesn't support buddy lists. When you first add a Jabber or Google Talk buddy to your buddy list, your buddy receives an authorization notice, and your buddy is temporarily added to the Offline area of the buddy list, with the status of Unknown, labeled "Waiting for Authorization." If your buddy clicks Decline, the buddy is labeled "Not Authorized." If your buddy clicks Accept, you can see your buddy's status.

Send Messages from One Mac to Another Mac
Simulate a chat between the users.

1 On your administrator computer, in the Messages window, in the To field, enter carl@server*n*.pretendco.com (where *n* is your student number).

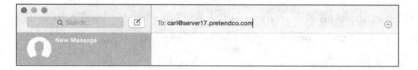

2   In the Jabber message field, enter some text such as Hello, Carl! as an example.

3   Press Return to send the message.

4   On your server, in the Messages window sidebar, select the new message from Sue.

5   On your server, confirm that the right side of the Messages window contains the message that you just sent from your administrator computer.

6   On your server, enter some text to reply such as Hi, Sue! and then press Return to send the message.

7   On your administrator computer, confirm that you see the reply from Carl.

Request Authorization

Note that in the Messages sidebar, the users are still listed as Offline. You cannot see their status in your Buddies window until you request authorization.

1   On your administrator computer, in the Buddies window, click the Add (+) button, and choose Add Buddy.

2   In the Account name field, enter carl.

You don't need to enter Carl's full Jabber address, which is carl@server*n*.pre-tendco.com (where *n* is your student number).

3   Click Add.

4   On your server, click the Jabber Authorization window that appears, and then click Accept.

5   On your administrator computer, confirm that the Buddy window displays the user carl with a green status indicator.

6   Confirm that the Messages window no longer has the word "Offline" in the sidebar for the messages with the user carl.

Restrict Messages Service Users

You can restrict who is permitted to use the Messages service by using service access controls. Like with many other services, you restrict user access via the Server app.

To restrict the user Sue Wu from chatting with others on the Messages service, follow these steps:

1   On your administrator computer, in the Server app sidebar, select Users.

2   Select Sue Wu, click the Action (gear icon) pop-up menu, and choose Edit Access to Services.

3   Deselect the Messages checkbox to turn off the user's access to the Messages service.

4   Click OK to save the change.

5   If you see the message "Do you want to manually manage service access for Messages," click Manage.

6   In the Server app sidebar, select Messages.

7   Confirm that the Permissions field reflects the new permissions (if you did not create a new local network user in the previous exercise, then the Permissions field will display "9 users" instead of "10 users").

```
Access

    Status:  ● Available on your local network at server17.local
                Learn about configuring this service ⊙

    Permissions:  10 users, All Networks
```

Disconnect and Attempt to Reconnect as the Restricted User

Now that you've restricted Sue Wu's access to the Messages service, disconnect her from the Messages service and then attempt to connect her to the Messages service again.

1   Disconnect Sue Wu. On your administrator computer, in the lower-left corner of the Messages window, click the Available pop-up window, and then choose Offline (or press Control-Command-O).

2   On your administrator computer, quit the Messages app.

3   Wait about a minute before reconnecting.

4   On your administrator computer, open the Messages app.

5   Attempt to reconnect Sue Wu. On your administrator computer, in the lower-left corner of the Messages window, click the Offline pop-up window, and then choose Available (or press Control-Command-A).

    If you are automatically reconnected, disconnect again, and wait another minute before attempting to reconnect.

6   When you are prompted for Sue Wu's password, enter net, and click Log In.

    Even after providing a valid password, you still can't log in as Sue Wu because you removed her access to the Messages service.

7   Click Cancel as many times as is necessary to close any authentication dialog.

Reenable Sue Wu's access to the Messages service, and connect to the Messages service again as Sue Wu.

1   On your administrator computer, in the Server app sidebar, select Users.

2   Select Sue Wu, click the Action (gear icon) pop-up menu, and choose Edit Access to Services.

3   Select the Messages checkbox to enable her access to the Messages service.

4   Reconnect Sue Wu. On your administrator computer, in the lower-left corner of the Messages window, click the Offline pop-up window, and then choose Available (or press Control-Command-A).

    If you are prompted for the password, click Cancel, and then try again after a moment.

5   Confirm that you can chat between the two computers again.

Remove the Custom Access Rule for the Messages Service

When you removed access to the Messages service for Sue Wu and then answered "Manage" to the question "Do you want to manually manage service access for Messages," this automatically created a custom access rule for the Messages service. Remove the custom access rule.

1   On your administrator computer, in the Server app sidebar, select your server.

2   Click the Access tab.

3   In the Custom Access section, select the Messages rule.

Custom Access			
Name	Users	Network	Ports
Caching	All users	Local Subnets	
Messages	11 users	All Networks	TCP/UDP 5060, 5222-5223, 52...

4   Click the Remove (–) button.

5   At the confirmation dialog, click Remove.

Restrict Messages Federation

By default, federation is not allowed with any other Messages service running on any other server or Jabber server. However, you can institute federation and then restrict the Messages service federation to approved Messages servers only.

1   On your administrator computer, in the Server app sidebar, select the Messages service.

2   Make sure that "Enable server-to-server federation" is selected, and then click the Edit button.

3   Select the "Restrict federation to the following domains" option and click the Add (+) button to add only those domains you want to participate within the federation.

4   As an example, enter the hypothetical server18.pretendco.com. For the purposes of this exercise, it does not matter that this server is not online.

5   Click OK.

6   To keep communication secure between federated servers, leave the "Require secure server-to-server federation" option selected. This option is dimmed if you have configured your Messages service to not use an SSL certificate.

7   Click OK to close the dialog.

View Messages Service and Chat Logs

To view the connection logs for the Messages service, you will use the Server app to view the Messages service log. Then, to view the archive of messages, you will use `sudo more` in a Terminal command.

Use the Logs Pane

1   On your administrator computer, in the Server app, select the Logs pane.

2   Click the pop-up menu, and in the Messages section, choose Service Log.

3   Browse the contents of the service log.

4   Enter `session started` in the search field, and then press Return.

```
Nov 10 12:52:22 server17.pretendco.com jabberd/sm[8067]: session started: jid=sue@server17.pretendco.com/client17
Nov 10 12:53:02 server17.pretendco.com jabberd/c2s[8069]: [10] [::ffff:10.0.0.171, port=50013] connect
Nov 10 12:53:02 server17.pretendco.com jabberd/c2s[8069]: Authentication succeeded, mech: DIGEST-MD5 client IP: ::ffff:
10.0.0.171 client port: 50013 username: carl
Nov 10 12:53:02 server17.pretendco.com jabberd/c2s[8069]: int od_auth_check_service_membership(const char *, const char
*): checking user "carl" access for service "chat"
Nov 10 12:53:02 server17.pretendco.com jabberd/c2s[8069]: int od_auth_check_service_membership(const char *, const char
*): mbr_check_service_membership returned 2
Nov 10 12:53:02 server17.pretendco.com jabberd/c2s[8069]: int od_auth_check_service_membership(const char *, const char
*): no access restrictions found
Nov 10 12:53:02 server17.pretendco.com jabberd/c2s[8069]: [10] DIGEST-MD5 authentication succeeded:
carl@server17.pretendco.com ::ffff:10.0.0.171:50013 TLS
Nov 10 12:53:02 server17.pretendco.com jabberd/c2s[8069]: [10] bound: jid=carl@server17.pretendco.com/server17
Nov 10 12:53:02 server17.pretendco.com jabberd/sm[8067]: created user: jid=carl@server17.pretendco.com
Nov 10 12:53:02 server17.pretendco.com jabberd/sm[8067]: session started: jid=carl@server17.pretendco.com/server17
Nov 10 12:54:15 server17.pretendco.com jabberd/c2s[8069]: [11] [::ffff:17.151.40.76, port=39704] connect
Nov 10 12:54:15 server17.pretendco.com jabberd/c2s[8069]: [11] [::ffff:17.151.40.76, port=39704] disconnect jid=unbound,
packets: 0
Nov 10 12:54:15 server17.pretendco.com jabberd/c2s[8069]: [11] [::ffff:17.151.40.76, port=59386] connect
Nov 10 12:54:15 server17.pretendco.com jabberd/c2s[8069]: [11] [::ffff:17.151.40.76, port=59386] disconnect jid=unbound,
packets: 0
Nov 10 12:54:15 server17.pretendco.com jabberd/s2s[8070]: [9] [::ffff:17.151.40.76, port=37219] incoming connection
Nov 10 12:54:15 server17.pretendco.com jabberd/s2s[8070]: [9] [::ffff:17.151.40.76, port=37219] disconnect, packets: 0
```

Service Log ◯   Q· session started ⊗ ?

This displays the date, Jabber account name, and computer name from which a new Jabber session started.

5   Note that each time you press Return, the Logs pane displays another entry.

The Messages service reports in the system log can also log any errors that may occur, and you can search for them using the search field in the toolbar.

6   Click the "X" in the search field to erase the contents, enter `authorized` in the search field, and then press Return.

```
Nov 10 13:03:47 server17.pretendco.com jabberd/c2s[8069]: int od_auth_check_service_membership(const char *, const char
*): user "sue" is not authorized to access service "chat"
Nov 10 13:03:47 server17.pretendco.com jabberd/c2s[8069]: [9] [::ffff:10.0.0.172, port=49506] disconnect jid=unbound,
packets: 0
```

Service Log ◯   Q· authorized ⊗ ?

This reflects the time you temporarily removed authorization for Sue Wu to use the Messages service.

Two additional logs are available in the Logs section of the Server app.

View the Archive

1   To view the chat transcripts, on your server computer, open Terminal (click Launch-Pad, click Other, and click Terminal).

2   To improve the readability of the command you enter and of the results, resize the Terminal window.

The toolbar of Terminal reflects the width and height of the Terminal window.

Drag the right side of the Terminal window to the right until the width dimension is displayed as 126 or more.

3   In the Terminal window, enter the following command, all on one line:

`sudo more /Library/Server/Messages/Data/message_archives/jabberd_user_messages.log`

Then press Return to issue the command.

The `sudo` command gives you root permissions for the command that follows it.

The `more` command displays the contents of a file one screen at a time; if there is more than one screen full of text in the file, press the Space bar to view the next screen full of text, or press q to exit the `more` command.

4   You are prompted for the password of the currently logged-in user; enter ladminpw, and press Return.

The chat transcripts appear; look for the conversation Carl and Sue had.

TIP ► You can use a spreadsheet app such as Numbers to improve the readability of the transcript.

5   You can drag the right border of the Terminal window to the right for better readability.

6   Quit Terminal.

In this exercise, you used two Mac computers to access the Messages service. You restricted access to the service for a user and then restored access (then you used the Access pane to remove the custom access rule for the Messages service). You used the Server app's Logs pane to view the service log, and you used Terminal to view the archived messages.

Index

Differentiate yourself. Get Apple certified.

Stand out from the crowd. Get recognized for your expertise by earning Apple Certified Pro status.

Why become an Apple Certified Pro?

Raise your earning potential. Studies show that certified professionals can earn more than their non-certified peers.

Distinguish yourself from others in your industry. Proven mastery of an application helps you stand out in a crowd.

Display your Apple Certification logo. With each certification you get a logo to display on business cards, resumés, and websites.

Publicize your certifications. Publish your certifications on the Apple Certified Professionals Registry (training. apple.com/certification/records) to connect with clients, schools, and employers.

Learning that matches your style.

Learn on your own with Apple Pro Training Series books from Peachpit Press.

Learn in a classroom at an Apple Authorized Training Center (AATC) from Apple Certified Trainers providing guidance.

Visit **training.apple.com** to find Apple training and certifications for:

OS X	Pages
OS X Server	Numbers
Final Cut Pro X	Keynote
Logic Pro X	

"The Apple Certification is a cornerstone of my consulting business. It guarantees to our clients the highest level of dedication and professionalism. And above all, the trusting smile of a client when you mention the Apple Certification can't be replaced."

– Andres Le Roux, Technology Consulting, alrx.net, inc.

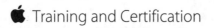
 Training and Certification